*BREAD AND FREEDOM*

Stanford Studies *in* Middle Eastern
*and* Islamic Societies *and* Cultures

# BREAD AND FREEDOM

*Egypt's Revolutionary Situation*

**Mona El-Ghobashy**

STANFORD UNIVERSITY PRESS
*Stanford, California*

Stanford University Press
Stanford, California

©2021 by the Board of Trustees of the Leland Stanford Junior University. All rights reserved.

No part of this book may be reproduced or transmitted in any form or by any means, electronic or mechanical, including photocopying and recording, or in any information storage or retrieval system without the prior written permission of Stanford University Press.

Printed in the United States of America on acid-free, archival-quality paper

Library of Congress Cataloging-in-Publication Data

Names: El-Ghobashy, Mona, author.
Title: Bread and freedom : Egypt's revolutionary situation / Mona El-Ghobashy.
Other titles: Stanford studies in Middle Eastern and Islamic societies and cultures.
Description: Stanford, California : Stanford University Press, [2021] | Series: Stanford studies in Middle Eastern and Islamic societies and cultures | Includes bibliographical references and index.
Identifiers: LCCN 2020050906 (print) | LCCN 2020050907 (ebook) | ISBN 9781503601765 (cloth) | ISBN 9781503628151 (paperback) | ISBN 9781503628168 (ebook)
Subjects: LCSH: Arab Spring, 2010– | Egypt—Politics and government—2011– | Egypt—History—Protests, 2011–2013. | Egypt—History—Coup d'état, 2013.
Classification: LCC DT107.88 .E415 2021 (print) | LCC DT107.88 (ebook) | DDC 962.05/6—dc23
LC record available at https://lccn.loc.gov/2020050906
LC ebook record available at https://lccn.loc.gov/2020050907

Cover art: *Revolution #3*, Hossam Dirar
Cover design: Rob Ehle
Typeset by Newgen North America in 10.5/14.4 Brill

*Contents*

|  | *List of Maps, Figures, and Tables* | vii |
|---|---|---|
|  | *Note on Transliteration* | ix |
|  | Prologue: We Won't Leave, He Must Go | 1 |
| 1 | Narratives of Egypt's Revolution | 27 |
| 2 | Let Them Say What They Want, and We'll Do What We Want | 47 |
| 3 | Fear Us, O Government | 86 |
| 4 | Let's Write Our Constitution | 127 |
| 5 | Down, Down with the General Guide's Rule | 166 |
| 6 | State Prestige | 206 |
|  | Conclusion: Bread and Freedom | 242 |
|  | *Acknowledgments* | 267 |
|  | *Abbreviations and Glossary* | 273 |
|  | *Notes* | 275 |
|  | *Bibliography* | 337 |
|  | *Index* | 357 |

*Maps, Figures, and Tables*

| | | |
|---|---|---|
| Map 1 | Egypt   x | |
| Map 2 | Tahrir Square and environs   6 | |
| Figure 1 | Tahrir protesters' demands, February 4, 2011   19 | |
| Figure 2 | Sign in Tahrir Square, February 11, 2011   29 | |
| Figure 3 | Hamdeen Sabahy surrounded by supporters on election day, November 28, 2010   49 | |
| Figure 4 | Police enclose an MB-Kifaya demonstration, September 1, 2005   76 | |
| Figure 5 | Protesters storm SSI Headquarters, March 5, 2011   87 | |
| Figure 6 | "Don't be afraid, I'm your friend! Nyahahahaha." Carlos Latuff cartoon, August 2011   118 | |
| Figure 7 | Activist sticker demanding transfer of power to parliament, February 2012   131 | |
| Figure 8 | Ballot in first round of presidential election, May 24, 2012   156 | |
| Figure 9 | Morten Morland cartoon, *The Times* (London), June 25, 2012   172 | |
| Figure 10 | President Mohamed Morsi meets with SCAF, April 11, 2013   196 | |
| Figure 11 | Funeral procession for former president Hosni Mubarak, February 2020   240 | |
| Table 1 | Repertoire of Political Contention in Contemporary Egypt, 1990s–2010   81 | |
| Table 2 | State Responses to Popular Contention, 1990s–2010   82 | |
| Table 3 | Results of the Parliamentary Elections, November 28, 2011–January 10, 2012   134 | |
| Table 4 | Results of the First Round of Presidential Elections, May 23–24, 2012   157 | |
| Table 5 | Results of the Final Round of Presidential Elections, June 16–17, 2012   161 | |

| | | |
|---|---|---|
| Table 6 | Composition of the 2012 Constituent Assembly | 180 |
| Table 7 | Protester Fatalities from Security Forces' Use of Force, 2011–2015 | 215 |
| Table 8 | Results of Three Constitutional Referenda, 2011–2014 | 220 |
| Table 9 | Transfers of Power during the Revolutionary Situation, 2011–2013 | 245 |

*Note on Transliteration*

I have used a simplified version of the transliteration system used by the *International Journal of Middle East Studies*. With apologies to purists, I omit diacritical marks (macrons and dots) except those denoting the letter *'ayn* and the *hamza*. Common English spellings of prominent figures' names are retained rather than meticulously transliterated; thus Gamal Abdel Nasser rather than Jamal 'Abd al-Nasir, Mohamed Morsi rather than Muhammad Mursi. The same goes for place names with common English spellings; Damietta rather than Dumyat, Port Said rather than Bur Sa'id, and Mohamed Mahmoud Street rather than Muhammad Mahmud. As much as possible, I have followed contemporary figures' preferred spelling of their names (e.g., Mohamed ElBaradei; Ziad Bahaa-Eldin; Nawal El Saadawi; Abdel Moneim Aboul Fotouh).

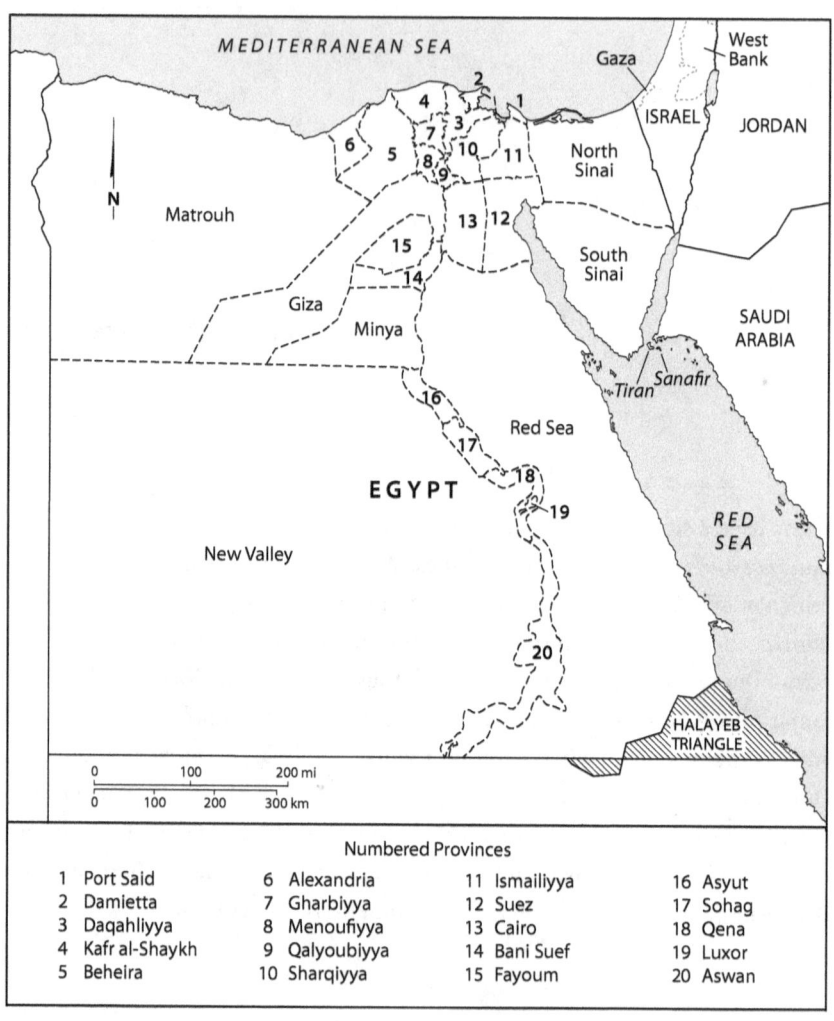

MAP 1. Egypt.

*BREAD AND FREEDOM*

*Prologue*

# WE WON'T LEAVE, HE MUST GO

مش حنمشي! هو يمشي!

> The oppressed masses, even when they rise to the very heights of creative action, tell little of themselves and write less. And the overpowering rapture of the victory later erases memory's work.
> —Leon Trotsky, *History of the Russian Revolution*

THE NIGHT OF JANUARY 14, 2011, ON THE DESERTED AVENUE HABIB Bourguiba in Tunis under curfew, an ineffable moment was captured by a cell phone camera. A man in a jumpsuit and white running shoes urgently paced up and down the eerily illuminated boulevard, gesturing with his arms and calling out over and over, "Ben Ali *harab*! Ben Ali *harab*!" It had already been hours since news broke that President Zine al-Abidine Ben Ali had fled the country after a twenty-nine-day popular revolt, but the man repeatedly cried out, "Ben Ali *harab*! Glory to the martyrs! There's no more fear, Tunisians! The criminal has fled! Ben Ali *harab*! Ben Ali *harab*!" Like a town crier after his own fashion, lawyer Abdel Nasser Laouini was heralding the unthinkable: the popular overthrow of an Arab president.[1]

In normal times, Arab presidents did not flee. They built formidable machineries of rule, with weak parliaments, useful constitutions, well-endowed government parties, ersatz opposition groupings, multiple media mouthpieces, and overlapping security services. They had steady foreign patrons in the governments of the United States, France, Italy, and Britain. And the presidents' sons and sons-in-law controlled top state institutions, their grooming for an imminent inheritance of presidential power. Of the nine Arab presidents in late 2010, observed historian Roger Owen, "seven clearly intended to stay in office for life and six were over sixty—a veritable kingdom of the old."[2]

The Tunisian people's routing of their gerontocrat electrified citizens across the Arab world. The day after, a major Egyptian independent daily ran a full-page headline: "Flight of Ben Ali."[3] The news came at a time of peak tension between Egypt's government and citizenry. Seven months earlier, after the savage police murder of twenty-eight-year-old Alexandrian Khaled Said in broad daylight, unusually large demonstrations had turned out in Cairo and Alexandria decrying police brutality.[4] After visiting Said's grieving mother and participating in the demonstration, retired Egyptian diplomat and newly minted opposition leader Mohamed ElBaradei told reporters, "It's a clear-cut message to the regime that the Egyptian people are sick and tired of practices that are inhumane."[5]

But the event most fresh in public memory was the government's violent rigging of general elections in December 2010. In district after district, tear gas–firing police and blade-wielding government musclemen blocked opposition voters from reaching polling stations, while inside the stations, civil servants calmly stuffed boxes with prefilled ballots. The government's party put a lock on all but 3 percent of parliament's seats, so dozens of ousted opposition deputies constituted themselves as a "shadow parliament," taking a symbolic oath on the steps of a courthouse and vowing to name-and-shame government policies.

Ben Ali's flight from Tunisia introduced a new ingredient into the routinized conflict between the Egyptian government and its diverse opposition: a perception that the president-for-life was vulnerable. For decades, even the most hopeful dissidents never imagined Hosni Mubarak to be in a precarious position. The eighty-two-year-old president had weathered an assassination attempt, an insurgency, a mutiny by riot police, growing opposition to his rule, and multiple ailments of old age. Dissidents' greatest ambitions were reforms that would check presidential power and end police impunity. Now the boundaries of the possible suddenly expanded. "The sight of President Ben Ali in his final speech convinces us that dictators are not as powerful as we imagine," mused influential neo-Islamist columnist Fahmi Howeidy. "It has also assured us that the people are more powerful than we think."[6]

\* \* \*

In the days after Ben Ali's flight, impression management took center stage in the jousting between government and opposition in Egypt. Hosni Mubarak donned the mantle of the unruffled statesman, concerned about the common man. While hosting an economic summit at his favorite Sinai resort of Sharm al-Shaykh, he lectured other Arab heads of state on the need for generating employment, calling young people "the most precious of all our resources."[7] The president's longest-serving police chief, untouchable Interior Minister Habib al-Adli, assured a television interviewer, "No Egyptian official trembled at what happened in Tunis. It's impossible to compare it to Egypt; the whole world acknowledges Egypt's stability."[8]

Indeed, the system that Mubarak had steered for three decades showed none of the telltale signs of instability: military defeat, elite schisms, or fiscal crisis. The government could even afford a package of preemptive measures to block any gales from Tunisia. Officials were particularly wary of antagonizing Egypt's 5.7 million government employees, among whom a wave of protests had spread since 2007. On January 18, it was prominently announced that a civil service reform bill would be shelved, and government ministers swiftly met the demands of several groups of protesting clerks and university graduates demanding public employment.[9]

By January 20, the independent press excitedly reported on calls percolating online for a national day of protest on January 25, National Police Day. In 2009, Mubarak had designated it a bank holiday, an attempt to link his abusive police force to a more heroic episode in its history.[10] Now, three youth-led opposition groups were planning to resignify the day as an occasion to chant against police torture and political repression.

With hope animating the opposition and an undertow of fear in the government's confident pronouncements, group after group announced its participation in what was branded a National Day of Wrath on January 25. The participant list read like a who's-who of the crowded opposition scene that had developed during Mubarak's third decade in power: the Facebook page commemorating

Khaled Said; the April 6 dissident youth movement; the shadow parliamentarians; workers in the militant textile town of Mahalla al-Kubra; a pensioners' rights group; the storied bar association; protest-prone university students and protest-shy gentlemen's dissident parties; liberal politician Ayman Nour and his following; the Revolutionary Socialists intellectuals' group; and the *Kifaya* (Enough!) movement established in 2004 to campaign for an end to Mubarak's tenure. Also joining was a social force new to opposition politics but seasoned in combat with police: hard-core soccer fans of Egypt's two main teams, the Ahli and Zamalek Ultras. Human rights lawyers announced hotline numbers to call for protesters facing arrest and needing legal aid. At the eleventh hour, cautious leaders of the Muslim Brothers (MB) and the Wafd party, Egypt's two oldest political movements, announced that they were leaving participation up to individual members.[11]

The organizing youth groups announced four consensus demands for what had been translated into social mediaspeak as #Jan25: an end to the permanent state of emergency; implementing a court ruling ordering a minimum monthly wage of £E1,200; sacking Interior Minister Habib al-Adli; and releasing all administrative detainees. Organizers reinforced the nonpartisan protest ethos by posting a video of Khaled Said's mother, Laila Marzouq, still in her mourning black, poignantly urging young people to turn out and find safety in numbers. Despite the anticipatory buzz, a small but nonnegligible assortment of strange bedfellows pointedly declared their nonparticipation: all three denominations of the Coptic Church; Salafi pietists, whose political posture was always with, not against, the government; and several tiny, government-licensed opposition parties that behaved as adjuncts to rather than critics of officialdom.

\* \* \*

The morning of Tuesday, January 25, began quietly enough, as people slept in on a welcome midweek day off. Demonstrations were not set to start until 2 p.m. But a peculiar thing began to happen. Well before 2 p.m., clusters of demonstrators were marching down narrow residential lanes and alleyways, drawing in more people as they filed past—passersby, residents sizing up the crowd from their balconies, men sitting languidly in coffee shops. By the time marchers veered onto broad avenues and even overpasses, they had swelled into impressive, briskly pacing crowds that took over traffic lanes. Car drivers amiably inched along beside them, tooting their horns in solidarity.

By design, the protest procession was rare in large Egyptian cities. Instinctively understanding the collective exuberance that permeates crowds, police only tolerated stationary assembly in a public place, to corral protesters and prevent bystanders from joining and augmenting crowd strength. Now, processions were freely roaming the streets, organically expanding in precisely the fashion police feared. Marching in central Cairo, Egyptian-British journalist Sarah Carr marveled, "As the numbers increased and reports of other marches in Mohandiseen and Shubra came in I wondered if we had all inadvertently entered some 5th dimension."[12]

The exceptionally compact layout of the city center explains police commanders' terror at the prospect of roving demonstrations. Visualize a plaza, Tahrir Square, ringed by several important buildings: the American University in Cairo campus; the huge government complex of al-Mugamma'; the Arab League headquarters; the Nile Hilton; the government's National Democratic Party (NDP) headquarters; and the Egyptian Antiquities Museum. Within a half-mile from the plaza in different directions sit more sensitive buildings: the Maspero state radio and television headquarters to the north; the two houses of parliament to the south; the Interior Ministry to the southeast; the British and US embassies to the southwest; and the bar association, High Court, press syndicate, and Judges' Club to the northeast. West of the square are two bridges spanning the Nile River, connecting central Cairo to the teeming western neighborhoods of the megacity.

By 2:30 p.m., outside the High Court building, a fierce tug of war over a metal barrier pitted irate shadow parliamentarians in their suits against black-helmeted riot conscripts with shields and batons. Half a block away, officers seemed to heave rows of riot policemen into masses of lawyers to prevent them from exiting the bar association and merging with the crowds heading to Tahrir Square. At the NDP headquarters on the Nile, liberal politician Ayman Nour fronted an energetic speed-walking procession of two hundred that stopped briefly to chant against NDP leaders and promise them the fate of Ben Ali before setting off for the television and radio headquarters, completely encircling it for a few minutes with no security forces in sight.

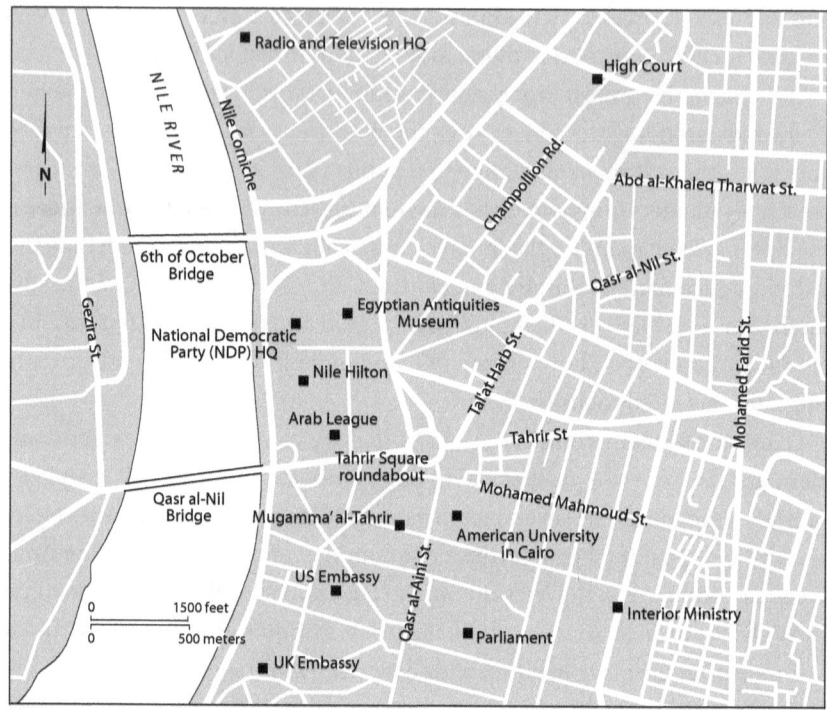

MAP 2. Tahrir Square and environs.

Around 3:30 p.m., separate processions from the extreme east and west of the capital poured into the plaza, overran all the police checkpoints, chased some policemen down side streets, and began chanting the Tunisians' litany, "al-Shaʿb Yurid Isqat al-Nizam!" (The people want to bring down the regime!). A group of fleet-footed protesters jogging in perfect lockstep broke through a tight formation of riot police desperately trying to block the way to parliament. A few steps further south, in front of the upper house of parliament, protesters faced a much thicker police battalion, five rows deep. They began energetically repeating the soccer Ultras' high-octane chant, three quick claps punctuated by "Masr! Masr!" (Egypt! Egypt!). Continuing south, on Qasr al-Aini Street, a stone's throw from parliament, a young man positioned himself directly in the path of an armored vehicle, forcing it to screech to a halt as it fired its water cannon. Drenched and hands defiantly on hips, the young man stood his ground as ecstatic videographers from a balcony above wildly cheered him on.

Further afield, in the port city of Suez (eighty-three miles east of Cairo), Mostafa Ragab Mahmoud, a twenty-one-year-old civil servant supporting a mother and four sisters, was walking with a friend for a long-planned outing to play pool when he heard the chants of demonstrators from far off. He apologized to his friend Yasser, saying he had to join the crowds massed on the main Arba'in Boulevard. Minutes later, he lay bleeding from a shot to the chest as police fired live ammunition at the unarmed demonstrators. Mahmoud was the first of the day's three fatalities in Suez.[13]

In Alexandria, protesters clashed with riot police outside Khaled Said's house and were engulfed by tear gas. Processions overran the city's tramways and brought the streetcars to a standstill; patients at one hospital looked on admiringly from windows at the marching crowds below. Eighty-five miles to the northeast in Balteem, a beautiful fishing town right on the Mediterranean that had seen street battles between opposition voters and police two months earlier during elections, demonstrators reprised the street fighting and breached police cordons, with the district's shadow parliamentarian Hamdeen Sabahy fronting the crowd. In Mahalla, a procession of thousands carrying banners walked to the main square, while elsewhere demonstrators ambushed the city's head of criminal investigations. They trapped him in the entryway of a residential building and delivered a beating: he had masterminded the rigging of the election, and now the score was settled.[14]

By sunset back in Cairo, people covered Tahrir Square and its grassy roundabouts, and they settled in to spend the night of an unplanned but now imperative occupation. Egyptians' picnicking prowess kicked in. Thick blankets were handed out, sandwiches, potato crisps, and juice boxes materialized, bonfires were lit for warmth against the stinging January chill, lutes were strummed to accompany beloved 1970s protest songs, and effigies of Mubarak and confederates were somehow produced and hung from traffic lights. In the evening, news trickled in of the civilian deaths in Suez and one policeman dead in Cairo. Heightening the sense that something extraordinary was afoot, American Secretary of State Hillary Clinton weighed in at this moment. "Our assessment is that the Egyptian government is stable and is looking for ways to respond to the legitimate needs and interests of the Egyptian people."[15]

A police lieutenant-colonel received the order at midnight. "The square had to be cleaned up, absolutely no one was to spend the night there," he recalled.[16]

Armored vehicles closed in, antiriot troops were arrayed, and the first tear gas canister was lobbed into the sit-in at 12:45 a.m. It took three hours to "clean up" the square, using two hundred armored vehicles, fifty public buses, three thousand special forces, and ten thousand antiriot policemen.[17] Under the eerie sirens of armored vehicles and billows of tear gas, defiant protesters exchanged stone-throwing with police and dodged rubber bullets even as they doubled over, heaving from the gas. One daredevil clambered onto an armored vehicle and nearly overwhelmed the helmeted policeman standing in its hatch, who subdued the protester only by maniacally pepper-spraying him in the face. Holding up bloodied hands to a cameraman, another protester cried out, "They shot at us! They shot at us! Who are we, the enemy?"[18] By dawn, municipal cleaners had washed away from the square all signs of the popular occupation.

\* \* \*

No one had expected the numbers, the national scope of the demonstrations, or the cross-class diversity of the crowds.[19] Government ministers quickly ordered consumer cooperatives to stock their shelves with large quantities of subsidized foodstuffs, hoping to peel off from the emboldened opposition those hardest hit by cost-of-living increases.[20] Police chiefs in the field were taken aback by the fluidity and fearlessness of crowd movements, leading some of them to abandon standard nonlethal tactics of crowd control and use live ammunition. This is what happened in Suez and North Sinai, two sparsely populated yet abundantly politicized frontier provinces. Adjacent to Gaza and Israel, North Sinai's Bedouin residents were systematically disadvantaged by the Egyptian central government, barred from state employment and land ownership, perceived as fifth columnists for their economic and cultural ties to Gazans, and ruled by an oppressive security regime of periodic mass arrests.[21] On January 25, protesters in the town of Shaykh Zuwaid blocked the highway with burning tires and staged a large procession through town that included scores of 4x4 vehicles. The turmoil continued for three days. Protesters encircled the police station and headquarters of State Security Investigations (SSI), and security forces used live ammunition, killing twenty-two-year-old Muhammad Atef on January 27.[22]

Second-class Bedouin citizens also lived next door in Suez province, but the port city had additional coils of social conflict, heavily micromanaged by police:

local workers' agitation at their displacement by workers from the Nile Delta and southeast Asia, and a drug-running and weapons-smuggling economy that led to the assassination of a police general by an erstwhile informant in 2009.[23] By the early hours of January 26, security officials had pressured the three dead victims' families to bury them quickly—without forensics reports—for fear that recording the true cause of death (live ammunition) would trigger angry funeral processions. But thousands of enraged townspeople and protesters had already encircled the hospital morgue, blocking ambulances from whisking away the bodies for hasty private burials. Over the next two days, January 26 and 27, Suez went into insurrectionary mode, with no pause in clashes between people and police; five hundred civilians and three high-ranking security officials were injured. Protesters stormed the traffic department and torched the NDP headquarters and the Arba'in police station, and two thousand workers at the Suez Steel Company staged an all-day protest on January 27. Reporters immediately christened Suez "Egypt's Sidi Bouzid," the province in central Tunisia where the uprising against Ben Ali began.[24] Not for the first time and not for the last, politics on the Egyptian periphery fed the center.

The Day of Wrath might have gone down as one of countless protest events in an Egyptian political script: the opposition harangues, the government is unmoved. But disproportionate police violence set in motion another familiar dynamic: domestic and international outrage that jump-started further rounds of protest. European Union High Representative for Foreign Affairs Catherine Ashton rebuked the government for the killings in Suez: "I deplore the reported deaths following the demonstrations taking place in Egypt."[25] Buoyed by the international scrutiny, the opposition alliance announced a second day of nationwide demonstrations, to follow Friday noon prayers on January 28, branding it the Friday of the Martyrs.

The cloud of expectancy was even bigger than for January 25. Mohamed ElBaradei cut short his international travels and returned to attend the Friday prayer-protest at a prominent Giza mosque. The Muslim Brothers officially threw their weight behind Martyrs' Friday, so State Security Investigations arrested five hundred of their branch leaders and an unprecedented eight of their eighteen-member politburo.[26] And some Coptic activists and congregations publicly broke with the Coptic papacy and announced their participation. In a move "unprecedented in scope and scale," the government ordered a blackout on internet and mobile phone communications that began on the evening of January 27, but that still did not ease officials' anxiety. For protesters had a ready-made national coordinating device that could not be extinguished: Friday noon prayers. So the government took all precautionary measures short of banning the prayers. Preachers were instructed to sermonize against "destructive protests"; police were stationed at large mosques to admit only those carrying national ID cards; and, for the first time, state television was to broadcast the sermon and prayers from its in-house mosque rather than the standard practice of live filming from a prominent mosque in the capital.[27]

\* \* \*

Minutes before prayers began on Friday, January 28, a young man paced up and down the tightly packed rows of congregants lined up outside Alexandria's al-Qa'id Ibrahim mosque, clapping his hands and coaching, "Today we have to stand firm, folks. Don't leave each other, stick together!" "Never leave each other!" echoed a congregant. No sooner had the prayer ended than an earth-rattling chant rose up from the huge gathering of men and women: "Allahu Akbar! Allahu Akbar!" Hands raised above their heads and clapping in unison, they segued into singsong calls of "We don't want him! We don't want him!" Then they began to inch along in a procession, chanting, "al-Sha'b Yurid Isqat al-Nizam!" (The people want to bring down the regime!). The roar of human voices nearly drowned out the plaintive sirens, clouds of smoke began to rise above the stately palm trees swaying in the sea breeze, and people buried their noses into the crooks of their elbows to shield themselves from the tear gas. They scattered and regrouped on the Mediterranean Corniche, and a new, larger procession took shape, marching down the wide seaside boulevard and merging with more crowds emerging from the side streets.[28]

Elsewhere on the boulevard, a marching human mass came upon a lone troop carrier stranded in the middle of the street, its load of conscripts quivering inside. Chanting "al-'Asaker Masreyin! al-'Asaker Masreyin!" (The conscripts are Egyptian!), young men in the crowd formed a protective aisle for the riot policemen to escape through, then chained their arms around the emptied vehicle to prevent hotheads from destroying it, all the while exhorting their fellows to continue the procession with "Silmiyya! Silmiyya!" (Peaceful! Peaceful!)

A majestic scene was unfolding all over Egypt, as congregants streamed out of mosques and some churches, beckoning residents watching from windows with appeals of "Inzil! Inzil!" (Come on down!). Residents unable to join pumped their arms in solidarity or threw down onions and bottles of vinegar to help relieve the effects of tear gas. In a countrywide synchrony, ever-expanding crowds encircled the trio of institutions that controlled their lives: provincial capital buildings; government party headquarters; and police stations. In Minya, Upper Egypt's most populated province, thousands marched in its major cities, blocked the main highway and Corniche with burning tires, and attempted to torch the Samalout General Hospital for refusing to admit the injured. In the port city of Damietta, huge processions of energetically clapping, speed-walking men bellowed "'Aysh, Huriyya, 'Adala Igtima'iyya!" (Bread, freedom, social justice!). In the labor stronghold of Kafr al-Dawwar, home to periodic intifadas since the 1980s, townspeople reprised their well-honed tactic of blockading the major highway; this time they ransacked the government party headquarters. Local patriotism infused citizens' direct actions. "They thought they could take on Shubra's men!" swaggered the residents of Cairo's teeming northern district as they made a bonfire of the local NDP building's furniture and files.[29]

On Cairo's Qasr al-Nil bridge, steps from Tahrir, an epic hours-long battle pitted riot policemen and armored vehicles against a civilian army determined to make the crossing and reach the square. Under clouds of gas and the statue of anticolonial leader Saad Zaghlul, his arm outstretched as if pointing the way toward Tahrir, demonstrators on the frontlines surged into riot police formations, clambering onto armored cars as their drivers plowed into the crowd. At 3 p.m., just as demonstrators were lining up to perform the afternoon prayer, an armored car sprayed water cannon from extremely close range. Instead of scattering and retreating, the prayerful stood their ground and others rushed to fortify their ranks. Unfazed by the torrents of water drenching them and the unnerving police sirens, they bowed their heads and folded their arms in collective serenity behind a white-clad, bearded prayer leader.

The five intense hours from 1 to 6 p.m. on Friday telescoped daily conflicts between civilians and police that had developed over thirty years. As the impossible happened and protesters overwhelmed police in street after street, enforcement vehicles were burned, helmets and shields seized as war trophies, and a third of the country's police stations were torched. In a startling inversion of reality, police officers fled from the people, not the other way round. Officer Ahmed M. recalled:

> Two of my colleagues and I jumped from the roof of the police station onto the roof of the adjacent building and ran down the stairs and knocked on the door of an old lady we knew from the neighborhood. She took us in but she was hysterical and in tears. She kept screaming, "Why are they doing this? Why are they burning the police station? What are all these gunshots I am hearing?" We tried to calm her down and asking [sic] her to keep her voice down so people outside would not discover we were in her house. We stayed there for maybe two hours until someone outside somehow found out that we were inside and they started calling people off the street to come into the building and find us. All the residents of the building were evacuating. So the lady, God bless her, gave us some clothes to be able to mingle with the residents. She gave me a pair of pyjamas and gave the other two *galabeyas* and thank God we were able to escape unharmed within the throng of residents running down the stairs and out onto the street.[30]

Communications between Alexandrian field commanders record the shock and awe police experienced in Egypt's second city. "We are still engaging very large numbers coming from both directions. We need more gas," a squadron head radioed to a superior. "The people have barged in and burned a security vehicle. The situation here is beyond belief. I'm telling you, sir, beyond belief," radioed another. In other parts of the city, police had run out of ammunition and resorted to throwing stones. A high-ranking commander got on the line to sternly instruct a field officer, "Stop engaging and secure the police stations! You don't have sufficient forces to calmly engage these numbers. Go and batten down the hatches!"[31]

At 4 p.m., President Mubarak ordered the military to deploy on the streets. By that point, police were still fiercely battling civilians all over the country, but it had become clear which way the balance of power was tilting. In the early evening, a curfew was announced and tanks rolled onto major city streets, quickly making a beeline for the state television building and the Interior Ministry to prevent citizens from capturing these two vital government organs. Jubilant crowds cheered soldiers and clambered onto tanks to hug their drivers, but skeptics wondered, "Who says the army is with us or will even be neutral?"[32] Away from the cameras, clashes continued outside some police stations, with police firing indiscriminately into crowds. Jails were broken open, some by their wardens, and high-end malls and nightclubs were ransacked and looted. The enormous government party headquarters fronting the Nile was a smoldering brown hulk, burning through the night. The civilians at Qasr al-Nil bridge had succeeded in making the crossing to Tahrir, joining thousands of their comrades who had flooded in from the east. Together they dug in for the second popular occupation since January 25, forming a human chain around the Egyptian Antiquities Museum to protect it from vandalism. Night descended on the largest policing failure in Egyptian history.

\* \* \*

When Hosni Mubarak stepped up to the podium after midnight on January 29, it was the first time he had been brought there by the actions of ordinary people. Breaking his silence since the January 19 economic summit, he announced the sacking of the government and the appointment of his intelligence chief Omar Suleiman as vice president, the post Mubarak himself had occupied under Anwar Sadat but had kept vacant for the twenty-nine years of his own presidency. "Sovereignty belongs to the people," Mubarak intoned, "There will be no turning back from the path of reforms that we have charted, and we will embark on it anew towards more democracy and freedom for citizens."[33] A little over an hour later, US President Barack Obama weighed in with unusually blunt words for his country's premier Arab ally. "I just spoke to him after his speech and I told him he has a responsibility to give meaning to those words, to take concrete steps and actions that deliver on that promise."[34]

Daybreak on Saturday brought to light what had transpired the night before. Protesters camped out in Tahrir fraternized with soldiers, who consented to the scrawling of graffiti on their tanks: "Down, down with Hosni Mubarak." Turning incinerated police trucks into dumpsters, protesters and street children cleaned up the square, and once again volunteer quartermasters secured blankets, food, and water for the second encampment. Official order was suspended and the logic of popular organization set in. Banks and courthouses were closed and the Stock Exchange shuttered for the first time since its 1992 establishment. Convinced that police withdrawal and the prison breaks were deliberate measures to terrorize the population, citizens began organizing themselves. Armed with bats and kitchen knives, young and old men formed neighborhood popular committees to defend their streets and homes from escaped convicts and looters, screening passersby and stopping cars to check drivers' IDs. Volunteers directed traffic, donated blood for the injured, and formed human shields around hospitals and other public institutions. Some mosques remained open round-the-clock, broadcasting Qur'anic recitation to calm frayed nerves.

Citizens exulted in their own capacities, exposing the authoritarian state's failure to provide violence-free public order. Collecting impressions from Tahrir, veteran journalist Anthony Shadid recorded this resolution from a man directing traffic. "If God is with us, we'll take a clump of dirt in our hand and turn it into gold. We're going to take care of our country. Who else is going to protect it but us?"[35]

At hospitals and morgues, the gravity of what happened on Friday came into view. Relatives wept and fainted at the sight of their loved ones' corpses, many shot in the head. Not all were protesters. After putting her two children to bed, Heba Hussein, twenty-seven, was hanging the wash on a clothesline as policemen on a rooftop nearby were firing live bullets into crowds at Waily police station in east Cairo. One hit her in the head, instantly ending her life.[36] A flash point of police violence was the fortresslike Interior Ministry half a mile southeast of Tahrir, known as the "death zone." Doctors reported a preliminary count of thirteen killed and seventy-seven injured near the ministry alone.[37] In Qasr al-Aini Hospital near Tahrir, overwhelmed doctors reported ninety-five deaths and six hundred injuries, with more cases coming in.[38] Funeral processions merged with the larger demonstrations roaming the streets, categorically rejecting Mubarak's government shake-up, chanting "Neither Mubarak nor Suleiman, both are stooges of the Americans!" His first line of defense defeated by the people, Mubarak activated his second apparatus of coercion. Low-flying F-16 fighter jets flew over Tahrir Square on January 30, to signal unshaken government power and deter spectators at home from heading to Tahrir. Ducking as a jet roared overhead, an American correspondent on the scene told the news anchor in the United States, "I can tell you that when those planes flew over the Square, it just inflamed the crowd."[39]

There was more at work here than a tone-deaf autocrat unable to process the youth revolt on his doorstep. Mubarak was in the grip of a structural problem bedeviling all governments facing mass protest: swinging back and forth between concessions and repression, "trying to find a combination that quells protest."[40] The root problem was imperfect knowledge of the level of popular support for the opposition. True, Tahrir was full of demonstrators and anti-Mubarak marches continued to turn out every day in provincial capitals, but there were millions of Egyptians at home watching the contest of wills between government and opposition without visibly committing to either side. On this population Mubarak's aides now worked. State television broadcast footage of the president as confident commander-in-chief in an operations room, flanked by his loyal Defense Minister Hussein Tantawi and new Vice President Suleiman. To address reports of long bread queues and price gouging, governors were instructed to set up extra distribution outlets for subsidized food and fuel. And to keep people at home, government television anchors relentlessly smeared the protesters as foreign agents, hyping the lawlessness allegedly spreading through the country.[41]

Mubarak's particular combination of repression and concessions—killing unarmed protesters then offering a partial cabinet reshuffle—did not do its work. The protest movement amplified its core demand from just Mubarak's departure to his and his cronies' departure *and* trial. More groups began to join the *Irhal* (Leave) bandwagon; on January 31, university faculty, Azhar clerics, Sufi associations, and the Coptic Secular Current announced their support for the opposition. Hand-wringing and crisis management at the highest levels instilled a sense that Mubarak was tottering. Israeli Prime Minister Benjamin Netanyahu broke his silence, worrying that "in a situation of chaos, an organized Islamist entity can take over a country. It's happened in Iran."[42] President Obama dispatched Washington lobbyist and former ambassador to Egypt Frank Wisner as his personal envoy to Mubarak, carrying the message that he ought not to run for reelection in September.

Piggybacking on the public's outrage at police killings of protesters and withdrawal from the streets, the protest movement announced a *milyuniyya* or "million-man" assembly in Tahrir on Tuesday, February 1, the one-week anniversary of the inaugural day of protest. Hours later, a military spokesman, General Ismail Etman, read out a statement on television lauding "Egypt's honorable sons" and respecting their right to peaceful expression. Internet communication was still blocked, but, to further depress turnout in Tahrir from the provinces, the government announced the suspension of all train service, a first in living memory. As all waited anxiously for the Tuesday gathering, some gave voice to profound thoughts. Brought to Tahrir by his mother to see that the tanks were not scary, six-year-old Michael told a reporter, "He has to go. If we leave him to be president, he's going to be scared and won't be able to leave his house again."[43]

\* \* \*

Tens of thousands left their homes to overfill the streets, marching and congregating in scenes that stunned observers. "The protest march in Alexandria has now exploded into a massive crowd," recorded Peter Bouckaert of Human Rights Watch. "We stood here for ten minutes watching solid crowds stream by. And now a second large crowd has come down. Very impressive numbers!"[44] Suez crowds reveled in their battle-hardened status as the uprising's spark, vowing to erect "the independent republic of Suez" if Mubarak did not resign. Despite the suspended trains and sealed-off roads, Tahrir Square filled to its 225,000-person capacity and thousands more blanketed the surrounding streets. Whole families turned out, including their infants and toddlers, as Egyptians beheld each other for the first time in all their diversity, unmediated by the distorting filters of a police state. Doctors and dentists marched in their white coats, Azhar clerics in their red-and-white turbans; protesters with white burial shrouds draped over their arms joined the crowds, signaling their readiness for martyrdom. The unifying chant this Tuesday was "*Mish Hanimshi! Huwwa Yimshi!*" (We won't leave! He must go!).

In Tahrir, homemade signs were the rule, voicing sentiments by turns playful and dead serious. "Go already, my arm hurts"; "The carpenters of Egypt want to know: what kind of adhesive is Mubarak using?"; "Israel, if you like Mubarak so much, why don't you take him?"; "Police = terrorism"; "Sovereignty of the people, rule by the people." Some messages were penned by self-styled regional delegations: "The youth of Dahshur say: Mubarak, scram." The signs were then carefully arranged on the pavement for all to peruse, a remarkable crowd-sourced exhibit of political opinion.

To provision the encampment, volunteers organized intricate systems of water and bread distribution and, as ever, trash collection. The impulse to gainsay the government's doctrine of a disorderly people ran very deep. "You see all these people, with no stealing, no girls being bothered, and no violence," Omar Saleh said to Anthony Shadid. "He's trying to tell us that without me, without the regime, you will fall into anarchy, but we have all told him, 'No.'"[45]

Captivated by Tunisia and now the unfolding revolt in Egypt, rulers and people in other Arab states were rapidly revising their calculations. Jordan's King Abdullah II fired his cabinet in response to protests, Syrian Facebook users announced February 4 as a Friday of Wrath, and Yemen's President Ali Abdullah Saleh said neither he nor his son would run for office in the next election. Further afield, foreign activists and Egyptian expatriates organized solidarity demonstrations and issued a stream of statements saluting Egyptians' mass mobilization. "We understand the tremendous odds faced by the Egyptian people struggling in the streets today," announced a socialist party in the Philippines. "However, we also know, based on our own experience in ousting the Marcos dictatorship in 1986, that people's power can be victorious and prevail against the most cruel regimes backed by the mightiest powers on Earth."[46]

On February 1, for the second time in four days, Hosni Mubarak made a late-night speech, this time to bargain with the protest movement. Within the first two minutes of his ten-minute speech, he insisted that the demonstrations had been "used by those who seek to foment chaos" and turned into "regrettable confrontations masterminded by political forces seeking to escalate and pour oil over the fire." Protesters who had assembled around screens set up in Tahrir Square roared their anger, brandishing the shoes off their feet in the ultimate sign of belligerent contempt. Though Mubarak heeded Frank Wisner's message and announced that he would not run for election in September, the calls circulating throughout the day for a second Friday mass protest now congealed. The upcoming Friday, February 4, was conceived as an ultimatum to the president. Branded the Friday of Departure, it was motivated in part by the United Nations' finding that three hundred people had been killed during the first four days of protests.

Taking immediately to his own podium, President Obama ratcheted up his government's pressure. Fulsomely praising "the passion and dignity" of the protesters and "the professionalism and patriotism" of the Egyptian military, Obama pointedly messaged to Mubarak that "an orderly transition must be meaningful, it must be peaceful, and it must begin now."[47]

On February 2, after a five-day blackout, internet services were restored and uniformed police made a cautious comeback, but not to their police stations. They roamed the streets in ambulatory patrols protected by the armed forces. Then, unexpectedly, another part of the state machinery made its appearance. The government's National Democratic Party dispatched sizable pro-Mubarak demonstrations to Alexandria and several Cairo districts, leading the government flagship daily to proclaim, "Millions Support Mubarak in Marches."[48] In a spectacle familiar from election times, the counterdemonstrators emerged from buses and carried identical signs and flags, telling reporters that they were civil servants ordered to perform allegiance to Mubarak in exchange for £E50.[49]

Perambulating in Tahrir that afternoon, Muslim Brother shadow parliamentarian Mohamed al-Beltagui had an ominous encounter. A military general identifying himself only by first name, Abdel Fattah, warned him to clear the square of protesters "to avert impending bloodshed." Disturbed, Beltagui asked what made the general think he had any power to empty the square, to which the officer simply repeated his cryptic message.[50] But this was General Abdel Fattah al-Sisi, Mubarak's chief of military intelligence, and he knew what was about to happen.

Around 2 p.m., armed pro-Mubarak gangs and plainclothes policemen entered the square and moved close to the antigovernment encampment. Shoving matches quickly turned violent as the government militia surged into the opposition with knives, batons, and Molotov cocktails. Other government forces arrayed themselves on rooftops and hurled down chunks of masonry, and a third battalion stationed itself on the 6th of October Bridge and hurled stones. Just then, in a surreal sight, men riding horses and camels and cracking whips charged into the anti-Mubarak protesters. The Tahrir denizens quickly set up barricades and set to ripping the pavement into pieces that others ferried to the frontlines using scarves and crates. In the middle of it all, war photographer Chris Hondros thought, "The only way I can describe the situation today is that it was totally old school, just people with rocks, sticks and fists. It felt almost historical . . . just thousands of people battling each other." But for the tanks stationed between the two sides, the scene evoked Ernest Meissonier's "La Barricade," down to the chunks of rock covering the street and the blood-soaked heads and shirts of the square's defenders.[51]

The Battle of the Camel lasted over twelve hours, leaving thirteen dead and 915 injured.[52] Outrage at this latest incident of government violence and the military's deliberate inaction propelled a huge turnout at the Friday of Departure protest. Battle veterans turned out with their heads still in bandages and arms in slings, their bloodied clothing hung on an iron railing in commemoration. International outrage also peaked; concurrent solidarity demonstrations on February 4 were held in Spain, Malaysia, Turkey, Venezuela, South Africa, the Czech Republic, Morocco, Thailand, and Brussels, where an EU summit had Egypt as one of its main agenda items. In Tahrir, a huge cloth banner was unfurled down the front of a nine-story building enumerating the protest movement's escalated demands: bringing down the president; dissolving the two houses of parliament; terminating the perpetual state of emergency; forming an interim national unity government; electing a new parliament to make constitutional amendments for presidential elections; and prompt trials of those responsible for killing the revolution's martyrs and of corrupt officials "and stealers of the nation's wealth" (fig. 1). In a definitive break with the pope's pro-Mubarak posture,

FIGURE 1. Tahrir protesters' demands, February 4, 2011; photo by Hossam el-Hamalawy, used under Creative Commons license CC BY 2.0.

Coptic protesters formed a human chain to protect Muslims as they prayed, and, two days later at another mass rally, Muslims protected their Coptic communards as they held a Sunday mass.[53]

But, far from the last gasp of a dying order, the violent attack on Tahrir augured a reenergized government using a fresh combination of repression and concessions. To stop the flow of independent information out of the square, journalists and human rights activists were arrested and al-Jazeera's office and equipment torched. The veteran human rights lawyer Ahmed Seif was arrested and interrogated for forty-eight hours, at one point by the chief of military intelligence himself, Abdel Fattah al-Sisi. "Sisi started to speak [about] to what extent we should respect Hosni Mubarak and the military leadership, and how we must return to our homes and leave Tahrir Square." When Seif retorted that Mubarak was corrupt, Sisi "became angry.... He acted as if every citizen would accept his point and no one would reject it in public."[54]

The substance of government concessions was thin, but it was part of a larger push to isolate Tahrir protesters as a disruptive gaggle, restore workaday routines, and instill confidence that the mighty Egyptian state's managers were back at the reins. Train service was restarted and banks and courts reopened, though markets and schools remained closed. Travel bans and asset freezes were ordered for sacked ministers, including the loathed Habib al-Adli, and a 15 percent salary raise promised for public sector workers. Under the close supervision of US Vice President Joseph Biden, Vice President Omar Suleiman began negotiations with a collection of opposition politicians on liberalizing the rules for the September presidential elections. Sitting at the roundtable was Muslim Brother leader Mohamed Morsi, who a mere ten days earlier had been a political prisoner, arrested in the sweep ordered by Adli on January 27 to deter the Brothers from turning out on Friday, January 28. Now the government televised the talks with the opposition to project an effortless resumption of its agenda-setting power. A dispirited human rights activist worried, "The government has too much muscle. I think the people are going to turn against the protesters. They've already started."[55]

Upholders of the status quo within Egypt and abroad rallied to get ahead of the popular movement. Establishment intellectuals and businessmen styling themselves a Committee of Wise Men embraced Suleiman's stewardship of a negotiated transition. Powerful regional leaders lobbied the Obama administration to temper its pressure on Mubarak, unprepared to accept a new reality of Egyptian presidents accountable to their publics. In dozens of phone calls to US officials, the Saudi and Jordanian monarchs and Israeli personalities cautioned against a transfer of power. "I don't think the Americans understand yet the disaster they have pushed the Middle East into," fulminated Binyamin Ben-Eliezer, Israeli lawmaker and close friend of Mubarak. "If there are elections like the Americans want, I wouldn't be surprised if the Muslim Brotherhood wins a majority."[56]

\* \* \*

Away from the expanding crowds and the scripted roundtable negotiations lurked an underground reality. A protester was plucked off the street by an undercover policeman, handed to army soldiers, and bundled into an ambulance.

> It wasn't a real ambulance, but they just used it to trick the protesters and transport detainees from one side to the other of Tahrir. We were inside the compound of the Egyptian museum, and several soldiers started kicking and punching me.... They took me deeper into the museum's compound, where there were more army officials. They said I had experienced nothing yet, and threatened to torture me with electric shocks and to sodomize me with a bottle, as they kicked me all over again.... One of them then told me that those in Tahrir Square had been brainwashed, and that the protests were incited by Hamas, and that he himself had caught four Kuwaitis in his neighborhood who were trying to incite these protests. I just pretended to listen and agree with everything he said.[57]

The protester was one of at least 119 others who were arbitrarily detained by the armed forces after their January 28 deployment on the streets. Some were tortured, others simply "disappeared." From the testimonies of those released, human rights advocates detected a campaign to incapacitate the protest movement by targeting protesters delivering medical and food supplies to the square.[58] Invisible to many, the military had quietly replaced the vanquished police as the unbroken arm of state violence.

Soldiers arrested another protester and took him to Abdin police station, one mile east of Tahrir, where an interrogator tortured him for two days with an electric shock machine.

> At one stage, the interrogator went out and personally stopped a car carrying medical supplies, and he was so angry that he tried to break the window by butting it with his head. Then, one of the members of the Muslim Brotherhood arrested with us tried to reason with the interrogator, saying that we weren't a foreign-inspired movement, explaining that it was ridiculous to believe that the Pakistanis, Iran, and the U.S. were doing this as they don't work together anyway, and that we really were all Egyptians in the movement. The interrogator actually listened to him and calmed down, and even apologized for losing his temper.[59]

Soldiers and State Security Investigations officers saw the organization and fortification of the Tahrir sit-in and could only conceive of a conspiracy backed by foreign governments. There was no room in their worldview for a popular assembly of that scale that was both disaffected and orderly, whose cohesion was achieved without, and against, constituted authority.

\* \* \*

The protests had turned into the biggest international story in the US media, surpassing coverage of the Iraq war, the 2010 Haiti earthquake, and the US war in Afghanistan.[60] But in Egypt anxiety and fear gripped supporters of the uprising. Seasoned journalist Amira Howeidy worried that "the number one demand of the demonstrators, that Mubarak step down, seems as distant as ever."[61] Yet the return to normalcy so coveted by the government entailed an unwelcome by-product: the return of routine politics. With civil servants back in their offices and industrial workers at their plants, both launched protests for decent working conditions. Now shipbuilders in Ismailia, textile workers in Kafr al-Dawwar, cement-makers in Helwan, and steel workers in Suez voiced their demands, while in Cairo public sector workers in the health, telecommunications, and printing sectors did the same. "They take millions, we get millimes!" chanted three thousand Egypt Telecom clerks, decrying the pay gap between managers and minions in the state-owned landline company.

That evening, Monday, February 7, a young man the public had never heard of was being interviewed on a popular talk show. Wael Ghonim was a Google executive and one of two anonymous administrators for the Khaled Said Facebook page that had helped organize the January 25 protest action. Arrested on the evening of the twenty-seventh, Ghonim was detained incommunicado for twelve days, knowing only the broad outlines of what had transpired in the country as he walked into the television studio. Now Mona al-Shazly, the show's host, was narrating a slideshow of portraits of the revolution's martyrs, beaming young men (and one woman) with heartrending smiles who had been killed by police. Overcome by the gravity of it all, Ghonim broke down in sobs of grief and walked off camera. His raw emotions moved many people; that moment was the closest Egypt had come to a public memorial for the fallen. The whirlwind fourteen days had left no time for silent reflection or proper commemoration.

The next day saw the biggest turnout yet in Tahrir. Ghonim addressed the adoring crowds, who feted him for his sincerity and reluctance to play the hero. Now that transport networks were back, sizable regional delegations filled the square. In a measured escalation, a contingent of Tahririites processed to parliament a few blocks away and set up an orderly camp outside the legislature, complete with tents and blankets. More luminaries added their heft to the protest movement: Nobel Prize–winning Egyptian-American chemist Ahmed Zewail visited Tahrir that day, and two prominent dissident judges harassed by Mubarak's government announced their return from exile in Kuwait to join the movement. In the Tahrir way, politics and ordinary life fused; the second wedding in the square saw the bride and groom clasping hands around an Egyptian flag that ruffled above their heads like a free-form canopy.[62]

In the Mediterranean city of Port Said, residents of the Zirzara shantytown seized their opportunity. After the police had withdrawn on January 28, they had squatted in vacant government-built housing units. Now they fought back the attempt to evict them, ransacking the governor's office, piling up its furniture in a heap, and torching it along with two police motorcycles and the governor's Mercedes.[63] In Fayoum, residents demonstrated to oust their governor, and in Aswan, five thousand unemployed youth stormed a government building and demanded the dismissal of their governor.[64]

Egypt's three protest strands—workplace, residential, and prodemocracy—now merged to make a potent countrywide rising. Oil workers in seven provinces, administrators at major universities, bus drivers, bakers, bankers, electricity and irrigation clerks, and military production workers walked out to bargain for better working conditions. Giza sanitation workers pointedly called for one of the initial January 25 protest's four points: a minimum wage of £E1,200. Meanwhile the anti-Mubarak pressure was building in Tahrir. Processions of doctors in their white robes and lawyers in their black robes streamed into the square from opposite directions, more determined than other professionals after two weeks of treating the wounded in field hospitals or advocating for the detained and tortured. It was a dry run for the third Friday mass rally planned for the next day, February 11, again branded the Martyrs' Friday. This one would honor the three hundred dead that had since come to light.

But suddenly on Thursday evening, February 10, white-knuckle anticipation held the country and the world in thrall. Word had spread that Mubarak was about to deliver a third speech. Certain it would be his last, people packed into Tahrir, ready with props of celebration. "Mood is beyond euphoric. Saw a Conga line chanting, 'Hosni's leaving tonight,'" tweeted journalist Ashraf Khalil from the square.[65] Then, top generals announced a Communiqué No. 1 declaring that the Supreme Council of the Armed Forces (SCAF) had convened, a first since the 1973 war with Israel. "The Supreme Council of the Armed Forces convened today, 10 February 2011, to consider developments to date, and decided to remain in continuous session to consider what procedures and measures may be taken to protect the nation, and the achievements and aspirations of the great people of Egypt." As the statement was read out, a television camera panned a large roundtable to show stiff-backed, stone-faced generals, without the presence of Suleiman or Mubarak. Then came a statement by CIA Director Leon Panetta in Washington, DC. Speaking before the US House Intelligence Committee, he forecast, "There is a strong likelihood that Mubarak may step down this evening." But Information Minister Anas al-Fiqqi sounded a discordant note: "The president is definitely not going to step down." Twitter users passed the agonizing hours with #ReasonsMubarakisLate: "You think it's easy packing gold bullion bars into vintage Louis Vuitton luggage?" "The thugs are surrounding him, demanding their money." "He's taking a conference call with Kim Jong-Il and Robert Mugabe."[66]

At 10:45 p.m., Mubarak started to speak: "I can tell you before anything else that the blood of your martyrs will not go in vain." People huddled around radios, straining to hear his words. "Fully recognizing the gravity of the current difficult crossroads, I have judged that the moment demands putting Egypt's interest above all, and have thus decided on delegating the President's powers to the Vice-President according to the constitution." Confusion, shock, and anger rippled through the crowd as people tried to make sense of what they had just heard. Then the chant went up again with ever more force: "We won't leave! He must go!" Crowds moved half a mile north to the radio and television headquarters and settled in for the night, as the army blocked the building's entrance with tanks. Another contingent of three thousand protesters began marching six miles northeast to camp outside the presidential palace in Heliopolis, where the army had also reinforced its defenses. At this point, the protesters had Tahrir occupied and encampments set up around three vital buildings, including parliament. With Mubarak hanging on so tenaciously, intense worry set in about violence on Friday.

Why on earth was Mubarak clinging to a lame duck presidency? Stubbornness, stupidity, denial—all were bandied about after his third speech. A major meme of the signs and slogans was Mubarak as a dim jackass, but the autocrat was no dunderhead. He and his backers worked strenuously for him to control the minutiae of his departure, for the precedent of masses chasing out the sovereign would not be easily lived down. For all their work edging out Mubarak, Egyptian generals and US officials were keen to ensure a dignified exit for the man, to limit the damage to the office. The protesters' imperative, "We won't leave, he must go" carried a profound political meaning, threatening to shatter a painstakingly built status quo. The president is not the locus of sovereignty. It is citizens who decide.

* * *

The masses that turned out on Friday, February 11, retread geographies they had carved out only three weeks earlier. Marching routes, public squares, and muster points with no particular significance before January 25 were now established venues of popular demand-making. Regular people with no ties to networks of power now laid claim to the local and national institutions that governed their lives. Suez crowds fronted by parents of the city's twenty-four fallen civilians encircled the provincial capital building, forcing the governor to flee in an ambulance and prevailing on soldiers to string up their dead sons' portraits on the building. Peppering the throngs that covered Alexandria's streets were symbolic funerals for its seventy-eight martyrs, and people proposed renaming the legion of Mubarak-branded streets and public institutions with the names of the dead. In Upper Egypt's Bani Suef province, with twenty martyrs, thousands camped outside the capital building and dared the governor to come down and face them. The mother of a martyred young man said, "His whole life he got nothing from the state, but before he died his share was five bullets from the police."[67]

Shortly before 6 p.m. in Cairo, SCAF General Ismail Etman clung to a videotape as he waded through the crowds surrounding the television building. When he made it up to the newsroom, he waited for the call. When it came, he gave the go-ahead to the news staff to interrupt regular programming and broadcast the tape.[68] An ashen Vice President Omar Suleiman appeared at a lectern, slowly reading out, "Citizens, during these very difficult circumstances that Egypt is going through, President Mohamed Hosni Mubarak has decided to relinquish the office of president of the republic and has charged the Supreme Council of the Armed Forces with administering the affairs of the country. And God is the Helper." It was over in thirty seconds. The celebrations, fireworks, tears, and outpourings of international support continued well past midnight. A new banner was quickly strung up in Tahrir: "Breaking news: the people have brought down the regime."

In a coda to two weeks of occupation, volunteers headed to the square on Saturday morning, February 12, to clean up rubble from the Camel Battle, repaint the curbs a gleaming coat of black-and-white, and whisk away mounds of trash on pickup trucks. At every step of the rising in Cairo and beyond, demonstrators were obsessively cleaning after themselves. There was a concern for public health in such prolonged, large encampments, to be sure, but there was something else. Egypt's rulers long claimed to be the uncontested guardians of public order, managing a violent, chaotic populace. The relentless policing of public space presupposed that popular assemblies were a source of defilement and danger, the people too unruly to be left to their own devices. The constant cleaning, provisioning, and collective problem-solving of the mass sit-in were a sharp counterpoint to rulers' claims. The message: We can manage ourselves.

*Chapter 1*

# NARRATIVES OF EGYPT'S REVOLUTION

> The demon of origins has been, perhaps, only the incarnation of that other satanic enemy of true history: the mania for making judgments.
>
> —Marc Bloch, *The Historian's Craft*

THE 2011 UPRISING WAS THE BIGGEST ACCIDENT IN EGYPTIAN political history, anticipated neither by its champions nor its adversaries. Every step during the Eighteen Days was marked by uncertainty. If on the evening of January 24, some imaginative soul had suggested that in four days' time, masses of people would vanquish the police and army tanks would roll onto streets, he would have been dismissed as a dreamer. If on February 2, an observer believed that the Battle of the Camel would eventually be won by the unarmed demonstrators, his judgment would have been impugned, and impugned again if he had forecast that on February 6, the return to a precarious normalcy would also bring the resumption of labor strikes. The uprising began as a familiar protest action within an established repertoire of opposition politics, then developed into something much bigger, not in the manner of a growing snowball hurtling down a slope but as an assortment of local incidents, miscalculations, extraordinary cooperation, escalation, and the sheer unpredictable logic of social interaction.

Knowing how things turned out makes us flatten and forget the many contingencies making up grand happenings. What if the Sidi Bouzid community protest a day after Mohamed Bouazizi's self-immolation had remained a hyperlocal Tunisian disturbance? What if January 25 had not been a public holiday that freed up citizens for political demonstration? What if Suez police had not killed three demonstrators on that day, breaking from the violent but nonlethal pattern of protest policing that had developed under Mubarak? What if civil servants had stayed at their desks and industrial workers at their machines, ignoring the Tahrir opposition movement as irrelevant to their concerns?

By the standards of statistical probability and expert analysis, the uprising was not simply contingent but highly improbable. Analysts have found that undemocratic regimes collapse more often through elite intrigue and palace coups than popular uprisings.[1] Before 2011, one scholar of Egypt considered that mass mobilization was the least likely scenario for regime change.[2] The revolt also departs from historical precedent. Egypt's nationwide anticolonial rising in spring 1919 had strikingly similar features to 2011—mass marches in Cairo and provincial capitals, use of lethal force by British-controlled police, torching of government buildings, a crippling strike by civil servants, and rousing nightly gatherings in al-Azhar mosque, the era's Tahrir Square.[3] But the early twentieth century movement pursued a comparatively modest goal: protesting Britain's deportation of Egyptian politicians seeking an audience at the Paris Peace Conference to negotiate Egyptian independence. In 2011, the demand was nothing less than upending the system of rule. "People should not be afraid of their governments, governments should be afraid of their people," read the English-language graffiti on an incinerated police-truck-turned-dumpster in Tahrir Square (fig. 2).

My central purpose in this book is to show how the unexpected uprising opened up several possibilities for how Egypt would be governed. It destroyed Hosni Mubarak's dynastic ambition to transfer power to his son, clearing other untrodden paths. Most observers expected a fledgling multiparty democracy with a lively civil society and culture of street demonstrations, essentially an unfettered version of Egypt's contentious politics that had developed during Mubarak's three-decade rule. Unknown was the precise constitutional form this would take; parliamentarism and a mixed regime had their impassioned advocates, and virtually everyone valorized the judiciary and supported granting it more independence. The corollary unknown was the position of the military high command that had responded to the growing Tahrir protest by edging out Mubarak on February 11. The Supreme Council of the Armed Forces (SCAF) declared themselves dictators, in the Roman sense of a temporary executive,

FIGURE 2. Sign in Tahrir Square, February 11, 2011; photo by Ramy Raoof, used under Creative Commons license CC BY 2.0.

and pledged to organize free elections and hand over power to elected civilians within six months.

Few seriously expected the generals to gallantly step aside and hand power to civilians without rigorous guarantees, but even fewer believed that the military wanted to or would be able to rule directly. Between these limits lay several possibilities for a civilian-military settlement, some form of a tutelary democracy. It could have been a constitutional veto role for the generals, on the model of Turkey before 2002; a presidential regime with a dual executive, one a transient civilian politician and the other a conclave of generals; a parliamentary regime with rigorous military reserved points, placing entire policy areas and public offices under exclusive jurisdiction of the armed forces. Three years after Mubarak's ouster, in February 2014, Egypt had gone through a sixteen-month period of interim military rule; one crisis-filled year under a civilian president; then a popularly supported military coup where the leading general was about to become president in plebiscitary elections. By 2019, the same general had built a personalized dictatorship, a counterrevolutionary regime dedicated to the erasure of practices of revolution using the state's ample resources of force, myth, and law.

How did this happen? The events constituting this juncture are so interlocking and multivalent that the overwhelming impulse is to evade them as noisy details and embark on a quest to uncover "what went wrong." Works in various genres repeatedly invoke "tragedy" as the lens to make sense of the Arab uprisings as a whole, the staggering state violence, population displacements, impoverishment, and regional realignments that continue to unfold ten years after the Tunisian revolt that started it all.[4] Of Egypt in particular, as soon as the 2013 coup occurred, perspectives shifted and the regime changes of 2011 to 2013 were forgotten, replaced by a determinist argument that the military was plotting to rule all along and merely engaged in strategic deception until their swift strike. Some lamented the pitifully divided state of the civilian opposition as the enabling condition for military intervention.[5] My study starts from a different premise: many-sided complexes such as uprisings are irreducible to the actions of single or even a handful of collective actors. Egypt's uprising is not well characterized as an epic misfortune, failed revolution, dysfunctional democratic transition, or master class in military planning. Moving away from dramaturgical tropes of hopeful beginnings and calamitous endings, I reexamine the uprising in the largest Arab state as a concrete political phenomenon, an example of what happens when, to paraphrase Vladimir Lenin, rulers and ruled cannot go on as before, but a new political order is by no means assured. I resurrect the forgotten concept of a "revolutionary situation" to illuminate the conflicts that ensue when state authority comes under fierce assault but does not collapse.

## DEMOCRACY'S NEW PIONEERS

At this point, ten years after the Tuesday protest that started it all on January 25, 2011, it is worth revisiting the heady international reception of Egypt's uprising to see why political analysis fell by the wayside as impassioned outpourings of acclamation took over, then gave way to expressions of consternation. In February 2011, celebrity philosopher Slavoj Žižek enthused, "The uprising was universal. It was immediately possible for all of us around the world to identify with it, to recognize what it was about, without any need for cultural analysis of the features of Egyptian society."[6] Citizens the world over who felt alienated from their own political institutions felt genuinely inspired by Tunisian and Egyptian protesters' revival of the power of mass politics. Representations of Arabs went from stubborn exceptions to the "Third Wave of Democracy" to "Democracy's New Pioneers."[7] Marxist philosophers Antonio Negri and Michael Hardt saw in the teeming public plazas of Arab countries an instantiation of their concept of multitudes, creating "original experiments that open new political possibilities, relevant well beyond the region, for freedom and democracy."[8] Political economists Daron Acemoglu and James Robinson opened their influential treatise with the Tahrir protesters' insistence that Egypt's economic ills were the outcome of misrule.[9] Judith Butler waxed philosophical about "the way a certain sociability was established within the square," announcing new relations of equality and nonviolence.[10] Less than two weeks after Mubarak's fall, American public workers protesting an antiunion bill in the state of Wisconsin held up signs that said, "Egypt, Save Us" and, in the words of the pop song, exhorted "Walk like an Egyptian!"[11]

The exultant mood left no room for or interest in reliving the precariousness of the days leading up to Hosni Mubarak's fall. A commemorative genre began to develop, featuring stories of the uprising and experiences of its participants, including a whole subgenre of Tahrirana recalling the ambience and civic spirit of the square.[12] Soon precariousness was expunged entirely and improbability forgotten, replaced by compelling stories of an expertly designed uprising. A dramaturgical storyline imputed shrewd planning and creative leadership to a core group of attractive protagonists. Not surprisingly, the leading role was assigned to social media-using youth.[13] A *Time* magazine cover featured seven young highly privileged Egyptians under the headline, "The Generation Changing the World."[14] Sociologist Jeffrey Alexander used a performance metaphor to portray the Eighteen Days as an expertly choreographed drama:

> The agents who were at the core of this performative project formed the revolution's "carrier group." It was they who projected the symbols, and after they made the connection with audiences, directed the revolutionary *mise en scène*. The "scene" of the revolutionary drama was peopled by the hundreds of thousands

of protestors, but this unfolding *mise en scène* was directed, not by the mass of people, but by movement intellectuals who tried to work out the script and choreograph street actions in advance.[15]

As the months wore on and the initial jubilation of winter 2011 gave way to high-stakes political conflict and the regrouping of ancien régime forces, dramatic tropes of tragedy, farce, and irony dominated representations of Egypt's political upheaval. Žižek returned in late 2011, sounding far less exultant than he had in February, voicing what had become an article of faith among the Egyptian and international Left. "Unfortunately, it looks increasingly likely that the Egyptian summer of 2011 will be remembered as the end of the revolution.... Its grave diggers are the army and the Islamists," he intoned. "The losers will be the pro-Western liberals ... and, above all, the true agents of the Spring events—the emerging secular left."[16] A year later, in July 2012, seasoned journalist Ashraf Khalil wrote of the "Fading of Tahrir Square" as the Muslim Brothers' Mohamed Morsi became Egypt's first elected civilian president. "Many of those revolutionaries have spent the last year slowly falling out of love with the place and what it has become," he rued.[17]

One year on, after President Morsi had been deposed by a popularly supported military coup on July 3, 2013, stories in the tragic mode were legion, exemplified by Jehane Noujaim's critically acclaimed documentary *The Square* (2013), tracking a handful of activists in a classic arc of hopeful beginnings that ends in disillusionment and dejection. Then the "prosecutorial narratives" set in, blaming particular political groups for the coup.[18] Some commentators took to task the "idealistic revolutionaries," faulting them for radical puritanism, while others inventoried the Muslim Brothers' failures, insisting that Egypt's largest political organization was "driven more by ideological zeal and delusions of grandeur than by a realistic assessment of the political environment."[19] One scholar opined that "Egypt's democracy debacle" lay not in the interactions of contending interests but in a deep-seated political-cultural *caciquismo*, a deferential attitude toward the military as the rightful arbitrator of all conflicts.[20] Arab leftists debated whether the Muslim Brothers were part of the counterrevolution or merely turncoats; Gilbert Achcar saw the Islamists and the ancien régime as two rival counterrevolutionary camps, while Sameh Naguib saw their role as "a classical betrayal by a reformist, non-revolutionary movement."[21] Exiled, imprisoned, in hiding, or deceased, the Muslim Brothers did not have space to air their own views, but a former minister in the overthrown government looked back on their experience and saw insufficient revolutionary action: "in some major areas we should have been less gradual than we tried [to be] because it turned out that being gradual is actually as if we are stagnant," said Amr Darrag.[22]

In this book, I do not offer yet another dramatic exposition nor my own distribution of praise and blame, preferring to steer clear of the inquisitorial mode of historiography that Marc Bloch warned against. Riveting stories and prosecutorial narratives make for emotionally satisfying reading but poor explanations, built as they are on redacting many pivotal facts and events, telescoping protracted interactions, reducing the set of relevant actors to two or three and then assigning them fixed motives and watching them hurtle directly to results. Thus outcomes are traced back to actors' intentions, unforeseeable consequences are cast as strategies, and unpredictability, miscalculation, and indeterminacy drop out of sight. In distant retrospect, highly complex intersections of events amenable to multiple readings are recast as morality tales, complete with flawed heroes, dastardly villains, wise fools, and a clucking, all-knowing audience.

## A REVOLUTIONARY SITUATION, A NONREVOLUTIONARY OUTCOME

The most exciting yet analytically troublesome aspect of the Egyptian and other Arab uprisings is their interstitial quality, occupying a *terra nullius* between revolutions and democratic transformations. From the earliest days, politicians and activists were acutely aware of living through this perplexing intersection. The late Maya Jribi, secretary-general of the Tunisian Progressive Democratic Party, reflected in February 2011:

> What happened is more than an intifada but less than a revolution, and puts us in a delicate intermediate phase through which we are forced in part to build on what came before. The transition must be made on the basis of the present. . . . Why? Because this revolution, although popular, did not provide a political direction.[23]

What the Arab uprisings brought together the social sciences have increasingly segregated, studying revolutions, uprisings, and democratic transitions with different literatures, each with its own specialized vocabulary. The uprisings' synthesis of revolutionary modes of action with democratic aspirations has meant that serious scholarly treatments differ on the basic issue of what to call these phenomena. Much hinges on the choice, since how we theorize the central object of study determines what we look for in the material and how we assess its significance; as James Rule reminds us, "all theories offer some distinctive way of slicing up reality for analytic attention."[24]

Reflecting on the Tunisia, Egypt, and Yemen uprisings, Asef Bayat characterized them as "political upheavals that were both revolutionary and nonrevolutionary, reflecting both a transition to democracy and revolutionary desires for economic distribution, social inclusion, and cultural recognition." Borrowing the neologism "refolution" from the East European regime changes of the 1990s, Bayat offers a thought-provoking account of how the current epoch of neoliberal triumph has cramped political imaginations so drastically that Arab activists and politicians had no vision of revolution even as they were enacting it. Focusing on the same three countries, Jason Brownlee, Tarek Masoud, and Andrew Reynolds's favored term is "authoritarian breakdown," seeing the uprisings as unseating long-standing presidents but leaving no enduring political effects, given the retrenchment of autocratic structures. Amy Austin Holmes argues that Egypt experienced a three-wave "revolutionary process" against three distinct kinds of authoritarian rule (Mubarak, SCAF, Morsi), followed by two waves of counterrevolution under Sisi. Saïd Amir Arjomand urges us to see the Arab uprisings as "constitutional revolutions," drawing illuminating parallels with the 1848 revolutionary wave that spread across continental Europe and featured a similar intersection of parliamentary, constitutional, and street politics.[25]

Taking a leaf from Arjomand's argument that revolution and democracy do not exclude one another, like a circle and square, but hold intriguing overlaps and historical affinities that it would be productive to reexamine, I propose the concept of a "revolutionary situation." I argue that this overlooked, minor entry in the lexicon of political analysis illuminates more of the many interlinked events and controversies of Egypt's upheaval than the concepts of revolution or democratic transition offer on their own. I was led to this way of thinking by the sense that "authoritarian breakdown" insufficiently articulates the magnitude of what happened during and after the 2011–2014 period, while "revolutionary process" carries an implication of distinct phases in a developmental trajectory rather than the continuous stream of compromises and confrontations that constituted the uprising's politics. I also do not classify Mohamed Morsi's one-year tenure as an authoritarian regime but as an increasingly besieged civilian presidency. My strongest motivation is to understand how the uprising's component events, or episodes, were related: how did the two military coups, protean protests and demonstrations, succession of governments, wrangling over the constituent process, competitive elections, collective violence, and court activism impinge on one another?

They were linked in a sequence of historical time, of course, but they fed off one another in confounding ways at synchronous points in time, composing the major controversies and dynamics of the uprising. State coercion and other forms of collective violence stoked deep suspicion and skepticism toward elections among many actors; judicial politics had a decisive influence on the constituent process; twice, a mass protest merged with a military coup, initially unseating the autocratic president in 2011 and later the first civilian president in 2013. Yet the division of labor in the social sciences is that political scientists handle coups, elections, and constitution-making, while sociologists' domain is mass protests, uprisings, and a venerable tradition in the study of revolutions.

Revolutionary situation is a niche concept in sociology but will sound familiar to historians, whether or not they explicitly use the term. The central analytical move is to disaggregate the master concept of "revolution" into its three distinct subconcepts: revolutionary intentions, revolutionary outcomes, and revolutionary situations. Rod Aya offers a clear summation:

> Revolutionary situations can start without revolutionary intentions and stop without revolutionary outcomes. Those who do much to start revolutionary situations and bring about revolutionary outcomes may not intend to. Those whose actions and decisions do most to change society may take them after the revolutionary situation itself is played out. And, lastly, those who start, support, lead, and ultimately profit from revolutions may be (and often are) "very different sets of people."[26]

The chief insight is that revolution is a happening and not necessarily a project or purposeful initiative launched by an energetic "carrier group," as Jeffrey Alexander terms it. The equation of revolution with revolutionary intentions is a post-1789 "myth of revolution as an act of redemption and liberation of oppressed masses and nations."[27] As with all marquee concepts in sociopolitical thought, revolution is a baggy construct that bundles together very different varieties of political experience. Over centuries, it has accrued contradictory meanings, layering them one on the other rather than shedding old meanings as it grows into new. Before 1789 "revolution" connoted regime mutations, as in Plato's notion of the cyclical degeneration of aristocracy into democracy and then tyranny (*The Republic*, bk. 8) and Aristotle's tracing of the permutations of monarchy, aristocracy, and democracy into variations of the same type (*The Politics*, bk. 5).

The 1789 French Revolution inaugurated the familiar modern idea of revolution as regeneration and rebirth, transporting societies from backwardness to modernity in a linear trajectory of historical progress. Revolution was pictured as an unstoppable force of nature, completely resetting a country's political life and transforming everything from public culture to gender relations. Out of this historical juncture emerged the figure of the carrier class, the bourgeoisie, breaking through the fetters of anachronistic ancien régimes to haul their societies into the modern epoch. The 1917 Russian October Revolution introduced the figure of the professional revolutionary vanguard, channeling the energies of the masses into a decisive seizure of state power.[28] Aya's point is that we should excavate and separate the distinct meanings of revolution and not hypostatize them into a unitary, capitalized, transhistorical Revolution.

Being explicit about which dimension of revolution we are interested in bypasses the morass of disputes about whether or not this or that uprising is *really* a revolution. In a similar conceptualist vein, Alexander Motyl observes, "revolution is situated in at least three different semantic fields—those of upheaval (sudden, mass), a type of change (rapid, fundamental), or a type of turmoil (sustained, all-encompassing). If revolution is in the realm of upheaval, then its semantic cousins are rebellion, revolt, uprising, and insurrection. If it is in the realm of change, then they are reform, transition, evolution, and collapse. Finally, if revolution is a type of turmoil, then semantically related concepts are breakdown, anarchy, chaos and riot."[29] This matters because it is not only scholars who mobilize different meanings of the concept. Participants in the events constantly invoked different shades of revolution in their discursive battles to define the situation. Youth activists privileged revolution-as-change; the main fissure between the Muslim Brothers, Egypt's largest political organization, and their secular interlocutors was a fight over what constituted change, reflecting a deeper divergence over what counts as politics. Liberals and leftists accused the Muslim Brothers of selling out by pursuing parliamentary politics, and the latter ignored them and held fast to the idea that change is impossible without an institutional perch in the state (see chap. 3). Unsurprisingly, governing authorities pushed revolution-as-turmoil; SCAF used it to delegitimize Tahrir demonstrations and workplace protests (chap. 3), and Mohamed Morsi's government adopted the same framing when he became the target of demonstrations (chap. 5). The doctrine of *haybat al-dawla*, state prestige, is the apogee of revolution-as-turmoil, and the bedrock ideology of the counterrevolutionary regime of Abdel Fattah al-Sisi (chap. 6).

This thumbnail conceptual sketch is necessary because "revolutionary situation" recovers the ancient meaning of revolution as regime change through factional conflict. It is a juncture of hectic political struggle over ultimate authority that does not depend on revolutionary intentions and need not terminate in a revolutionary outcome, that is, the seizure of power by insurgents. The concept is open about the consequences of the struggle. Revolutionary situations can end with the triumph of insurgent forces, but they can equally well end in the reconquest of the state by a reconfigured old elite or by a settlement between new and old interests. The dynamics of the conflict determine the outcome. As Eric Hobsbawm wrote, "Revolutionary situations are thus about possibilities."[30]

Historical sociologist Charles Tilly transported the concept from the domain of revolutionary strategy to render it usable for social analysis, defining revolutionary situations as moments of deep fragmentation in state power, as distinct from revolutionary outcomes, the rapid, forcible, and durable transfers of state power from incumbents to a new elite. Revolutionary situations appear when three features converge: (1) coalitions of contenders advance strong claims on the state or some segment of it; (2) there is commitment to those claims by significant segments of the citizenry; and (3) rulers are unable or unwilling to suppress the alternative coalitions and/or commitment to their claims.

> Revolutionary situations drive to the extreme a political condition that is more common and equally crucial outside of revolutions: a shift in power over the state that threatens every group having a stake in the existing structure of power at the same time as it offers new opportunities to every group—including

existing power-holders—having the capacity to enhance its interests by acting quickly. While the acuteness of the conjunction between opportunity and threat sets off full revolutionary situations from their cousins, it is precisely this conjunction that helps us recognize their kinship. Ends of lost wars, disintegration of empires and cycles of protest may occur with or without open splits in polities, but they all have some recognizable traits of revolutions.[31]

Rather than a sudden, volcanic eruption that pushes society into a new epoch, Tilly's conception is explicitly deflationary, seeing revolutions (both how they start and how they end) as outgrowths of everyday political contention. What distinguishes them from routine politics is the presence of "multiple sovereignty," or competing claims for state control by two or more irrepressible power blocs, segments of public opinion that support the contenders, and the inability of the state's coercive apparatus to crush rival claims. Another distinction implied is that, given the high stakes of the struggle and the explosion of the political field to contenders and their supporters, opponents and their constituents, the undecided public, the state elites' vested interests, and international stakeholders, the exigency of acting quickly to secure or enlarge positional advantages will lead to a great deal more accelerated and volatile interaction than politics in less turbulent times.

Skeptics will find this an unacceptable loosening of the concept of revolution. This framing makes it capacious enough to include everything from regional revolts that establish temporary autonomy to national rebellions that may change governing personnel but not structures to a cluster of state governments coalescing against a federal government.[32] Yet that is the point of distinguishing between revolutionary situations and outcomes; the latter directs attention to the reconstruction of a new order by a new elite (Motyl's revolution-as-change); the former moves a step back, to the dynamics of the conflict before it is clear who will prevail, so that we can understand why the winners triumphed (revolution-as-upheaval). The notion of a revolutionary "situation" assumes that the dynamic of high-stakes conflict over state power is worthy of study for its own sake, regardless of the outcome. Or, more precisely, it holds that why things turned out as they did is illegible without tracing the sequences of interaction that led to the outcome.

Other skeptics may accept the disaggregation of revolution into its component subconcepts of intention, situation, and outcome but wonder how Egypt can possibly be considered a revolutionary situation when the military backbone of the Mubarak regime had control of the state throughout the upheaval. It is worth fleshing out how Egypt's events look from this angle because there is a patent truth to it. In this view, Egypt experienced an uprising, but no revolution, for the simple reason that no multiple sovereignty, or competing power centers, ever materialized. Only in a figurative sense can the Tahrir protest movement be interpreted as a countergovernment. It had nothing of the solidity of the self-constituted French National Assembly of June 1789 or the Petrograd Soviet of 1917, nor the audacity of Ayatollah Ruhollah Khomeini in appointing a provisional government five days after returning to Iran in February 1979. Indeed, it was to abort just such an alternative concentration of power that the military generals hastily assembled to remove Hosni Mubarak on February 11, 2011, and to prevent vital institutions such as parliament and the radio and television headquarters from falling into the hands of the swelling crowds. The generals then quickly seized all executive and legislative power and even expanded the purview of the military's judicial power, trying a dozen thousand civilians before military tribunals in 2011 alone.

In this light, each juncture from 2011 to 2014 was a calculated, well-played move by the military high command to encircle and defeat the uprising. In 2012, shortly before the first elected president took office, the generals again granted themselves key executive powers and dissolved the first legislature chosen by universal suffrage, seizing its legislative power and ensuring that the new president entered office unmoored, without the aid of another elected institution. A year later, the generals carried out their coup d'état, suspending the constitution, imprisoning the president, and killing over a thousand of his supporters. A year after that, they installed one of their own in the presidency in stage-managed elections and then packed parliament with their loyalists. The sine qua non of a revolutionary situation—multiple sovereignty—never happened.

Yet from another angle, this was no ordinary uprising. In the days and months after Mubarak was toppled, the Tahrir protest movement, claiming popular sovereignty, compelled the generals to put Mubarak and his cronies on trial; appoint two new governments; remove provincial governors; and backtrack from designs to control constitution-writing and stay in power for two years instead of the transitional six months. On the first anniversary of the uprising, January 2012, the first freely elected parliament since 1951 was seated, wresting legislative power from the military and establishing itself as a new claimant to popular sovereignty. Six months later, a contested presidential election brought to office the first civilian outsider president in Egyptian history, former parliamentarian Mohamed Morsi of the Muslim Brothers. When a fierce protest movement crystallized against him, it did so in the name of the people's right to replace the president, and Morsi's government retorted on the same terrain of popular sovereignty as embodied in his democratic legitimacy. In this view, multiple power blocs vied throughout the revolutionary situation; Tahrir versus the generals in 2011; parliament, Tahrir, and the generals in 2012; the president, Tahrir (with some old regime allies), and the generals in 2013.

The challenge taken up by this book is to plausibly reconstruct the dynamics of these conflicts between old-regime power holders, a variety of newly enabled, confident contenders, and the hordes of other actors who were pulled into the fray of revolutionary politics to defend and advance a multitude of causes. Tilly's notion of an acute conjunction of opportunity and threat brings into focus pivotal actors left out of most accounts of Egypt's uprising. These are the state agents who mobilized either defensively to ward off the threat of popular oversight over their affairs or offensively to improve their power positions. The military generals are only the most visible among this collection, but there are also judges on different kinds of courts; low-ranking policemen and untouchable police chiefs; humble civil clerks and elite bureaucratic barons; and the most disruptive, and short-lived, state actors, the newly elected parliamentarians of 2012 who quickly turned the legislature into a perch from which to confront the generals and then the courts over constituent power. By bringing them into the frame side by side with the more familiar cast of politicians, youth activists, and protesters, the following pages will re-present familiar events in a new light and bring to the surface events and interactions buried in the maelstrom of revolutionary politics.

## THINKING SYNOPTICALLY ABOUT THE UPRISING

Paying attention to the politics of revolutionary situations is not the customary way that sociologists approach the study of revolutions. In the Anglo-American social sciences, to talk of revolution is to talk of causes and consequences. The standard procedure begins with the outcome of a durable transfer of state power to a new elite, then reasons back to pick out only those factors that the analyst is looking for, guided by the chosen theoretical lens. A state-centered theory looks for crises of rule—fiscal, military, or succession-related. A class-centered model looks for escalating conflicts between owners and workers or landlords and peasants. A hegemony-centered theory looks for fatal cracks in the dominant ideas of the epoch or for a rising revolutionary consciousness among subalterns. The selected causes are explicated and arranged, then marched through the pages to their expected consequences.

The field-defining work in the discipline, Theda Skocpol's *States and Social Revolutions* (1979), compares three momentous "social revolutions" (France, Russia, China) that transformed types of rule, class relations, and dominant ideologies. Her causal argument fixates on the structures of ancien régime states, structures that broke down from severe geopolitical pressures, accelerated by class-based revolts from below. Jeff Goodwin's *No Other Way Out* (2001) builds on Skocpol's model and applies it to Third World states, but with a new twist: "states largely construct... the revolutionary movements that challenge and sometimes overthrow them."[33] The difference between these perspectives and my own is not just that they examine cases of revolutionary outcomes while I concentrate on a negative case, it is in the nature of the central research question. Skocpol and Goodwin ask, What is it in the nature of agrarian bureaucracies and postcolonial peripheral states that made them vulnerable to revolutionary overthrow? I ask, How did an unlikely contest for state power emerge in a durable authoritarian state, terminating with the victory of a counterrevolutionary coalition? Their work is about causal origins, mine traces trajectories.

Let me also distinguish my approach from another influential sociological contribution, a cogent critique of the causes-and-consequences school. Charles Kurzman makes the case for an alternative "anti-explanation," seeking to plumb the experiences of the 1978–79 Iranian revolution's participants, their motivations, emotions, and, above all, their overriding sense of confusion as they lived through a national political upheaval. Reflecting on the Arab uprisings, he counseled, "We might look past our obsession with causation and seek instead to understand the lived experience of the uprisings."[34] Kurzman's revival of Max Weber's *verstehen* aims to bridge the gap between subjects' self-understandings and social scientists' analyses of their subjects. The attractions of verstehen are overwhelming, especially for a region such as the Middle East, long accustomed to the condescending gaze of social scientists and experts.

Yet, though this book's pages are filled with the arguments, metaphors, and reflections of the revolutionary situation's participants and observers, this is not a hermeneutic study that recovers and represent subjects' inner states (emotions and dispositions).[35] My obsession has been the density and multiplicity of the revolution's events and how they ought to be conceptualized together. So I maintain a strict epistemological line between subjects' self-understandings and my own analytical narrative of events. Readers familiar with some or all of those events may disagree with my choices and arrangement, or wonder why certain episodes are magnified and others barely mentioned. That is as it should be. As a work of interpretive selection, governed by an analytical framework centered on the competition over state powers and authority, the narrative is bound to depict familiar events in unfamiliar ways and to highlight episodes such as the brief five months of parliamentary wrangling (chap. 5) that are completely absent in other studies of Egypt's uprising.

My method has been influenced by philosopher Louis Mink's conception of historical thinking as a "configurational" mode of comprehension. For Mink, historical understanding is more than the study of the past. It is a kind of conceptualization, giving analytical form to history's details and reciprocally marshaling details to refresh or revise concepts. "It would be misleading to suggest that historical inquiry consists of the indefatigable collection of facts and *then* a grand swoop of synthesis."[36] What distinguishes history as a mode of reasoning is "synoptic judgment," as in the original Greek meaning of "seeing all together":

> That events occur sequentially in time means not that the historian must "relive" them—by reproducing a determinate serial order in his own thought—to understand them, but that he must in an act of judgment hold together in thought events which no one could experience together.[37]

The concept of a revolutionary situation is my synoptic device to make sense of the analytically separable kinds of politics that we see in the uprising, namely elections, judicial politics, parliamentary contention, mass protests, constitution making. These political interactions occurred simultaneously, sequentially, and in an overlapping fashion, not on separate tracks. Analysis and synopsis work in tandem, breaking things down into their components to better understand their lines of connection, mutual influence, and contradiction. So many of the uprising's most baffling features come down to the intersection between these different ways of doing politics, interactions that we should untangle and yet see together in one mental act.

The varying modes of approaching revolution—causal, verstehen, and configurational—reflect basic philosophical differences in understanding the social world. Causal approaches seek mastery, abstracting from many-sided realities to identify the deep-seated forces and impersonal structures that foster human action and set its limits. Verstehen plunges the analyst into the concreteness of social life; in the case of revolution, it seeks to relive the chaos "as it really was," recovering how participants constructed meaning as they wrestled with overwhelming new experiences.[38] Configurational treatments share with the causal an impulse to abstract from manifold realities, not by reducing their complexity but reordering it into a legible arrangement of components, the better to see them together in a single frame. My hewing to this mode derives from a social ontology that I ought to make explicit. It rests on a relational view of social life, in contrast to the structure versus agency dichotomy that organizes studies of regime transitions and revolutions. When thinking about moments of peak sociopolitical conflict, actors are neither prisoners of structures inherited from the past nor self-directed agents calculating optimal strategies but individuals enmeshed in webs of relations with other actors. They construct their courses of action through mutual influence and pressure by allies, adversaries, potential and actual constituencies, and international parties. The unit of analysis is the interaction as it unfolds through time, generating new cleavages, shifting coalitions, episodes of brinkmanship, cooperation, and violent collision.[39]

Temporal reconstruction will show how provisional results at different points in the conflict were products of multilateral interactions, not a unilateral design. No election outcome, court decision, local or mass protest, law decree, military or judicial coup, political argument, or piece of legislation was produced by a single will. This is so evident as to border on the banal, but, as I hope to show in the following chapters, when we pursue this systematically over the course of the revolutionary situation, we see the political world differently. Caricatures of masterminding generals, hapless politicians, naive youth activists, and faceless masses give way to a sharper, more precise delineation of who was taking whom into account, why, and with what effects.

## A PASSAGE THROUGH CONTESTED SOVEREIGNTY

More than at any time in its contemporary history, the revolutionary situation exploded Egypt's political diversity. New partisan subcultures emerged, substantive political issues proliferated, and different kinds of social actors demanded political recognition. Newly politicized citizens wrestled with a disorienting mixture of past legacies and new conundrums. Time itself became a pivot of contention, especially the timing of elections in 2011; the sequencing of elections versus constitution writing in 2011–12; and the controversy over early presidential elections in 2013.

Egyptians wrote and spoke and sparred endlessly about what was happening to them, and their debates traced bedrock issues in political theory. The Islamist-secular divide which has received the lion's share of attention was hardly the only political cleavage that mattered. New axes of division emerged, chiefly: what to do about the agents of the ancien régime (and who counts as *fulul*, or such remnants); Do elections reproduce or subvert the status quo? Do protests undermine or deepen democracy? Is constitution making a form of politics or above politics? And the biggest issue of all: who commands sovereignty, or supreme political authority. Matters went further, as major contenders claimed constituent power, the originary power to establish a political order. The Tahrir *milyuniyya* (mass gatherings) claimed constituent power in the name of popular sovereignty; the military council did so as well, leaning on the constitutional article of 1956 vintage that stipulates, "the armed forces belong to the people"; parliament clashed with the military council over who had sovereignty over constitution making and the government; the judiciary claimed supremacy over parliament. The revolutionary situation was made up of struggles over power *and* authority, that is, its mutually recognized justifications. As Sidney Tarrow put it, revolutionary situations are "passages through openly contested sovereignty."[40]

The copious documentary by-products of this passage are the primary sources on which this study is based. The revolutionary conjuncture produced a torrent of documents—official fact-finding reports; rulings by criminal, administrative, and constitutional courts; procès verbal; decree-laws; parliamentary plenary sessions; constituent assembly deliberations; election returns; campaign manifestoes; partisan *prises de position*; slogans and couplets; tweets and Facebook posts; leaflets and broadsheets; unofficial archiving platforms; reports by human rights organizations; autopsy reports; pop-up books of personal experience or score-settling; protest petitions; martyr commemorations; letters from prison; photos and videos of every conceivable collective event during the conjuncture, from protests to election queues to parliamentary proceedings. Both partisan and professionalized newspapers printed many of these documents in full or abridged form, in addition to valuable regional and local news reports that, besides videos and the rare published personal testimony, are our only sources for the many important events taking place outside of the Greater Cairo conurbation. On several occasions, newspapers were carrier pigeons during peak political conflicts, publishing threats and exhortations on their front pages, as when SCAF and the Muslim Brothers traded barbs in spring 2012, or when military and police officials invited the public to the streets during the weeks leading up to the June 30, 2013, anti-Morsi protests.

There are two reasons why I rely on documents as my sole primary sources rather than the more common method of interviews with participants. For this study of political history, as distinct from political memory, my interest is in contemporaneous sources or material produced immediately after events. Indelible documents recording political positions, impressions, and facts in the moment are less prone to the misrepresentations, retrospective glosses, or hazy recall that impinge on actors involved in controversial or traumatic events. Certainly, documents cannot be read at face value; their contexts of production and the positions of their producers must inform their use. Their unrestricted availability enables readers to check my interpretations and develop their own readings. Still, interviews would have been a valuable complement, to access undocumented knowledge and buried information that might illuminate the many inscrutable and/or intensely contested episodes of revolutionary politics. But this book has been written in the time of counterrevolution; revolution participants are either exiled, in prison, deceased, or otherwise silenced. I can only hope that conditions might change to enable a work of political memory, to preserve participants' testimonies and honor their experiences.

Each of the book's chapters takes its name from a revolution-era slogan (or prerevolution maxim as in chap. 2), a crowd-sourced claim or counterclaim invented during the period under study to reflect some key dynamic. The chapters trace three political temporalities: the political environment that developed under Hosni Mubarak; the sovereignty contests during the revolutionary situation;

and their termination in a nonrevolutionary outcome and construction of a counterrevolutionary regime. Chapter 2 is a conceptual map of the political world out of which the revolution grew, analyzing how elections, street protests, and courtrooms became the three most salient arenas for doing politics during the thirty years of Mubarak's incumbency. Chapters 3 through 5 parse the contested sovereignty that is the nub of a revolutionary situation, "seeing together" its component political forms of elections, collective violence, mass protests, judicial politics, and civil-military relations. Chapter 3 examines how the generals' seizure of legislative and executive powers from Mubarak in early 2011 was first widely welcomed, then challenged by renewed mass protests, forcing the military to abandon its plans to rule for two years.

Chapter 4 reconstructs the first six months of 2012, the maximum moment of sovereignty conflicts, with the intersection of parliamentary politics, the first competitive presidential elections, and the constituent process. The political turbulence of the first elected president's twelve months in office is the subject of chapter 5, due in no small measure to the continued wrangling over constitution writing. Chapter 6 returns to the three political arenas identified in chapter 2 to see why the state-led counterrevolutionary thrust targeted these spaces under the revived autocratic doctrine of *haybat al-dawla* (state prestige). The conclusion reflects on what such a study of political volatility can contribute to our understanding of political contention more generally.

If alert readers suspect a "normalizing" conception of revolution at work here, they are correct. This study recovers Charles Tilly's observation made en passant decades ago, "Revolution dissolves as a phenomenon *sui generis*, for it becomes simply the maximum moment of conflicts which endure long before and long after the transfer of power."[41] By this I do not mean to flatten the richness of revolution or downplay its magnitude, most of all for those whose lives were upended by it. Indeed, Egypt's revolutionary situation holds within it many instances of awe and wonder, most as yet untold. This book clears a middle space, explaining the revolution as a set of struggles with histories while relating some extraordinary moments that have been buried under the tonnage of diminishment and forgetting.

*Chapter 2*

# LET THEM SAY WHAT THEY WANT, AND WE'LL DO WHAT WE WANT

هما يقولوا اللي هما عاوزينه، و إحنا نعمل اللي إحنا عاوزينه

> A widening scope for opposition can still be reconciled with the continuation, even the strengthening, of one-party rule.
> —Roger Owen, "Review," *Middle East Report*

PERCHED ON EGYPT'S NORTHERNMOST TIP, BALTEEM IS A SEASIDE town of haunting beauty, swept by gentle Mediterranean winds and dotted with majestic date palms. White-sailed feluccas silently glide down Lake Burullus; fishermen ply the lagoons, standing atop wooden canoes colored a faded turquoise and deep ochre; wintering white cranes daintily pick their way through dense reed swamps.

In late November 2010, I was taken by Balteem's natural charms, but I was there to observe its roiling politics. The town came to national attention in 1995, when an opposition figure ran against the government incumbent in parliamentary elections; police violence against his supporters led to the death of two elderly female would-be voters. The challenger was Hamdeen Sabahy, a journalist who was born in Balteem and developed a reputation as a Nasserist rabble-rouser in Cairo. Yet it was unusual for a dissident like Sabahy to participate in parliamentary elections. One of Hosni Mubarak's achievements was to corral the small political class in the capital, blocking it from developing a nationwide constituency. Dissidents could publish their niche newspapers, hold talk shops to preach to the converted, and appear on television talk shows to fulminate against the government. But organizing on the streets with the potential to mobilize a wider range of disaffected citizens was rigorously policed.

The 1995 elections were a turning point, auguring a trend of increasingly competitive parliamentary elections between rival government loyalists, on the one hand, and between loyalists and opposition figures, on the other. Sabahy lost the 1995 round but went on to win both the 2000 and 2005 elections. His voters fought running street battles with tear gas–wielding riot police in collusion with the government candidate, and three of Sabahy's supporters lost their lives trying to vote—the two women in 1995 and one man in 2005.

Balteem gained a reputation as a troublemaking place, and not just during elections. In summer 2007, townspeople blocked the highway for twelve hours with burning tires to protest the chronic lack of potable water, forcing the governor to rush to the scene and negotiate. A year later, they used the same tactic, blockading the highway with their fishing canoes for seven hours to protest the governor's abrupt decision to end distribution of flour rations to households.[1] No surprise then that the autumn 2010 elections in the flashpoint district were keenly watched. A local magnate backed by Hosni Mubarak's National Democratic Party (NDP) was determined to unseat Sabahy. Two days before polling, one of Sabahy's campaign managers was kidnapped, severely beaten, and left lying in a ditch.

Election day started at 6:30 a.m., with a pink sunrise and a polyphony of birdsong blanketing the hushed streets. I accompanied Sabahy's campaign flotilla of diehard local supporters, volunteers from Cairo, and photojournalists who knew that elections in the town yielded newsworthy photos. Our first stop was Balteem junior high school at 7:10 a.m., to drop off Sabahy's representatives for that polling station; each candidate was allowed at least one proxy in each polling station to monitor the vote. Though voting did not officially begin until 8 a.m., I saw an elderly woman voter already there, panting from the strain of hurrying to the station. I looked at her quizzically and she broke out in a huge smile. "I always vote for him," she said bashfully.

At 9:10 a.m., the first reports of foul play began to trickle in. Sabahy's proxies at twelve polling stations in the district phoned in that they were being ejected by poll workers (often municipal clerks). An hour later, campaign workers convened in the yard outside Sabahy's house to plan next steps. The pressing issue

FIGURE 3. Hamdeen Sabahy surrounded by supporters on election day, November 28, 2010; photo by author.

was how to get Sabahy's campaign workers to the adjoining town of Hamoul, to check on the conduct of polling there. The rival candidate hailed from Hamoul, which has a larger share of the district's votes than Sabahy's base in Balteem. At 1:25 p.m., reports of rigging in Hamoul started rolling in; a sense of defeat and disappointment seeped into the Sabahy campaign. A male journalist and ardent Sabahy supporter began to weep quietly. The town's main street was lined with somber-faced men congregating and sitting on sidewalks. Suddenly, a flotilla of cars and pickup trucks loaded with angry young men sped past in the direction of the highway. Seemingly spontaneously but actually replaying the town's well-honed tactic of collective action, residents decided to blockade the highway to protest what was now a certain sense of coordinated election rigging. The news traveled quickly and some campaign cars abruptly changed route and joined the caravan speeding toward the highway.

By 2:30 p.m., huge billows of black smoke wafted up from the burning tires and tree branches blocking the highway. Traffic was at a standstill, with freight trucks backed up as far as the eye could see. A campaign worker in the car I was sitting in said to no one in particular, "Didn't I say that this morning was the quiet before the storm?" As we made our way back to the unofficial campaign headquarters in the clearing outside Sabahy's house, I saw crestfallen residents gathered outside their houses, some cursing the government and others sitting in complete silence on their front stoops. At 4 p.m., Sabahy came out to address the large crowd that had gathered. Standing atop a pickup truck and clutching a microphone, the hoarse-voiced parliamentarian visibly struggled to control the crowd as livid young men repeatedly climbed onto the truck next to him and delivered angry harangues demanding revenge for the rigging.

Suddenly, a fully veiled woman dressed entirely in black materialized atop the truck and pulled the microphone from Sabahy in midsentence, screaming, "Don't you dare give up on this election, Sabahy! Don't you dare withdraw!" The crowd roared and chanted, "Balteem boxes won't leave! Balteem boxes won't leave!" Fearing that their ballot boxes would be destroyed or stuffed en route to counting stations in Hamoul, the crowd was intent on keeping the boxes in Balteem.

A contingent of the chanting crowd broke away like a renegade train car and headed for polling stations to confront the clerks engaging in ballot-stuffing. Riot police were activated and began firing tear gas canisters, blocking streets, and chasing down any young men. I accompanied a handful of journalists trying to get close to a polling station to take photos, but the gas burned my eyes and I couldn't see through the tears. I approached a matronly woman standing outside her house and asked for onions. Without a word, she rushed inside and was back fifteen seconds later, stuffing into my palm two small red onions slit through the middle. The journalists and I snorted the onions, immediately clearing our sinuses and eyes.

It was 6 p.m. now and turning dark, but people were still milling about on the side streets. I came upon a group of mirthful women and children clustered outside a house, clapping, laughing, and loudly chanting one of Sabahy's campaign slogans: "*Shemal!* (Left) *Yemeen!* (Right) We love you ya Hamdeen!" Astonished by this corner of joy on such a grim day, I started laughing too. By 7 p.m., a large crowd had again formed outside Sabahy's house, as rumors swirled that elections in the district had been officially suspended. The crowd's mood suddenly turned jubilant, and people waited for Sabahy to come out and give a speech. He was immediately mobbed when he emerged, lifted onto shoulders and given a hero's welcome. He gave a rousing speech denouncing the government and announcing his official withdrawal from the elections. The crowd pressed him to authorize and lead a peaceful protest march to the police station to protest the rigging, but Sabahy feared security forces' violent response and did not want casualties among his supporters, which had occurred in the past. The back-and-forth went on for an hour but in the end he prevailed. The crowd was dejected, though no one took matters into their own hands as they had that afternoon. People began to disperse, but some sat in silence out in the open, mulling over their stolen election.

## CONCEPTUALIZING THIRTY YEARS OF AUTHORITARIAN POLITICS

As police forces and poll workers were fixing the vote in Balteem to prevent an opposition incumbent from reentering parliament, the same was happening across dozens of other districts across Egypt. The Mubarak regime had resolved to eject all opposition figures from the 2010 parliament, to reverse the gains they had made in the previous election cycle, when they had controlled a quarter of seats. When final election returns were announced in 2010, the opposition's share had dropped to 3 percent. The election capped a three-year surge of repression by the regime to block advances by both the parliamentary and extraparliamentary oppositions, part of a larger bid to prepare the ground for upcoming presidential elections in 2011 that Hosni Mubarak's son Gamal was widely expected to contest.

The dynamics of government-opposition interaction drop out in retrospective accounts of politics in the Mubarak regime, constructed after the fact with the knowledge that Mubarak was toppled by the January 25, 2011, uprising. We are so accustomed to thinking of prerevolutionary eras as years of decline and decay that it was unsurprising to read after 2011 assertions that the revolution was inevitable. "The extent of socioeconomic and political deterioration that occurred during the last 20 years gradually pushed the country towards an inevitable explosion," wrote one observer. Another backward glance at the Mubarak period saw a regime based on nothing but fear and lies. "Egyptian media did not report news that reflected badly on the government, especially news about protests," asserted Zeynep Tufekci. "People feared talking about politics except with their close family and friends—and sometimes even with them." An opposite view saw protests under Mubarak as a dry run for the 2011 mass rising, infusing with portent every worker strike and student demonstration. "The 2011 uprising did not come out of nowhere," wrote Jeroen Gunning and Zvi Baron, "but emerged from a decade of intense protest waves which had forged, and been forged by, activists in ever-widening protest networks. Each wave built on the previous ones, strengthening existing networks, extending network links and bringing in more sectors of society."[2] In hindsight, the Mubarak era takes on epic dimensions, a progressive march toward either liberation or a void of silent paralysis.

This chapter skirts the dual impulses to discount or inflate political dynamics in the Mubarak period, taking up the challenge of understanding prerevolutionary politics on their own terms without succumbing to teleological thinking and other retrospective fallacies. The particular struggles of Balteem and dozens of similar electoral districts with opposition challengers underscore a defining feature of the Mubarakist political order: the government's careful management rather than outright banning of public political opposition. If we take public politics to mean "all externally visible interactions among constituted political actors and agents of government,"[3] what is striking about Mubarak's era is the range of public politics over its three-decade span. By 2010, both parliamentary and extraparliamentary politics had crystallized into visible, adversarial confrontations between collective claims and counterclaims, almost always involving government officials as their target. Even the casual visitor to Egypt noticed the freewheeling public criticism of authorities, including biting takedowns of Hosni Mubarak himself in opposition newspapers and street protests. This was not the sort of political system where people looked over their shoulder or spoke in code while in public. The public dissimulation of privately held oppositional views that Timur Kuran identified as the hallmark of dictatorship does not capture prerevolution Egypt.[4] In fact, political activists ruefully noted the government's stratagem of letting people talk politics while rigorously managing their practice of it. "Let them say what they want, and we'll do what we want" is how many dejected cause lawyers and opposition politicians described the government's philosophy, with its clever toleration of dissenting political speech but rigorous policing of political organization.

Scholars too have long pinpointed the management rather than crushing of interest groups as Egyptian authoritarianism's trademark. Clement Henry

Moore emphasized the Gamal Abdel Nasser regime's (1952–70) "tremendous elasticity in its ability to absorb new groups in plastic structures, control them, and satisfy an occasional demand without sacrificing resources needed to satisfy other groups." Surveying Egypt's "unruly" associational life under Anwar Sadat (1970–81) and Hosni Mubarak, Robert Bianchi made this insightful obiter dictum: "The plasticity of Egyptian authoritarianism is evident... in its willingness to be worn down by protracted struggles arising from the daily defiance of unpopular and unenforceable laws." Robert Springborg formalized the dissidents' lament: "Less oppressive than the pure authoritarian model, this mixed polity draws a sharp line between political expression and political action." And in the most sustained study of the variety of opposition groups under Mubarak, Holger Albrecht went further, adopting a functionalist approach to emphasize the regime's instrumental use of opposition to stabilize its rule, albeit noting the limits of this strategy.[5]

Yet while the absorptive capacities of the Egyptian authoritarian state are duly noted, they are seldom demonstrated. After all, Mubarak ruled Egypt for as long as Nasser and Sadat combined, a long three decades in which the same man occupied the presidency, but both his inner circle and the broader citizenry experienced multiple mutations. The material underpinnings of public politics were also transformed, with economic management shifting from state capitalism and central planning to crony capitalism and market-led growth. Given these changes, how did Mubarak and his shifting inner circle undemocratically rule such a large population (84 million in 2010) for twenty-nine years? How did successive governments achieve the balancing act of superintending a contentious public politics while never allowing opposition to threaten the ruling group's hold on power?

Authoritarian rule entails a paradoxical combination of popular participation and governmental domination. This Janus-faced trait of modern authoritarianism preoccupied classic works in the field. Scholars have long tried to pin down how it is that authoritarian rulers channel public political practices within safe boundaries. Juan Linz, analyzing Francisco Franco's regime in Spain, extrapolated from it this foundational observation that continues to structure our understanding of modern nondemocracies: "Authoritarian regimes are characterized by a limited (legal or de facto) pluralism, not only within the governing group but within institutions and social forces."[6] Linz chronicled the arenas where plural social forces parried with government control, noting the latter's master strategy of promoting apoliticism in the broader population so as to handily deal with a narrow circle of activists. "The population that does not become involved in politics or withdraws from politics can be large.... [they] are in the background of the conflicts between the governing group and its critics, dissidents, and opponents."[7]

Political sociologist Charles Tilly goes one level deeper, devising a helpful schematization of how state managers code and categorize popular political practices ("performances" as he called them) in all regimes, not only nondemocracies:

> Every government distinguishes among claim-making performances that it prescribes (e.g., pledges of allegiance), those it tolerates (e.g., petitioning), and those it forbids (e.g., assassination of officials). The exact contours of the three categories vary from regime to regime as a result of accumulated bargains between rulers and their subject populations.[8]

We can conceptualize public politics under Mubarak not as a top-down master template engineered by the ruling elite en bloc but as a set of adversarial bargains continuously negotiated between different government agents and social groups in the course of repeated confrontations. These settlements constituted the Egyptian polity under Mubarak as a patchwork of occasional prescribed performances (e.g., bussing of civil servants to vote for government party candidates); several forbidden performances (e.g., popular election of the president, opposition control of parliament); and a wide range of tolerated acts. Unlike the Syrian government's obsessive staging of outlandish prescribed performances under Hafez al-Assad, or the Tunisian government's long list of forbidden performances under Zine El Abidine Ben Ali, Mubarak's regime stands out for its toleration of a relatively broad array of open political practices.[9]

Unintentionally, the term "toleration" has an avuncular whiff, as if governments benevolently indulge citizens' boisterous behavior. In fact, toleration is a far more adversarial operation, involving relentless government policing and revision of the boundaries of the politically permissible. Regulation of the political arena is driven not just by bottom-up political innovations but reflects the ruling group's own changing internal dynamics. One of the main developments during Mubarak's years in power was the increasing salience of the president's party, the National Democratic Party (NDP), both as a mechanism of intra-elite spoils division and as a vehicle for hereditary succession.[10] Putting these conceptual elements together—Linz's idea of depoliticizing the general public to better manage the politicized public, Tilly's insight on the boundaries of political action as ever-shifting results of interaction—we can analyze the making and remaking of the political arena during Mubarak's tenure without falling into idealizations of "popular resistance" facing off against "authoritarian resilience." As in Balteem, in the rest of Egypt government agents openly struggled with demand-making constituencies, neither side able to fully subdue the other. Over time, we see not a linear trajectory of a weakening state and an emboldened society, still less a placid arena of effortless state control, but recurrent cycles of mobilization, state repression, provisional settlements, and new rounds of conflict. We see election contests turn into demonstrations, courtrooms turn into political stages, and a set of protest practices attain familiarity through repetition and begin to diffuse across diverse interest groups. Tracing how elections, courts, and protests became fields of political maneuver, this chapter unfolds its epigraph, Roger Owen's prescient 1991 prediction that Egyptian politics would develop not into a zero-sum game but a set of struggles that would mutually strengthen both power holders and their diverse interlocutors.

## COMPETITIVE ELECTIONS AND A PEASANT INTIFADA

Examined up close, rigging elections is a gargantuan feat of manipulation. As Andreas Schedler notes, "For authoritarian governments striving to contain the uncertainty of electoral outcomes, multiparty elections with universal suffrage involve problems of agency control at a massive scale."[11] The primary goal for Mubarak's governments was to reserve for the president's party the all-important two-thirds parliamentary supermajority needed to pass legislation, constitutional amendments, and nomination of the president for term renewals.[12] No less important was to abort linkages between voters and opposition politicians on the campaign trail, to promote the generalized apoliticism that Juan Linz described. For example, the 1987 general election showed a ruler in full control; the president's party obtained 80 percent of seats while opposition parties combined (including the Muslim Brothers) secured 20 percent. As Erika Post noted at the time, "The most striking thing about the poll was the general lack of popular enthusiasm it evoked."[13] A legislature full of government supporters enabled the smooth nomination of Mubarak by parliament for a second six-year term in 1987, a choice that was approved in a referendum by 97 percent.

The 1995 general election took place under very different conditions.[14] In 1991, the government had begun implementing an economic restructuring plan mandated by the International Monetary Fund (IMF) that required trade liberalization, tax increases, public spending cuts, subsidy removals, and a first wave of privatizing state-owned enterprises. However, despite the austerity policies, the government increased social spending but directed it to what political economist Samer Soliman called "political control expenditures."[15] The context was that Mubarak was facing the first (and as it turned out, only) armed opposition to his rule. The militant Jihad group that had assassinated president Anwar Sadat, murdered Speaker of Parliament Rifʿat al-Mahgub and secular intellectual Farag Foda, along with another Islamist organization, al-Gamaʿa al-Islamiyya, launched attacks on security forces, Coptic Christian businesses and homes, and tourist sites. The state's violent confrontations with the groups led to 1,442 deaths and 1,779 injuries,[16] a "war on terrorism" that targeted all forms of association. Between 1993 and 1995, new laws effectively ended elections in professional associations; ended elections of village mayors and faculty deans (replacing them with appointment by governors and university presidents who are in turn appointed by the president); extended the terms of office for incumbent leaders in state-controlled unions; and increased penalties for journalists accused of libeling government officials.

This domestic context was nested in a broader regional reality, an early "Arab Spring" in Algeria that had far-reaching consequences across the Arab world and beyond. After mass protests led president Chadli Benjedid to switch from a one-party to a controlled multiparty system in 1991, the new legal Islamist party Front Islamique du Salut (FIS) gained more than 80 percent of the seats in the first round of elections. However, before the second round could be held in January 1992, the Algerian military suspended the elections, banned the FIS, and ordered mass arrests of its members, plunging the country into a decade-long civil war. For Arab autocrats and their American supporters, the Algerian experience held one unambiguous lesson: even controlled elections could displace rulers. A major 1992 US policy statement on the Middle East warned that Islamists would use elections to destroy democratic institutions and retain power, coining the widely circulated phrase "one person, one vote, one time" to characterize this purported Islamist ploy.[17] It was at this juncture that Arab state elites resuscitated a wooly concept from the annals of statist political thought to frame their violent repression of Islamists as a matter of restoring "state prestige" (*haybat al-dawla*), or the reverential awe owed the state. At a 1993 meeting in Cairo with supportive Egyptian government newspaper editors and other establishment intellectuals, the military-installed Algerian acting president Ali Kafi said:

> Algeria is committed to uprooting terrorism and violence, and confronting attempts to use religion as a means to attain power. . . . We do want to build democracy, but should we sacrifice the state for the sake of democracy? We are in no need of elections that sweep away the state, we will not sacrifice Algeria for the sake of democracy. We must recover the prestige of the state and reestablish its foundations.[18]

Echoing the American policy document and indigenizing it with a statist theory that equated electoral contestation with state collapse, Kafi's argument would become Arab rulers' stock position on parliamentary opposition. Algeria's aborted democratization launched the public career of a concept that would surface two decades later, when Arab presidents-for-life were toppled by the mass uprisings of 2011.

The Mubarak regime was thus determined that the first round of the Algerian elections not be repeated in Egypt's 1995 poll. Months ahead of the vote, the State Security Investigations Directorate, Egypt's domestic intelligence agency, arrested members of the Muslim Brothers to prevent them from running in the autumn polls. They were referred to trial before military tribunals on charges of subversion and sentenced to three or five years' hard labor. The election results saw the president's party securing 94 percent of parliament seats, its largest share ever, at the cost of the most electoral violence seen up to that point or since; fifty-one died and 878 were injured. At the same time, the election broke another record as the most competitive general poll yet, with 4,277 candidates vying for 444 seats.[19] Government incumbents faced non-Islamist opposition challengers, including journalist Hamdeen Sabahy, who did not secure a seat. But the real competition took the form of intramural rivalry between the NDP's official candidates and those passed over for nomination; one-third of the 4,277 aspirants were disgruntled loyalists who decided to run anyway, leveraging their local ties to defeat the official candidates handpicked by the party leadership. Violent street battles between followers of rival NDP bigwigs contributed to the lethal nature of the election.

If the elections were not a true barometer of public opinion or the relative weight of government and opposition forces, they did accurately reflect a different social process: the political debut of Egypt's new capitalist class. The Oslo Accords between Israel and the Palestinians (1993) followed by the Barcelona Process (1995) had pulled Egypt into a new "Mediterranean" economic arena linking southern European, Israeli, and Egyptian business interests and propelling their political ascent in both Egypt and Israel.[20] The Egyptian variant of crony capitalism had a dynastic undertow. The US-Egypt Presidents' Council, a new lobby group of thirty top Egyptian and American businessmen established in 1995 by Hosni Mubarak and US Vice President Al Gore, included Mubarak's younger son Gamal, an investment banker who began promoting himself as "an important force behind Egypt's efforts at economic reform."[21] Gamal's official political debut would come in 2000, when he joined the politburo of his father's party, the same year that Bashar al-Assad inherited the Syrian presidency from his father Hafez.

The competitive and violent elections, Mubarak's inaugural dynastic gestures, and the economic thawing of a heretofore frosty Arab-Israeli peace came together in the new network of business associates linked to Mubarak. Two top tycoons married into the Mubarak family, while the rest held positions of privilege in the upper house of parliament and the American Chamber of Commerce in Egypt (Amcham), owned niches within the burgeoning print and satellite media market, and were exclusive agents of American and Gulf corporations. For this business elite, parliamentary seats had become "increasingly attractive investments."[22] Businessmen on the make craved the immunity and insider knowledge of important economic legislation that a spot in parliament made possible. The legislature seated in 1995 contained the largest number of businessmen of any Egyptian parliament, seventy-one deputies compared to thirty-one in the 1990 legislature.[23]

Manifestations of Egypt's changing political economy were also visible below the commanding heights of state and economy. The largest mobilization against privatization began not on shop floors but in fields, when 900,000 tenant farmers and their families rose up to defend their way of life. A new law raising land rents by 315 percent went into effect in October 1997, evicting tenants off land that they had tilled since the 1950s and passed on to sons in perpetuity under a system of quasi-property ownership. Anticipatory repression began months before the law's activation, with police forces working alongside landowners' guards to break up peaceful protest gatherings and tear down the black banners hung up in streets and at town entrances as an emblem of protest.[24] It is all but forgotten now, or shrugged off as an ineluctable by-product of globalization, but a wave of peasant civil disobedience spread across provincial towns in Upper Egypt and the Delta throughout the second half of 1997, powered by a repertoire of practices that a few short years later would seep into the routines of Egyptian urban politics. The left-wing newspaper *al-Ahali* was one of only a handful of outlets that documented the farmers' resistance to their dispossession:

> Tuesday, July 1 was the date set by Agriculture Minister Yusuf Wali for transferring ownership deeds from tenants to owners, with procedures taking place at the agricultural associations. On Tuesday morning, in Tawfiqiyya village (pop. 8,000), Markaz Samalouṭ, tenants did not make their way to the Tuesday market as usual but headed to the headquarters of the agricultural association, where landowners were present. Villagers destroyed the association's door, windows, and land registers to stop the transfer of land ownership, then they set the building ablaze. At that point, the crowds had swelled to 5,000, occupying the Minya-Cairo highway, blocking traffic and setting a public bus on fire after allowing its passengers to disembark. They then made their way to the railroad tracks to block them. For an hour and a half, security forces chased down farmers in the village's narrow streets and alleyways and fired 3,000 bullets, leading to the death of three fellaheen. The Minya governor hastily ended a meeting and accompanied the director of security to the scene. Nineteen villagers were arrested.
>
> In Attaf village in Mahalla, as with news of deaths, accidents, and natural disasters, the mosque loudspeaker was used to announce that owners had begun evicting tenants from their lands. Villagers went out in droves and made their way to the agricultural association, throwing rocks and stones at its door and windows and seizing some of its land registers to burn outside in a heap. Thirty-six villagers were arrested and charged with rioting, resisting authorities, destroying a government building, and burning official documents.[25]

Elsewhere in Egypt, farmers staged die-ins and sit-ins on their fields, marched in huge processions, organized communal hunger strikes that lasted for days, sabotaged roads and railway tracks as their predecessors had in the 1919 anticolonial uprising, and torched agricultural cooperatives' buildings. To suppress what the opposition press called the "peasant Intifada," security forces used live ammunition and mass arrests, causing over two dozen deaths.[26]

## COLLECTIVE BARGAINING BY RIOT

On March 5, 2000, on her way back from school, fifteen-year-old Samah Mostafa Abdallah was struck and killed by a truck as she crossed the hazardous Cairo-Alexandria highway where it bisected her town of Mit Nama in Qalyoubiyya. Three thousand townspeople assembled and blocked the highway, demanding the building of a pedestrian footbridge to prevent recurring road fatalities. Security forces used tear gas, injuring twenty-five people and arresting seventy-five. Prosecutors later referred seventy-seven "rioters" (plus thirteen minors) to the Supreme State Security Court.[27] One week later, in the town of Awlad Seif in neighboring Sharqiyya province, a speeding tour bus careened into a group of women waiting to cross the highway, killing fifteen-year-old student Doaa' El-Sayed and nineteen-year-old textile worker Hanan Abdel 'Al. One resident announced the news on the mosque's loudspeaker, bringing out a crowd that blocked the highway for four hours, torched the tour bus, and stoned a train that happened to halt near the scene. Residents clashed with firemen and security forces, and seventeen were arrested. The Sharqiyya governor ordered the swift disbursement of compensation to the families of the dead and injured girls.[28]

No accounts of politics before or after 2011 mention the Nile Delta towns of Mit Nama or Awlad Seif. Their direct actions are coded as riots (*ahdath shaghab*) and relegated to the crime pages of government newspapers and the municipalities' pages of the opposition press, reflecting an entrenched legal, policing, and reporting tradition that parochializes such events as public-order offences. Yet as Eric Hobsbawm famously argued about eighteenth-century popular action, the purposefulness of crowds' actions points not to spasmodic eruptions of rage but targeted pressure on authorities, what he called "collective bargaining by riot."[29] Implicitly recognizing the political logic of riots, Egypt's Law 10/1914 on Assembly (*Tagamhur*) criminalizes unauthorized public gatherings of more than five persons "with the purpose of influencing authorities" (art. 2), preempting popular pressure on government by rendering it a crime. A relic of the colonial era promulgated upon the outbreak of World War I, Law 10 was the basis for prosecuting the Mit Nama protesters.

Mit Nama and Awlad Seif are urban versions of the peasant intifada, helping us see the concrete effects of the state's transformed role from producer, public goods provider, price-setter, and employer to seeker of foreign investment, implementer of austerity programs, and steward of privatization. Residents in the two towns called attention to the lack of safe crossings on hastily built new highways, part of infrastructure policies to facilitate commerce with no regard for the impact on locals' daily lives and no mechanisms to incorporate their input during decision-making. An official with the Roads and Bridges Authority admitted that footbridges were not part of the agency's budget allocations and were built only following citizens' complaints.[30] Residents in other locales protested to call attention to the dearth of potable water; they wrecked mobile phone towers erected without their consultation (fearing that their signals cause cancer); and they camped outside municipal government headquarters to protest the demolition of their homes.[31]

By the mid-2000s, disruptive direct action had become a recognizable means of citizen voice on a range of local problems. Any robust patterns in local protests lay less in how each was settled (through concessions or repression) and more in the diffusion of tactics such as highway blockades to compel responsiveness from officials. A year after the Mit Nama and Awlad Seif protests, in the wake of more blockades induced by road fatalities, a provincial police chief admitted to devising a new countrywide strategy to pinpoint particularly accident-prone locations, presumably not to build more pedestrian walkways but to abort incipient risings.[32] Two years later, a parliamentary inquiry was launched into the continuing practice of angry residents blocking highways. Engineering professor and future revolution-era Prime Minister Essam Sharaf expressed outrage, not at the frequency with which schoolchildren were dying while crossing highways, but that 90 percent of speed bumps on highways were makeshift structures built by residents and violated all technical specifications. "This is a crime against roads," he said.[33]

An episode from Coptic politics in 2004 is perhaps the best illustration of how a dispute rooted in local conflicts can scale up to a bargaining situation at the national level. At the turn of the millennium, Egypt's largest minority community of Coptic Christians, who had long chafed under official discrimination and social bigotry, began airing their grievances in more confrontational forms. In November 2004, Wafaa Constantin, the wife of the priest of Abul Matameer town in Beheira province, left her home under mysterious circumstances; some believed she had been abducted and forced to convert to Islam, others that she had eloped with a Muslim coworker. When news surfaced that Constantin was in police custody in Cairo, Abul Matameer parishioners packed into buses and made their way to the seat of the Coptic papacy in Cairo, beseeching Pope Shenouda to demand that police return Constantin to the church. To signal his displeasure at the government's detention of Constantin, Pope Shenouda went into seclusion as a crowd of about a thousand camped out on the cathedral grounds for six days and clashed violently with riot police. Even after SSI officials acceded to their demands and handed over Constantin (church leaders ordered her placed in seclusion in a monastery), the pope remained in retreat to draw attention to other Coptic grievances, particularly government restrictions on the building of churches and the trend of Coptic women's conversion to Islam—which Copts believed were coerced and sectarian Muslims insisted were voluntary.[34] The Constantin case pushed Coptic politics from a pattern of closed-door deliberations between church elders and government officials to visible, contentious bargaining powered by the disruptive direct actions of the Coptic citizenry.[35]

## DEMONSTRATE, SIT IN, BLOCK ROADS, THAT IS THE RIGHT WAY TO GET LOST RIGHTS

At this point let us pause to make some distinctions. Mit Nama, Awlad Seif, and Abul Matameer were a genus of direct action organized by neighborhood or locality, but they were not the only kinds of protests filling Egypt's streets. There were at least two other organizational bases for political demand-making: (1) associational protests launched by students and professionals in their unions and activists through their networks, and (2) workplace protests, by both industrial workers and civil servants. This classification goes against the grain of labeling protests by separating the content of their claims as either "economic" or "political." Besides the staggering diversity in the content of protests and their blending of economic and political demands in a single action (e.g., think of workers' objection to abusive verbal harassment by their bosses), the conventional classification skirts too close to authorities' own understandings and labeling practices, coding subaltern claim-making as "riots" and workers' demands as "economic grievances," while recognizing only middle- or upper-class and urban activists' initiatives as properly political. Better to heed the advice of social historian E. P. Thompson, who advised "turning over the bland concepts of the ruling authorities and looking at their undersides. If we do not do this we are in danger of becoming prisoners of the assumptions and self-image of the rulers ... and important kinds of social protest become lost in the category of crime."[36] Freeing conceptual categories from rulers' coding scheme, we are better able to see how by the mid-2000s, through emulation and diffusion, protesters of different classes expressing very different grievances were using the same tactics, particularly the sit-in (*i'tisam*).

Regional wars and the Egyptian regime's response to them caused an intense wave of associational protests from 2000 to 2003 organized by student unions, professional associations, and a new activist umbrella network, the Egyptian Popular Committee for Solidarity with the Palestinian Intifada (EPCSPI). The second Palestinian Intifada of 2000 and the two major invasions in the twenty-first-century Middle East—Israel's reinvasion of the West Bank in 2002 and the US invasion of Iraq in 2003—were crucial feeders of Egypt's emergent protest culture. The televised suffering of Palestinians and Iraqis under military occupation redefined the framing of public issues, as Marc Lynch has shown, and led to a process of politicization among both politics-prone and politics-shy sectors of the Egyptian and broader Arab public, angry at their governments' complicity with US and Israeli policies.[37] It was at this juncture that Tahrir Square became a commonsense locale to oppose the Mubarak regime's national and foreign policies. On September 10, 2001, a larger-than-usual protest against Israeli policies that drew many onlookers first alerted police to the square's centrality as a protest hub.[38]

Israeli Prime Minister Ariel Sharon's reinvasion of the West Bank on March 29, 2002, spurred a six-week surge of nationwide demonstrations that journalists called an "Egyptian Intifada." Nearly every university witnessed large demonstrations that spilled out onto streets, leading to the police killing of one student with live ammunition in Alexandria. Countless public meetings were organized, a stream of protest letters and petitions were lodged with the American and European embassies, and a coordinated consumer boycott of businesses supporting Israel eventually forced the Sainsbury's British supermarket chain to shutter its hundred outlets in Egypt. The outpouring of fellow feeling with Palestinians extended beyond urban activist circles; in the Delta town of Sinba al-Maqam in Daqahliyya, farmwives donated their sole asset of four hundred ducks to the EPCSPI relief efforts.[39] University faculty petitioned Mubarak to sack Interior Minister Habib al-Adli for the killing of the Alexandria student, a seemingly quixotic request that would fester for years and resurface as one of the four core demands of the January 25, 2011, protest action.

To counter the mass mobilization and its sharp antigovernment edge, authorities unsurprisingly used both coercion and co-optation. Police banned the Port Said custom of burning the malefactor-of-the-year in effigy, an annual spring ritual dating back to 1917 when residents burned an effigy of General Allenby, the commander of British forces stationed in Egypt.[40] Top-tier regime figures appropriated popular solidarity innovations. The president's wife, Suzanne Mubarak, personally fronted a street procession of government officials to deliver humanitarian supplies to Gaza, and, along with other presidential wives, organized an "Arab summit for women," ostensibly to support Palestinian women.[41] Realizing that they could no longer physically prevent multiplying street demonstrations without fatally overstretching their resources, police switched to a strategy of minimizing their consequences. The technique was to encircle protesters within associational headquarters, university campuses, or dead-end streets and street corners with thick corrals of riot police, to prevent demonstrators from spilling out onto streets and merging with bystanders. In police thinking, activists' agitation was tinder to ambient public grievances, liable to erupt into conflagration. "People can shout as much as they want inside," said a police officer about a thousands-strong public meeting against Israeli policies at the bar association. "But we won't let them out and risk major chaos in the streets."[42]

In the lead-up to the US invasion of Iraq in 2003, careful not to cede ground to popular initiatives, the NDP orchestrated a large antiwar rally in Cairo stadium, with the president's son Gamal and other party grandees in attendance. The occasion served as the public political debut of the president's son, who had been promoted to head a new policy unit in his father's party and marketed to the public as renewing Egypt's liberal tradition and modernizing the NDP.[43] The attempt to use the Iraq war to burnish the government's nationalist credentials failed. As soon as the first US cruise missiles were dropped on

Baghdad on March 20, crowds descended on Tahrir Square in what grew to be a gathering of 20,000, for the first time outnumbering the startled contingent of antiriot police deployed continuously near the square since 2001. In hindsight as well as in the moment, the ten-hour occupation of Tahrir Square that day registered as a signal event. Journalist Amira Howeidy captured the scene: "For 10 hours, the capital's most famous and strategic square was occupied by people from all age groups and walks of life; activists; politicians; students; children; passersby; families; housewives; professors; beggars; journalists; and downtown Cairo residents."[44] Politicians delivered fiery speeches against US war-making, activists sang 1970s-vintage protest songs, young people chalked the pavement, and dozens of candles were lit at sunset. By the next day, police used overwhelming force to clear Tahrir and abort any further mass demonstrations. In the ensuing street battles with police, a quick-moving band of protesters tore down a huge poster of Hosni Mubarak from the NDP headquarters. Police violently dispersed a sit-in at the nearby bar association and arrested Hamdeen Sabahy and another parliamentarian, along with eight hundred activists and at least six children.[45]

The continuous associational protests and solidarity activities from 2000 to 2003 yielded a new, negotiated settlement between protesters and police, where demonstrators began to be managed rather than crushed across the board. There was no uniform policing tactic of repression or co-optation but a flexible mix of the two that responded to the tactical exigencies of each situation. As Tamir Moustafa observed at the time, "Although the Egyptian government still hems in demonstrations with an overwhelming security presence, the mere fact that protests are tacitly permitted outside the gates of university campuses marks a qualitative shift in Egyptian political life."[46] Sometimes the forces of order broke up gatherings by force; other times they corralled protesters to prevent them from swelling their ranks with curious onlookers; sometimes they arrested them or referred them to prosecutors; and still other times they appropriated the protest performance, as when Suzanne Mubarak led a relief convoy to express solidarity with Palestinians. At all times, police agents were present in large numbers, proactively monitoring protesters, writing down their chants, enclosing them within building grounds or street corners, negotiating with their leaders, and wielding force.

A series of labor protests across the country in 2004 prompted a new leftist daily to gleefully headline its year-in-review, "To Those Who Proclaim the End of the Era of Labor, Workers Cry Out: We Are Here!"[47] Earlier that year, Mubarak had appointed a new cabinet headed by technocrat Ahmed Nazif that had several members of the new business class assume ministerial portfolios and redouble the flagging privatization drive. Joel Beinin and Marie Duboc tracked a wave of labor protests against the Nazif government's policies that saw a more than twofold increase in the incidence of workplace actions, from 266 in 2004 to 609 by 2008. Though organized at the plant level with no regional or national coordination, in terms of participants the labor wave constituted "the largest social movement Egypt has witnessed in more than half a century," observed Beinin. "From 2004 to 2008, over 1.7 million workers engaged in more than 1,900 strikes and other forms of protest."[48] The government's changing response to protests can be seen in the largest industrial action since 1947, at the public-sector Misr Spinning and Weaving Company in the Delta town of Mahalla al-Kubra, site of one of the largest textile factories in the Middle East and North Africa.

In December 2006, thousands of Mahalla workers launched a four-day strike and sit-in to protest unmet government promises and fears that the company would be privatized. Taken aback by workers' defiance, especially that of the female garment workers, panicked officials restored nearly all of workers' abridged entitlements.[49] Labor Minister Aisha Abdel Hadi first repeated the government's reflexive argument that the Muslim Brothers were behind the strike, despite the Islamists' weak ties to the labor sector. Then she expressed her real fear: copycat strikes. "If some think that we will bow to demands made outside the legal channels, that's a fantasy. No one can twist our arms."[50] Abdel Hadi's fears were not groundless. In the ensuing weeks, a wave of strikes spread through ten mill towns in Alexandria and the Delta, in nearly all cases successfully wringing concessions from the government.[51] State officials then changed their discourse, framing the strike wave as a product of the enlarged freedoms under Mubarak. Minister Abdel Hadi lectured reporters in February 2007, "The strikes are not a disturbing thing but a result of the democratic climate experienced by Egypt for quite a while, as well as the past history of protest in Mahalla and [second labor stronghold] Kafr al-Dawwar."[52] The government's rhetorical normalization of protest did not mean that repression of work stoppages ceased altogether but, as with the associational protests, signaled authorities' admission that protests could no longer be uniformly repressed and therefore had to be managed.

Workers' resistance to the downgrading of their labor was not confined to the industrial sector. Scores of low-ranking civil servants protested their abysmal pay compared to that of higher-status peers in privileged government bureaus. Problems of entrenched inequalities within the vast public bureaucracy predated market-driven economic reforms but were only exacerbated by them.[53] A protest during the final days of 2007 made this issue headline news. In what we now know as the largest occupation in downtown Cairo before the 2011 revolution, 55,000 property tax collectors organized a strike and sit-in across from the cabinet headquarters.[54] Their chief demand was pay parity with their better-compensated counterparts in the Ministry of Finance. The clerks and their families slept in tents in the bitter cold and drew avid, sympathetic media coverage, upending the negative image of the lowly civil servant (*muwwazaf*) from a duty-shirking, bribe-seeking functionary to a creative human being with real grievances that most citizens could relate to. At first, Finance Minister Youssef Boutros-Ghali echoed Labor Minister Abdel Hadi a year earlier, proclaiming, "I don't like anyone to twist my arm."[55] Strike leaders then escalated, announcing the imminent arrival of 15,000 more tax clerks from the provinces to swell the Cairo sit-in. But just before that happened, on Day 10 of the sit-in, State Security agents, acting as official emissaries of the blustering Boutros-Ghali, relayed to the protesters the minister's accession to their demands. One year later in 2009, half of the tax collectors succeeded in establishing the first independent union in Egypt since 1957.[56]

The tax collectors, textile workers, local residents, and crowds of people who did not know each other but came out en masse to express solidarity with Palestine and Iraq all had different grievances against different levels of government. When seen together, what is significant is how, without coordination but with knowledge of each other's actions, attained via coverage by competitive media outlets, they wrested recognition for the practice of assembling at their own initiative in public space to make demands on government agents. Through repeated interaction between protesters, police, governors, ministers, and journalists, a new way of doing things was taking shape, as expressed by an opposition newspaper editor who exhorted, "Demonstrate ... sit in ... block roads ... for that is the right way to get lost rights."[57] By the spring of 2010, different groups of striking and protesting industrial workers and civil servants were camping out across from parliament, side by side and for weeks on end.

By the summer, the Nazif government quietly announced the end of its privatization policy.[58]

## STATE OF MOTION

By the early 1990s, administrative courts began to emerge as a third field of political contention alongside elections and protests. Despite its dry-sounding name, the administrative court system, Majlis al-Dawla, lies at the heart of public politics, virtually by design. Like their French models, these are courts "before which the humblest citizen could arraign and call to account the all-powerful and interfering state."[59] As the branch of the judiciary tasked with finding facts and rights in disputes between individuals and government officials, administrative judges developed a strong professional identity as monitors of the arbitrary exercise of bureaucratic power. Since the 1946 founding of Majlis al-Dawla, they have produced a body of case law upholding citizens' rights and liberties by asserting their right to review any act of a public official at any level, including the president and all his ministers, the head of al-Azhar (the state religious establishment), and the Coptic Patriarch. The nature of administrative law is what gives these courts latent political significance. As a French jurist explained:

> While private law is essentially a law of equality where all persons find themselves on the same level, subject to the same laws and same judges, *droit administratif* figures as a law of inequality which recognizes and deals with two distinct classes—on the one hand, officials invested with exceptional prerogatives, nay with real privileges; on the other hand, private individuals compelled to submit to this official dominance.[60]

Filing a lawsuit against executive officers draws in judges as arbiters in the asymmetric relation between a citizen and the functionary, with the possibility of annulling the administrator's power and officially vindicating the humble citizen.

Since courts are reactive institutions by design, they depend on the initiative of litigants and lawyers. Similar to the uncoordinated yet cumulative way that groups of citizens turned the streets into sites of political claim-making, individuals' and interest groups' increasing resort to the administrative courts activated judges to weigh in on numerous public issues, over time thrusting them into the center of heated political controversies. One of the first cases to contest a high-stakes executive action came in 1992. When Hosni Mubarak began referring Islamist activists to military tribunals, their lawyers contested the presidential decree before the courts, arguing that it was an abuse of power to try civilians in military courts. In a decision that was hailed as "the most significant in the history of Majlis al-Dawla," judge and historian Tareq al-Bishri struck down the president's decree.[61] Though it was quickly overturned by the apex Supreme Administrative Court (SAC), the legal and media attention to Bishri's decision signaled to other cause lawyers that administrative courts could be a viable channel to amplify complaints against government abuse of power.

In the same year, wholesale produce merchants contested in court the Cairo municipality's urban beautification plan, which ordered the removal of their historic wholesale market from the central Cairo district of Rod al-Farag to an outlying area far removed from the wholesalers' dense networks. Opposition newspapers closely tracked the legal drama, printing evocative photos of female vegetable peddlers filling the courthouse courtyard as they awaited judges' deliberations, while inside the courtroom, prominent cause lawyers hired by the merchants sparred with government attorneys before the bench as spectators looked on in rapt attention.[62] The court ruled in favor of the merchants, but the government appealed and, in February 1994, the SAC overturned the lower court order and green-lighted the transfer of the market well outside the city center. Though the government secured its preferred policy and the merchants lost, this particular case was significant because (1) it generated publicity about a peremptory policy affecting thousands of livelihoods that would not otherwise have become widely known, and (2) the publicity was actively constructed into a controversy by the opposition press, selecting from the thicket of daily governance conflicts a particular issue that it weaponized in its sparring with the government.

By the mid-1990s, the tactic of administrative litigation as political position-taking began to appear. In 1996, the chairmen of opposition political parties and several prominent cause lawyers filed a lawsuit contesting the second round of public-sector privatization. "Government Policies on Trial in the Administrative Judiciary," blared the front-page headline of an opposition newspaper. The exasperated government attorney pointed out, not unreasonably, that parliament was the proper venue for putting the government on trial.[63] Some maverick lawyers then crafted public profiles as crusaders for citizens' rights. One of the first was Mamdouh Nakhla, who launched a career of petitioning the administrative courts to strike down sundry regulations discriminating against Copts. Nakhla filed a flurry of lawsuits against the scheduling of school and university exams on Copts' holidays; the imposition of admission fees on Coptic historic sites; the mandatory religion field on national identity cards; the rule requiring presidential sanction for church renovations; and he set a model for others. The courts sometimes found for Nakhla and other times for the government, but as important as the judicial disposition of the cases was his strategy for building a public opinion against the daily disadvantages imposed on Egypt's minority community.[64]

To process increasing caseloads, in 1996 new circuits were created in Cairo and three other cities.[65] Officials fretted about the unstoppable litigation against the government and passed a new law in 2000 creating arbitration committees attached to ministries, in hopes of diverting disputes away from the courts and back into the bureaucracy. That failed to put a dent in litigation rates; between 2000 and 2009, cases filed before the courts went from 13,470 to 59,200, a 440 percent increase.[66] Yet caution should be used when interpreting this aggregate figure. Without a more specific breakdown of cases by the ministry sued or a representative sample of cases' contents, we run the risk of reproducing the bias of media focus on select high-profile cases. At the same time, it is this subset of mediated cases that is of interest, since it was print (and later television) journalists, as well as Egypt's deep reservoir of cause lawyers, who diffused information about administrative litigation as a tactic to contest public policies.

An example is the Society of Friends of the Environment (SFE), a citizens' group in Alexandria that began filing multiple suits against the governor for allotting public gardens to real estate developers erecting malls and high-rises. SFE's successful litigation was transmitted by opposition journalists, who translated the dense information in the court rulings into accessible feature stories: they exposed the opaque government-business dealings that were hastening the privatization of the commons.[67] While disseminating public information about such administrative litigation, at the same time the print media shaped public understanding of the administrative courts by framing every decision counter to the government as a small victory. When the SFE secured a ruling against the privatization of prime beachfront properties in Alexandria's tony Rushdi neighborhood, a leftist weekly narrated it as a "historic court decision."[68] Editors assigned reporters to cover protracted court proceedings, and photographers documented an emergent ritual: litigants amassing on courthouse steps with signs and banners, chanting slogans against the government to draw public attention to their lawsuits.[69]

It would be only a slight exaggeration to say that the courts became the most effective forum to challenge the creeping privatization of public services and its attendant regime of new fees, duties, and taxes. The case that affected the largest number of citizens and drew sustained national attention was a new rule pegging sanitation fees to consumers' electricity bills, threatening power cut-offs if households and businesses failed to pay for garbage collection. The fees were the government's attempts to pass on to consumers a new fifteen-year agreement subcontracting trash disposal to multinational companies, despite the existence of efficient, indigenous trash collectors (*zabbaleen*) in every major Egyptian city. Citizens' groups in Alexandria, Giza, and Cairo filed separate lawsuits disputing the corporatized waste collection scheme, and, in December 2004, "to the government's utter confusion and shock," the Supreme Administrative Court harmonized conflicting lower court rulings into a final decision invalidating the new fees as illegal and unconstitutional.[70]

The tactic of legally contesting public policies made out of public view eventually reached the most insulated policy domain of all: the Mubarak regime's foreign relations. In November 2008, the *New York Times* tersely reported: "An Egyptian court ordered the government to stop piping natural gas to Israel, saying the 15-year contract was improperly awarded because it was not approved by Parliament."[71] A group of activists, led by former diplomat Ibrahim Yousri, had filed suit as soon as the gas began to flow in May of that year, accusing the government of making the deal in secret and selling the gas at below-market prices. The ruling came in the midst of intense public anger at Mubarak's complicity with the Israeli blockade on Gaza; the strip was under a relentless bombing campaign during the winter of 2008–9. The court decision launched a two-year debate over presidential cronies' role in selling Egypt's natural resources to Israel (Mubarak's personal friend Hussein Salem co-owned the consortium selling the gas) and the lack of any parliamentary or popular oversight of such export agreements. Ultimately, as with the wholesale market case, in 2010 the Supreme Administrative Court overruled the lower court decision, invoking the controversial doctrine of "acts of sovereignty" that placed executive decisions beyond the reach of judicial scrutiny. But the plaintiffs had got what they wanted—a protracted public controversy, with countless televised court sessions, talk show debates, and opinion pieces that dragged out into the open what several stakeholders worked to shield: the deep personal business ties underpinning Egypt-Israel relations.

By the last years of the Mubarak regime, administrative courts had become a hyperactive site of government-citizen contention. Abdel Razzaq al-Sanhuri, the second chief justice of Majlis al-Dawla, could scarcely have imagined how far his observation would extend when he wrote in 1950, "It has been said that the constitutional law describes the different parts of the state in repose, while administrative law describes it in a state of motion and labor."[72] Thinking of administrative law as a law of inequality that mediates between powerful officials and defenseless civilians illuminates the political logic of administrative litigation. By activating the judicial machinery—compelling government attorneys to show up in court and defend government decisions, inviting judges to issue authoritative rulings, creating courtroom spectacles—relatively powerless people deliberately created something out of nothing, building a halo of controversy around well-concealed government decisions, extracting answerability out of unaccountability. "Accountability is what many bureaucrats invest enormous amounts of effort in short-circuiting or avoiding," writes anthropologist Michael Herzfeld, "A cynic might define power as the right to be unaccountable."[73] Journalists, activists, and even judges took to using the term "public opinion case" (*qadiyyat ra'i 'am*) to refer to high-impact lawsuits likely to receive domestic and international attention. Judges allowed unrestricted public attendance and numerous television cameras in their courtrooms, hinting at their interest in publicizing their self-definition as defenders of citizens' rights. Harassing unaccountable executive power, litigants understood that they were not bringing down the whole edifice, or even changing policies, but leveraging judicial power to publicly air rampant executive privilege. Timothy Mitchell's general definition of political conflict illuminates the rationale of seemingly tame legal contentions:

> Democratic struggles become a battle over the distribution of issues, attempting to establish as matters of public concern questions that others claim as private (such as the level of wages paid by employers), as belonging to nature (such as the exhaustion of natural resources or the composition of gases in the atmosphere), or as ruled by laws of the market (such as financial speculation).[74]

In the definitional battle over what counts as a matter of public deliberation, strategic litigants pulled in a segment of the state—judges—to authoritatively weigh in on the actions of another—the administration—exploiting the latent friction between these two public powers. As with so much in Egyptian politics, these initiatives against executive privilege were inescapably spatial. The people's appropriation of the administrative court steps to stage protests and shout slogans became so routinized that even some judges were offended, concerned about the downgrading of the building's prestige by turning it into a permanent location for unruly protest. Someone devised the solution of filling the steps with dozens of huge, scrawny potted plants, leaving only a narrow aisle for the public to enter and exit the courthouse, single file.

## THE EGYPTIAN MOVEMENT FOR CHANGE

On December 12, 2004, a small but attention-grabbing protest of several hundred EPCSPI activists, veteran cause lawyers, young journalists, intellectuals, and families of political prisoners massed on the steps of the High Court in downtown Cairo, encircled by hundreds of riot policemen and dozens of police trucks. They brandished a large yellow banner and round yellow stickers bearing one word in bold red lettering: *Kifaya!* (Enough!). Calling themselves the Egyptian Movement for Change, a spokesman told reporters that the nascent movement was a self-styled irritant, aspiring "to become a thorn in the side of Mubarak's re-election for a fifth term."[75] When, two months later, Mubarak suddenly announced a constitutional change to switch to multicandidate presidential elections that he would contest in September 2005, the movement launched an energetic agitation campaign against what was widely understood as the penultimate step in the regime's careful preparation for Mubarak's succession: the father would run in a stage-managed election in 2005, paving the way for the son, Gamal, to run in 2011.

The electoral calendar for 2005 in fact contained three important dates: a May constitutional referendum authorizing the switch from plebiscitary to multicandidate presidential elections; the new presidential elections in September; and parliamentary elections at the end of the year. The uncertainty in these contests lay not in who would win and govern but in the nature of the struggle; by what margin would the president claim a victory over his ostensible challengers? How many seats would the opposition secure in parliament? How would judicial supervision of elections, the game-changing new rule stipulated by a landmark constitutional court ruling in 2000, impact the outcome?[76] Kifaya's signature performance became a weekly Wednesday anti-Mubarak protest in some central Cairo location, always encircled by hundreds of policemen and sometimes personally monitored by Cairo police chief Nabil al-Ezabi. On referendum day, May 25, a Kifaya crowd in downtown Cairo chanted "Down, down with Hosni Mubarak!" and urged the public to boycott the vote. The NDP organized counterdemonstrators who charged into the Kifaya gathering, dragged and beat protesters, and sexually assaulted scores of women activists as plainclothes policemen facilitated and joined the attack. US First Lady Laura Bush's coincidental visit to Cairo in the same week had riveted media attention on Egypt, and the NDP-orchestrated violence became the focal point of the news disseminated to an international audience. The government tried to redirect the narrative to its pitch about a regime marching toward democracy, claiming 54 percent turnout and 83 percent approval in the referendum. That prompted a faction of 1,500 independent judges (out of a total of about 7,000) overseeing the vote to issue their own countercount in a scathing report, finding proper judicial supervision in only 5 percent of polling stations and turnout not exceeding 3 percent.[77]

More unpleasant surprises surfaced in the September presidential election. A handful of aging leaders of loyalist opposition parties had been handpicked to "run" against Mubarak and lose, but a forty-one-year-old liberal politician named Ayman Nour entered the race unbidden. With the support of the Muslim Brothers, the opposition organization with the largest voter base, Nour came in a distant second with 7 percent of the vote to Mubarak's 88 percent. Soon after the election, he was tried on politicized charges and sentenced to a five-year jail term. Even those anticipating more surprises during the November parliamentary elections did not foresee the actual chain of events. To the astonishment of their own leaders and despite government violence against voters that caused fourteen fatalities, candidates of the Muslim Brothers secured eighty-eight seats, a fivefold increase of their representation in the 2000 parliament. Factoring in the additional seats won by non-Islamist opposition members, the total proportion of opposition seats in parliament was 27 percent, the highest since the return of multiparty elections in 1976. In no small part, this outcome was enabled by the concerted mobilization of independent judges who asserted their authority to oversee the count. In one of the most high-profile districts pitting a crony of Hosni Mubarak against a Muslim Brothers (MB) candidate, supervising judicial officer Noha al-Zainy blew the whistle on government ballot-tampering to favor their man, publishing her account, endorsed by 137 of her colleagues, in a credible independent daily. For decades Egyptians knew that the government rigged elections and for that reason stayed away, but this was the first time that a credible official was willing to go on the record and relay details of the fraud.[78] Al-Zainy became a revered public personality whom activists tagged with Egyptians' highest praise for a woman: "She's worth a hundred men."

The three elections mattered both for what happened inside polling stations on election day and the unpredictable interactions between a large number of actors long before and after polls had closed. From a relational perspective, the significance of a loose opposition network such as Kifaya was less what it did than what it compelled others to do. The NDP's taboo-breaking violence against Kifaya's female activists drew copious negative media coverage and increased sympathy for the movement among various publics. Small yet energetic and novel, Kifaya's weekly protests prompted Egypt's largest opposition organization, the MB, to take calculated risks and organize what was described as their first street demonstration on domestic issues, quickly broken up by police.[79] This febrile political atmosphere in turn activated the dissident judges to confront the government on its election rigging, publicizing evidence of electoral fraud and offering their alternative turnout figures. International observation teams relied on the judges' work to produce their own assessment of the polls; "perhaps the most encouraging element in the presidential election was the effort of the Judges' Club—the primary association of all judges in Egypt—to ensure a transparent election process," concluded a US election-monitoring organization.[80] The signal that an independent core of judges would protect ballots in turn motivated opposition candidates and their supporters to brave police violence, leading to the highest-ever opposition representation in parliament.

It is often thought by sympathizers and critics alike that Kifaya was a phenomenon of "expressive" politics, breaking the barrier of fear that muzzled Egyptians from attacking the president directly and collectively in public. However, confrontational out-of-doors action was already well under way in Egypt's other protest sectors of workplaces and neighborhoods. As Beinin and Duboc caution, it is a misreading of history to consider Kifaya the early riser

FIGURE 4. Police enclose an MB-Kifaya demonstration, September 1, 2005. Khaled Desouki/AFP via Getty Images. Reprinted with permission.

that stimulated other sectors' collective action.[81] The significance of Kifaya is not that it goaded the working classes to action but that it forged a new middle-class oppositional identity and collective action frame. Kifaya activists consciously sought to transcend the existing options for middle-class dissent: the thoroughly tamed political parties licensed by the government; the disciplined cadre organization of the Muslim Brothers, who recoiled from joining broad fronts that they did not initiate; and the professional associations that hosted Kifaya gatherings but were ultimately answerable to a dues-paying membership not yet ready to yield their associations to a motley mosaic of confrontational activists. Given these limited options, Kifaya helped broaden the politically engaged public by modeling a new political identity: an urban, middle-class, cross-ideological dissenting posture that kept at arm's length existing oppositional organizations with their accumulated baggage. Through a persuasive counternarrative to the government's reformspeak, it tied Hosni Mubarak's pliant pro-US and pro-Israel stance to his ever-narrowing ruling coalition of crony businessmen and cosseted military generals. The revolution-era chant "Yasqut Yasqut Hukm al-'Askar" (Down, down with military rule) first appeared at a July 2005 Kifaya demonstration in Alexandria.

The 2005 year of elections was planned as a showcase of the regime's steady democratization, but it ended with an augmented parliamentary opposition and a new extraparliamentary movement. Immediately after the elections, the two came together in an alliance of support for the judges who had challenged the regime's falsified counts, an alliance that attracted enthusiastic international support. In early 2006, the judges used the public platform they had gained to press their twenty-year-long demand for judicial independence, drafting a bill and promoting it in the media. The government sensed danger in the growing public respect for the judges and referred two of their most outspoken representatives to a disciplinary tribunal. Judges parried by converting the disciplinary occasion into a show of strength. Borrowing the disruptive tactic from the humble workers' repertoire, they announced a sit-in at their downtown Cairo associational headquarters, the august Nadi al-Quda (Judges' Club), to protest the disciplining of their two colleagues. Hundreds of judges from across the country descended on the club to take turns manning and financially supporting the sit-in, which lasted for four weeks in what turned into a public relations fiasco for the government.

On the days of the hearings, the two judges, flanked by hundreds of their colleagues, marched in a solemn procession to the High Court building as activists, onlookers, the newly elected opposition deputies, and the press processed parallel to them, separated by thick cordons of riot police to prevent the merging of the judges and their sympathizers. In a visually striking performance, hundreds of judges staged a one-hour silent vigil outside the club, donning the red and green sashes of the bench over their starched suits. For that month in spring 2006, the Judges' Club served as the headquarters of the emergent prodemocracy coalition. Kifaya led solidarity marches and pitched a parallel tent sit-in across from the club (violently disbanded by police), and delegations of admiring social worthies, politicians, and celebrities visited the club's leadership. If the Mubarak regime had hoped to intimidate outspoken judges into quiescence, it had instead brought them national and international adulation. "All rise for the judges of Egypt," hailed the *Christian Science Monitor*.[82] As the political scientist Mohamed Sayed Said reflected on this remarkable moment in Egyptian politics, "The conflict centers on the principle of the independence of society—all of its institutions, not only the judiciary—from the state. Authoritarianism does not spare any social institutions but works to control them all through monitoring and stringent subordination to security."[83]

That principle of independence animated a burst of public-interest litigation before the administrative courts, inspired by the heavy media attention accorded the case over piping natural gas to Israel. A variety of cause lawyers, rights groups, and individual controversy-seekers filed petitions before the courts, with no connections to one another other than their knowledge of administrative law and media coverage of Majlis al-Dawla. In 2010, a raft of court rulings against government interests on high-profile matters helped generate a sense of an administration under siege. Judges invalidated the sale of state-owned land to a Mubarak crony; ordered police officers removed from university campuses; called on the government to institute a minimum wage; struck down the interior minister's banning of mobile phones in police stations; and struck down the Coptic pope's banning of a second marriage for divorced Coptic Egyptians. The court reporter at one of the two leading independent dailies enthused, "Instead of resorting to parliament and its members to solve their problems, or appealing to dispute resolution committees within ministries, citizens in 2010 found refuge in Majlis al-Dawla to compel the government to abide by the law and roll back its unconstitutional decrees."[84]

To remember the final years of Mubarak's rule as a crescendo of popular mobilization culminating in the 2011 revolt would be to ignore some inconvenient facts. During its final three years, the regime engaged in a concerted counteroffensive aimed at demobilization, to diminish the resources aggregated by political actors over the years. The government campaign was both reactive and preemptive, a response to aftershocks of the 2005 elections and a preemption of any renewed mobilization in the lead-up to general and presidential elections scheduled for 2010 and 2011. Power holders sought a pacified national political arena as the delicate matter of presidential succession approached. In the electoral sphere, the regime for the first time broke with its clockwork scheduling of elections, pushing back the 2006 municipal polls two years to weather the political firestorm of the judge–civil society alliance. In the months prior to the rescheduled vote in April 2008, security forces waged a sweeping campaign against the Muslim Brothers, the only opposition organization capable of competing for a chunk of the 53,000 municipal seats nationwide. Fearing a replay of their 2005 general election performance, government clerks and policemen worked round the clock to prevent the Muslim Brothers' candidates from registering, harassed would-be candidates and campaign workers, and arrested 831 members of the organization. Not a single MB candidate secured a seat, while the NDP took 97.5 percent of the seats and the rest went to government-licensed parties of loyal opposition.

In the protest arena, the year 2008 saw an important new development: an attempt to link the associational and workplace-based protest subcultures. Youth members of Kifaya supported Mahalla textile workers' calls for a general strike to demand a raise in the monthly minimum wage, envisioning a nationwide day of action on April 6, 2008, that they advertised heavily through online forums. However, one day before the scheduled action, police occupied the Mahalla factory complex to prevent workers from massing. On April 6, the thwarted strike gave way to street battles between townspeople and police that killed one fifteen-year-old boy. Demonstrators set ablaze shops and schools, blocked railway tracks with blazing tires, and trampled underfoot a huge poster of the president that they tore down from a party building. In Cairo, police arrested two hundred activists and chased Kifaya demonstrators out of Tahrir Square. As Beinin and Duboc observe, for the government, "the specter of a nationally coordinated workers' action was intolerable."[85] To reinforce the message, forty-nine demonstrators were tried before an exceptional court, of whom twenty-two were sentenced to three- and five-year jail terms. Authorities blocked Kifaya's website and issued new regulations requiring internet café users to provide detailed personal information before accessing the internet.[86]

The police's unhesitating preemption of the April 6 general strike and its thorough pursuit of any follow-up attempts may be understood as an effort to abort "brokerage," or the "linking of two or more currently unconnected social sites by a unit that mediates their relations with each other."[87] The youth activists' ambitious attempt to connect the parallel streams of labor and associational protest could have escalated into what all undemocratic regimes strive to prevent: a broad cross-class coalition combining the organizing experiences of workers with the rhetorical skills of urban activists, and this at a time when the regime was under international scrutiny for its impending succession scenario. Naturally, the government acted quickly to reassert the limits, but the repression had an enduring effect on public politics. It midwifed a new political actor, the April 6th youth movement, the first social movement of young, postgraduate politicized Egyptians; its members had graduated from university student politics but were still locked out of leadership positions in existing opposition formations. The youth movement joined the crowded field of Egyptian opposition and would go on to become a major player in post-Mubarak politics.

As the scheduled 2010 general elections approached, the government's next goal was to deprive opposition forces of a platform in the national legislature from which they could harass the incoming presidential heir. The central plank of the government's plan was to remove judges as poll monitors, the wildcard factor that had exposed the government's election rigging and enabled unprecedented opposition gains in 2005. First, the constitution was amended to wrest responsibility for vote-counting from judges to state functionaries under the aegis of a Higher Election Commission, which had no authority beyond announcing election returns. Then the government moved to shut down the locus of judicial mobilization, sparing no financial or human resources to oust the dissident judges from leadership of the Judges' Club.[88] The effects of terminating judicial supervision were immediately clear on election day: the president's party secured 93 percent of seats and loyalist opposition parties won 3 percent. Not a single member of the outgoing parliamentary opposition retained his seat, including Hamdeen Sabahy, whose election battle opened this chapter.

The election results were nearly identical to the 1995 elections but occurred in an altered political environment teeming with political dissidence, worker protests, and everyday displays of collective assertion. The 121 opposition deputies from the outgoing parliament vowed to maintain the new corporate identity that they had formed inside the chamber during the 2005–10 term. They created a "parallel parliament" (Barlaman Muwazi) that served as the nucleus of a new oppositional alliance bringing together the April 6th youth movement; the Muslim Brothers; Kifaya activists; followers of politician Ayman Nour; followers of former international diplomat Mohamed ElBaradei, who had returned to Egypt in 2010 and entered political life; and several prominent public intellectuals. On December 14, 2010, as Hosni Mubarak addressed the inaugural session of the parliament packed with his loyalists, a score of ex-deputies arrayed themselves on the steps of Majlis al-Dawla, the now commonsense gathering space for

Egypt's wronged and evicted, and recited in unison the parliamentary oath to protect the republic and defend the people's interests.

* * *

The Mubarak regime's toleration of a range of public politics was not an inherent attribute that came with the man's assumption of the presidency in 1981. It developed through repeated confrontations, bargains, and provisional settlements between state agents and distinct social groups that, over time, turned streets, administrative courts, and elections into recognized spaces of political wrangling. A more accurate term than government "toleration" may be "policing," in the antique, broad sense of that term denoting the close regulation, not ceding, of public space that toleration implies. Interacting repeatedly over time, citizens and policing agencies exercised reciprocal influence and acquired mutual knowledge. Tables 1 and 2 summarize the varieties of popular action that developed into a recognizable repertoire of contention over time along

TABLE 1. Repertoire of Political Contention in Contemporary Egypt, 1990s–2010.

| |
|---|
| Massing on the steps of a prominent building carrying banners and chanting slogans (*waqfa ihtijajiyya*) |
| Canvassing, campaigning, and voting in national and subnational elections |
| Demonstrating or marching in streets or on university campuses (*masira*) |
| Filing lawsuits against government officials in administrative courts |
| Organizing sit-ins (*i'tisam*) in a factory plant, union offices, or parched field |
| Organizing a sit-in (*i'tisam*) in a church or the cathedral in 'Abbasiyya, Cairo |
| Assembling inside and/or streaming outside a mosque after Friday noon prayers |
| Convening public conferences and meetings |
| Picketing parliament, the cabinet headquarters, a ministry, or other state institution |
| Withholding or slowing down labor from fifteen minutes to several weeks (*idrab*) |
| Blockading streets, highways, or railway lines with burning tires or branches |
| Besieging a government building such as hospital, morgue, or police station |
| Burning/destroying government property (vehicles, buildings, documents, ballot boxes) |

TABLE 2. State Responses to Popular Contention, 1990s–2010.

| |
|---|
| Issuing laws and administrative regulations to control, restrict, or criminalize demonstrations, political organizations, and civic associations |
| Engaging in administrative manipulation, obstruction, fraud, and violence to control national and subnational elections |
| Establishing exceptional courts and military tribunals to try civilian dissidents and political activists |
| Corralling demonstrators within pens formed by riot police formations |
| Facilitating and funding counterprotests, front organizations, and individual loyalists |
| Controlling media outlets and creating media content for political propaganda |
| Using tear gas, rubber bullets, birdshot, and live ammunition to break up crowds |
| Applying torture in police stations, detention centers, and prisons |
| Engaging in covert surveillance to monitor, infiltrate, and sow dissension within opposition networks and organizations |
| Practicing administrative detention, enforced disappearances, and extrajudicial killing of political activists |

with the government's range of management procedures, crystallized "as laws, registers, surveillance, police practice, subsidies, organizations of public space, and repressive policies."[89]

Despite the heaving energy of these political interactions, it would be misguided to read them as evidence of a rising revolutionary consciousness. That would construct a fable of methodical prerevolutionary rehearsals to be enacted in 2011. Before the revolution, those who fought to get an opposition seat in parliament, challenged the government's policies in court, or blocked highways to defend land and life were acting to regain abridged rights or decry government inaction. Revolution was not part of the vocabulary of Egyptian politics, so well had the Mubarak regime evicted the possibility of revolution from thought and deed. The implication is that had there been no uprising in 2011, the patterns of public politics traced here would have rumbled on, perhaps intensifying during the succession.

However, it would be equally mistaken to dismiss these conflicts as lively but ephemeral campaigns that did not fundamentally change the political system. We could echo Juan Linz's attractive formulation as he surveyed the varieties of opposition in the last years of Francisco Franco's rule in Spain and concluded, "It is the same system, but things have changed within the system."[90] But systems thinking, with its functionalist vocabulary of maintenance, adaptation, resilience, decay, and breakdown, forces us into rigid dichotomous mental models where system maintenance and system breakdown become the sole objects of explanation. Does a protest wave or an opposition movement feed into system breakdown or system resilience? When courts rule against government interests, does that undermine the system or stabilize it by channeling discontent into safe legal channels? There are no good answers to these questions because the questions themselves contain a misprision: political regimes are not systems that function in terms of inputs and outputs. They are also not structures whose strength can be tested by the loads placed upon them, surviving unscathed if they bear the weight, "breaking down" like a building if not.

Starting from a different ontology that sees social and political life as relational rather than system-structural, this study looks at politics under Mubarak and detects changing relations between rulers and ruled. Over the decades, many separate interest groups were increasingly able to act collectively on matters large and small; but the greater frequency of protests, increasing competitiveness of elections, and rise in administrative litigation rates were a sign of shifts in power, not impending authoritarian breakdown or unaltered authoritarian functioning. The vastly unequal relations between a ruling group that controlled nearly all parts of the state and fragmented interest groups, some of whom occupied strategic nodes in the state (tax collectors, judges, opposition parliamentarians), were incrementally approaching some elements of equality. In the contest over political ideas, the Mubarak regime's complacent self-packaging as a steward of economic reforms paled in comparison to the opposition's counterframe of corrupt familial rule allied with Israel against the Palestinians. The regime had the unequivocal backing of governments in the US, EU, Israel, and the Gulf monarchies, but the opposition had the succor of other actors in the international network of influence: human rights organizations, international media, and the democracy-promotion branches of the US and EU states. Domestically, the government's media apparatus and army of publicists rarely offered more than defense, reacting to the terms and arguments set by the more energetic and creative opposition and independent press.

Still, the Mubarak regime philosophy—"Let them say what they want, and we will do what we want"—has more than a bit of truth to it. The regime may have evolved to tolerate opposition opinion, but it never failed to thwart opposition organization. Political party formation was regulated by a jumble of laws and regulations to the point of strangulation, and professional associations were swiftly frozen when they began to behave as shadow political parties. For all the popular collective capacity-building, very rarely did it lead to organization-building; the tax collectors' union formed in 2009 was an exception that proved the rule. Yet the political patterns surveyed in this chapter can hardly be classified under "opinion." Midway between the poles of organization and opinion, we can identify two kinds of popular capacity-building, two forms of social power, that were built up by interest groups over the span of three decades as they confronted the government. The first was an opposition alliance that combined the separate, small endowments of its heterogeneous components into an anti-Mubarak "negative coalition," as Robert Dix conceptualizes, an alliance without an elaborate program but with a single target: "ridding the country of an isolative, corrupt, and repressive clique of rulers."[91] The alliance threw together entities of very different bases and vintage in a common project to discredit their more powerful foe, the Mubarak ruling group and its hereditary succession plans. It encompassed Egypt's only durable opposition organization, the Muslim Brothers, with the activist networks that had fused into Kifaya; its offshoots in the April 6th youth movement; mavericks such as Ayman Nour, Hamdeen Sabahy, Abul Ela Madi, Mohamed ElBaradei, and their followers; cause lawyers as individuals and in their NGOs; the parallel parliamentarians; and intellectual groupuscules such as the Revolutionary Socialists and various small networks of liberals and communists. Their power was in producing an effective mobilizing idea, a frame, to make sense of their collective experience and to launch action, as they did on January 25, 2011.

Distinct from the alliance but with parallel effects were the hundreds of protest acts in streets and workplaces that diffused during the first decade of the new millennium. Hopelessly parochial and ephemeral when looked at singly, when seen as an accumulation of practices and understandings, the significance of Hobsbawm's "collective bargaining by riot" becomes clear. Without formal union organizations or municipal representatives, groups of workers and town residents represented themselves, massing in disruptive public gatherings to induce bargaining situations with government representatives over a host of problems. Their direct action had no ties to the oppositional alliance nor could it be thought to endorse an anti-Mubarak stance, much less harbor revolutionary sentiments. Their posture toward Hosni Mubarak and other political preferences are unknown, since no free elections or surveys existed, and the opposition's organizing of broad constituencies was prohibited by definition. Their targets were those who ruled them directly, the provincial governors, police chiefs, patrol officers, and petty bureaucrats with whom they negotiated their demands, amassing tactical knowledge of their movements and methods. Their power lay in disrupting the daily functioning of social domination. Acting together to discredit the regime, and acting together to disrupt its operations: these were the forms of power that escalated the January 25, 2011, protest action into a revolutionary situation.

*Chapter 3*

# FEAR US, O GOVERNMENT

خافي مننا يا حكومة!

> We exist and have a right to exist. We have strength, coherence, and determination. National politics must take us into account.
> —Charles Tilly, "Political Identities"

### Alexandria, March 4, 2011

After Friday prayers, demonstrators streamed out of al-Qa'id Ibrahim mosque and made for the headquarters of State Security Investigations (SSI), propelled by rumors that officers of Mubarak's notorious domestic intelligence agency were feverishly shredding documents. The crowds encircled the building and demanded that the agency be dissolved and its documents safeguarded. By sunset, a hard core of protesters readied themselves to spend the night camping outside. Suddenly, tear gas and rubber bullets were fired from the building. Demonstrators responded by setting cars alight and by 9 p.m. had succeeded in storming the headquarters and trapping SSI officers inside. Military personnel arrived to negotiate the release of the officers while demonstrators fanned out, searching for documents. They found heaps of shredded paper in huge trash bags; some spirited away as many intact files as they could carry, and others handed them over to military police, insisting that their sole objective was to prevent SSI agents from destroying evidence of their surveillance of the population.[1]

### Cairo, March 5, 2011

When the Alexandria news reached Cairo, crowds encircled the SSI behemoth in east Cairo's Nasr City neighborhood as well as the one in the October 6th suburb. Among the Nasr City crowd was Judge Zakariyya Abdel Aziz, former head of the dissident judges. Someone cried out that police trucks loaded with shredded files were attempting to exit at the back of the building. Overwhelmed by the surge of angry citizens, military policemen unlocked the gates, and demonstrators rushed in to find huge trash bags overflowing with shredded paper. They huddled around office desks, reading from the files stacked from floor to ceiling. One excited young man recorded his walk-through of former interior minister Habib al-Adli's private quarters; "Yes, this is Habib al-Adli's office," he narrated breathlessly. Panning his phone camera over a bathroom with a Jacuzzi, exercise bike, and matching his-and-her terry bathrobes hanging in a closet, he hyperventilated, "I wonder whose these are, ya Habib!" Outside, many people were hurrying out, arms loaded with dossiers. "The SSI's archive," wrote journalist Amira Howeidy, who found files on her father, journalist Fahmi Howeidy. "Or to be more accurate, our archives, details of our lives, secrets, relationships, phone calls, networks, interests, movements, compiled by the massive spy networks maintained by Mubarak's police state."[2] Ten days later, the interior minister announced the dissolution of SSI and its replacement

FIGURE 5. Protesters storm SSI Headquarters, March 5, 2011; photo by Hossam el-Hamalawy, used under Creative Commons license CC BY 2.0.

with a National Security Sector, vowing that it would serve "the nation without interfering in the lives of citizens or their right to exercise their political rights."[3]

### Cairo, March–May 2011

When universities reopened for the delayed spring term on March 5, students immediately began organizing free student union elections, energized by the revelations in SSI documents of intelligence agents micromanaging campus polls. At Cairo University's Faculty of Mass Communications, students began a sit-in demanding Dean Sami Abdel Aziz's resignation, accusing him of being a chief publicist for the Mubarak regime. As the days turned into weeks, the sit-in drew many more students and supportive faculty seeking to expunge Mubarak *fulul* (remnants) from their college. When the university president tried to convince them to disband, they shouted him down, chanting "Irhal! Irhal!" (Leave! Leave!). At a rally by female students, one held up a sign that read, "Either we live free or we die as revolutionaries." Dean Abdel Aziz sighed, "God help me, I have no recourse but dialogue, then more dialogue."[4]

On March 24, Abdel Aziz called the head of military police to disband the sit-in. Armored personnel carriers entered the campus grounds and military policemen tore down the students' posters, beat them with electric batons, and detained several professors and student ringleaders. The next day, prominent journalists visited the sit-in to express outrage and solidarity, and faculty began organizing a formal vote on the dean. Students processed around campus, chanting "We won't leave! He must go!" They compiled Abdel Aziz's pro-Mubarak opinion pieces into a "black book" that they delivered to the university president. He responded by expelling nine of them. The faculty voted to dismiss Abdel Aziz by twenty-four to eighteen votes. On May 23, the sit-in's eightieth day, the university president met with the faculty and announced that he was relieving Abdel Aziz of his duties and reinstating the nine students.[5]

### Qena, April 15–25, 2011

Under pressure from demonstrators in Tahrir Squares across the country, the interim military authorities relented and replaced Mubarak-appointed provincial governors with new executives. For Qena province in Upper Egypt, the interim government followed Mubarak's precedent and appointed a Coptic police general named Emad Mikhail. His predecessor, Qena's first Coptic governor, had

had a controversial tenure that alienated many groups.[6] Incensed townspeople organized a large protest procession to the provincial government headquarters and began a sit-in, chanting "Irhal! Irhal! We don't want him! We don't want him!"[7] The next day, thousands blocked the main highways and train tracks with makeshift barricades, planting their bodies astride the province's major communication lines. On the third day, with Upper Egypt cut off from the rest of the country, Interior Minister Mansour Essawi, a Qena native, headed to the province and attended a meeting with clan notables, political activists, and security chiefs, requesting that roads and railways be reopened and promising to relay Qenawis' concerns to the military generals in Cairo. No sooner had he left than the prime minister sent a team of three emissaries (two Salafi preachers and a Qena-born journalist) to negotiate with the protesters, but they too returned empty-handed.

A protester held up a sign, "Wanted: A Governor for Qena. Qualifications: Muslim, Civilian." Theories circulated about who was really behind the protests. It was the Salafis, who had recently assaulted a Coptic schoolteacher and incinerated his car. It was leaders of the Hawwara and Ashraf clans, manifesting their clout to the central government. It was disgruntled officers of the SSI, seeking revenge for their agency's dissolution. A local shaykh explained why many Muslims did not want a Coptic governor. "He could not enforce the law. We Muslims felt that he was biased against us, and Copts felt that he was biased against them. Neither Muslims nor Copts are wrong."[8] A Coptic activist explained why many Copts were supporting the protests, "Ayoub [the previous Coptic governor] refused us a permit to renovate St. Dumyana Church, and removed a fence put up by the diocese, in defiance of a court ruling." Bishoi Narouz of the Qena diocese addressed the encampment, taking them to task for using coarse terms to describe their Coptic brethren but joining their demand not to repeat the "bad experience" of a Coptic governor.[9]

On the eighth day of the insurrection, a joint statement was authored by Qena's revolutionary youth, the diocese, Salafi groups, and the local bar association. They proposed that Qena be governed by a transitional military figure for three months who would organize a direct popular election of a civilian governor. A strong regional pride infused the statement, framing Qena as a potential pioneer in bottom-up governance rather than a testing ground for inscrutable top-down policies. A protester exclaimed, "We are simply sick of being laboratory rats for the government. There was no Christian governor before and they chose us to have the first ever Christian governor. Now without telling us they chose another Christian governor."[10] As similar large protests against newly appointed governors began to spread to Alexandria, Minya, and Daqahliyya, the prime minister sent a personal aide (another Qena native) to meet with the demonstrators blocking the railways, unaccompanied by any other officials or a security detail. On the eleventh day, using a face-saving bureaucratic contortion, the government announced it was "suspending the activity of Emad Mikhail" for three months and delegating his powers to the province's secretary-general. Protesters removed their barricades and cleaned up the train tracks, but those camped outside the government headquarters decided to stay there, just clearing the way for government employees to reenter.[11]

## PARSING A REVOLUTIONARY SITUATION

If an Egyptian Rip Van Winkle had slumbered in December 2010 then awakened to behold these scenes of spring 2011, we would expect him to feel disoriented. The crowds, their righteous anger, the sabotaging of railways, the large encampments in front of public buildings—all of these were familiar features of Egyptians' disruptive repertoire of collection action. But there were unthinkable new scenes—impregnable security buildings stormed and their classified documents seized, deans holed up in their conference rooms by impertinent students, Egypt's south cut off from the rest of the country for *more than a week* by protesters. What is going on? Why were the protesters using the word "revolutionary" and what did *fulul* mean? What were Salafis doing, barging into a world of politics that they had long repudiated? Above all, why did the government appear so intimidated and indecisive, dissolving an untouchable police agency, sacking bureaucratic barons, and everywhere negotiating fecklessly so as to encourage this popular disobedience?

The fall of Mubarak unleashed new popular initiatives to remake state institutions. The four protest episodes typify the goals of citizens' direct action in spring 2011: purging ancien régime officials, dismantling the hated institutional core of Mubarak's police state, and demanding the election of provincial executives, the mini-presidents who set the regulations most directly affecting people's daily lives. A new lexicon of political communication rapidly circulated in the form of slogans, daily expressions, and assertions of collective identity;

*thawri* (revolutionary) became the self-identification of anyone demanding thoroughgoing change, and *fulul* (remnants) the derogatory label slapped onto high-ranking apparatchiks of the Mubarak regime. To the interim authorities, citizens sent the message: "Fear Us, O Government" (*Khafi minnina ya hukuma*), as a ubiquitous graffito from 2011 encapsulated. Fear here carried the weighty political connotation of "take us into account"—as coauthors and not merely subjects of national politics—what Charles Tilly calls the assertion of political identities.[12] But for all the bold new citizens' initiatives, the four examples also reveal that the state did not crumble or wither away in response. If anything, its operations became more visible, as its many agents and organizations scrambled to satisfy and contain popular direct action while also straining to preserve their own positions.

This chapter confronts the inherent ambiguity in the strategic situation after Hosni Mubarak's fall. On February 11, the revolution was over, and the revolution had just begun. When the generals seized power from Mubarak on the uprising's eighteenth day, they extinguished the possibility of Tahrir turning into a countergovernment. But their emergency action inaugurated a juncture of uncertainty over who would govern Egypt and on what basis they would rule. The chapter analyzes how the generals built their claim to rule and how that claim came to be fiercely contested after a brief period of popular jubilation and trust in the military as "protectors of the revolution." Egyptians' collective capacity-building and powers of disruption, analyzed in chapter 2, enabled them to effectively challenge the generals' claim to rule, yet without being able to eject the military from the political arena and install themselves as masters of the state. This two-power contest between ancien régime personnel and new and old civilian contenders is the defining feature of the revolutionary situation.

We owe the concept of revolutionary situations to a curious mix of Russian revolutionary activists and American social scientists. In 1915, Vladimir Lenin unbundled the singular notion of "revolution" into three distinct components: revolutions, revolutionary organizations, and "revolutionary situations." He was at pains to distinguish revolutionary situations from revolutionary outcomes where state power changes hands; "it is not every revolutionary situation that gives rise to a revolution." To get from situations to outcomes, the crucial connectors are revolutionary organizations that direct mass energies for an effective seizure of state power. But revolutionary situations are significant in their own right as interludes when constituted public authority is under assault, when the "ruled do not want to live in the old way and the ruling classes are unable to rule as before."[13] To Lenin the revolutionary strategist, such transitional periods when a stable political order comes undone are pregnant with possibilities, not inevitabilities, for change.

Two years later, after the outbreak of the Russian February Revolution, Lenin built on his initial insight by extracting a general idea from the specific experience of the standoff between the liberal Provisional Government and the Petrograd Soviet from March to November 1917:

> The highly remarkable feature of our revolution is that it has brought about a *dual power*. ... What is this dual power? Alongside the Provisional Government, the government of *bourgeoisie, another government* has arisen, so far weak and incipient, but undoubtedly a government that actually exists and is growing— the Soviets of Workers' and Soldiers' Deputies.[14]

Leon Trotsky sharpened this image of a deadlock between two organs of rule in his concept of *dvoevlastie*, or dual power. Inspired by the Russian events, Trotsky looked back in history to theorize all revolutions, including the seventeenth- and eighteenth-century English and French Revolutions, as epic battles between "double governments," or rival organs of public authority. These are "essentially incompatible governmental organizations—the one outlived, the other in process of formation—which jostle against each other at every step in the sphere of government." The politics of revolution is conceptualized as a battle between contending sovereignties; "to overcome the 'anarchy' of this twofold sovereignty becomes at every new step the task of the revolution—or the counterrevolution."[15]

The analytically and empirically interesting problem thrown up by the 2011 revolts in Egypt, Tunisia, and Yemen is not that they created countergovernments in the form of revolutionary organizations, for then they would be full-fledged revolutions in Lenin's terms, but that they opened up revolutionary situations. Millions of citizens filling public squares for weeks on end rendered it impossible for the authoritarian states to rule in the old manner, while leaving indeterminate what the new power configurations would be. Emboldened by their unexpectedly large numbers and victories in defeating the police, occupying public spaces, and unseating monarchical presidents, the mass movements advanced a claim that they alone had sovereignty, that is, the ultimate power to authorize political rule. "Sovereignty is best understood as a set of claims made by those seeking or wielding power," reminds historian James Sheehan, "claims about the superiority and autonomy of their authority."[16] The heterogeneous popular movements toppling Arab autocrats did so in the name of popular sovereignty and claimed the right to build the new order on the same basis.

What made the sovereignty claim effective was the active support of segments of the public in each Arab state, and of publics the world over that were closely watching and cheering the uprisings. As Tilly underlines:

> The claims themselves do not amount to a revolutionary situation. The question is whether some significant part of the subject population honors the claim. The revolutionary moment arrives when previously acquiescent members of that population find themselves confronted with strictly incompatible demands from the government and from an alternative body claiming control over the government, or claiming to *be* the government... and those previously acquiescent people obey the alternative body.[17]

What developed during the Eighteen Days narrated in the prologue is this split in the general population between allegiance to the Mubarak regime (think of the proregime demonstrations and the February 2 attempt to violently disband the Tahrir encampment) and support of the Tahrir opposition. For the vast majority of citizens at home watching on their television sets, we can reasonably assume a similar split, though we have no way of knowing the size of each camp or the number of fence-sitters. But we do know that on February 9 and 10, the diffusion of strikes throughout the civil service and industrial sectors buoyed the mass uprising (if not endorsing every demand of the protesters), prompting the generals on the hastily convened Supreme Council of the Armed Forces (SCAF) to step in, remove Mubarak on February 11, and take control of the state before it could fall into the opposition's hands.

SCAF's seizure of power after edging out Mubarak created two claimants to sovereignty: the self-constituting generals claiming to "protect the revolution," and the Tahrir movement claiming popular sovereignty, each with a constituency of support in Egypt and abroad. Few had illusions that the US-backed generals would simply cede control to the farrago of groups constituting the Tahrir opposition, but fewer expected a restoration of the status quo ante. Between these poles of radical transformation and authoritarian restoration stretched a large middle space, a yet-to-be defined synthesis of democratic arrangements and military prerogatives that could take several forms: a presidential regime with a dual civilian-military executive; a parliamentary republic with military veto points; or a mixed regime of strong presidency, empowered legislature, and military jurisdiction over specific policy domains. Given the number of domestic and international actors with an existential stake in how the largest Arab state was to be governed after Mubarak, and an incentive to act quickly to press their advantage, the only certainty was that Egypt was headed into a volatile transitional period.

At the most abstract level, Arthur Stinchcombe helps us understand the unscripted politics of revolutionary situations:

> By a political revolution I mean a time of rapid, often erratic, change in the relative power of social classes, ethnicities, regions, political parties, legislatures, military groups, royal or noble lineages, and so on.... For such instability of relative power to continue, different groups and people have to have different estimates of how it will all come out; otherwise they would make deals in light of who was going to win and so produce stability.[18]

Stinchcombe's twin emphasis on objective and subjective perceptions of uncertainty helps us get some grip on the most confusing attribute of revolutionary dynamics: the seeming chaos and formlessness of politics in times of exceptional flux. The perpetually shifting balance of power between contending claimants to sovereignty is the chief attribute of political revolution, the main thread we must follow to understand what happened when a three-decade-old undemocratic regime was unexpectedly toppled by a dual force: mass action and military coup.

## A TSUNAMI OF MINI-REVOLUTIONS

The days and weeks after Mubarak's fall exhibited much of what one historian of Russia has called "the motifs of release, liberation, and devolving power that infuse the rhetoric and symbolism of the revolutionary moment."[19] A flurry of political activity began the day after Mubarak's departure. The network of seven youth movements that had organized the January 25 protest action constituted themselves as the Revolution Youth Coalition (I'tilaf Shabab al-Thawra; hereafter

RYC); in a striking self-limiting strain reflecting their ambivalence toward party politics, the RYC explicitly disavowed competing for power. Instead, they cast themselves as a broad front to "monitor the realization of the revolution's demands and the peaceful transfer of power to civilians."[20] An assertive Coptic youth movement was born, defying the tutelage of Pope Shenouda. Baptizing itself the Maspero Youth Union (Ittihad Shabab Maspero), it took the name of the radio and television building where it sited its rallies to demand equal citizenship rights.[21] Presidential hopefuls began wooing the public, cozying up to the suddenly famous youth activists and stumping in historically neglected provinces far from Cairo. Suppressed associational energies rekindled; the two-million-strong teachers' union vowed to purge NDP operatives and hold clean internal elections, and the engineers' union met for the first time since 1995 when it had been placed under government receivership. Editors of the leading independent daily *al-Shurouq* tracked a "tsunami of mini-revolutions" across government bureaus, public sector factories, banks, hospitals, museums, schools, state-owned media, and courthouses, as subordinates moved against entrenched bosses.[22] Workers and civil servants did not simply demand higher wages but an overhaul of authority relations under the banner of *tatt-heer* (purification); by one count, between forty and sixty workplace protests occurred every day between February 12 and 14.[23] Whether or not they participated in his removal, after Mubarak's ouster many Egyptians rose up against misrule in their daily lives.

One week after Mubarak's fall, on February 18, Tahrir filled in celebration, but the crowds pointedly reminded the generals that many demands were still unmet, principally lifting the state of emergency and releasing political prisoners. Activists envisioned turning the Friday *milyuniyya* (million-man rally) pioneered on February 4 into a new mode of pressure on the interim authorities, extending through time and space the crowd power that had brought about Mubarak's toppling. The milyuniyya should be "the general assembly of the Egyptian people," declared Kifaya activist Karima al-Hifnawy.[24] The months after Mubarak's removal bore out her aspiration. A dialectic emerged between crowds filling Cairo and provincial Tahrirs every Friday and SCAF decisions. On February 18, the Friday of Victory (Jum'at al-Nasr), protesters demanded the purging of Mubarak loyalists from the caretaker cabinet. Four days later, the generals ordered a cabinet reshuffle, appointing for the first time two members of opposition parties, including leftist economist Gouda Abdel Khaleq as minister of social solidarity. Unsatisfied, crowds rallied on February 25, Purification Friday (Jum'at al-Tatt-heer), for a completely new cabinet. The following Thursday, hoping to head off the Friday rally, SCAF forced the resignation of Mubarak crony Ahmed Shafiq as prime minister and appointed the engineering professor Essam Sharaf, who had been proposed to the military council by the RYC. Still, on Friday, March 4, Insistence Friday, the rally went ahead as planned, so Sharaf made his way to Tahrir, where, flanked by dissident judge Zakariyya Abdel Aziz and the Muslim Brothers' Tahrir leader Mohamed al-Beltagui, he insisted to the delighted crowds that his legitimacy derived from them but stopped short of reciting the oath of office then and there as some demanded.[25]

What had been improvised as a bargaining instrument between rulers and crowds during the Eighteen Days now turned into a weekly practice of popular deliberation, acclamation, and denunciation, an open-air parliament to organize pressure on SCAF until the onset of civilian rule. A new protest performance thus accrued to the repertoire of contention, an instrument of popular voice in national politics that was inconceivable before the revolutionary situation. The milyuniyya was not a gathering of literally one million people; at capacity, Tahrir Square holds one-quarter of a million people. Rather, *milyuniyya* came to mean a mass assembly of thousands to tens of thousands in Cairo and the provinces, usually scheduled on Fridays, to make demands on the interim authorities, advance various causes, or commemorate events. The Friday rallies punctuated political dynamics for all of 2011, aggregating the most radical flank of public opinion, airing rival *prises de position* from the square's different stages, and forcing the generals to constantly perform their incongruous self-definition as "protectors of the revolution." We saw how the storming of SSI headquarters began in Alexandria on Insistence Friday, as news spread outside Qa'id Ibrahim mosque that SSI agents were shredding documents. The Qena imbroglio was also the outcome of a milyuniyya. On Friday, April 8, demonstrators stepped up their demands that Hosni Mubarak and his security officials be prosecuted for the murder of protesters. Balking at the prospect of humiliating their former commander and opening the Pandora's box of the state's mass killings, SCAF temporized by appointing new governors on April 14, setting off the protests in Qena, Alexandria, and elsewhere. Continued Friday mass rallies and threatened reoccupations of Tahrir finally forced their hand, and Mubarak was referred to trial on May 24. By year's end, a massive November milyuniyya triggered a series of events that escalated into SCAF's first governance crisis.

Where Tahrir Square became revolutionary Cairo's speakers' corner, central bulletin board, and campground combined, Mostafa Mahmoud Square in the west Cairo neighborhood of Mohandiseen turned into the antirevolution's muster point. During the Eighteen Days, pro-Mubarak crowds claimed the space as a counter-Tahrir; after February 11, they did not disappear but deliberately styled themselves as defenders of order against revolutionary chaos.

Even further from Tahrir and far beyond Cairo, many Egyptians were experiencing newly assertive regional political solidarities. Where most had never heard of Suez's Arba'in Square before January 25, it was now nationally recognized as the revolution's early riser, vindicating its townspeople's fierce pride in their history of resistance.[26] Alexandria, Egypt's second city, earned its own laurels as the early riser against the SSI apparatus on March 4 that led to the intelligence agency's dissolution ten days later. Some of the neighborhood popular committees (*lijan sha'biyya*) that had sprung up to protect streets and homes on January 28 remained active and even convened a national conference in April 2011.[27] When a spate of arson attacks on shrines reached Abu Mashour village in Menoufiyya, residents quickly pooled their resources to rebuild the structure, to avoid police involvement and stave off an escalation between Sufis who venerated the shrines and Salafis who saw them as a dangerous heterodoxy.[28] In Bani Suef, fine arts students launched a "revolution of colors," painting the concrete wall that ran along their cornice with "simple designs and mirthful colors," inspiring local business owners to donate supplies and passersby to lend a hand in the daily afternoon beautification sessions.[29] To paraphrase geographer Doreen Massey, in the process of constructing their new and overlapping political identities, Egyptians resignified urban geographies in the capital and across the provinces' cities and towns.[30]

Yet performances of collective identity were not friction-free, nor the preserve of groups that progressives would applaud. When two hundred feminist women and a few supportive men tried to rally in Tahrir on March 8, International Women's Day, they were surrounded and heckled by hostile men (some from the permanent protesters' encampment in the square), who then violently pushed through the rows of women and took over the raised platform on which they were standing.[31] In April, thousands of Salafis massed outside the Coptic cathedral in 'Abbasiyya, demanding the release of Coptic women like Wafaa Constantin who had been placed in church custody after converting to Islam. The demonstrators demanded legislation to protect converted Copts, whom they called "new Muslims," and called for subjecting churches to the same level of government control as mosques.[32] In a counterdemonstration days later, thousands of Copts filled the cathedral courtyard in what protesters called an *istishhad* (martyrdom), announcing their readiness to perish to protect the church and its leadership from any attacks by Salafis.[33]

It is a truism that revolutionary situations portend heightened social conflict. As many groups exercised newfound political agency, often directly on the streets, they called into being countermobilization to defend rival visions. Old social conflicts reignited and new ones were brought forth, harmonic creativity coexisted with emboldened bigotry, and civic cooperation jostled with mutual misrecognition. Before the men broke up the feminists' rally, the antagonists were arguing about whether women could run for the presidency. The revolutionary situation revealed, and did not resolve, irreducible political differences among Egyptians that had found no occasion to be aired prior to 2011.

## CONSERVATIVE REVOLUTIONARIES

Built into the same moment of mass collective action was a powerful countervailing force: interim rule by a military junta. All but one of the eighteen senior generals who had ousted Mubarak were unknown to the public; Minister of Defense Mohamed Tantawi was the only recognizable figure by virtue of the cabinet position he had held since 1991. The first time Egyptians had seen the generals was on February 10, when television footage showed them meeting at a roundtable without Hosni Mubarak as their Communiqué No. 1 was read out, declaring that the Supreme Council of the Armed Forces (SCAF) was in continuous session. From the newspapers on the morning of February 12 Egyptians learned that SCAF was the apex of the military, consisting of the armed forces' senior command, and that it was an emergency conclave that had convened only twice before, during the 1967 and 1973 Arab-Israeli wars.[34] Outside military academies, the biographies of the generals, their collegial dynamics, and their worldviews remained unknown, an obscurity cultivated by Hosni Mubarak after sidelining a charismatic military rival in 1989.[35]

Yezid Sayigh's adroit description helps explain why many in Egypt and abroad welcomed SCAF's intervention to remove Mubarak: "One of the most remarkable things about Egypt is how ubiquitous the Egyptian Armed Forces are and yet how little anyone outside their ranks, and possibly within them, knows about their social composition."[36] The armed forces had a distinct mystique, at once familiar and well-regarded in public culture yet insulated and inscrutable, furthering the perception that they were a professional, neutral third party ridding Egypt of a reviled autocrat. It helped that the generals' most powerful patron swiftly certified their status as legitimate interim rulers. Hours after Mubarak's departure, US President Barack Obama declared, "The military has served patriotically and responsibly as a caretaker to the state, and will now have to ensure a transition that is credible in the eyes of the Egyptian people."[37] But this is hardly the whole story of why military intervention did not immediately raise hackles. As sociologist Atef Said reflected from his ethnographic vantage in Tahrir Square during the Eighteen Days, Egyptians had contradictory perspectives on the armed forces; "on the one hand they want a strong military regionally, but at the same time they do not want military intervention in politics."[38] They were also keenly aware of and ambivalent about the armed forces' elevated economic status as producer of both military equipment and consumer goods and as default custodian of public land, a veritable military aristocracy built on the labor of conscripts and an annual stream of $1.3 billion in US military aid.[39] The complex embeddedness of the military in state and economy portended a reckoning that would unfold in the political arena.

The major uncertainty opened up by the revolutionary situation was what sort of status this powerful state elite would seek in the new political order. Would the generals seek to be kings or kingmakers of post-Mubarak politics? Whether they opted for direct rule or behind-the-scenes influence, what specific forms would "military involvement in politics" take? After all, this catchall label covers many different arrangements. In the modern world, men in uniform can reserve positions within the state for one of their own, from seats in the legislature and cabinet to the presidential seat; claim "reserve domains," entire policy areas walled off from civilian control, such as defense and foreign relations;[40] secure total autonomy of the armed forces' budget and appointments from civilian oversight; institutionalize their control over a range of policies through a National Defense or Security Council in which they hold the majority of seats; and constitutionalize their status, inscribing themselves as permanent guardians of a state where elected civilians are mere transients.

No wonder contemporaneous observers had conflicting assessments of the generals' goals. Despite assurances from SCAF that they would not field a presidential candidate, the Pentagon was not shy about divulging that its favorite SCAF member was Chief of Staff Sami Anan.[41] A foreign diplomat who said he knew SCAF chairman Mohamed Tantawi assured, "My strong sense is there is no real desire to prolong this period. The field marshal does not seem really interested in being the government of Egypt. He would prefer to take the armed forces back, to have their very large and very comfortable arrangement in Egyptian society and let the civilians take charge of government."[42] A thirty-five-year-old protester in Tahrir Square was less sanguine. "Over the next six months, I am afraid the army will brainwash the people to think that the military is the best option."[43] Leading military-watchers downplayed that possibility, forecasting that direct military rule would lead to political instability and ultimately another revolution.[44]

In the three days following Mubarak's ouster, the generals acted quickly to "slow down rates of change of relative power and decrease uncertainty about who, and what policies, will rule in the near and medium-range future," in Arthur Stinchcombe's terms.[45] They signaled continuity of Egypt's position in international alliances, especially the 1979 peace treaty with Israel, pledging to abide by all of Egypt's regional and international treaties. Acting as dictators in the Roman sense of a temporary executive, with SCAF chairman Mohamed Tantawi as interim head of state, the generals promised to steer a transition to civilian rule, giving themselves six months to fulfill Tahrir Square's banner of demands unfurled on February 4: dissolving the 2010 parliament, organizing new general and presidential elections, and amending the 1971 constitution which they had just suspended. But they pointedly ignored the demands to prosecute ancien régime officials and police commanders who had ordered the killing of protesters, and they retained as a caretaker government the Ahmed Shafiq cabinet appointed by Mubarak on January 29. In three weeks, the Friday milyuniyyas pressured them to concede to these demands by appointing a new cabinet and putting on trial police commanders and Hosni Mubarak himself.

Their self-designation as both "protectors of the revolution" and guardians of the state compelled the generals to perform a hybrid identity as at once pro-change and prostability. A pro-SCAF academic helped disseminate this framing, seeing no incongruence in arguing:

> The armed forces are revolutionary but they are conservative. The best revolutionaries are those who have the capacity to brake their idealistic ambitions so as not to overturn the car and lose everything that we have achieved, all because we wanted something before its time.[46]

The generals themselves were keen on public outreach, scheduling back-to-back meetings with newspaper editors, the Tahrir youth activists, and party politicians. They presented themselves as clean-handed men of honor who cherished their bond with "the people" and had gladly "adopted the revolution" once the masses rose up. In their first television interview ten days after taking power, they praised January 25 as "the greatest revolution in Egypt's history," smiling genially at the camera in their simple military fatigues and speaking without baroque formalities. Notwithstanding the free-flowing conversation that lasted for over two hours, they were intent on communicating a key point: the armed forces "belong to the people, as Article 180 of the constitution states," quoted SCAF's legal specialist, General Mamdouh Shahin, referencing the suspended 1971 constitution.[47] The clause, dating from Egypt's first republican constitution of 1956 under Gamal Abdel Nasser, enabled military men to claim sovereignty during ordinary and unsettled times, equating themselves with the state *and* nation.[48] SCAF generals resurrected the idea in 2011 as the linchpin of their claim to power after the mass uprising. To a group of journalists and activists, they were blunt, "We must know that SCAF sees the *regime* as having collapsed, but the *state* did not and will not collapse, except over everyone's dead body, army and people."[49]

The only time the generals lost composure and talked animatedly over one another and the television interviewers was when the conversation turned to the Friday milyuniyyas. They bristled at the host's suggestion that the Friday gatherings were necessary to monitor SCAF's progress in fulfilling the revolution's demands. "You cannot deny that these continued gatherings are destabilizing," maintained General Mohamed al-Assar. "We don't want these revolutionary atmospherics now, we want to go back to normal life and enjoy the accomplishment of the revolution."[50]

To stem what they saw as the dangerous wave of disobedience diffusing across universities, workplaces, and neighborhoods, SCAF deployed the armed forces to shore up state authority. With the police still in disarray and facing a mutiny by low-ranking officers, the military essentially took over policing during the early months of 2011. Military policemen were repeatedly dispatched to evict squatters from vacant public housing units; the scope of the military justice system was dramatically expanded, trying 11,879 civilians and convicting 8,071 in military tribunals by August; the penal code was amended to stiffen penalties for a range of transgressions; and SCAF rebuked the mounting strikes by workers and civil servants, issuing a decree criminalizing strikes and sit-ins.[51] Having already conceded Tahrir's demands for a new cabinet and referred Mubarak and his associates to trial, the military council was careful not to yield any further changes in governance structures. Perhaps the most striking example was inaction on reforming the police, the most publicly loathed state organ and the catalyst for the inaugural January 25, 2011, protest that led to the uprising.

In April, an official fact-finding panel established that police had killed 846 citizens and injured 6,467 during the Eighteen Days, including more than a thousand eye injuries resulting in complete loss of sight. It was perhaps the first official acknowledgment in Egypt's contemporary history that the state had engaged in mass killing.[52] The dead were sanctified with the honorific "martyrs" (*shuhada'*) and folded into Egypt's historical "martyr-scape."[53] Activists petitioned courts to efface Mubarak's name from metro stations and city squares and replace it with martyrs' names; and the faces of the fallen were memorialized by artists on city walls and on banners hung up in Tahrir and the neighborhoods where they lived.[54] Martyrs' surviving families were iconized in ways surpassing recognition of Egypt's war veterans; they were feted by luminaries at gala events, courted by presidential hopefuls, and offered recompense by the government.[55]

But their quest for justice told a different story. Police officials pressured families to halt their legal pursuit of the policemen who murdered their children and accept financial compensation. When hospitals' death certificates falsified the cause of death, families' next port of call in the bureaucracy was the Forensic Medicine Authority, to establish the true cause of death as a policeman's bullet. When prosecutors actually referred policemen to trial, family members and their advocates had to ensure that they would not be barred from attending the proceedings and that police defendants would be compelled to be present in court. To this point, only one police officer had been sentenced for the murder of protesters, but in absentia. The battle to establish responsibility for mass killing traces the power of the bureaucracy to temporize and dissipate attempts to subvert a cornerstone of the modern state: police impunity.[56] Although crowds had ransacked SSI headquarters and forced the institution's dismantling, the interior minister merely relabeled the agency as *Qita' al-Amn al-Watani*, the National Security Sector.

It was the martyrs' families who catalyzed what came to be called the "second wave of the revolution." After police attacked martyrs' families as they attempted to enter a commemorative event at a theater house, demonstrators reoccupied Cairo's, Alexandria's, and Suez's Tahrirs for three weeks starting on July 8. Initially, the Interior Ministry sacked 500 police generals and 164 officers, but on July 15, Tahrir overfilled with unsatisfied protesters on Final Warning Friday, and, two days after that, SCAF announced a partial cabinet reshuffle, replacing fourteen out of twenty-seven ministers but retaining the ministers of justice and interior, whom protesters blamed for delaying prosecutions of ancien régime figures. Two weeks later, on August 1, seizing the opportunity of the first day of Ramadan when energies were low, soldiers and police forcibly disbanded the sit-in, shredding tents, beating protesters with batons, and storming the Omar Makram mosque where protesters had fled.[57] The conflict went into a brief hiatus as public attention shifted to a scene that many had feared would never happen. On August 3, shortly before 10 a.m., Hosni Mubarak made his first appearance since February 10. He was wheeled into a courtroom cage on a hospital gurney for the opening session of his trial for murdering protesters, flanked protectively by his sons in prison whites. In an adjoining cage were former interior minister Habib al-Adli and his six senior lieutenants. Millions of viewers across the Arab world and beyond gaped at what Egyptian newspapers branded the "Trial of the Century." An Arab autocrat stood accused in an ordinary courtroom. "I am dreaming," said Hossam Muhammad as he watched. "Somebody pinch me."[58]

## WHAT'S THE HURRY? I NEED TIME

The six-week period between February 11, 2011, and SCAF's promulgation of a provisional constitution on March 30, 2011, had an abiding impact on the course of revolutionary politics, cementing the generals' sovereignty claim and revealing the first significant schism within the opposition coalition that had taken down Mubarak. The core dispute hinged on the generals' unilateral dictating of the transition roadmap and refusal to countenance any form of power-sharing with civilian politicians. The controversy began with SCAF's decree of February 14, appointing an eight-man panel of constitutional experts to amend and liberalize the constitutional rules for free general and presidential elections. The body came to be known as the Bishri panel, after its chairman Tareq al-Bishri, the esteemed judge respected for his rulings upholding citizens' rights (see chap. 2). Bishri's reputation as a bold critic of the Mubarak regime signaled the military council's attunement to public opinion, but some on the Left mistrusted him due to his ideological drift from leftist thought to Islamist sympathies.

However, the real misgivings centered on the only nonjurist and partisan figure on the panel: the attorney and former parliamentarian Sobhi Saleh, one of the Muslim Brothers' most outspoken members. No one on the military council explained why only the Muslim Brothers and not any of the country's numerous other political factions were represented on the panel. Activists then pointed to other salient exclusions, notably female legal experts and young people, and the inexplicably rushed ten-day schedule set by SCAF for the panel to complete its work.[59] It was but a short step to a gathering sentiment that the generals had cut a deal with Egypt's largest political organization to pacify the mass anti-Mubarak ferment by channeling it into safer formal electoral institutions. The two sides stood to reap great benefits—the generals would get unruly crowds off the streets and into orderly election queues, and the Muslim Brothers would receive the lion's share of any free and fair vote, based on their experience in contesting national elections since 1984.[60]

When they were revealed in ten days, most of the panel's revisions were widely welcomed as undoing the worst features of authoritarian presidentialism. The president's term was reduced to four years and a two-term limit was imposed; Mubarak-era restrictions on presidential candidacy were scrapped; the president's power to declare a national emergency was restricted; and the game-changing judicial supervision of elections that had enabled opposition gains during the Mubarak years was restored and expanded.[61] It was the panel's unusual procedure for constitution-writing that caused controversy and became a major driver of conflict throughout the course of the revolutionary situation well into 2013. The panel designed a two-step process for drafting a new constitution: the future deputies of both houses of parliament would first select a hundred-member Constituent Assembly; then that body would draft the new constitution that would be put to a public referendum. The rule change deliberately left unspecified *how* legislators would elect or select the hundred constitution-drafters, considering this a prerogative of the future legislators.[62]

A torrent of counterproposals for the transition were then put before the public via print and electronic media by politicians such as Mohamed ElBaradei, judges and political scientists, civil society collectives, and emergent political parties. Their chief argument was that it made no sense to amend a constitution that had been suspended by SCAF, and that the transition should instead begin with an elected constituent assembly to write a new constitution from scratch rather than "patch up" (*tarqiʿ*) the 1971 charter. While there was no single opposition body collating the proposals into a common list of demands, from the sea of pamphlets we can identify a handful of recurrent elements: an elected, joint civilian-military presidium of three to five men to act as interim executive alongside SCAF; a national unity government; direct elections to a constituent assembly to write a new constitution; and a longer transition period than SCAF's six-month timeline, ranging from twelve to eighteen months.[63] The rationale was that more time was needed for new political groupings, especially youth activists, to organize and build constituencies before entering the electoral fray. A pamphlet circulating in Tahrir Square argued for a moratorium of at least one year on elections, to "grant more time for the people to identify their true representatives after long decades of the liquidation of their parties and unionist organizations."[64] Another leaflet tackled why self-defined democratic revolutionaries would be leery of free elections: "What's the hurry? I need time. For the first time in many years my vote will mean something and I'll be able to determine my own fate. I need time to catch my breath and think and see and participate."[65]

This first grand divide of revolutionary politics created what became known as the constitution-first versus election-first camps, but it was the body to be elected that was the point of contention, not elections per se. Election-firsters thought it logical that a freely elected legislature be the constituent power to draft the charter for the new political order; constitution-firsters feared the legislature would be a stomping ground of Muslim Brothers and reinvented Mubarak loyalists and insisted on a separate, directly elected Constituent Assembly. Underlying the dilemma were rival views of the distribution of power in the revolutionary situation, especially the power exerted by the still-palpable authoritarian past over the indefinite future. Forgotten now but very salient at the time, members of Mubarak's National Democratic Party (NDP) were loudly and enthusiastically stumping in favor of the constitutional amendments. And as we saw at the beginning of the chapter, there was intense popular agitation against tenacious Mubarak fulul in the security forces, universities, and provincial governments. It was this context that informed a leftist member of the RYC to urge:

> We need a year to prepare for the elections . . . there is no reason to be in all this hurry. This is a fundamental moment: if we hurry we will only succeed in reproducing the old regime, but with a new look.[66]

Responding to the same concern—that parliamentary elections would only result in Muslim Brother and NDP dominance—Tareq al-Bishri argued:

> I'm much more optimistic about the results of the coming elections and don't think they'll be limited to these two. . . . I think [the people] are capable of ensuring they are represented in any elections that are held. Given the current revolutionary momentum elections held sooner rather than later will best express the revolution and unity. This might change later when cultural, social or class particulars surface.[67]

More than optimism versus pessimism, the two visions register the depth of uncertainty constituting the situation, where two opposing conceptions of reality appeared equally plausible, founded on different assessments of an uncertain future. Would quick elections transport revolutionary dynamism into state institutions and defeat the old order, or would they instead empower old interests to reconstitute themselves in refurbished institutions?

The military council ignored all the proposals, especially calls for a joint civilian-military council to manage the transition. Rushing the process to leave no room for debate and deliberation reinforced their command of the situation and prevented any counterproposals from gaining traction. So the opposition took its case to the public. The two weeks leading up to the referendum on the constitutional amendments on March 19 were a frenzy of public outreach and mutual recrimination as the revolution's factions realigned themselves on either side of the emergent boundary. A very similar coalition to the one that had organized the original January 25, 2011, protest action brought together leftist, liberal, and nationalist politicians, the April 6th and RYC youth groups, Coptic groups, and presidential hopefuls in a "No" campaign. Using television talk shows, print media, and a promotional video featuring film celebrities, the "No" camp urged the public to reject the constitutional amendments as cosmetic alterations that would put the counterrevolution back in the saddle, and it castigated the Muslim Brothers as inveterate opportunists for supporting the amendments.[68] The Muslim Brothers relied on their mainstay of mobilization, canvassing neighborhood by neighborhood and holding large public meetings to lobby for a "Yes" vote as the pathway to a new era of honest politics, accusing their critics of being elitist antidemocrats fearful of facing voters in a free poll.[69] Salafi preachers and local activists took shape as a new collective actor, using their own media of mosque pulpits and neighborhood networks to spread the idea that a "Yes" vote was a religious duty, drawing the ire of both the Muslim Brothers and the "No" advocates for cynically inserting religious appeals into a political dispute.[70]

In the event, out of 45 million voters, 18.5 million (41.2 percent) turned out to stand in orderly, cheerful queues, a historic figure given the authoritarian past of electoral fraud and minuscule single-digit turnouts. The results were a surprising 77 percent for the "Yes" vote and 22 percent for "No," defying expectations that the Tahrir coalition's appeals would sway the public. A competitive rush ensued to interpret the results in self-validating terms. International observers took it as proof of their long-held belief that a catchall category of "Islamists" would dominate any post-Mubarak political order.[71] A Salafi preacher proclaimed that Islam had triumphed in the "battle of the ballot boxes," inviting Egyptians who did not like the result to decamp for Canada or the United States. The military council's legal affairs specialist read the results in plebiscitary terms as a 77 percent vote of confidence in the generals themselves rather than the constitutional amendments.[72] As Egyptians wrestled with the ambiguous meanings of the results, ten days after the referendum SCAF promulgated an interim constitution that included over fifty articles that the public had not voted on. The March 30 Constitutional Declaration included verbatim articles from the 1971 constitution that laid out fundamental rights and liberties and the powers of major state institutions, but it also contained two articles codifying the armed forces' status: Article 53 was the old clause that the armed forces "belong to the people," and article 56 was a new addition formalizing the ad hoc SCAF as the holder of executive and legislative powers until the election of a president and parliament. Article 56 constitutionalized the military council's de facto seizure of power, purposely bypassing public input on this controversial measure. "As such," Nimer Sultany observes, "the March 30 declaration resembled a 'grant' in which the ruler bequeaths a constitution to the people."[73]

The referendum began the first of a series of realignments that would span the three-year course of the revolutionary situation from 2011 to 2013, decomposing the original anti-Mubarak Tahrir coalition over disagreements on how the transition should go. It is easy to lament the breakup of this potent alliance, but it is important to appreciate the source of the split: divergent assessments of the Mubarak regime's staying power. All revolutions in their early months are haunted by the specter of the ancien régime's comeback. Egypt's political factions had good reason to fear that Mubarak's party bosses would regain control of parliament, since the fulul were unabashedly active on the political scene, lobbying for a "Yes" vote. It was a month later, in April, that a lawsuit succeeded in dissolving the NDP by court order, yet even then prorevolution groups of all persuasions continued to operate on the assumption that the *nizam*, or regime, was still alive and plotting a comeback. Political fears of hidden power, whether a deal between generals and Islamists or dormant counterrevolutionary forces biding their time, reflected great uncertainty about the real distribution of power. "The sense is that things are not what they seem, that the surface of events does not show what lies beneath—and that the obscurity is intentional and dangerous," observed Talal Asad.[74] What is important about such fears is not their veracity but their reflection and reinforcement of the revolutionary situation's key trait: genuine confusion about the balance of power between new and old groups.

The referendum controversy was revealing in another sense too, offering a first indication that the generals were not a neutral "caretaker to the state," as US President Barack Obama had characterized them on February 11. In ignoring civilians' demands for a partnership role in planning the transition and unilaterally inscribing the military council in the provisional constitution, the generals made clear their intention to have a more substantial role in the post-Mubarak political order. From that point forward, they acted as a constituted body of guardians over the state as a whole rather than the apex of the military hierarchy alone, and civilian factions revised their stances accordingly. Some sought to ally with the generals against their civilian political rivals, others vowed to oust them as illegitimate usurpers and arch-fulul.

SCAF appeared victorious, securing what it wanted in the March 30 interim constitution and rebuffing civilian demands for power-sharing during the transition. But the final constitution was still to be drafted. The Bishri panel had inadvertently planted a "time bomb" in the transition plan, to borrow a phrase from Nathan Brown, vesting parliament with the authority to select the drafters of the new constitution.[75] This presented an acute dilemma for the generals: How would they control constitution-writing if it was the prerogative of legislators? It was the attempt to square this circle that, by the end of 2011, brought the military council to the brink of the same governance crisis that had felled Mubarak at its beginning.

## EVERY EGYPTIAN IS A WALKING POLITICAL PARTY

With the stakes now doubled for the parliamentary elections as the route to both legislative power and constitution-writing, political factions fell to constituting themselves as registered parties and electoral alliances to contest the election. The liberalization of Mubarak-era restrictions on party organization led to not only considerable public engagement with partisan life but the formation of sixty-two parties by the eve of the November poll.[76] At the same time, another fraction of the political class dreaded general elections, fearing that they would usher in a majority of Islamists who would monopolize constitution-writing. They began to think of ways to bind the legislators, eventually settling on the idea of immutable "constitutional principles" in the name of preserving the foundations of a modern secular state.

The new parties on the scene fell into the four ideological currents that have structured politics in Egypt and the Arab world since the early twentieth century: liberal, leftist, Nasserist, and Islamist. The Wafd (est. 1923), standard-bearer of Egyptian liberalism and leader of the anticolonial mass rising in 1919, was joined by three newer liberal outfits: the Tomorrow (Ghad) Party, headed by politician Ayman Nour, who had competed against Mubarak in the 2005 presidential elections; the Democratic Front (al-Jabha al-Dimuqratiyya), a clique of intellectuals formed in the late Mubarak era; and the Free Egyptians (al-Misriyeen al-Ahrar), a new organization founded by telecom billionaire Naguib Sawiris, who framed his party as a cosmopolitan competitor to the Muslim

Brothers.⁷⁷ The Free Egyptians was by far the weightiest of the new liberal contenders, owing to its founder's wealth and the support of the Coptic Church. Leftists broke away from the state-funded loyal opposition to Mubarak to form the Socialist Popular Alliance (al-Tahaluf al-Shaʿbi al-Ishtiraki), counting several figures of the Revolution Youth Coalition (RYC) as members. Straddling liberals and the Left was the Social Democratic Party (al-Hizb al-Dimuqrati al-Ijtimaʿi), a diverse group of academics, cause lawyers, and intellectuals upholding the indivisibility of the revolution's tripartite slogan "Bread, Freedom, and Social Justice." Also claiming the social justice banner were Nasserists, a distinct brand of leftism in Egypt. Nasserists capitalize on a significant current within public opinion that venerates the former president for his redistributive policies and anticolonial resistance. Hizb al-Karama, the Dignity Party, was the most visible Nasserist collective, headed by former parliamentarian Hamdeen Sabahy, whose 2010 election battle opened chapter 2.

The Islamist political field expanded dramatically, with four distinct subcurrents ranging from those with extensive experience in public politics to newcomers who had long spurned political participation on principle, albeit for different reasons. The Muslim Brothers, Egypt's oldest Islamist electoral movement (est. 1928), founded the Freedom and Justice Party (FJP) under the chairmanship of Mohamed Morsi, bringing to an end the Egyptian state's foundational prohibition on its largest opposition movement since the monarchy's ban on the MB in 1948.⁷⁸ The FJP enjoyed the advantage of the MB's extensive nationwide grassroots network and experience in contesting elections since 1984. The neo-Islamist Center Party (Wasat) was a breakaway from the Muslim Brothers, modeling itself on Turkey's ruling Justice and Development Party (AKP) and proudly advertising two Copts and three women among its leadership. The referendum controversy had revealed the Salafis as an assertive new force, though they had sat out the uprising as an extension of their pietist, nonconfrontational stance. After Mubarak's fall, they rushed into the political arena to proselytize and combat what they perceived as the dual threats of Sufi and Shiʿa heterodoxy on the one hand and secular domination on the other. Three new Salafi parties came into being; the largest, al-Nur (the Light), was compelled by law to nominate women on its party lists and open its membership to Copts. Salafis justified these violations of their conception of shariʿa as the lesser evil to leaving the field open to secular parties and the MB, with whom they had a history of animosity.⁷⁹ Finally, the Gama'a al-Islamiyya established the Building and Development Party (Hizb al-Bina' wa-l Tanmiya), culminating its evolution from commitment to overthrowing the government and establishing an Islamic state to deradicalization and ideological revision after its leaders' imprisonment in the 1990s.

The crowded partisan arena should not obscure important asymmetries. While the Muslim Brothers and Wafd predated the republican authoritarian regime and enjoyed national and international name recognition, the 2011 parties were largely Cairo-centric cliques of notables with no experience in party-building or electioneering. Yet the different resources that the new and old parties brought into politics partly offset their highly unequal vintage. If the FJP was the only party that boasted a nationwide organizational presence developed over decades of MB mobilization, the new parties commanded ideational and financial resources that would prove significant. Liberal and Salafi parties purveyed compelling ideas about Egypt's future to emergent constituencies; liberals preached a secular doctrine of equality of citizenship and economic growth, and Salafis upheld a return to the pure tenets of Islam, undistorted by decades of corrupt tradition and neglect of the poor. Leftists and Nasserists positioned themselves as bearers of the revolution's demand for social justice. Financial resources and media access were also hedges against the "liability of newness."⁸⁰ Billionaire Naguib Sawiris put his considerable wealth at the disposal of his party, including his popular satellite television channel; the Salafi parties had their own licensed channels and streams of funding from like-minded groups in Gulf states.⁸¹ And the small parties of prominent personalities enjoyed copious, positive media coverage in the independent and opposition press. The parties' electoral agreements pooled these different resources of ideas, money, and media into alliances that were governed less by ideological affinity and more by the imperative of attaining the 0.5 percent electoral threshold required for parliamentary representation.⁸²

There is contemporaneous evidence of high public engagement with emergent partisan politics. A Pew poll capturing attitudes in March and April found highly favorable views toward all political actors, including the military, the April 6th youth movement, several prominent politicians, and the Muslim Brothers. Another poll showed a marked enthusiasm for new parties; 68 percent of respondents said they would support a new party compared to 14 percent who would support a pre-2011 party and 18 percent who did not know.[83] At a public debate in April, queues of young people extended for blocks outside the venue, chattering with anticipation as they waited to witness Islamist versus liberal visions of Egypt's future between two loquacious young politicians with devoted followings: al-Wasat's Essam Sultan and political scientist Amr Hamzawy. Among the piles of political books and tracts churned out during this juncture, one complained, "In Egypt today, there are 80 million political parties, every Egyptian is a walking political party."[84]

Concurrent with party politics, other members of the political class were building public opinion for revising the roadmap spelled out in the March 30 interim constitution. At the largest political conference since Mubarak's removal, hundreds of non-Islamist nationalist, leftist, and liberal politicians and intellectuals, including two representatives from the Sharaf cabinet, gathered at the "First Egypt Conference" in May to constrain parliament's authority to select the hundred constitution-drafters.[85] Fearful that an Islamist majority would control writing the new constitution, conference participants developed the idea of "essential principles" that ought to be part of any new constitution and to which future legislators would have to declare fealty. The most prominent advocate and author of the principles, Tahany El Gebaly, Egypt's only female judge, framed the argument as protecting the "civil state" against Islamists' putative intention to found a religious state. Her proposal envisioned a partnership between the Supreme Constitutional Court (on which she was a sitting justice) and the armed forces to "face any legislative violation that threatens the civil character, democratic system, national or geographic unity of the state, or the basic rights and freedoms of the citizens."[86] Gebaly later acknowledged that she began working directly with the generals at this point to enshrine military guardianship in the constitution.[87]

As with other cases of transitional polities, the significance here is that military tutelage over the political process was not the brainchild of generals alone but a joint construct of civilian politicians, jurists, cabinet ministers, and the military. The goal was to constitutionalize guarantees against the unknown outcomes of a competitive electoral process, empowering countermajoritarian state institutions to act as a bulwark against the first freely elected legislature. Guillermo O'Donnell and Philippe Schmitter's observations about Latin American and southern European transitions resonate here:

> The political tradition of the countries examined here has been plagued (and continues to be plagued) by civilian politicians who refuse to accept the uncertainties of the democratic process and recurrently appeal to the armed forces for "solutions," disguising their personal or group interests behind resounding invocations of the national interest; in no case has the military intervened without important and active civilian support.[88]

In Egypt, the banner under which military tutelage began to be articulated was the concept of the "civil state" (*dawla madaniyya*), a term that Gebaly and other conference participants invoked against a religious state (*dawla diniyya*). Islamists retorted on the same conceptual terrain, arguing that they too were fighting for a civil state but against its real antithesis of a military state (*dawla 'askariyya*).[89] The split in the original anti-Mubarak coalition that had surfaced in the referendum was now recomposing into, on the one hand, situational alliances between parties in preparation for the elections, and, on the other, an embryonic civilian constituency for military guardianship as a hedge against the election's unknown results.

## WE ARE NOT SHEEP

Concurrent with renascent partisan politics was a wave of labor protests that had not stopped since February 9. We have seen that nationwide strikes by civil servants and industrial workers were instrumental in buoying the Tahrir opposition and spurring the military council to intervene on February 11. Two generals told an American newspaper that it was these protests that prompted SCAF's intervention: "On February 10 [when SCAF first convened], there were demonstrations that amounted to millions of people all over the country ... it made us worry that the country was going into utter chaos."[90] When continuing civil service strikes paralyzed the banking sector days after Mubarak's departure, a SCAF member read out a communiqué on television on February 14, demanding an end to workplace protests as destabilizing and harmful to national security. This set the tone for a widespread stigmatization of worker protests as *muzaharat fi'awiyya*, or "sectional demonstrations," a framing that was widely adopted by all media outlets and even prorevolution activists and intellectuals.[91] They accepted that protesting workers were selfish and parochial in contrast to the pure and worthy demands of Tahrir. Ironically, instead of seeing workers' collective clout as a motor of the revolutionary situation, an emblem of refusal to be ruled in the old way as Lenin wrote, activists and politicians reproduced the authorities' discourse of narrow "economic" protests undermining serious "political" demands.

A more careful analysis of what workers said and did reveals why the military council was so perturbed by their spreading disobedience. Looking at only the civil service, employer of 5.7 million Egyptians and explicitly targeted in SCAF's communiqué, we see some 301 white-collar strikes or sit-ins during the first three weeks after Mubarak's ouster, more than the total number of protests in both the civil service and the industrial workforce in all of 2004, for example.[92] Virtually all protesters demanded better pay and permanent contracts (many civil service employees work on rolling temporary contracts), but this ostensibly economic demand was enmeshed in a deeper critique of authority relations in the bureaucratic workplace. At both the summit and the street level of the bureaucratic hierarchy, government employees sought to purge the "mini-Mubaraks" who controlled workplaces; 124 out of the 301 protests, 41.2 percent, demanded the resignation of bosses, be they postal supervisors, school principals, university deans and presidents, hospital directors, cabinet ministers, or provincial governors. As did the mass communication students who opened this chapter, clerks in all nooks of the bureaucracy chanted the slogan invented in Tahrir, "We won't leave, he must go!"

A close reading of functionaries' grievances reveals four principal categories of complaint that framed both the universal demand for higher salaries and the frequent call for new management:

1. Managers' arbitrary authority
2. Managers' ill-treatment and abuse
3. Unfair bylaws
4. Large pay differentials between employees in the same unit or equivalent employee positions across units

Over and over again, protesters focused on bosses' abuse of power, both in terms of degrading treatment and verbal abuse but even more in terms of impersonal, pervasive practices of cronyism in hiring; arbitrary dismissal or transfer of refractory employees; and blocking new leadership by extending incumbent managers' tenure past the legal retirement age of sixty. Clerks repeatedly pointed to draconian workplace bylaws that imposed stiff penalties for minor infractions, a tool frequently used by bosses to punish and harass employees.

Anonymous functionaries rarely feature in dramaturgical accounts of revolution that privilege self-professed revolutionaries. But in Egypt the revolutionary situation was made just as much by clerks refusing to be ruled in the old way as politicians and activists demanding a new constitution. Consider one example. In its April 14 governors' reshuffle, SCAF had included a redrawing of administrative boundaries to reabsorb Helwan, an industrial suburb seventeen miles south of the capital that had been made its own province in 2008, back into Greater Cairo. Incensed that residents had not been consulted, three members of the Helwan municipal council (including one woman and one Copt) organized a demonstration of hundreds of people in a Helwan public square, then made their way to cabinet headquarters in downtown Cairo to demand a meeting with Prime Minister Essam Sharaf. The local development minister hurried outside to remonstrate with them. Unappeased, they demanded a referendum on "self-determination" and penned a petition to Sharaf that read in part:

> Save Helwan province! We categorically refuse this decree, which has no meaning and brings only chaos, confusion, and lack of vision. Must we waste our time assembling Helwan's people in Tahrir so that the world can see how far Egypt has reached in arbitrariness and floundering? We are not sheep to be pushed around by the government wherever it wants.[93]

There are surely details to this episode that we do not know, and score-settling and opportunism were certainly ingredients in the civil service protests. The point is not to cast them in a heroic light but to rethink their dismissal as prosaic "economic" demands with no relation to the main political dynamic of challenging unaccountable state authority. From the generals' point of view, the spreading mutinies within the bureaucracy, a structure they could hardly do without for day-to-day administration in a volatile situation, portended the disintegration of the entity that SCAF had called itself into being to preserve. It must have appeared as "the supreme political crisis: a crisis of the state not only ... as an apparatus, but in its primary aspect as guarantor and organizer of social domination."[94] Guillermo O'Donnell has an indelible articulation of how threatening mass mobilization appears to the bureaucratic-authoritarian military worldview:

> Such situations manifest themselves in daily life in "improper" attitudes toward social "superiors," in unusual forms of interpersonal relations among socially "unequal" persons, in the questioning of traditional patterns of authority in such settings as the family, the school, and even the street, and—specifically characterizing this crisis—in the challenging of the bourgeoisie's claim to the right to organize the work process and to appropriate and allocate the capital it generates.[95]

When their February 14 communiqué failed to deter the protests, the military council issued Decree-Law 34/2011, "On the Criminalization of Attacks on Freedom of Work and the Destruction of Facilities," penalizing work stoppages with one year in prison and a hefty fine; but ultimately the decree was enforced only once.[96]

It remains to understand the fourth category of grievances, pay differentials between employees in the same unit or across divisions. Recall that this was the chief demand of the striking property tax collectors in 2008, who wished to attain parity with their better-compensated counterparts in the Cairo Ministry of Finance. Expert on the Egyptian bureaucracy Abdel Khaleq Farouq sheds light on the endemic inequalities running through the state behemoth. There are three main tiers in the civil service: the Cairo-based Administrative Apparatus, which includes all ministries and agencies in the capital; the Municipal Administrations, and the Service Agencies (mostly composed of the public universities). The Cairo-based bureaus employ 24 percent of civil servants but receive 42 percent of public salary spending; the starved Municipal Administrations employ 60 percent of public functionaries but receive 46 percent of the salary budget, and the Service Agencies are the only sector allotted salaries proportional to its size, at 12 percent. Further, within the Cairo-based Administrative Apparatus, an elite stratum are paid the highest salaries, including police officers, university professors, and the judicial, diplomatic, and consular corps. At the very top of the civil service pay structure, above even the elite, are twenty peak units whose employees receive the highest compensation. These include the presidency, the general secretariat of the cabinet, and the General Tax Authority, where the spouse of the no. 2 general on SCAF occupied a top position.[97]

The workers' grievance exposed the enduring fault-line in Egypt's political economy between a capital city receiving the lion's share of resources and provincial cities lacking basic infrastructure where functionaries are paid a pittance. The apparent hyperlocalism of protesters was used by SCAF to tar them as threatening national interests. In reality, civil servants were agitating against the geographic inequalities and networks of familial privilege embedded in the state, not unlike the Tahrir protest movement's struggle to break the monopoly of the Mubarak clan on the summit of the state. They were up against a twenty-first-century version of venality, where ambitious clans built franchises within and across state enclaves, not least the police, judicial, diplomatic, and university teaching corps, cemented by ties of marriage, school cohorts, and a natural respect and affinity for hierarchy. Nor were they circumspect about guarding their privileges. Relatively elite employees of the state broadcasting and telecom sectors seized the opportunity and staged their own legacy "protests," prevailing on managers to increase annual hiring of their offspring from 10 to 20 percent.[98]

In his study of Portugal's revolutionary situation, Robert Fishman identifies two dimensions that bring into focus what was happening in Egypt in 2011. "Crucial to the impact of the revolutionary configuration is the confluence in historical time of the partial inversion of existing hierarchies with the unleashing of new cultural and expressive energies—as well as the rapid accumulation of intense new experiences within a broad sector of the population."[99] We have seen above the expressive energies and intense new experiences of political fear *and* active citizenship. The self-assertions of the bureaucratic plebeians against the patricians was a "partial inversion of hierarchies," a warning that things could not go on as before, that rampant favoritism and abuse by corrupt leaderships was intolerable. They were undeterred by either SCAF's repression or its concessions: first the decree criminalizing strikes and sit-ins, then an increased minimum monthly wage of £E700 ($117). But they stopped short of ejecting their bosses and taking their places.

## MILITARY LIARS

The military council entered the fourth quarter of the year in a different position than when it first appeared on the scene in February. The stresses of direct rule over a relentlessly demand-making society had begun to manifest. Public mudslinging between individual generals and the April 6th youth movement, and the violent break-up of the Tahrir sit-in on August 1 revealed a more sinister face to SCAF than the image of benevolent stewards they sought to project. Activists' campaigns to expose ancien régime corruption began to uncover the personal wealth of SCAF members, so the generals went on the offensive, summoning critics for questioning in the name of upholding "respect for the [military] institution." Quietly, away from indignant pronunciamientos, they rewrote the law to block civilian prosecutors from investigating the finances of serving and retired military personnel.[100] At the same time as military law trespassed on civilian spheres, putting 11,879 civilians on trial before military tribunals, the military was carefully insulating itself within its own system of laws and courts. The disillusionment with SCAF is captured by Brazilian political cartoonist Carlos Latuff, one of the most sensitive visual chroniclers of the revolution. In an August 2011 cartoon, the generals are depicted abusing

FIGURE 6. "Don't be afraid, I'm your friend! Nyahahahaha." Carlos Latuff cartoon, August 2011.

vulnerable Egyptians with trials of civilians by military tribunals, intimidation of martyrs' families, and sexualized violence against female protesters (so-called "virginity tests").[101]

As summer segued into autumn, the decree-law criminalizing strikes had no effect on the diffusion of workplace protests demanding management shake-ups. In their first strike since 1951, teachers forced a shutdown of 85 percent of schools; bus drivers shut down Greater Cairo's twenty-four depots; postal workers shuttered half the country's post offices; air traffic controllers grounded four-fifths of flights; and thousands of low-ranking policemen organized a sit-in at the Interior Ministry, demanding a purge of ancien régime police commanders.[102]

The challenges of governance compelled the SCAF generals to angle for more time to fashion their role in the new political order than the original six-month timeframe they had codified in the March 30 interim constitution. They found ready allies in the civilian elites who dreaded an Islamist victory in elections. Generals began to coordinate with Justice Tahany El Gabaly and other jurists, adopting the idea of essential principles for the constitution that the drafters would not be able to alter.[103] Then, with US backing, they announced a change to the transition timetable, delaying presidential elections until the seating of parliament and ratification of a new constitution, which meant SCAF would hold executive power into 2013.[104] As activists and the political class were absorbing this turnabout from SCAF's repeated declarations that it did not seek power, the first mass killing of civilians by military personnel occurred in full view of television cameras. The cascade towards SCAF's governance crisis had begun.

On October 9, a large protest procession of Copts and Muslims in Cairo, demonstrating against the burning of a church in Aswan, was met with deadly force by the military. As the procession reached its destination at the Maspero television building, site of Coptic protests throughout the year, two armored military vehicles careened onto sidewalks, crushing and killing at least ten protesters and bystanders. Another fourteen died of bullet wounds, blows to the head, and knife slashes.[105] Appearing ten days later on a talk show to address outraged public opinion, two tense SCAF members cut very different figures from the genial informality of their public messaging eight months earlier. They categorically denied any responsibility for the killings and framed the attacks as a brazen assault on both Copts and the military by mysterious third parties.

Asked by the host what had happened in the span of eight months to "tarnish the pristine image of the armed forces," General Mohamed al-Assar answered:

> I'll tell you. The army's principles have not and will not change, what has changed is that there are enemies of this nation, and enemies of the revolution for whom it is important to obstruct the transition to democracy. We have to accept that the soldiers guarding the Maspero building were assaulted and the Copts in the demonstration were assaulted. We have to accept that the armed forces did *not* assault protesters but were themselves assaulted. All forces in Egypt should find out who did this.[106]

What became known as the Maspero massacre made visible what had been hidden from view since the initial Eighteen Days: the military's use of force against unarmed demonstrators. It introduced the generals' consistent rhetorical strategy from then on, shunting responsibility for mass killing onto a spectral "third party" (*al-taraf al-talet*) to maintain the founding myth that the armed forces, unlike the police, were a disciplined, professional state institution that "belonged to the people."

With the general election set for November 28, SCAF hastened to unveil the plan it had worked out with the jurists to curb parliament's role in constitution-writing. On November 1, deputy prime minister Ali al-Silmi presented a "Declaration of the Fundamental Principles for the New Egyptian State," a twenty-two-article document of mostly uncontroversial basic rights. What drew immediate condemnation from across the political spectrum were articles 9 and 10, which granted SCAF exclusive control over the armed forces' budget and bills as well as a decisive role in foreign policymaking. The document further trespassed on parliament's authority to elect the hundred constitution-drafters, establishing detailed criteria for the makeup of the Constituent Assembly (CA) and granting SCAF veto power over its deliberations and the authority to form a new CA should parliament's CA not complete its work.[107]

Though it was presented by a civilian cabinet minister with ties to the Wafd party, the Silmi document was instantly recognized as a SCAF creation enshrining military supremacy over constitution-making and the incipient democratic order. A statement from the Muslim Brothers lambasted articles 9 and 10 as "wresting sovereignty from the people and consecrating dictatorship." Labor lawyer Mahienour al-Masry of the Revolutionary Socialists called them "a back door for SCAF to impose its will on the people."[108] The document did what no other issue was able to achieve since February, recomposing the original anti-Mubarak coalition for a November 18 milyuniyya branded Single Demand Friday. It was the first cause to bring together all Islamists and most non-Islamists in a joint pressure campaign to get SCAF to scrap the offending articles. The April 6th youth movement, several presidential contenders and their partisans, the Muslim Brothers, the Salafis, and the Ghad party announced their participation, while the RYC, the Coptic Maspero Youth Union, the Wafd, and the Socialist Popular Alliance refrained, leery of the milyuniyya's dominance by Islamists.

The mass protest was one of the largest since the Eighteen Days, escalating from opposition to the Silmi document to an explicit demand for SCAF to hand over power no later than April 2012. But the day is remembered most for what happened after the crowds went home. A small group of two hundred injured during the Eighteen Days settled back into a Tahrir sit-in they had organized to protest the government's neglect of their health care entitlements. The following morning, November 19, riot forces and military policemen violently disbanded the tent encampment and made arrests. As the news circulated, thousands of protesters descended on the square in solidarity, beginning six continuous days of clashes between protesters and police in downtown Cairo and fifteen provinces; for the first time since January, several police stations were attacked. In Cairo, Mohamed Mahmoud Street southeast of Tahrir Square became the epicenter of state violence. Human rights reports and field doctors documented use of force "on a scale not seen since the '25 January Revolution,'" including live ammunition, shotgun pellets, and the extraordinary use of tear gas that led to sixty-one deaths and 3,256 injured.[109] Video footage captured soldiers dumping the corpses of protesters on trash piles on the fringes of Tahrir and a police sniper methodically targeting the eyes of demonstrators.

The Battle of Mohamed Mahmoud became one of the most iconic episodes of the revolutionary situation, freighted with meanings far beyond its barebones empirical description as a lethal six-day encounter between protesters and security forces. For its civilian combatants, not all of whom considered themselves protesters against military rule, "it is remembered as something legendary," writes Lucie Ryzova, "euphoric, intoxicating, at once doomed and victorious."[110] In the collective memory of non-Islamist revolutionaries, it is a metonym for betrayal by the Muslim Brothers. Critics of the MB tied the street battle to its prior milyuniyya through the trope of the MB's reflexive opportunism, accusing the MB of abandoning the square to participate in elections and selling out revolutionaries at a moment of confrontation with the army. Though other political parties also left the square to focus on the final stretch of their campaigns, the charge of betrayal was pinned only on the MB, an Egyptian version of the hallowed revolutionary script casting calculating politicians against uncompromising purists.[111] On the first anniversary of the battle in November 2012, a large banner was strung across the street, declaring "Muslim Brothers Not Allowed."

The scale of the violence compelled SCAF chairman Mohamed Tantawi to address the nation on television, repeating that hidden hands were driving a wedge between army and people but conceding the milyuniyya's demand for a transfer of power in 2012. He pledged that presidential elections would be moved up to June 2012 but stopped short of retracting the two articles in the Silmi document.[112] The Essam Sharaf cabinet resigned and Tantawi appointed a new government headed by Mubarak apparatchik Kamal al-Ganzouri as prime minister, the third government in 2011 installed amid crisis. Unlike SCAF's appointment of Sharaf at the behest of the RYC, Ganzouri's resurrection signaled the military council's uncompromising stance. Opposing Ganzouri became the focal point for a large milyuniyya on November 25 demanding an immediate transfer of power to a civilian presidential council. On the same day, the milyuniyya received an unexpected boost when the Obama administration issued its first public criticism of the generals. Throughout the year, the United States had backed SCAF's shifting timetable for holding power until 2013. Now the White House declared "we believe that the full transfer of power to a civilian government must take place in a just and inclusive manner that responds to the legitimate aspirations of the Egyptian people, as soon as possible."[113] As Mubarak had been in February, SCAF was caught between the converging pressures of Tahrir and Egypt's chief foreign patron.

Despite acute fears that renewed violence would accompany the general elections, voters headed to the polls on November 28 as scheduled, reaching a 62 percent turnout by the end of balloting six weeks later.[114] As initial results showed the FJP and Salafi parties securing two-thirds of the vote and non-Islamists one-third, a SCAF general convened an invitation-only meeting with eight American journalists to communicate a message to Washington: SCAF would not cede power to an incoming parliament dominated by Islamists.[115] Restating the provisions in the Silmi document, General Mokhtar al-Molla insisted that the military would retain control of constitution-making and full authority over the Ganzouri government. He cast doubt on the legitimacy of the yet-to-be-seated legislature; "In such unstable conditions, the Parliament is not representing all the Egyptians."[116] Given the armed forces' foundational claim to "belong to the people" and their newfangled identity as "protectors" of the revolution, these remarks telegraphed to audiences within and outside Egypt the military council's hostile posture toward the revolution's first remade state institution. Even before it was seated, parliament represented a rival conception of popular sovereignty that challenged the generals' primacy and their claim to embody the will of a mystical unitary "people." Parliament embodied popular sovereignty defined as the will of concrete, diverse voters. The making of the collision between parliament and the military that would come to pass in 2012 began at this point, in the military's flouting of its own rules in the interim constitution that granted parliament authority over constitution making.[117]

The Mohamed Mahmoud clashes had ceased, but a group of protesters and families of those killed during the battle established a sit-in outside the cabinet headquarters, arranging mock coffins draped in Egyptian flags along the length of the street, blocking the new ministers from accessing their offices. They rallied against SCAF's appointment of a Mubarak stalwart as prime minister and demanded restitution for the Mohamed Mahmoud martyrs. On December 16, security forces' detention of a protester escalated into five days of clashes, with the government again using maximum force to disband the sit-in. Field hospitals were burned, doctors attacked, and the Institute of Egypt, housing tens of thousands of inestimable manuscripts, burned and its roof caved in. Twenty-six civilians lost their lives and 926 were injured.[118] Video footage of three soldiers dragging an unconscious female protester and stomping on her exposed midriff circulated around the world so that she became known as the "blue bra girl." Thousands of women turned out for a mass march in downtown Cairo, many for the first time, to express outrage at SCAF's enabling of violence against women; the US Secretary of State said the violence "disgraces the state and its uniform."[119] Concerned that the public was seeing only the SCAF's denials of state violence and its blaming of protesters and a "third party," a collective of activists and filmmakers sought to bring the footage of state abuses to people outside of Tahrir. On street corners and in clearings in dense residential neighborhoods, some just blocks away from Tahrir, they set up large projectors for public screenings of the military's violence at Maspero, Mohamed Mahmoud, and the cabinet sit-in, calling their campaign 'Askar Kadhebun (Military liars).[120]

We do not know the impact of this effort, but we do have a glimpse into public sentiments about the military at this juncture. A Gallup poll found that 63 percent of respondents felt that the military remaining in politics after the presidential elections was bad, but a sizable 27 percent saw it as a good thing, indicating some public support for the idea of the military as a guardian. A vast majority, 87 percent, said it would be a bad thing for the presidential election to be delayed.[121] If the questions had more explicitly addressed the military's responsibility for violence, perhaps the approval ratings would have looked different. But the results speak to the same imbalance that worried the activists: the gap between the general public's positive stance toward the military, and the smaller, politically engaged, activist public's view of the generals as Mubarak henchmen.

\* \* \*

Contesting rank and hierarchies, doffing and donning new political commitments, battling police impunity, fighting over the constitution, defending threatened identities, wrestling with grand dilemmas of democracy and revolution, seeking recognition for the living and the dead—this was the stuff of Year 1 of Egypt's revolutionary situation. A staggering diversity of events and agendas characterized these dense months, geographic particularities, varying conditions of work, vivid pasts, rival estimates of the future, along with a searing realization of the momentous promises and perils of the post-Mubarak order. "The revolution that happened in February, however beautiful it was, left us with a coup," said a fifty-two-year-old chemist who joined the Mohamed Mahmoud protests. "Tantawi was never persuaded there was a revolution. All he wants to do is renovate the old system."[122]

SCAF generals began the year confident in their ability to conduct a transition in which they would be the pacesetters and content-makers. They did not anticipate that by year's end, despite the rapid divisions and permutations of civilian political forces, they would face a rebellion rivaling that which brought down their former commander. What they had reasonably estimated was that with strong international backing, and a generous fund of public goodwill, they would manage a transition to a contained democracy and be lauded as enlightened modernizers. What they faced was a deepened revolutionary insurrection of the sort that they had intervened to forestall. Banking on the surge of public support and admiration that reigned for a few fugitive weeks in February and March, they did not foresee that "in power," as Alain Rouquié observed of Latin American militaries, "the military suffer a dangerous 'desacralization.'"[123] Still, they emerged from the experience remarkably free of internal splits and clearer about their interests, if no closer to realizing them. There was no royal road to a secure status in the midst of a turbulent infant democracy, but controlling the constitution emerged as the generals' best path to carving out institutional certainty, putting them on a collision course with the new parliament.

For all the chaotic alignments and realignments of civilian political groups and activist collectives, the shifts from schism to solidarity and back did have a logic. The ever-present past structured the rhythms of unity and fission. Signs of the ancien régime's resurgence motivated the factions to band together against the common threat, as at year's end, despite months of acrimony. But the Mubarak regime's practice of stoking mutual fears and animosities cast a long shadow over revolutionary politics; Islamists lived in fear of a secular-military alliance that would crush them and send them back to prisons, and secularists were convinced that they were victims of an Islamist-military deal to share power and obliterate everyone else. These political fears were not delusions; in a revolutionary situation, the ancien régime is battered but not dead. In Egypt, the coercive arms of the state not only survived but continued to attack civilians with impunity, giving rise to a strain of revolutionary antipolitics that valorized battling the state on the streets and rubbished electoral politics as contemptible treachery. The elections-versus-protests division rehearses the enduring political schism between negotiating politicians and unyielding activists.

Year 1 of the revolutionary situation defined the main axes of conflict and division, but it did not produce any certainty about how Egypt would be governed. Despite bitterly contesting SCAF's sovereignty claim as "defenders of the revolution," the civilian factions did not coalesce into a robust all-party front against the military council, much less institutionalize themselves in a countercouncil. Some openly allied with SCAF, and others found expression in different kinds of politics in different arenas—in streets, on television talk shows, and in electioneering. Year 2 of the revolutionary situation would see the opening of a new arena of political contestation: the first freely elected legislature under universal suffrage.

*Chapter 4*

# LET'S WRITE OUR CONSTITUTION
تعالوا نكتب دستورنا

> Dual power in revolution is a situation in which alternative paths for constructing consensus-forming and constitution-creating processes are always present.
> —Arthur Stinchcombe, "Lustration as a Problem of the Social Basis of Constitutionalism"

JANUARY 23, 2012, WAS NOT AN ORDINARY MONDAY MORNING. CAFÉ owners arranged rows of chairs in front of television sets that were all occupied before 11 a.m., many by young men watching such proceedings for the first time. Civil servants tuned their radios to listen while conducting the public's business. Pedestrians stopped to gawk at the live coverage on televisions mounted in stores and alleyways. At five muster points near Tahrir Square, marchers assembled, adjusting their placards and banners before embarking on their processions. "No, this isn't the World Cup final or a match between Ahli and Zamalek," quipped social media users. "Breaking: The elected Egyptian People's Assembly!"[1]

Minutes before 11 a.m., members of the first freely elected parliament under universal suffrage filed in to take their seats. On their way into the building, many waded through crowds of supporters so thick that they were carried on well-wishers' shoulders, and some were serenaded and given flowers. In the chamber, the 498 members appeared as a sea of men in dark-colored suits. Four women deputies of the Muslim Brothers' Freedom and Justice Party (FJP) sat bunched together, smiling and holding the single red roses handed to them by supporters. Five more women were sprinkled among the rows of men, representing the Wafd and the Social Democratic Parties, for a total of just under 2 percent female MPs. Scores of secular MPs draped gleaming yellow sashes across their blazers emblazoned with the slogan "No to Military Trials!" in solidarity with the activist campaign of the same name. Astonishingly, Salafi MPs with no prior electoral experience occupied 24 percent of seats; many of them sported the long beards they believed emulated the Prophet Muhammad and his companions. There was less surprise that the FJP held 45 percent of the seats, given their accumulated experience with parliamentary elections since 1984. Only three members of the Revolution Youth Coalition (RYC) were now members of parliament, and a lone trade unionist: Kamal Abu Eita, leader of the property tax collectors who had founded the first independent union in 2009.

A new kind of solemn convocation began. Instead of the standing ovation and applause for the head of state accorded to Hosni Mubarak by every new parliament for twenty-nine years, deputies stood for a moment of silence to honor the fallen civilians of the revolution. Instead of unbroken control of the speakership by a member of the president's party, a post held by the same NDP politician for twenty years, the new deputies held a contested election between two Islamist deputies. Saad al-Katatni, secretary-general of the FJP, won with 399 votes to his rival's 87, the Wasat Party's voluble attorney Essam Sultan. A noisy rumble over the oath-taking broke out, reflecting the new body's symbiosis between established parliamentary ritual and extraparliamentary passions. Salafi lawmaker Mamdouh Ismail started it, appending to the oath of fealty to the republic and constitution the phrase "as long as it does not violate God's law." Outraged non-Islamists retorted with their own amendments, swearing loyalty to the revolution and its martyrs. An exasperated master of ceremonies, the senior-most parliamentarian Mahmoud al-Saqqa of al-Wafd, repeatedly scolded the new deputies for flouting the rules.[2]

Beyond the chamber, five separate processions of several hundred each were heading toward Parliament to urgently petition the new deputies. Carrying photos of their slain children, families of those killed during 2011 demanded accountability from security forces; "Remember, without their life you wouldn't have made it here," read one placard. Campaigners from "No to Military Trials!" vowed to pressure parliament to put an end to trials of civilians by military courts. In linked arms, several hundred actors and celebrities of the culture industry set off from the Cairo Opera House to warn Islamist legislators that they would fight any attempts to interfere with free expression. And reprising one of the four demands of the January 25, 2011, protest action, trade unionists and their cause lawyers appealed to deputies to decree a living wage and repeal SCAF's ban on strikes and sit-ins. The workers' march merged with a fifth procession of those injured in the chronic clashes with police, demanding that legislators compel government to make good on its promises of restitution. As she watched parliament's twelve-hour inaugural plenary on television, journalist Mona Anis reflected, "Parliaments that are elected following great political and social upheavals are problematic, and in the Egyptian case they have been ill-fated."[3]

Two days later on January 25, 2012, enormous crowds filled the streets of Cairo, Alexandria, Suez, and other provincial capitals to mark the one-year anniversary of the revolution, retracing the same routes that protest processions had tread during the Eighteen Days. Protesters chanted ""ʿAysh, Huriyya, ʿAdala Igtimaʿiyya!" (Bread, freedom, social justice!), adding a biting new addendum: "Yasqut Yasqut Hukm al-ʿAskar!" (Down, down with military rule!). Outrage at the military's violence against women in December motivated the chant: "Come down from your houses! SCAF has stripped your daughters!" The anger crystallized into a demand for the military's immediate removal from power; "politics is not for the army" read the banner of Cairo University students' procession to Tahrir. Suez's Arbaʿin Square mirrored the mosaic of jostling political identities constituting revolutionary politics: families of the province's two dozen fallen civilians demanding justice; FJP partisans with banners proclaiming, "Freedom Yes, Chaos No"; and jobless residents denouncing rampant cronyism in the local petroleum industry. In Alexandria, the navy and military police organized celebrations with a brass band, free t-shirts, and flags emblazoned with "Glory to the nation, glory to the martyrs." Recovered from the shock of 2011, the state was determined to reassert its presence, drowning out remembrance of the popular revolt with an official commemoration of a bond between state and people. In a televised address, SCAF chief Mohamed Hussein Tantawi defended the military against popular suspicions, reminding the populace that "the nation and the armed forces have one aim: for Egypt to become a democratic state." As if in retort, a sign in Tahrir read: "You ever seen a wolf defend a lamb?"[4]

## THE RESPECTABLE MAJORITY IN THE FIRST PARLIAMENT AFTER THE REVOLUTION

It is difficult to overstate the conflicting demands targeting Egypt's first democratically elected legislature. "This domed white building is now a magnet for national expectations," observed journalist Jack Shenker. "Many wonder whether it will sag under the weight of so much anticipation."[5] At 62 percent participation, elections for the legislature saw the highest turnout of any of the revolution's polls, indicating voters' interest if not their varied motivations.[6] The five processions toward parliament voiced a litany of demands festering since Year 1 of the revolutionary situation. Anti-SCAF activists, outraged by the military's violence against protesters in late 2011, articulated a new demand for an immediate transfer of executive power to the speaker of parliament (fig. 7), one that the FJP quickly rebuffed as violating the terms of the interim constitution. An international human rights organization enumerated a to-do list for parliament, urging that it begin undoing a raft of authoritarian laws to push forward the democratic transition.[7] Even those who felt alienated from the legislature could not ignore it. In a pointed query sent to lawmakers the day before they took their seats, the Maspero Youth Union wrote, "To the respectable majority in the first parliament after the revolution, we approach you with all respect, although you never once respected us." It went on to ask whether the Islamist majority would treat Egypt's Copts as equal citizens, especially Coptic women who did not cover their hair or faces.[8]

This chapter fleshes out how the arrangements for transferring power to civilians in the first six months of 2012 constituted the maximum moment of conflicts in Egypt's revolutionary situation. At first glance, the seating of parliament appears as a moment of demobilization and deflection, redirecting mounting social pressures and criticisms to a new national target. This is the understanding of elections articulated by Guillermo O'Donnell and Philippe Schmitter: "One of the primary motives of transitional authorities in convoking elections for significant governmental positions may well be to get that

FIGURE 7. Activist sticker demanding transfer of power to parliament, February 2012.

multitude of disparate and remonstrative groups 'off their back.'"[9] By contrast, this book's core concept of a revolutionary situation puts elections and the parliament they produced in a very different light, not as a step on the path to pacification but as a new arena for multiple conflicts over state powers. The seating of the legislature began a new phase of multiple sovereignty. Legislative power was now held by a parliament under popular control for the first time since Egypt's last free election in 1950; executive power remained with SCAF; and Tahrir retained protean crowds' power to certify and delegitimate national authorities and their policies. Sovereignty claims collided on three intersecting issues: a row over control of the government between SCAF and parliament; fights over setting the rules for the competitive elections to the post-Mubarak presidency; and the ongoing maneuvers over the constituent process. Parliament stood at the center of all three battles, claiming authority to form a new government; using legislative power to set presidential election rules; and jealously insisting on its supreme authority to choose the hundred constitution-drafters, against the military's unflagging insistence on a veto role in constitution-making.

Sidney Tarrow's sketch of a revolutionary situation illuminates why a legislature seated as a result of a founding election has politicizing rather than demobilizing effects:

> One group's actual seizure of some portion of state power, furthermore, immediately alters the prospects for laggard actors, who must immediately choose among alliance, assault, self-defense, flight, and demobilization. Consequently, rivalries, coalition making, demand making, and defensive action all spiral rapidly upward.[10]

What this helps us see is that well before parliament made a single decision, its very existence as a democratically constituted state institution dominated by historically excluded political forces sounded alarm bells for powerful vested interests, while spurring new interest groups to ratchet up their demand-making. Already on its opening day, we see the range of responses sketched by Tarrow. Cultural celebrities marched on parliament in self-defense against potential freedom-restricting legislation. Martyrs' families and victims of police abuse demanded restitution. Coptic activists put Islamist legislators on notice that their majority status did not license them to run roughshod over minority rights. Labor lawyers and trade unionists sought legislation codifying the long-standing demands for a minimum wage as well as the repeal of SCAF's March 2011 decree criminalizing strikes and sit-ins.

For its part, the military council launched not a full assault on parliament but some opening salvos. In December, as discussed in chapter 3, a SCAF general had announced that parliament was not representative and would not exercise unhindered authority to choose the hundred constitution-writers. Four days before parliament's convocation, SCAF issued two major pieces of legislation by decree, asserting its lawmaking power even as parliament was constituted, drawing pointed criticism from legislators and presidential contenders from across the ideological spectrum.[11] From SCAF's perspective, with its bruising experience of direct rule in 2011, the prospect that the new parliament would join forces with an elected president to subject the armed forces to civilian control must have seemed intolerably real, compelling the generals to devise alternative means of influencing constitution-writing. That they had the wherewithal and willingness to craft these alternative paths is an instantiation of Arthur Stinchcombe's obiter dictum: one way of understanding dual power in revolution is that no rules or agreements, even constitution-making rules, are irreversible.

## AL-BARLAMAN WA-L MIDAN

It is worth looking more closely at the composition of the parliament seated by the first free elections in decades, unmarred by police officials and poll workers using force and fraud to contrive a supermajority for the president's party.[12] Clément Steuer notes that "the most spectacular innovation of these elections was the unprecedented diversity of the political offer."[13] Though twenty-three political parties were represented in the legislature, five were little-known micro-outfits occupying one seat each, so effectively parliament consisted of eighteen parties from across the ideological spectrum, compared to the maximum of seven parties in the Mubarak-era parliaments. Eighty-one percent of deputies were first-time MPs, a 20 percent increase over previous parliaments, and 92.5 percent were under the age of sixty, higher than the 80 percent high recorded for the 2005 parliament. The only visible continuity with pre-2011 parliaments was the deputies' occupational backgrounds; civil servants, professionals, businessmen, and farmers were the leading employment categories.[14] Yet these indices of new blood and partisan variety were not what shaped public perceptions. Far more visible were the paltry numbers of female, Coptic, and youth deputies; at nine, six, and three, respectively, they just barely filled two rows in the chamber, dashing hopes that the revolution would catapult them into its first institutional creation. The salient fact was that the revolution-era legislature had a 72 percent supermajority of Islamists.

This was at once predictable and surprising. The FJP's position as the plurality party was widely expected, given its parent organization's decades of voter outreach and reputation as an uncorrupted opposition.[15] The "double surprise," as Ellis Goldberg remarked at the time, was the legitimation of a new political actor, the Salafis, and the unmaking of a feared specter, the NDP.[16] The Salafi groups, which had burst onto the political scene after Mubarak's fall but had no prior electoral experience, now occupied the second largest share of seats, 25 percent. The fulul, remnants of Mubarak's NDP that nearly all the revolution's

TABLE 3. Results of the Parliamentary Elections, November 28, 2011–January 10, 2012.

| Party/Alliance | PR Votes (m.)* | % Vote | Seats | % Seats |
|---|---|---|---|---|
| FJP-led Democratic Alliance | 10.1 | 37 | 235 | 47 |
| FJP | | | 222 | 45 |
| Karama | | | 6 | 1.2 |
| Civilization | | | 2 | 0.4 |
| Ghad Thawra | | | 2 | 0.4 |
| 'Amal | | | 1 | |
| Arab Egypt | | | 1 | |
| Independent | | | 1 | |
| Nour Alliance | 7.5 | 28 | 123 | 25 |
| Nur | | | 107 | 22 |
| Construction and Development | | | 13 | 2.6 |
| Asala | | | 3 | 0.6 |
| New Wafd | 2.5 | 9 | 38 | 7.6 |
| Egyptian Bloc | 2.4 | 8.9 | 34 | 6.8 |
| Social Democratic Party | | | 18 | 3.6 |
| Free Egyptians | | | 13 | 2.6 |
| Tagammu' | | | 3 | 0.6 |
| NDP Offshoots | 1.3 | 4.8 | 18 | 3.6 |
| Wasat | 0.99 | 3.3 | 10 | 2 |
| Reform and Development | 0.6 | 2.2 | 9 | 1.8 |
| Revolution Continues | 0.75 | 2.8 | 7 | 1.4 |
| 'Adl | 0.18 | 0.7 | 1 | |
| Independents | | | 23 | 5.4 |
| Total | 498 elected members + 10 appointed | | | |

*The Electoral Commission announced only the Proportional Representation (PR) votes per party, in millions. For the one-third of seats filled under the individual candidacy system, only the name of the winner was announced.
Valid ballots: 27,065,135 million.
Sources: *Al-Ahram*, January 22, 2012; Amr Hashem Rabi', ed., *Intikhabat Majlis al-Sha'b 2011/2012* (2012).

factions had feared would reassert themselves through elections, gained eighteen seats, a mere 3.6 percent. The elections that were widely expected to rehabilitate the autocrat's political machine had instead issued its death certificate, as voters summarily rejected ancien régime associates. The distribution of seats among non-Islamist forces reflected a similar mix of the familiar and the insurgent. Egypt's oldest mass party, the Wafd of 1919 vintage rechristened as the New Wafd, occupied the third-largest share of seats, 7.6 percent, while the Egyptian Bloc alliance of two leading 2011 parties, the Social Democratic Party and the Free Egyptians, had the fourth-largest share with 6.8 percent, challenging the venerable Wafd for leadership of the secular-nationalist caucus against the hegemony of the Islamists.

The lopsided 72–28 composition of parliament into Islamists and non-Islamists should not conceal an important distinction: the Islamists did not run for parliament on one slate and would not act as a united bloc in parliamentary politics. The Islamist supermajority was composed of four Islamist brands: the Muslim Brothers' FJP, the three Salafi parties, the neo-Islamist Wasat Party, and the former militants of the Construction and Development Party. Only the Construction and Development and Salafi parties ran on a unified slate and maintained this coherence under the rotunda. Inter-Islamist rivalry began on Day 1 with the Wasat-FJP competition over the speakership, and the Salafis saw themselves as insurgents against *both* elitist secular parties and the paternalistic condescension of FJP deputies. The Salafis' swaggering, maximalist posture on key issues, prefigured by the ruffles they raised over the oath-taking, sowed fear in the secular minority and frustration for the FJP, undermining the prospects of an all-party parliamentary front against SCAF's machinations in the looming presidential election and constituent process. That in turn worked against a grand civilian coalescence of parliamentary and extraparliamentary groups to limit SCAF's room for maneuver. Instead, a rift widened between *al-Midan* and *al-Barlaman*, square and parliament, two warring conceptions of the rightful embodiment of popular sovereignty. Salafi and not a few FJP deputies saw the new parliament as the only legitimate carrier of democratic aspirations and came to fear mass demonstrations as dangerous and uncontrollable. The Maspero Youth Union and other activists, and those segments of the public put off by the Islamist preponderance in the legislature, felt no stake in parliament and came to see it as a counterrevolutionary bulwark against the more genuine, open-air paraparliament that Tahrir Square had become since the first milyuniyya of February 4, 2011.

## WE WILL CONTINUE ESCALATING

The irony is that the fledgling parliament began its tenure with two crises that built up deputies' esprit de corps across partisan divides and found them audaciously asserting the principle of ministerial responsibility, even as the country's constitutional framework remained undefined. An event far from downtown Cairo became parliament's first skirmish with the generals, just one week after legislators swore their oath. In Port Said, a soccer match on February 1 between al-Ahli and home team al-Masri turned violent. At the end of the game, al-Masri fans invaded the pitch, attacking Ahli players and fans with small weapons; the Ahli players fled into their changing rooms while their fans struggled to escape, only to be crushed against locked stadium gates. Harrowing eyewitness accounts described Ahli fans thrown from bleachers, trampled in the stampede, and suspicious behavior by stadium security.[17] The violence led to seventy-four dead Ahli Ultras and a thousand injured. Recognizing the potential fallout so soon after the autumn 2011 mass killings of civilians, SCAF chief Mohamed Tantawi acted quickly, ordering a military helicopter to airlift the Ahli players back to Cairo and greeting them at the airport; dispatching another military plane to transport fifty-one bodies to the central Cairo morgue; and declaring three days of national mourning. Incensed Ahli fans thronged platforms in the Cairo rail station that night, awaiting the train from Port Said carrying the injured. As it creaked into the station at 3:30 a.m., they chanted "The people want the execution of the Field Marshal!" The widespread conviction was that SCAF had looked the other way as local police and criminal elements attacked Ahli players and fans as revenge for the Ahli Ultras' frontline role in major encounters with riot police in 2011.

In a stormy three-hour emergency session the next day, one deputy after another rose to insist that this was no ordinary stadium brawl but a catastrophic result of police negligence and inaction. Not a few deputies framed the violence as the latest in the 2011 series of security forces' attacks on protesters, reeling off the dates of January 28, February 2 (the Battle of the Camel), the March 9 violent disbanding of the Tahrir sit-in, and the mass killings of Maspero, Mohamed Mahmoud, and the cabinet sit-in. Independent Islamist MP Mustafa al-Naggar proclaimed, "The military council lost its legitimacy today given the blood that has been shed."[18] The prime minister, minister of the interior, and local development minister sat together with hunched shoulders as deputies heaped on them denunciations and demanded their resignation, unappeased by Prime Minister al-Ganzouri's announcement that the Port Said governor and security chief had been relieved of their posts. Parliament resolved to immediately dispatch a fact-finding mission of parliamentarians to Port Said to gather evidence before it was destroyed.[19] The strong implication was that prosecutors investigating cases of mass killings throughout 2011 were suppressing evidence of security forces' culpability. One street over from parliament, Ahli Ultras were marching on the Interior Ministry to avenge their fellow fans. Five days of running street battles between protesters and police led to a further thirteen dead and two hundred wounded, the highest death toll since the violent November–December 2011 clashes that had rapidly soured the public on SCAF's governance.

The seventy-four Ahli victims were folded into the iconography of the revolution's martyrs, their beaming faces painted on the walls of downtown Cairo and the number seventy-four attaining totemic status in Egyptian soccer lore.[20] Egypt's worst soccer disaster was the first test for parliament, gauging how the people's representatives would respond to the touchstone issue of police management of crowds. The incident and its ramifications dominated parliamentary business for days. The fact-finding report confirmed witness accounts of police inaction when Masri supporters stormed the pitch, blamed stadium management for sealing the exits, in defiance of FIFA regulations, and failing to conduct pregame searches.[21] In the plenary discussing the report, MPs not known for hyperbole criticized the sober tone of the report, echoing the ambient perception that the generals enabled the violence to punish the Ahli Ultras. "The question is why the army, which has participated in safeguarding several previous soccer matches, refrained from doing so this time," said the liberal, secular political scientist Wahid Abdel Meguid, elected on the FJP-led Democratic Alliance. "The army bears the greatest political responsibility for the tragic events in Port Said," said lawyer Ziad al-Ulaimy, one of three MPs from the Revolution Youth Coalition. "The events in Port Said serve the interests of SCAF, giving it an excuse to stay in power for a longer period."[22] Deputies' anger aligned with that of major sectors of extraparliamentary opinion—youth activists, presidential hopefuls, nearly all political parties, and the families and friends of the Ahli Ultras. Once again, violence against civilians, this time abetted by police *inaction*, brought together disparate constituencies in a potent coalition of rage.

A second confrontation ensued one month later over the worst crisis in US-Egypt relations in decades. In December 2011, as SCAF faced a domestic outcry against military police attacks on women demonstrators, both President Barack Obama and Secretary of State Hillary Clinton publicly rebuked SCAF for the first time. On December 29, police raided seventeen international NGOs, including the US-based Freedom House, the National Democratic Institute, and the International Republican Institute (IRI), which operated freely in Egypt and had government permission to observe the parliamentary elections. Prosecutors accused forty-three NGO staffers, including Sam Lahood, Egypt director for IRI and son of a US cabinet secretary, of receiving foreign funding to stir up unrest and had barred them from leaving Egypt. In what was described as the worst row in Egypt-US relations since the "strategic partnership," President Obama warned SCAF chief Tantawi in a phone call that American military aid in 2012 would be jeopardized if the prosecution continued. The US chairman of the Joint Chiefs of Staff traveled to Cairo to discuss the matter with SCAF leaders Mohamed Tantawi and Sami Anan.[23] With no face-saving retreat, the government hastily lifted the travel ban on the American citizens among the NGO staff, and a US-government charter plane flew Lahood and coworkers out of the Cairo airport—after their organizations had paid nearly $4 million in bail.

In a boisterous March 11 plenary, legislators were incensed at the "slap in the face" to Egyptian sovereignty by acceding to US pressures, thundered Nasserist MP Amin Iskandar. Leftist MP Mohamed al-Sawi demanded an official apology from SCAF to the Egyptian people for mishandling the NGO debacle. Deputies railed against the Ganzouri cabinet and demanded its resignation and replacement with a new government "free of SCAF influence," building into a groundswell of support for a motion to withdraw confidence from the government. In a show of hands, almost every MP voted in favor of the motion. Coming on the heels of the still-raw anger over the Port Said stadium disaster, SCAF's submission to US pressure mobilized parliamentarians of all persuasions to speak with one voice and claim for themselves the power to remove Ganzouri and his cabinet and install a new cabinet reflecting the balance of forces in parliament. FJP MP Farid Ismail insisted that the vote was "a public declaration that the government isn't accepted by the street. We will continue escalating until the military council responds."[24] SCAF chief Tantawi first ignored the deputies, then offered to discharge two ministers but retain the rest of the cabinet and the prime minister until the election of a president in June; deputies roundly rejected this. Confident now that SCAF would not submit to the deputies, Ganzouri and several ministers pointedly ignored the legislature and stopped attending its sessions, leading to more fire-and-brimstone speeches in the chamber about the government's unacceptable contempt for the democratically elected parliament.[25]

On the face of it, this appears nothing more than the bluster of novice legislators, as one seasoned parliamentary correspondent interpreted the deputies' escalation.[26] The parliamentarians spoke ex cathedra when their authority to control the government was at best ambiguous. Article 33 of the interim constitution allowed that parliament exercised oversight over the executive but said nothing about appointing the government. As Kristen Stilt and Nathan Brown noticed at the time, "it is simply not clear what would happen if the new parliament ... decided to bring down (or even question) a minister."[27] When this transpired in March 2012, SCAF appeared cornered and widely maligned. Judicial circles were up in arms at the blatant intervention in the judicial proceedings of the NGO case and the sudden lifting of the travel ban. On the presidential campaign trail, by then in full swing with a dozen hopefuls, candidates warned the generals against maneuvering to delay the elections until they could find a pliant civilian front-man. And some US officials showed no gratitude for the resolution of the NGO case, openly voicing their low estimate of the generals. "When we met with SCAF, we had no clear idea about where they stood. They had no answers ready on anything," an aide to a US Congressional delegation led by Senator John McCain said.[28]

To be sure, grandstanding and hyperbole were rife in the infant legislature.[29] But in a political history marked by executive supremacy and parliamentary subordination, a democratically constituted legislature brashly assuming the prerogatives of an entrenched Westminster-style parliament was the point. More than its legislative capacity, the significance of the new parliament was that it showed what happens when a rubber-stamp slips from the grip of the executive and comes under the influence of groups put there by a free vote. It emerged as a beachhead within the state from which to contest the generals' claim to rule, bolstering the public opinion that had been building up in the same direction since December.[30] "What Parliament did reflects the growing feeling that it must have effective instruments besides summoning ministers and yelling at them to no avail. Parliament must wrest the powers not granted it in the constitutional text," wrote Social Democratic MP Ziad Bahaa-Eldin, one of the first to raise the demand for parliamentary formation of a new government.[31] As this ancient tussle over government between insurgent parliaments and entrenched executives unfolded, parliament was plunged into its most anticipated charge.

## A CONSTITUTION IS NOT LIKE AN ELECTION

When the election of both the upper and lower houses of parliament was complete by early March, deputies fell to the task of selecting the hundred constitution-drafters. There was a double significance here. There was the *content* of a document that would pronounce on weighty matters of civil-military relations; citizenship rights of minorities; reform of the monarchical Arab presidency and its police foundations; the powers of parliament; and provisions for the equity and redistribution thoroughly eroded by Mubarak's predatory rule. Substantively, many aspired for a charter enshrining the revolutionary slogan's nexus of "'Aysh, Huriyya, 'Adala Igtima'iyya" (Bread, freedom, social justice). But before content there was the *procedure* by which specific persons would be designated to write the principles of the emergent order. Article 60 of the interim constitution stipulated that both houses would gather to elect one hundred drafters to the Constituent Assembly (CA), but left open the criteria for who could become a candidate. The Silmi document, discussed in chapter 3, was an attempt to set these criteria along corporatist lines, specifying the number of seats to be held by jurists, professionals, representatives of state institutions, religious groups, farmers, youth, and women, in a bid to limit the role of political parties in the constituent process.

The Silmi document's added maneuver—building in guarantees of military autonomy from civilian oversight—led to the November 18, 2011 milyuniyya that roundly rejected it, instilling a sense of urgency in future legislators to retain full authority over selecting the Constituent Assembly. But when parliament's supermajority Islamist composition became clear, secular deputies grew more apprehensive about being sidelined in the constituent process, while Islamists feared *they* would be excluded by a resurrected SCAF-judicial alliance like the one that had produced the Silmi document. Both went into the constituent process with considerable political fears and heaps of mutual suspicion. But judges, military generals, and party politicians were not the only stakeholders in constitutional politics. The intelligentsia, youth activists, feminists, religious and cultural minorities, and cause lawyers had a keen interest in it as well. A certain solemnity attended their conception of constitution-making in a new, democratic Egypt, with deeply felt aspirations for inclusion, representativeness, and accommodation. The act of constitution-making was envisioned as a restitutive forum where those silenced by decades of authoritarian politics, and yet still disadvantaged in the rough-and-tumble of the new electoral politics, would find a seat at the table. "A constitution is not like an election outcome that pleases some and angers others," wrote human rights lawyer Gamal Eid. "A constitution must have consensus and unanimity."[32]

This vision is reflected in a campaign launched by a group of young activists in June 2011 under the invitation, "Let's Write Our Constitution" (Ta'alu Naktub Dusturna). Not content to wait until the constituent assembly was seated or watch from the sidelines as constitution-writing turned into a turf war between rival sets of elites, the volunteers, centered in the Hisham Mubarak Law Center, a rights organization, started collating the voices and experiences of regular citizens to guide the yet-to-be selected drafters. Their manifesto articulated a critique of Egypt's history of formally unimpeachable, elite-drafted, toothless constitutions:

> Despite its flaws, the epoch of despotism's 1971 constitution has many articles preserving several rights and liberties; torture was hardly a constitutional act. Nonetheless, this constitution did not protect the people from the violation of their rights and the divestment of their liberties. We must ask, then: what is the value of a constitution drafted without real popular participation? Even if it is an ideal constitution, it remains ink on paper if there is no balance of forces activating and protecting it.[33]

The campaigners sought an organic document springing from "the direct concerns and issues of all, without being restricted to conventional constitutional questions." Their aspirations chimed with the arguments of theorists such as Jeremy Waldron, who has argued that constitutional*ism* is not the only compelling notion of what a constitution is:

> Constitutions are not just about restraining and limiting power; they are about the empowerment of ordinary people in a democracy and allowing them to control the sources of law and harness the apparatus of government to their legitimate aspirations. That is the democratic view of constitutions, but it is not the constitutionalist view.[34]

But the popularly authenticated document that the activists envisioned as a guide and check to the hundred potential constitution-drafters never materialized. Campaign volunteers were overtaken by the crisis atmosphere enveloping the last quarter of 2011, and one leading member of the initiative, blogger Alaa' Abdel Fattah, found himself in prison for joining the massive Coptic demonstration that ended in the Maspero massacre.[35] By the time he was released in late December 2011 and set to resume work on the campaign, all attention had shifted to security forces' violence against demonstrators and the parliamentary elections. Even if the campaigners had resumed their work, they would have run up against the implacable reality of constitution-making in frenetic conditions. As the scholar of constitution-making Jon Elster concludes, "There are very few instances of either constitutional conventions or constituent legislatures deliberating "*à froid*," in the absence of any internal or external crisis. . . . It seems to be a near-universal rule that constitutions are written in times of crisis and turbulence."[36]

Perhaps the most visible attribute of crisis conditions was parliamentarians' panicky rush to compose the CA. Though article 60 of the interim constitution granted them six months to deliberate on how the hundred drafters should be selected, anticipating the delicate nature of accommodating the plurality of interests and identities in crafting the basic law, the legislators crammed the matter into three weeks. They acted speedily not because they did not understand article 60 but because of the open conflict with the constitution-obsessed generals. If they did not act quickly to claim their constituent power, parliamentarians feared that SCAF would seize it and draw up a CA to its liking.

Deputies' first order of business at a meeting on March 3 was to decide the proportion of MPs to be elected to the CA. Given parliament's Islamist majority, the issue of MPs' self-selection to the CA became a proxy for the Islamist presence in the CA. The FJP proposed a forty/sixty parliamentarian/nonparliamentarian distribution of delegates that the secular parties agreed to as a fair compromise between their own preference for between twenty-five and thirty legislators and Salafis' insistence on a minimum of seventy MPs. Yet on March 17, when the joint houses of parliament convened to vote on the final distribution, the FJP abandoned its earlier proposal and adopted a fifty/fifty distribution, bowing to Salafi pressure to increase the number of legislators. Sensing the impending Islamist takeover of constitution-writing that they feared, secular MPs, journalists, and activists began to agitate in the press and on the streets for a CA not dominated by Islamists. A week later, on March 24, when the elected members of parliament's two chambers convened in Cairo's largest convention center to elect the hundred drafters, protest marches from several points in the city converged on the convention to pressure the lawmakers for an inclusive assembly. A young man held up a sign reminding, "We didn't die so the Brothers could write the Constitution."[37]

Balloting and counting were logistical feats, as hundreds of MP electors had to choose from a slate of 2,078 candidates. Confusion reigned; many MPs wrote in their choices, and many complained of being handed the slate only that morning without sufficient time to review and finalize their choice of drafters.[38] After a thirteen-hour marathon of handwriting-deciphering and vote-counting, results were announced in the early morning hours: sixty-four of the hundred CA members were Islamists or had close ties to them; six were women (two of them FJP members); and six were of various Christian denominations. Even before the results were officially announced, the CA began hemorrhaging members in protest at its Islamist majority. Eight leaders of secular parties who were elected to the assembly resigned in protest. Al-Azhar withdrew its representative and the Holy Synod of the Coptic Church followed suit. The Wafd Party pulled out its five members, as did the bar association, journalists' union, and actors' guild. Enumerating the prominent legal scholars and social interests that had been excluded from the assembly, the SDP MP Ziad Bahaa-Eldin, who was elected but resigned his seat, wondered, "Where is Egypt in this composition?"[39]

When the Islamists forged ahead anyway and convened the CA's first meeting four days later on March 28, a full quarter of its members absented themselves in protest. Before the meeting was over, the Supreme Constitutional Court's representative had walked out. When parliament speaker Saad al-Katatni was elected as CA chair by seventy-one of the seventy-two members in attendance—so that the same man now chaired parliament *and* the constituent assembly—the signal sent was that Islamists had been instructed on how to vote. "From there it is a very small step to assume a new constitution has already been drafted for which the Islamist majority would vote regardless, rendering the deliberations of the assembly redundant," pointed out MP Wahid Abdel Meguid, one of the handful of non-Islamist CA members who was in attendance.⁴⁰ Faced with the prospect of an inquorate assembly and the growing public outcry at the Muslim Brothers, FJP members worked at cross-purposes. While MP Mohamed al-Beltagui scrambled to win back the boycotters by arranging for some Islamists on the assembly to give up their seats to marginalized interests, MP Sobhi Saleh embraced the unyielding majoritarian position. Dismissing what he said was "minority bullying," he sniffed, "Egypt has no minority veto, this is not Lebanon."⁴¹

Yet both public interest in constitution-making and the gathering anti–Muslim Brother sentiment revealed that there was more to the matter than an insignificant obstructionist minority. A coalition of thirty political factions and women's groups, trade unions, and youth groups banded together in a "Constitution for All Egyptians Front," identifying MB dominance of both parliament and CA as the greatest challenge to the revolution. On March 30, a *milyuniyya* they called for brought out demonstrators across the country to demand a more inclusive CA. In a new development in the geography of protests, demonstrators gathered in front of the MB's headquarters in Daqahliyya, chanting, "Yasqut Yasqut Hukm al-Murshid!" (Down, down with the General Guide's rule!).⁴² The growing suspicion was that FJP deputies had no autonomy, but took their marching orders from their parent political organization, the Muslim Brothers, and its leader Mohammed Badie, known as the General Guide (*al-Murshid al-'Am*). The chant entered the lexicon of revolutionary politics, reflecting the general political fear of hidden power in all its forms, as well as considerable distrust of the Muslim Brothers as they moved deeper into the thicket of parliamentary and now constitutional politics.

FJP leaders now faced a dilemma. They could insist on the soundness of the CA selection procedure and begin constitutional deliberations, in the absence of the twenty-five boycotters. This risked confirming their adversaries' contention of an Islamist cabal intent on cooking Egypt's constitution, thereby amplifying the street-based opposition and increasing the probability of public rejection of the document. Or they could concede the need for a reset, returning to the negotiating table with the boycotters to hammer out a new CA with more procedural legitimacy. In the pressure-cooker atmosphere of intense mutual suspicion and mistrust, this risked a costly loss of face. Anti-Islamist civilian politicians and hostile military generals would peg the retreat as a defeat and set the new CA on their own terms. Ironically, it was one of the FJP's critics and constituent assembly boycotters who pithily captured their predicament, partly because he shared their motivating fear of military intervention. Ziad Bahaa-Eldin wrote:

> Unfortunately, the nature of politics, not just in Egypt but the world over, makes admitting mistakes out to be a vice, not a virtue. . . . In this heritage of political action, admitting mistakes means weakness, hesitation, and loss of control leading to more concessions. . . . What makes the matter more grave, however, is the sense that parliament and the whole constitutional experience is being ambushed, by those hoping for the collapse of the whole process in favor of direct military rule.[43]

Beyond the particulars of a deadlock between an intransigent Islamist majority and an obstreperous secular minority, the general dynamic here was the rapid erosion of conditions for compromise. Seeing only a hostile SCAF keenly interested in controlling the constitution, the FJP and some Salafis dismissed the boycotting parties as a cat's paw for military sabotage of the constituent process. Secular parties could not see the increasingly open conflict between the generals and the FJP in parliament, since they were still convinced that SCAF and the MB were in cahoots and were now poised to codify their deal in the constitution. We might throw up our hands at the hopeless myopia and poor judgment of these bickering politicians, incapable of carving out common ground to avert the greater disaster of military intervention. Andrew Arato articulates this view, faulting the actors for not seeing how inclusion, negotiation, consensus, and preassembly binding mechanisms work together to produce effective constitution-making.

But pinpointing the actors' lack of vision ("it is the actors that failed in Egypt, ultimately") tidily shifts the focus to politicians' dispositions, ignoring the structure of a volatile situation that downgraded the value of compromise and elevated intransigence as the only means of political survival.[44] Compromise is viable only when the contending parties believe they will fare better if they compromise than if they do not. But "under conditions under which compromise solutions are highly uncertain each party will be better off seeking a full realization of its interests, that is, seeking to assert itself over others by whatever means."[45] Adam Przeworski's important reminder is that not all political situations are conducive to peaceful settlement. The uncertainty and reversibility of rules, agreements, and institutions in a revolutionary situation means that contending parties are virtually pushed to become fearful and unyielding, since it is neither clear nor likely that a compromising overture will be reciprocated or enforced.

Before the FJP could act on its dilemma, another major actor entered the fray. Constitutional jurists and several public figures had resorted to the familiar political tactic of administrative litigation, honed during the Mubarak years, to draw the courts into the controversy, arguing that the fifty/fifty distribution of the CA granted an unfair advantage to legislators. On April 10, an administrative court invalidated parliament's formation of the CA, agreeing with the plaintiffs and going still further. The ruling explicitly adopted a countermajoritarian logic, rebuking the parliamentary majority for abusing its power and coming down clearly on the side of secular critics, interpreting article 60 of the interim constitution to *require* that the assembly ought to be composed exclusively of nonparliamentarians.[46] The decision was swiftly framed as a stinging slap in the face of grabby Islamists; their ecstatic critics hailed it as a "landmark ruling." A highly placed unnamed "official source," presumably a SCAF member, told the editor of a leading privately owned newspaper that the court ruling offered the FJP a face-saving way out, after they had been carried away by "the arrogance of power and the ecstasy of victory."[47] Backing down from a costly confrontation with the widely respected judiciary, parliament speaker and CA head Saad al-Katatni issued a terse press release affirming respect for the court ruling and suspending the CA's deliberations.

The defeat of the CA before it could start deliberating had far-reaching political effects. It validated critics' views of a shambolic CA selection process, and, by extension, the swaggering behavior of the parliamentary majority. The budding unity among deputies as they wrenched authority for their institution came to a halt, and a strong rift emerged between the Islamist majority and the secular minority. Then the Islamist majority split; the Salafis parted ways with the FJP over the issue of appointing the government, leaving the largest parliamentary party isolated and rapidly hemorrhaging its hard-earned political capital in an increasingly desperate quest to dismiss the Ganzouri cabinet. When speaker Saad al-Katatni took a hasty vote on shuttering parliament for one week to protest what he said were Ganzouri and SCAF's contempt for the legislature, the vote passed by the FJP's plurality, but 103 Salafi and secular deputies recorded their opposition in writing, criticizing the speaker for acting without due deliberation.[48]

The April 10 ruling thrust the courts into the center of the protracted constitutional contention, where they would remain for the duration of the revolutionary situation. It was not the first significant judicial ruling after Mubarak's ouster; other administrative court panels had dissolved the NDP and rolled back some major Mubarak and SCAF policies, in an extension of the courts' activism during the Mubarak years.[49] But the ruling was the first to weigh in on the contested constitutional framework and compel a re-do of the CA, countering parliament's claim to be the sole constituent power. But courts do not act on their own. The minority parties and their extraparliamentary allies who had brought the suit discovered a resource in this countermajoritarian strategic litigation and pursued it systematically henceforth. With such an effective form of "exit," the minority lost what little incentive remained to negotiate with an intransigent majority.

## UPLOADING A PRESIDENT

The first competitive presidential elections in Egypt's history were scheduled to take place on May 23 and 24. More than a dozen contenders were energetically battling it out at the hustings, delivering speeches before thousands and seeking the endorsements of regional notables and social worthies. Given the central role of the president in charting Egypt's domestic and especially foreign policies, competition over the office after Mubarak's twenty-nine-year tenure was tracked punctiliously by the former president's close friends in the region and the world, principally Israel, Saudi Arabia, the UAE, the EU, and the US. But a cloud of uncertainty hung over the campaigns. Suspicions were rife that the military council would stage-manage elections to place a token civilian in the role or delay the poll until they had a constitution to their liking. When an aged former minister from the Sadat era who was assumed to be SCAF's man withdrew from the race, fears mounted that the generals planned to delay elections until they could find another front.[50] Thus, candidates' stump speeches were as much about Egyptians' right to a timely and honest election as wooing voters with their programs and promises. A graffito scrawled on a public wall in the Nahiya neighborhood in Giza reflected the anticipation and uncertainty: Gari Tahmil Ra'is (Uploading a president).

The major contenders were a set of ancien régime stalwarts, seasoned dissidents, and post-2011 personalities. Mubarak's former foreign minister and secretary-general of the Arab League, Amr Moussa, had resigned his post just hours after Mubarak's ouster on February 11, 2011, and begun his campaign shortly thereafter. He recast himself as a liberal who had always been at odds with Mubarak and who possessed the necessary diplomatic experience to revive Egypt's standing in the world: "We're Up to the Challenge" read his campaign motto. Ahmed Shafiq, Mubarak's last prime minister dismissed by SCAF under popular pressure in March 2011, made a remarkable comeback as he capitalized on the fickle public mood after fifteen months of upheaval. He appealed to and fed on fears of Islamists taking over, pegging himself as the reliable statist insider who would maintain an "Egypt for All."

Four familiar dissidents tapped into the still-salient public desire for a complete break from the Mubarak system, presenting themselves as carriers of the spirit of revolution. In June 2011, Abdel Moneim Aboul Fotouh was expelled from the Muslim Brothers for defying the party line and announcing his candidacy. By spring 2012, his "Strong Egypt" campaign was led by a professionalized team of young advisers of various ideological commitments, positioning their man as a progressive Islamist-centrist who could bridge the Islamist-secularist divide and restore Egypt's international stature. Hamdeen Sabahy presented himself as "One of Us," a democrat and Nasserist who would work for social justice for the millions of families hurt by decades of austerity; he declared, "my first war is against the internal enemies of poverty, corruption, and unemployment," rather than fighting Israel.[51] Hisham al-Bastawisi, a dissident judge censured by the government in 2006, embarked on a long-shot campaign on the leftist Tagammu's ticket, his slogan a slightly modified version of the revolution's triptych, "Change. Freedom. Social Justice." The youngest candidate in the race, rights lawyer Khaled Ali, ran a similarly quixotic campaign on a shoestring staffed by eager volunteers who saw themselves as the true embodiment of Tahrir Square. "A President from Tahrir" was their preferred chant at mass meetings; their official slogan was "We'll Realize Our Dream."

The campaign with the largest corps of committed volunteers alternately inspired, frightened, and amused many Egyptians and international observers. Lawyer and Salafi preacher Hazem Salah Abu Ismail was a curious amalgam of effective political orator, unabashed patriarch, revolutionary Salafi (for his unrelenting criticism of the generals), and maverick political operator who refused to align himself with either the FJP or the three Salafi parties. The only candidate to loudly oppose Egypt's 1979 peace treaty with Israel, his fierce partisans called themselves "Hazemoon" (The Determined) and plastered what seemed like the entire country's public walls with posters of his broadly smiling, bearded face. Social media users lost no time in disseminating the meme of Abu Ismail posters blanketing the universe: on ocean beds, held up by astronauts on the moon's surface, and framed on a wall in the Oval Office as President Barack Obama took a call. His slogan, "We'll Live with Dignity," echoed the revolution's bedrock aspiration, with particular appeal to the pious, culturally conservative segment of the population historically held in contempt by the self-professed modern political and cultural elite.[52]

Per the March 30 interim constitution, there were three pathways to get on the ballot: endorsement by thirty parliamentary deputies; affiliation with a political party represented in parliament; or the notarized signatures of 30,000 voters from at least fifteen of Egypt's twenty-seven provinces. To advertise their electability, serious contenders opted for the third option, even if they could have gotten on the ballot through parliamentary endorsements. Submitting the sealed file boxes of signatures to the Presidential Election Commission (PEC) became an elaborate display of political mettle, with large processions of supporters, luminaries, and news media accompanying the candidate to the PEC's headquarters and reverently carrying the boxes into the building. Amr Moussa submitted 44,000 endorsements; Abdel Moneim Aboul Fotouh, 33,000; Shafiq, 35,000; Sabahy, 39,000. Abu Ismail's was by far the largest cavalcade of cars and buses, processing ceremoniously for hours from west to east Cairo to present 120,000 citizen signatures and forty-three parliamentary deputies' endorsements. Opinion polls of varying methodologies tracked the oscillating fortunes of the contenders. Based on some repeated results, Moussa and Aboul Fotouh were dubbed the frontrunners, though one widely cited poll put Abu Ismail in second place with 28.8 percent to Amr Moussa's 30.7.[53]

## A GAME OF CHICKEN

On March 31, the Muslim Brothers made a major announcement: they were joining the presidential race, fielding their deputy leader and chief strategist Khairat al-Shater. It is an understatement to say this decision caused widespread trepidation. To the MB's adversaries, the news confirmed the group's essentially untrustworthy nature, making a mockery of their constant reassurances that they would not seek the presidency, under the motto "participation, not domination." With their plurality in parliament and domination of the constituent process, the fear was that the MB was now realizing its latent project of total political control over Egypt's institutions. At the March 30 "Constitution for All Egyptians" milyuniyya, protesters chanted, "Abdel Nasser Alha Zaman, al-Ikhwan Malhumsh Aman!" (Abdel Nasser said it long ago, al-Ikhwan [the Muslim Brothers] can't be trusted!).[54] To their friends, the decision reflected a grave misreading of the Egyptian public's readiness for an Islamist president. "Do they not realize that the masses voting for them in parliamentary elections is completely different than the case of the presidential election?" wondered Islamist columnist Fahmi Howeidy. He underscored the hostility of "certain Arab states" to the MB as an added difficulty, referring to the Gulf kingdoms of Saudi Arabia and the UAE, leaders of the counteralliance against the region's democratic uprisings. Even within the group's ranks, the move generated considerable resistance, especially given the organization's expulsion of Abdel Moneim Aboul Fotouh in 2011 for defying the party line on not contesting the presidency. The internal vote approving Shater's candidacy was an extremely close 56 to 52; we know this because the losing faction was unusually vocal, publicizing the vote to the press. Leading the dissenters was previous MB leader Mohamed Mahdi Akef, who went out of his way to announce his opposition, yet affirmed that he would abide by the majority vote.[55]

Given the highly diverse field of candidates which, after all, included three other Islamist presidential contenders, why should the largest Islamist organization's entry into the race generate so much consternation?[56] Partly it was the sudden about-face from the MB's self-limiting posture after Mubarak's fall, not least to reassure anxious foreign governments and investors that the group did not seek to Islamize the revolution or lead an abrupt transformation in Egypt's foreign relations.[57] And partly it was the high-risk nature of the decision, seeming to confirm decades of government propaganda that the MB were wolves in sheep's clothing; "They Have Fallen into the Trap," Howeidy's column was titled. In terms of political prudence, the decision seemed irrational, shouldering sole political responsibility (parliament and presidency) during the most turbulent juncture in Egypt's contemporary political history.

Close observers of the MB interpret the move as the group's seizure of an unrivaled political opportunity. The group's gains in the March 2011 referendum and the parliamentary election results emboldened it to go for the presidency; "it seemed like now or never," wrote Yasser El-Shimy. Similarly, Carrie Rosefsky Wickham explains the group's interest in both the parliamentary and presidential contests in terms of its "eagerness to 'seize the moment,' that is, to maximize its influence at a crucial early phase in the transition process."[58] But this does not explain why they would seize the opportunity at what was a highly inopportune moment, when the political class and segments of public opinion were mobilizing against them due to the CA fiasco. I propose a different interpretation that brings to the fore more of the contextual factors that impinged on the decision, showing it to be as much a defensive reaction to threats as a serial conquest of opportunities, an example of what O'Donnell and Schmitter call "a hurried and audacious choice" in unstable junctures of transition.[59]

The MB's about-face emerged directly out of the mounting conflicts in which it was embroiled in the parliamentary and constitutional arenas. On the evening of March 24, the same day that the legislators were electing constitutional delegates, the MB issued an unusually blunt statement of fighting words. It listed the Ganzouri cabinet's failures to solve pressing economic problems, accused SCAF of plotting to rig the presidential elections, and referred to a threat to dissolve parliament as an "unbecoming act of blackmail."[60] For weeks prior, as FJP-led deputies clamored for parliament's right to replace the Ganzouri cabinet, news had circulated that the Supreme Constitutional Court (SCC) was reviewing a legal challenge to the law under which parliament had been elected, for infringing on the rights of independent candidates by allowing party-list candidates to contest the 166 seats available for independents. The implication was clear: if the parliamentary majority did not cease pressure to change the government, parliament would be dissolved pursuant to a court order.[61] This was a credible threat. There was precedent for the SCC ruling election laws unconstitutional for discriminating against independents; twice under Mubarak (in 1986 and 1990), the SCC struck down election laws and invalidated the parliaments under which they were seated, requiring new elections. If the threat was carried out, it would appear not as a military-judicial coup against the most democratically elected parliament since 1950, but as one of the county's three apex courts deepening its tradition of prodemocracy jurisprudence.

This began a very public game of chicken between the generals and the Muslim Brothers, a mutual test of strength to see who would flinch first. Each side claimed sovereignty: the FJP by virtue of its status as the parliamentary plurality, and SCAF by referencing article 56 in the interim constitution that it had authored, granting itself the presidential prerogative to appoint and discharge cabinets. The next day, SCAF issued a counterstatement broadcast on television, lashing out at the MB's accusation of imminent election rigging as "mere baseless slander" and taking full credit for the clean legislative elections that gave the MB their place in parliament. The statement issued another direct threat, invoking the specter of 1954 when Gamal Abdel Nasser ordered mass arrests of MB cadres and banned the movement. "We ask everyone to be aware of the lessons of history to avoid mistakes from a past we do not want to return to." The Revolution Youth Coalition, April 6th youth movement, and secular political parties were consumed by the struggle with the FJP over the Constituent Assembly and kept their distance from the MB-SCAF escalation, seeing it as a base fight for spoils between dueling religious and military autocrats.[62]

The brinkmanship was more than a two-player game; there was a powerful third party that shaped the MB's calculations. In February and March, as US and Egyptian officials bargained out a resolution to the US NGO crisis at the highest levels, a visiting US Congressional delegation led by Republican Senator John McCain met with MB leaders and FJP parliamentarians. Back on the Senate floor, Senators McCain and John Hoeven engaged in a colloquy on how "impressed" they were with the FJP legislators and commended the MB leaders' role that "helped break the logjam."[63] US policymakers in other quarters were also sending positive signals. The surge in Hazem Salah Abu Ismail's popularity had terrified State Department officials; US diplomats "who once feared a Brotherhood takeover now appear[ed] to see the group as an indispensable ally against Egypt's ultraconservatives, exemplified by Mr. Abu Ismail."[64] The MB's risky decision to contest the presidency was thus pushed by a dual threat and pulled by an opportunity: the prospect of being completely shut out of the political arena for the foreseeable future if parliament was dissolved, and possibly having its leaders and cadres hauled to prison, was counterbalanced by US signals that it would not oppose an MB presidency. Not insignificantly, the decision to field their own candidate also enabled the MB leadership to reassert authority over the rank and file, rallying members behind the organization's own choice and away from the popular renegade Abdel Moneim Aboul Fotouh.

With the MB now in the race, Egypt experienced one of the most bewildering fortnights in the revolutionary calendar. On April 7, one day before the close of the nomination period, a surreal scene transpired as former intelligence chief Omar Suleiman presented his candidacy papers to the PEC, flanked by military police officers and a member of SCAF. Mubarak's short-lived vice president had not been seen in public since his thirty-second announcement on February 11, 2011, that Mubarak was stepping down. His audacious resurfacing as a presidential contender caused genuine alarm that he was SCAF's new candidate to counter the MB's Khairat al-Shater and that the election would be fixed to ensure his victory. A flurry of urgent political action ensued. In a five-hour emergency session in parliament on April 12, MPs delivered rousing orations on how to confront the looming threat of Mubarakism's return via the ballot box. Islamist and secular deputies momentarily closed ranks, passing a "Political Ostracism Law" barring any high-ranking member of the ancien régime from holding high office for ten years, overruling the reasoned objections of two ministers (and former judges) against retrospective legislation.[65] In a seven-minute peroration that received a standing ovation, independent MP and former dissident judge Mahmoud al-Khodeiry voiced the wrenching dilemma of employing unconstitutional means to block Mubarak's aide-de-camp from winning the presidency:

> I declare before you that in 46 years of judicial work, I have not faced a law that has tormented me as much as this law. In the end, I asked myself a question: are we now in a revolutionary phase or a normal phase where ordinary principles apply in the constitution and laws? The answer came quickly that we are in a revolutionary stage, for two reasons. [applause] First, state institutions have yet to be constituted, we still have coming up very important elections for the presidency. The second reason is that out of the goals of the revolution that you sacrificed and confronted death for, only the most tenuous have been achieved. All that we have done is remove the president and some courtiers.[66]

Tahrir Square saw the two largest milyuniyyas since the revolution's first anniversary. On April 13, Islamists overfilled the square while on April 20 secular groups had their turn; both were outraged by Suleiman's recrudescence but not enough to overcome their divisions over the Constituent Assembly. A grassroots campaign under the banner Mayuhkumsh ("He Won't Rule") plastered the streets with posters warning the public against voting for Mubarak's man. Activists renewed their pleas to prorevolution presidential candidates to put aside their personal ambitions and rally behind a single candidate, to prevent splitting the prochange vote and enabling the counterrevolution to recapture the presidency.

Into this maelstrom came the decision of the PEC on April 14 disqualifying ten presidential candidates, including the trio generating the most controversy. Hazem Salah Abu Ismail was disqualified on the grounds that his mother was a naturalized American citizen (violating the rule that candidates' spouse and both parents be Egyptian nationals with no dual citizenship); Khairat al-Shater was ruled ineligible for his past conviction in a political trial under Mubarak; and Omar Suleiman was declared thirty-one signatures short of the 30,000 required citizen endorsements.[67] While legally sound, the disqualifications were interpreted as a purely political maneuver by the SCAF-influenced PEC, with Suleiman's sudden resurfacing and disqualification now appearing as a makeweight for the elimination of the two candidates most threatening to the military council.[68] However, the MB had anticipated Shater's disqualification and also registered FJP chairman Mohamed Morsi as its backup choice. As he entered the race, Morsi was quickly tagged as *El-Stebn* (the spare tire), a smear that would prove difficult to dislodge throughout the campaign. Out of some two dozen presidential hopefuls, the ballot now contained thirteen final candidates.

Relief at Suleiman's disappearance did not put to rest fears of foul play. Renewed violence against protesters fed suspicions that SCAF was fomenting unrest to delay the handover of power. A sit-in by Abu Ismail partisans in Cairo's 'Abbasiyya neighborhood to protest his disqualification was attacked by armed plainclothes assailants, killing twelve and injuring hundreds. Several presidential candidates suspended their campaigns in protest, prompting the generals to hold a two-hour press conference on May 3 to reiterate to the nation their good intentions. "Today, we're announcing it honestly and clearly: the armed forces and the Supreme Council are committed to handing over power before the 30th of June, 2012."[69]

But for the stubborn fact that the election occurred in the shadow of military rule, the final weeks looked like any dynamic electoral contest, with an hourly news cycle reporting on celebrity endorsements, the creative and humorous tactics of the candidates' campaigns, and polls showing a sizeable 37 to 40 percent of respondents undecided.⁷⁰ The two largest Salafi parties' surprise endorsement of Aboul Fotouh rather than the FJP's Morsi capped the rift between the Islamist parties and created a bandwagon effect for Aboul Fotouh, who was also supported by al-Wasat. Virtually all observers anticipated that he and Amr Moussa would be the top two candidates to vie in the run-off. On May 10, the two faced off in the Arab world's first televised presidential debate, transfixing viewers well past midnight in a five-hour joust. On the eve of the debate, a Brookings Institution poll showed Aboul Fotouh leading Moussa 32 percent to 28 percent. Significantly, the poll showed that voters thought differently about presidential candidates than contenders for parliament. Political party affiliation was the leading factor in choosing a member of parliament, whereas personal trust was ranked highest in electing a president. Seventy-one percent thought it was a mistake for the Muslim Brothers to reverse their promise not to field a candidate.⁷¹

## THE SAMSON OPTION

Voters went to the polls on May 23 and 24 with a mixture of elation and anxiety at what would happen next. Ballot-counting began immediately after polls closed on the evening of the twenty-fourth and stretched into the morning hours. In its first piece of legislation in February, parliament had amended the presidential election law to seal any openings for fraud, especially at the counting phase. The law allowed NGOs, news media, and candidate agents to observe the count and enabled judges to announce final results at polling stations.⁷² Well into the wee hours, television split-screens broadcast live proceedings from inside polling stations, with clerks and judges huddled around tables, reading aloud the choice on every ballot and arranging them in piles in full view of all. When every last paper had been counted, all stepped back to take in the cluster of surprises presented by the results.

The first surprise was the relatively low rate of participation in the first competitive presidential election: 46.42 percent turned out, compared to 62 percent for the general election. Perhaps the very attributes that drove some voters to turn out made others stay home, namely the intense media coverage, wrangling over candidacies, and fears that the military would meddle with the process to shape the outcome. Five of the thirteen contenders captured 98 percent of the vote, suggesting that the electorate preferred established politicians who could

FIGURE 8. Ballot in first round of presidential election, May 24, 2012; photo by Jonathan Rashad, used under Creative Commons license CC BY-NC-SA 2.0.

win. The biggest surprise was that the two candidates who consistently brought up the rear in opinion polls, Mohamed Morsi and Ahmed Shafiq, emerged as the top two vote-getters, with a difference of merely 259,625 votes. The presumptive frontrunners who had received the lion's share of media attention ended up fourth and a distant fifth; speculation raged over whether their mutual personal attacks in the televised debate had put off voters. Perhaps benefiting from the underdog effect, Nasserist Hamdeen Sabahy became the contest's dark horse, astonishingly coming in first in the top two cities (Cairo and Alexandria) and in his home province of Kafr al-Shaykh. There was considerable crying over spilt milk, as activists rued the decision by Sabahy and Aboul Fotouh to compete against each other rather than consolidate the prochange vote on a joint ticket. The 38 percent of the vote that they both secured would have put them in good stead to capture the presidency in the run-off. But election rules did not require a candidate to select a vice president for the ticket, so there was no incentive or mechanism for either Sabahy or Aboul Fotouh to yield and settle for second fiddle.

For many voters, the results embodied the dreaded choice framed by Hosni Mubarak for decades: the only alternative to stable undemocratic rule was

TABLE 4. Results of the First Round of Presidential Elections, May 23-24, 2012.

| Candidate | Votes | Percentage |
| --- | --- | --- |
| Mohamed Morsi | 5,764,952 | 24.78 |
| Ahmed Shafiq | 5,505,327 | 23.66 |
| Hamdeen Sabahy | 4,820,273 | 20.72 |
| Abdel Moneim Aboul Fotouh | 4,065,239 | 17.47 |
| Amr Moussa | 2,588,850 | 11.13 |

Source: Presidential Election Commission, http://pres2012.elections.eg/round1-results.

domination by the Muslim Brothers. Despite entering the race at the eleventh hour as his party's second choice, and despite the MB's alienation of nearly all political allies with its go-it-alone conduct in parliament and the makeup of the Constituent Assembly, Mohamed Morsi still came at the head of the contenders, testifying to the MB's national outreach network and disciplined voting for the organization regardless of the candidate. However, the MB had suffered significant losses in the five months between the parliamentary and presidential elections, its vote share dropping from 10.1 million to 5.7 million votes for Morsi, indicating that many voters either stayed home for the presidential poll or granted their vote to other candidates that they deemed a better fit for the presidency. Furthermore, Morsi came in third in major metropolitan centers, including Cairo, Alexandria, Daqahliyya, and Gharbiyya, and second in his home province of Sharqiyya; his lead was in the most populous Upper Egypt provinces. Conversely, Ahmed Shafiq underwent a remarkable rehabilitation from political pariah to presidential frontrunner, coming in first in the major Delta provinces of Menoufiyya, Qalyoubiyya, Daqahliyya, and Sharqiyya, and second in Cairo. Multiple motivations likely drove his voters: fatigue from the relentless turmoil and instability of revolutionary politics; fear of the Muslim Brothers; risk aversion (better the devil you know); and principled commitment to a statist insider as the new president. These point to a stubborn fact about Egypt's revolutionary situation: the old regime had been dealt a major blow, but was not dying. It had proved that it could muster sizable popular support in a contested election.

Shafiq's strong showing was read as the generals' checkmating of the revolution, using the instruments of open, competitive politics to hoist one of their own into the presidency while remaining the supreme power behind the throne. Protests were organized outside Shafiq campaign offices and led to violence; in the Cairo headquarters and the Fayoum branch, protesters stormed the offices and set fire to the buildings. In the lead-up to the run-off on June 16 and 17, organizers of the two campaigns geared up to woo more voters along the basic cleavage of the "party of order" versus the "party of change." Shafiq's campaign changed its slogan to "Actions, Not Words" and harped on fears of an Islamist "takeover" of state and society, warning that the MB would pack ostensibly neutral government organs with their partisans and roll back the rights of women, Copts, and nonreligious Egyptians. Morsi strategists rebranded their motto to "Our Strength Is in Our Unity," framing the campaign as a resurrection of the unity that had toppled Hosni Mubarak and reminding voters that it was Shafiq who was prime minister when pro-Mubarak armed gangs attacked Tahrir Square on February 2, 2011.

Celebrities and other public figures aligned themselves with either pole; Aboul Fotouh's campaign and the April 6th youth group endorsed Morsi; Sufi orders, the families of former presidents Nasser and Sadat, and the Social Democratic and Socialist Alliance Parties endorsed Shafiq; and Hamdeen Sabahy and Amr Moussa declined to back either contender. Many prochange voters confronted the novel experience of having to choose between sincere and strategic voting. The latter, reasoning that it was imperative to hold one's nose and vote for Morsi to short-circuit a victory for Shafiq, became known as *'asiri al-laymun*, or lemon-squeezers, a reference to the culinary trick of adding citrus to a rich dish to render it digestible. Two distinct camps emerged among sincere voting advocates: *al-muqati'un* or boycotters, refusing to partake in a ritual that did not accommodate their true beliefs, and *al-mubtilun* or ballot-spoilers, reasoning that defacing one's ballot was a purposive political act that registered protest while observing the civic duty of turning out.[73]

Days before the run-off, a raft of game-changing decisions stoked intense anxieties about the integrity, even the meaning, of the election. On June 13, the minister of justice issued a decree granting military officers police powers, including arrest of civilians, until ratification of a new constitution. The next day, the Supreme Constitutional Court delivered two highly anticipated verdicts concerning parliament. The Political Ostracism Law passed in April to block fulul from running in elections was deemed unconstitutional, allowing Ahmed Shafiq's candidacy to continue. The SCC then ruled that the law under which parliament was elected was also unconstitutional. The ruling stated that by allowing party-slate candidates to compete with independents for the one-third of seats available for the latter, the law granted undue advantages to party candidates. "The formation of the whole assembly is null and void," pronounced the court, ordering the disbandment of the first democratically constituted legislature in sixty years "without the need for any other measure."[74] The next day, police barricades went up around parliament to prevent deputies from accessing the building. Egypt's 144-day legislature thus joined the shortlist of disbanded parliaments in other revolutionary situations—the 378-day Frankfurt Parliament of 1848–49, the 1906 Duma in session for 72 days—but is distinguished by the fact that the reassertion of executive supremacy was achieved by judicial writ.

With barely any time to digest the momentous decision, voters headed to the polls on June 16. Then, one hour before polls closed the next evening, another major bundle of edicts was promulgated, this time by SCAF. In what they called an "addendum" to the interim constitution of March 30, 2011, the military council divested the incoming president of significant powers that they assumed for themselves. They seized legislative power until the election of a new parliament; made themselves the sole arbiters of matters related to the armed forces; rendered the head of SCAF rather than the president as the commander-in-chief of the armed forces; claimed war powers; and stipulated that the incoming president take the oath of office before SCC judges, the same men (and one woman) who had just dissolved parliament. SCAF also granted itself two inroads into the constitution-drafting body. First, "if the constituent assembly encounters an obstacle that would prevent it from completing its work, the SCAF within a week will form a new constituent assembly to author a new constitution." Second, SCAF gave itself and other high state officials, including the president, veto power over the deliberations of the Constituent Assembly, and set up the SCC as the final arbiter of any dispute that might arise between the Constituent Assembly and the state.[75] What the military council had failed to achieve seven months earlier with the Silmi document was now basic law.

SCAF's brinkmanship with the MB that had started in March had terminated in a one-two punch, with parliament disbanded and the presidency subordinated and stripped of significant powers. In March, other political players had deemed it unlikely that the generals would activate "the Samson option," as Salafi Nur party leader Bassam al-Zarqa characterized it.[76] Three months later they had, but unlike the Biblical figure who perished in the course of defeating his enemies, the generals brought down the house while remaining very much on their feet. To address the wave of opposition that had peaked by the afternoon of the next day, they held a two-hour press conference to "clarify to the news media, the Egyptian people, and the world" the document they had promulgated. SCAF's legal specialist Mamdouh Shahin presented their takeover of lawmaking power as a logical solution to parliament's court-ordered dissolution, to prevent the president from fusing executive and legislative powers in his hands. "So now there is a balance between SCAF and the president," said Shahin, placing both his hands on a level to illustrate. Invoking the familiar rhetorical trope of a moderating role invariably used by interventionist militaries, the general presented the disbanding of parliament and the hamstringing of the president as restoring balance to an out-of-whack political system. Shahin then made a remarkable claim:

> We have three powers: constituent power (*al-Sulta al-Ta'sisiyya*), which is SCAF. What is constituent power? That which generates all state institutions. If there is no parliament, it brings parliament, it organizes matters until there is a parliament. There is no president until it brings a president. There is no constitution until it brings a constitution. When these state institutions are constituted, the founding power's work is considered complete.[77]

This simply spelled out SCAF's doctrine and practice since its formation on February 10, 2011, as not just *a* constituted state authority but *the* constituting power. As such, it had the right to make, and break, the constituted authority of the new elected state institutions as well as the entire constitutional framework. What this meant for popular sovereignty was clear. Forms of democratic participation were to be upheld and even facilitated, but as an adjunct to the originating power. After all, a "bond" between the armed forces and "the people" was inscribed in the March 30 interim constitution, declaring the armed forces "the property of the people" (art. 53). Grafting the armed forces onto a unitary notion of the people, the military justified its power in terms of popular sovereignty.

SCAF's assault on the fledgling democratic institutions spurred the last significant coalescence of civilian parties against military rule. At the invitation of candidate Mohamed Morsi, two dozen prominent party leaders, youth activists, and public figures held a five-hour meeting to begin patching up the debilitating rifts between the Muslim Brothers and other Islamists and non-Islamists, and to close ranks against any eleventh-hour fraudulence to enthrone Ahmed Shafiq. With security forces surrounding parliament, a resurgent SCAF, and military officers granted arrest powers, there was apprehension and dread at an impending hard coup. Morsi's campaign had been exceptionally vigilant, maintaining an independent tally of the count at all 13,000 polling stations around the country; within twenty-four hours of polls closing, the Morsi campaign had released its figures showing a narrow win for Morsi.[78] In what became known as the Fairmont Meeting (after the hotel where the meeting was held), the presumptive president pledged to install a national unity government headed by a non-MB prime minister and with a diverse team of presidential advisers. The political theorist Heba Raouf Ezzat, one of three women in attendance, explained that the meeting was not to forgive the Muslim Brothers' mistakes nor grant Morsi carte blanche but to brake the alarming polarization that endangered the democratic experiment.[79]

On the afternoon of June 24, all waited to hear the official results as they were announced live on television. Morsi supporters filled Tahrir Square, where leaders and members of the April 6th youth movement had also turned out in solidarity. In a large public square in the provincial capital of Mansoura, many paced nervously, held their heads in their hands, and shushed one another as PEC head judge Farouq Sultan read out an interminable, florid preamble before announcing the number of registered voters, turnout figures, the number of spoiled ballots, and then the results. Mohamed Morsi became the first civilian, Islamist, elected national leader in Egypt's history. When Sultan finally read out the vote tally for Morsi, the Tahrir crowd broke out in ecstatic cheering

TABLE 5. Results of the Final Round of Presidential Elections, June 16–17, 2012.

| Candidate | Votes | Percentage |
| --- | --- | --- |
| Mohamed Morsi | 13,230,131 | 51.73 |
| Ahmed Shafiq | 12,347,380 | 48.27 |

*Source:* Presidential Election Commission, http://pres2012.elections.eg/round2-results.

and flag-waving that lasted for a continuous three minutes; in Mansoura, they hugged one another, wept, chanted "Allahu Akbar!" and jumped up and down like spring-loaded puppets.[80]

With a 51.85 percent turnout, slightly more than the first round, the most striking takeaway of the results was the exceedingly thin margin by which Mohamed Morsi won, just 882,751 votes. The implication for the new president's governance prospects was that half the electorate stayed home, half of those who turned out voted against him, and millions of those voting for him did so not out of enthusiasm but out of aversion to his opponent. Morsi now had electoral legitimacy but quite thin public support, a tension that would prove central to his tenure.[81] Seen from the heady days of March 2011, when Ahmed Shafiq's tenure as prime minister was abruptly terminated by SCAF after only thirty-three days in office, making him the most ephemeral Egyptian premier since 1954, his 48 percent of the vote was astounding. It was a tangible measure of how mistrust of the Muslim Brothers drove millions to prefer a revival of the Mubarak order. Shafiq led in the populated and politically central provinces of Cairo (55.7 to 44.3 percent), Daqahliyya (55.6 to 44.4 percent), Gharbiyya (63 to 37 percent), and Menoufiyya (71.5 to 28.5 percent), including Morsi's own home province of Sharqiyya (54.3 to 45.7 percent), and Morsi led in Alexandria (57.5 to 42.5 percent), Giza (59.7 to 40.3 percent) and the provinces of Upper Egypt.[82] While the spoiled ballots (843,252) were double the number of the first round, the increased turnout in the run-off renders it unknown what percentage of the invalid papers were due to the *mubtilun*. The ballot-spoilers received much media attention, as they reflected the passions and stresses accompanying the elections. "I'm not obliged to choose between a murderer and a traitor," wrote one ballot-spoiler, referring to Shafiq and Morsi respectively. "Down with military rule, glory to the martyrs."[83]

The ceremonies for the handover of truncated powers to the president were a protracted affair, mirroring the struggle for primacy that had already begun. SCAF's decree required that Morsi recite the oath of office before the SCC judges who had dissolved parliament, normally the institution where the president was sworn in. In defiance, Morsi headed to Tahrir Square the day before the official ceremony to recite the oath before ecstatic crowds of his supporters. Much to the annoyance of presidential bodyguards, he strutted back and forth on stage, his blazer pulled open to show that he wore no bulletproof vest. He read out the oath, then delivered a pointed counteraddress to SCAF's claim of constituent power:

> I came to talk to you today because I believe that you are the source of power and legitimacy. There is no person, party, institution or authority over or above the will of the people. The nation is the source of all power; it grants and withdraws power. I say to everyone now, to all the people, the Ministries and the government, the army and police of Egypt, men and women, at home and abroad, I say it with full force. "No authority is over and above this power."[84]

The next day at the official ceremony, Morsi sat stony-faced as the robed Supreme Court judges delivered speeches about their institution. He stood to recite the oath encircled by the judges, then read out brief prepared remarks stressing the separation of powers.[85] Next, the president headed to a Cairo University hall packed with foreign dignitaries, politicians, and ministers, where he recited the oath again and delivered a more expansive address of assurances that Egypt would not export its revolution and would not deviate from the "great heritage of the Egyptian state" under his leadership. Then he headed to a military base for a ceremony organized by the armed forces, where he was greeted with a twenty-one-gun salute. SCAF chief Tantawi gifted Morsi a plaque bearing a military shield, and he and chief of staff Sami Anan sat on either side of the president to watch a parade. "The Egyptian people and the world are witnessing a unique model," said Morsi, "not seen before, of how power is transferred from the Egyptian military forces by the will of the people to an elected, civilian power."[86]

\* \* \*

It would not be wrong to see the first six months of 2012 as a three-cornered struggle between the power holding generals, a fractious Islamist-dominated parliament, and secular MPs breaking from their Islamist peers and linking up with extraparliamentary allies in a budding anti-Islamist coalition. But it is a rather tame depiction of the highly charged context of those months, where parliamentary politics, the constituent process, and an unremittingly tense presidential election intersected and fed off one other, drawing in many more interest groups than a stylized three-actor game. Politics in the winter and spring of 2012 also involved the agency of Salafi MPs, judges on administrative and constitutional courts, cabinet ministers, protesters advancing various causes, presidential contenders and their partisans, influential international parties with a keen stake in how Egypt would be governed, and a hyperactive domestic news media that reported the interplay of these interests but also acted as a conduit for signal-sending and mutual testing between contending groups.

Actors' cognitive construction of opportunities and threats helps explain their political action, and how they made sense of their situation was fundamentally interactive. Political fear of the ancien régime's resurgence impelled parliamentarians to hastily pass a dubious lustration law; a loudly assertive parliament reawakened judges' belief in their supralegislative status as guardians of the constitution, motivating them to check and ultimately dissolve the new parliament; uncertainty about the future wracked prochange voters as they contemplated dismal options; aversion to being governed by a disciplined ideological party drove prostability voters to cast their lot with the ancien régime; fear of repression and an opportunity for international recognition shaped the calculations of Egypt's largest political organization; outrage at their sidelining in the constituent process motivated minority parties to pursue permanent opposition, leaving an opening for the generals to reassert their power and autonomy in ways that had failed only months earlier.

The vexed transfer of power to civilians transported the conflict between political contenders into conflict between state institutions. The constitution of a new parliament and president activated the powerful unelected military and judicial state enclaves to claim that they held constituent power. There are two ways to see these dynamics. The literature on revolution frames it in terms of multiple sovereignty, or the copresence of multiple "constitution-creating processes," as Arthur Stinchcombe has it. Parliament, SCAF, and the courts all claimed supreme power to organize the constituent process. The literature on democratic transitions emphasizes a power apparatus claiming a perpetual right of overrule. Adam Przeworski puts it clearly: "The crucial moment in any passage from authoritarian to democratic rule is not necessarily the withdrawal of the army into the barracks or the opening of the elected parliament but the crossing of the threshold beyond which no one can intervene to reverse outcomes of the formal democratic process."[87] We have to hold on to both conceptual frames to understand the structure of conflict in the revolutionary situation. Warring sovereignty claims emerged out of a shifting power distribution that rendered no outcome irreversible and no newly constituted institution immune from dissolution.

The state's elected institutions were turning out to be fragile things compared to the energized judicial and military enclaves. With international endorsement, the presidency seemed to resolve into a diarchy. When US Secretary of State Hilary Clinton made her first trip to Egypt after the presidential election, she met separately with president Mohamed Morsi and SCAF chairman Mohamed Tantawi. Midway into Year 2 of Egypt's revolutionary situation, an isolated, precarious president faced an array of powerful state institutions, buttressed by his organization and the fraying patience of an exhausted public.

*Chapter 5*

# DOWN, DOWN WITH THE GENERAL GUIDE'S RULE
يسقط يسقط حكم المرشد!

> The messianic expectations aroused by most revolutions are likely to lead some disappointed supporters to challenge sooner or later the government which they had helped to establish.
> —Peter Amann, "Revolution: A Redefinition"

TWO DAYS BEFORE THE REVOLUTION'S SECOND ANNIVERSARY, hundreds of Ahli Ultras staged a warning to the government by paralyzing downtown Cairo. Authorities had announced a possible delay in the trial verdict on the Port Said stadium disaster of February 2012, when seventy-four Ahli fans were murdered in brawls with Masri team fans. The Ahli Ultras surrounded the Stock Exchange building, then marched on the tracks of the underground metro to the Tahrir Square station, leaving packed train cars stranded in the tunnels for an hour. Exiting the station, they moved to the Mugamma' complex where they blocked clerks from entering or exiting, then stopped traffic on the October 6th overpass nearby. The Ultras' show of force was a message that they would brook no delay in the scheduled January 26 verdict.[1]

The revolution's second anniversary on January 25, 2013, was a different affair from the first anniversary. In Bani Suef, Ahli Ultras and partisans of the new opposition National Salvation Front (NSF), formed just one month prior, blocked train tracks and denounced the government's betrayal of the revolution, chanting the master slogan of 2011, "al-Sha'b Yurid Isqat al-Nizam!" (The people want to bring down the regime!). In Ismailiyya, hundreds stormed the provincial government headquarters and set a fire inside. In Damanhour, crowds broke into two branch offices of the Muslim Brothers, tore up awnings, and threw the building's contents onto the street. In Cairo, former presidential contender Hamdeen Sabahy, Mohamed ElBaradei, and other opposition leaders fronted a procession from Mostafa Mahmoud Square to Tahrir as the crowd behind them chanted for the downfall of the Muslim Brothers' rule, seen as the real power behind the throne of President Mohamed Morsi: "Yasqut Yasqut Hukm al-Murshid!" (Down, down with the General Guide's rule!). Khaled Ali, the youngest former presidential contender, led the procession coming from Imbaba, calling for the downfall of the government because of its policies that hurt the poor, as had those of the Mubarak regime. Near Tahrir, at the Maspero radio and television headquarters, protesters cut through the barbed wire and began throwing stones and tearing surveillance cameras off the building. A new group of black-masked young men calling themselves the Revolutionary Black Bloc vowed a "revolutionary escalation" against President Morsi's government, vowing to lay siege to vital institutions. A forty-two-year-old female journalist in Tahrir sensed danger in the square and prepared to leave but was quickly encircled by a mob of men, disrobed, and sexually attacked for forty-five minutes. At least nineteen other cases of group sexual assaults occurred that day.[2]

In Port Said, the families of the men on trial for the soccer disaster camped out by the prison where they were incarcerated, putting up banners imploring the court convening in Cairo not to submit to the pressures of the Ahli Ultras. On January 26, as soon as the judge's verdict was broadcast live on state television, sentencing twenty-one men to death, the Port Said families and local Masri team Ultras moved to storm the jail. Other residents tried to storm the governor's office, police stations, the power station, and the main court building, cutting off all access to the city. Police fired tear gas, rubber bullets, and live rounds, leading to thirty-one deaths and 322 injuries. As the government lost control of Port Said, President Morsi cancelled a foreign trip and met for the first time with the National Defense Council, a new body of senior military leaders and cabinet ministers. Military forces were then deployed in Port Said and Suez where the protests had spread; Amnesty International noted that, two years into the revolution, Suez was again the site of police killings of protesters, with no one held accountable.[3]

As a large funeral cortege processed down the streets of Port Said on January 27, unknown assailants opened fire, killing five and injuring 536. In a finger-wagging speech on state television later that evening, President Morsi announced a month-long state of emergency and imposed a curfew in Suez, Port Said, and Ismailiyya, warning, "This cannot be but the ugly face of the counterrevolution." He extended a formal invitation to fifteen party leaders to deliberate with him on a path out of the crisis. Morsi's most vocal opponents in the National Salvation Front refused to attend, demanding that the president first acknowledge political responsibility for the deaths of citizens by police violence. In Port Said, years of built-up grievances against a remote Cairene authority framed the court verdict as yet another indignity. "They wanted to please Cairo and the people there, so they decided this verdict at the expense of Port Said," said a thirty-two-year-old street vendor whose brother was killed by a police bullet on January 26.[4] A twenty-four-year-old man expressed his anger in autonomist terms. "We'll declare Port Said a separate state and we'll only have relations with Ismailiyya."[5]

### MOHAMED MORSI MUBARAK

For the second time in just under a year, the Port Said soccer disaster was thrust into the center of national politics. Six months into his presidency, as he reckoned with his declining political capital, Mohamed Morsi found himself bearing sole political responsibility for the country's worst stadium disaster. From the beginning, the catastrophic brawl between two teams pointed to police collusion, and now police violence ramified the issue into a regional insurrection, carrying canal cities' long-standing resentments toward Cairo into the center of the revolution's politics. The precarious president, himself the object of police negligence in December 2012, inherited the same problem that the generals had faced one year earlier and that had felled Mubarak one year before that: an unreformed police force's unleashing of violence against civilians. Other forms of political violence that were in part by-products of police inaction—the new nonpeaceful protest tactics, mob attacks in Tahrir, factional street fighting between the president's partisans and his opponents—created a dangerous coup climate that reactivated the military into politics and eventually led them to oust Morsi 368 days after he took office.

This chapter reconstructs Mohamed Morsi's crisis-filled one-year presidency, focusing on how the first civilian president struggled to build governing authority amid mounting problems. There was the destabilizing effect of political violence; a new opposition alliance against the president bringing together losing presidential candidates and Mubarak regime personalities; increasingly vocal threats by the military generals; and the second round of constitution-writing that exploded into controversy, landing on Morsi's doorstep. The president's energetic diplomacy, negotiating a loan with the IMF, drumming up new foreign investment sources, and reorienting Egypt's foreign policy away from the Mubarak regime's line antagonized both his political opponents and the military generals observing menacingly from the sidelines. Unlike the widespread view that lands the blame on Morsi for his aborted tenure, my account places his year in office in a wider context, that of first-time elected civilian chief executives facing hostile entrenched interests. This is not to downplay the June 30, 2013, mass demonstrations calling on Morsi to leave office but to see them together with the resistance by the bureaucracy and courts. Morsi was ousted by a popularly supported military coup not because he brought it on himself but because of the unpredictable interaction of several wills and agencies, including Morsi's. Recovering the main lineaments of those interactions is the task of this chapter.

Alternative explanations propound the view that the president was to blame for his fate. Invariably, they pinpoint a specific decision as "the beginning of the end for the MB": a November 22 emergency decree Morsi issued immunizing presidential decrees and the constitution-writing body from annulment by court order, as parliament had been dissolved in June 2012. In the words of two analysts, the decree marked "the twilight of a presidency."[6] Similarly, Jason Brownlee, Tarek Masoud, and Andrew Reynolds classified Morsi's action as a case of "executive overreach," rightly centering attention on the conflict between state institutions within which Morsi was operating.[7] But in borrowing a label from American politics' interbranch conflicts denoting a president's unambiguous violation of the separation of powers, they skirt the difficult question for turbulent situations such as Egypt's: how much power did the first elected civilian president actually exercise, given the military's dominant presence and the courts' reversal of electorally constituted institutions such as parliament and the Constituent Assembly?

Other analysts shift focus from notions of abuse of power to choice of political strategy. Patrick Haenni argues that "the Brotherhood's basic problem was not its authoritarianism, but the fact of having placed all its bets on governance and not enough on the political process. . . . It believed that politics boiled down to a big fight against state bureaucracy. Despite its pragmatism, it oddly underestimated classic party politics."[8] In the same vein but reaching the opposite conclusion, Daniela Pioppi finds that the MB's cautious measures emboldened vested state interests to strike back. "The MB-FJP did not try (at least not in the short time it had) to purge or alter radically the balance of power inside state institutions and administrations, especially if compared to other post-revolutionary national cases. What the Brothers were doing instead was trying to find a *modus vivendi* with former regime representatives, flanking them with their own people when possible."[9]

That the scholars arrive at contradictory conclusions is par for the course for such turbulent and contested events. But all of the postmortems share an explanatory approach: they reach back for a single critical decision or strategy that is then projected forward in a straight line, with Morsi's removal as the endpoint. Instances from other times and places of newly elected executives deposed from office should give us pause. There is Venezuela's first democratically elected president, Rómulo Gallegos, who was in office for nine months in 1948 before being threatened and then removed by a military coup. In 1953, the experienced politician and former minister Mohammad Mossadegh was the prime minister of Iran for one-and-a-half years when he was deposed by an American-British–orchestrated coup. And Salvador Allende, the Western Hemisphere's first elected Marxist head of state, was in office for three of his constitutionally mandated six years until his ouster in September 1973 by a US-backed military putsch.[10] We need not jump to a law-like determination that all first-time elected outsiders are destined to be overthrown. Instead, this chapter argues that Egypt's first elected president faced a common situation that cannot be reduced to an individual disposition or decisive fatal mistake. It reconstructs the main features of the hazardous situation that Mohamed Morsi faced, where both the scope of his authority and his room to govern were obstructed at every turn by powerful state actors ready and willing to block him: the courts, the military, and the bureaucracy, especially its police, diplomatic, and judicial enclaves.

At the same time, by virtue of being the first democratically chosen national leader after a popular uprising, the new president faced extraordinary demands for immediate and total change, from raising stagnant wages to fixing shoddy municipal services to ending institutionalized police brutality. Months after he assumed office, and well before the November 22 decree, Morsi faced a wave of public disillusion; Tahrir Square protesters hung up posters fusing Morsi's and Mubarak's visage with the caption, "Mohamed Morsi Mubarak." This angry sentiment of "meet the new boss, same as the old boss" was twined with the contradictory yet equally livid slogan that titles this chapter. A range of the president's opponents claimed that while Morsi may have been the official president, real executive power lay elsewhere, in the inner sanctum of his parent political organization, the Muslim Brothers. Morsi was cast as a dopey front for the MB's leader, the General Guide (*al-Murshid al-'Amm*).[11] As historian Peter Amann reminds us, this is no accident. New representative governments created in the wake of popular uprisings may command immediate loyalty, but "loyalty freely given may be freely withdrawn."[12] The basic fact of the Morsi presidency is that it was part and parcel of a revolutionary situation, not a new phase of normalized democratic politics.

### PLEASE WELCOME OUR NEW DEMOCRATICALLY ELECTED PRESIDENT

On assuming office on June 30, 2012, Morsi's situation looked to be as Daniel's in the lions' den. A public weary of sixteen months of economic instability and political turmoil impatiently awaited quick results; in a poll taken in the lead-up to the presidential election, respondents ranked job creation, wage increases, and improvement in the security situation to be their top three priorities.[13] Morsi faced downgraded public support after the FJP's bungling of the Constituent Assembly composition, the conflict we saw in the previous chapter. The same poll data found a 24 percent drop in support for the FJP, from a high of 67 percent in February 2012 to 43 percent by April.[14] Yet the new president's powers were abridged before he set foot in the presidential palace by the generals' June 17 edict that reserved some executive powers for themselves, without oversight. Nor was the battle with the military over sovereignty Morsi's only significant political hurdle. There was the civilian politico-intellectual class whose luminaries gave their votes to Ahmed Shafiq or abstained from voting altogether out of ideological hostility or distaste for Morsi and the Muslim Brothers. The many Copts, women, trade unionists, heads of clans, and Sufi orders who had also voted for Shafiq had diverse reasons for dreading an Islamist president, converging on a master fear that Islamists in power would overturn their settled modes of belief and practice.

The extent to which powerful elites in the ministerial bureaucracy would obey an elected Islamist president was unknown. For a half century, ministers and deputy ministers, police officers, intelligence professionals, and diplomats had built their professional esprit de corps on the exclusion of Islamists, and it was a mystery how they would deal with the first elected civilian chief executive who also happened to be an Islamist. Furthermore, the bad blood between judges and Islamists that had developed over the first half of 2012 caused many judges to look askance at the new president before he took a single decision. No less vexed was Morsi's most intimate political relationship. From the moment of his forwarding as the Muslim Brothers' backup candidate in April, MB critics smeared him as *El-Stebn* (the spare), a stand-in for the MB's "real" chief, Khairat al-Shater, a label Morsi could never quite shrug off. Seen together, these

FIGURE 9. Morten Morland cartoon, *The Times (London)*, June 25, 2012. Reprinted with permission.

challenges led to a common understanding at home and abroad that Morsi was a transient "president without power."[15] A cutting cartoon by the Norwegian political cartoonist Morten Morland depicted beefy generals sitting on ornate gilded armchairs, whisking out a rickety folding chair and placing it in their midst as one of them announces, "Please welcome our new democratically elected president..."

Before contemplating specific policies or a broad agenda, Morsi's first brief was to establish that he was a real *and* democratic president, a move that required symbolic as well as concrete actions. His first acts sought to reassure his clamorous constituencies, alternately projecting accessibility, accountability, and responsible statesmanship. Gestures of accessibility were necessary to signal an end to the tradition of a remote, heavily fortified presidential apparatus. While he did not quite fling open the doors of the presidential palace to the masses, Morsi ordered security officials not to interfere with citizens congregating outside the building seeking aid and redress. On July 7, borrowing an institution common in Saudi Arabia and other Gulf states, Morsi decreed a Board of Grievances (*Diwan al-Mazalim*) that received more than three thousand petitions on its first day, though the dispensation of petitions left much to be desired.[16] Inside the palace, he received a stream of delegations of social worthies, assuring church officials, university professors, and journalists that their concerns had his ear. He decreed modest increases in the bonuses and pensions of civil servants and public sector workers as well as debt write-offs for small farmers. To signal his commitment to the new concept of presidential accountability, just before the runoff vote candidate Morsi borrowed the American presidential tradition of projecting his first hundred days in office, promising to deliver on the five chronic problem areas of security, traffic congestion, fuel and bread shortages, and sanitation. After his swearing-in, activists immediately designed a website, the "Morsi Meter," to track the president's progress.[17]

Projecting capable statesmanship was crucial for the first Arab Islamist head of state governing a country deeply reliant on international financial aid and tourism revenues. To signal continuity in Egypt's foreign policy despite being under new management, Morsi chose Saudi Arabia as his first foreign trip as head of state. Saudi investors were a major cash stream for Egypt; after Mubarak's fall, the Saudi monarchy had pledged $2.7 billion to sustain Egypt's economy. But relations had reached a nadir in April 2012, when the Saudis closed their embassy in Cairo and recalled the ambassador after weeklong protests against the jailing of an Egyptian rights lawyer in the kingdom. Morsi sought to reassure the Saudis of his administration's pragmatism, prioritizing bilateral economic and security ties over the maltreatment of Egyptian guest workers in Saudi Arabia. Repairing relations was also the agenda for Morsi's next foreign trip, to the African Union Summit in Addis Ababa, the first time in over a decade that an Egyptian head of state had attended in person. Morsi sought to manage a tense dispute between the nine Nile Basin countries over their respective shares of the river's waters. While in Addis Ababa, the president attended to an individual matter of larger import. A twenty-five-year-old Egyptian journalist had been arrested in Sudan while covering street protests against incumbent president Omar al Bashir; protesters and human rights groups in Cairo called on Morsi to intervene. A few hours after Morsi's meeting with Bashir, Shaimaa Adel was released and taken to Addis Ababa where she flew back to Cairo on the president's plane.[18]

## A MASTERSTROKE

Well before installing his new cabinet, Morsi demonstrated that he had no intention of being a figurehead president. On the ninth day in office, July 8, he issued Presidential Decree 11/2012 overruling SCAF's executive decision disbanding parliament after the June 14 SCC ruling. The decree called the legislature back into session until the completion of the constitution, after which new general elections would be held within sixty days. In effect, Morsi struck down SCAF's seizure of legislative powers in their June 17 addendum, vesting it back in parliament. Reactions cascaded swiftly. While the generals issued a calm statement urging "all state authorities to respect the constitutional addendum," various judicial bodies (including the SCC, the Judges Club, and the bar association) signed a statement giving the president thirty-six hours to reverse his decision. The next day, in the most forgotten fifteen minutes of the revolution's politics, parliament heeded the president's decision and met briefly to deliberate on how to implement the SCC's ruling dissolving it. After posting armed guards to the building for weeks, SCAF now did nothing to prevent the lawmakers from entering the chambers, but many non-Islamist deputies boycotted the session in support of the legislature's dissolution, even though it cost them their own seats. Before adjourning for good, the FJP and Salafi deputies resolved to appeal the SCC's dissolution decision before a different apex court, the Court of

Cassation. Incensed again, the SCC rebuked both president and parliament later that evening, insisting that the latter remain shuttered and threatening the president with contempt of court if he continued to defy its decisions. The next day, the president's office issued a statement affirming his commitment to judicial verdicts, and "the need to prevent collision" between state authorities.[19]

In this chain of events, legal hairsplitting and a raw contest over power are inseparable. Morsi's decree was a direct challenge to the generals' peremptory closure of parliament and seizure of legislative power. In a double maneuver, he challenged the generals' decree while asserting the legislature's authority to self-determine how best to implement the SCC ruling. But because SCAF had justified its action in terms of simply executing the SCC ruling, it was inevitable for the SCC to view Morsi as defying that ruling, and for other anti-Islamist judges to attack the new president in the lofty terms of upholding the rule of law. The synthesis of the legal and the political caused intense confusion. Some erstwhile critics praised Morsi's action as both politically and legally sound. Lauding it as a "masterstroke,"[20] rights lawyer Gamal Eid argued that "it abolishes an executive order, and it is not related to the constitutional court. It negates the decision of the military council."[21]

Opponents made three distinct claims about Morsi's move. First was that it was a power grab, as asserted by think-tank expert Amr Hashem Rabi'. "President Morsi reinstated the parliament because his Muslim Brotherhood Party had a majority there, and because he wanted to use that majority to issue legislation that would allow him to control the state."[22] Second was that Morsi was a proxy for the US, as told by Rabi's colleague Diaa Rashwan. "The decree came hours after his meeting with [US Assistant Secretary of State William] Burns on 8 July. It was intended to send a message to the military and other authorities, warning them that the Americans want him to assume full powers and that they are ready to protect him to achieve this objective."[23] Third was that Morsi was a tortured proxy not of the US but of his parent organization, as Social Democratic Party lawmaker Emad Gad opined. "Most of his advisors are Brotherhood cadres. They have no experience of governing, and they have dragged him into damaging battles with the judiciary and with the press."[24] The same three contradictory claims would tail Morsi throughout his time in office, that he was at one and the same time a bit pawn of much bigger players and a cunning Machiavellian plotting domination over the whole state. What was at issue in all three views was not opposition to specific policies or proposals but Morsi's exercise of presidential power. Opponents focused not on what he did but whether he had the *right* to do what he did. The crisis was defused by lawmakers' decision not to convene again, but its other lasting legacy was permanent: a combustible conflict between the new president and judges across Egypt's diverse courts.

Percolating in the background was intense speculation over the composition of the new cabinet, as news circulated of respected non-Islamists declining to work with the new president.[25] On August 2 the government was sworn in with Hisham Qandil as premier, a little-known American-educated technocrat and irrigation minister in the outgoing SCAF-appointed caretaker government. Continuity prevailed in nine other portfolios, including the so-called sovereign ministries of defense, interior, finance, and foreign relations, where Morsi retained SCAF chief Mohamed Hussein Tantawi as defense minister as had been expected. Among the holdovers was the sole Copt, Nadia Zachary in the Ministry of Scientific Research. To the dismay of human rights professionals and revolution activists pushing for police reform, Morsi selected a Mubarak regime stalwart as interior minister; Ahmed Gamal Eddin had been security chief in Asyut during the eighteen-day revolt, where he zealously swept the streets clean of protesters on the second day.[26] The president's FJP took only five out of thirty-five portfolios (information, housing, higher education, youth, and labor), but the most change-oriented choice was in the Ministry of Justice with the appointment of Ahmed Mekky, dean of the dissident judges who had challenged the Mubarak regime in 2005 and 2006.

The prevalence of bureaucratic insiders reflected the outsider president's realism; he feared antagonizing the apparatus that he needed to implement governance goals. But it left him open to charges of betraying the revolution. Pursuing a logic of administrative continuity rather than the calculus of political coalition, Morsi conciliated powerful state actors leery of an Islamist president at the cost of alienating the political allies who made his win possible.[27] Sure enough, immediately after the announcement of the insiders' cabinet, several respected public figures who had lent candidate Morsi their support at the Fairmont Meeting in exchange for a pledge to appoint a national unity government publicly withdrew their backing of the president.[28]

Signaling the inclusion and change missing from the cabinet was left to the president's advising team. Four senior policy advisers were chosen, both for their bona fides and to appease important constituencies. Political scientist Pakinam al-Sharqawy, Coptic intellectual Samir Morqos, Salafi Nur Party chairman Emad Abdel Ghaffour, and prominent MB entrepreneur Essam al-Haddad were given the briefs of domestic policy, democratic transition, social outreach, and foreign relations, respectively. Seventeen additional intellectuals, journalists, and politicians were retained as an informal advisory group, though a hypervigilant press corps hastened to point out that eleven of the twenty-one total advisers were Islamists.[29]

## COMPLETE RESPONSIBILITY

On the evening of August 5, just as they were sitting down to break their Ramadan fast, sixteen Egyptian border guards in North Sinai were killed by militant gunmen, who then tried to storm the border with Israel before being killed by Israeli airstrikes. To hunt down the attackers and live down the debacle, the Egyptian army launched its largest operation since the 1973 war. The president seized the opening. Three days after the attacks, Morsi fired the chief of intelligence, the North Sinai governor, and the chief of the presidential guard for security lapses that prevented the president from attending the state funeral for the soldiers. On August 12, he ordered SCAF's two senior leaders into retirement, moved three other top generals into government sinecures, and promoted the youngest generals. Abdel Fattah al-Sisi succeeded Mohamed Tantawi as defense minister and Sidqi Sobhi took over from Sami Anan as army chief of staff, replacing the two men who had led Egypt since Mubarak's fall. The reshuffle was a negotiated agreement with both the departing and rising generals, but its timing was wholly unexpected.[30] Even the most optimistic observers had expected that SCAF's disengagement from politics would take years. The emboldened president did not stop at asserting his supreme command over the armed forces but also annulled the generals' June 17 edict, wresting back the legislative power they had seized upon parliament's dissolution and transferring to himself the authority to reconstitute the Constituent Assembly should it fail to complete its task. Finally, though it was overshadowed by the reshuffling of the military high command, the president also named his vice president on August 12, selecting

Mahmoud Mekky for the post, another dissident judge from the Mubarak era and the younger brother of the new justice minister.

Six weeks into his tenure, it appeared that Morsi had turned the poisoned chalice of a hamstrung civilian presidency into a post with real power, turning the tables on the generals and reclaiming the full scope of executive authority. The dual civilian-military executive that seemed to be the new post-Mubarak political settlement after Morsi's election had suddenly given way to unabridged civilian leadership that had boldly terminated the political role of the military council and restructured its personnel. The decision was hailed by Morsi's partisans, supporters, and segments of international media as a decisive win for an infant democracy; a British commentator lauded it as a signal political maneuver.[31] The April 6th youth group applauded it as "the first step towards establishing a civilian state," and MB members massed in Tahrir Squares around the country and chanted "President of the republic, your decree gets 100 percent!"[32] But the president's opponents in the political class, media, and judicial corps focused not on the assertion of civilian control but on the president's holding of both executive and judicial power. Leftist intellectual and newspaper editor Salah Eissa warned, "Now with the army out of the political scene, secular forces—including political activists and judges—must prepare themselves for a battle against Egypt's first Islamist pharaoh."[33]

Acutely attuned to just such an opposition mobilization, Morsi held a series of meetings with politicians and judges in the days after his decision to reassure them that his use of decree powers would be sparing, and that he would not seek to control the Constituent Assembly.[34] Ironically, the unexpected exit of the generals isolated the president rather than rallying more civilian groups to his side at the realization of a consensus revolutionary goal. Having neutralized the military and recovered his full powers, the president now faced not only a fearful anti-Islamist opposition but unabridged political responsibility. Former MP Ziad al-Ulaimy, one of the most vociferous critics of the FJP in the short-lived parliament, supported Morsi's sweep of the generals but spelled out the implications of eliminating the diarchy. "Just as we have welcomed his decree, we have the right to assign him and his organization complete responsibility for any failure in the coming period."[35]

Morsi marked his hundred days in office with a triumphal rally in Cairo Stadium packed with his supporters. By that point, he had completed a busy diplomatic itinerary to message a vigorous new independence in Egyptian foreign policy. After the Saudi Arabia and Sudan trips, Morsi had traveled to China seeking investment; the European Union in search of loans; Iran for the Non-Aligned Summit, the first visit by an Egyptian head of state since the 1979 Iranian revolution; Turkey for economic and moral support from a friendly Islamist government; and the UN General Assembly in New York, where he delivered a well-received address projecting a new leadership role for Egypt on sovereign Palestinian statehood and regime change in Syria. At Day 97, the Morsi Meter had counted only four out of sixty-four promises delivered and twenty-three in progress, but Egypt's leading private polling firm put the president's approval rating at 78 percent. Pollsters theorized that it was the president's effective foreign policy overtures that won him high marks, even from Ahmed Shafiq voters. Among eligible voters who had not turned out, 73 percent approved of the president.[36] A month later, Morsi made the cover of *Time* with the headline, "The Most Important Man in the Middle East."[37]

## CONSTITUTION-WRITING IN THE OPEN SEA

When the first Constituent Assembly (CA) was invalidated by court order on April 10, secular groupings hailed the ruling as a vindication of their point that Islamists sought to dominate constitution-making. Two months of intense negotiations followed to hammer out a more inclusive seat distribution for a reconstituted CA. On June 12, two days before its own dissolution by a Supreme Constitutional Court ruling, parliament elected a new body according to the new formula. The new composition dropped the share of political Islamists from 64 to 39 percent and seated more representatives of groups defined along corporatist lines (labor, youth, state bodies, constitutional law experts). At 7 percent, the presence of women remained minuscule. Table 6 shows the membership distribution of this second CA, which went on to draft the constitution.

Despite the reduced presence of Islamists and the eighty-three new faces compared to the first CA, secular politicians cried foul, accusing the Muslim Brothers of surreptitiously packing the assembly with supporters, if not official members.[38] The new body's elected head, Judge Hossam al-Ghiryani, a leader of the 2006 dissident judges, was compelled to publicly affirm that he was not an Islamist. Far from starting with a clean slate then, delegates carried over into the chamber the enmities and mutual suspicion that had ripened

TABLE 6. Composition of the 2012 Constituent Assembly.

| Faction | Number of Seats |
| --- | --- |
| Muslim Brothers | 20 |
| Nur Party | 11 |
| State Organs | 10 |
| Writers and Intellectuals | 10 |
| Azhar (and other Islamic religious institutions) | 8 |
| Wafd Party | 8 |
| Women* | 7 |
| Professional Associations | 7 |
| Islamist Wasat Party | 4 |
| Other Islamists | 4 |
| Churches | 4 |
| Coptic Politicians and Public Figures | 4 |
| Labor and Farmers' Groups | 4 |
| Revolution Youth Groups | 3 |

Source: Calculated from the list of names in "Ha'ula' Yaktubun Dustur Misr al-Thawra," al-Shurouq, June 14, 2012, 5.
*Three of the seven women drafters were members of the MB.

since the first iteration of the CA in spring. The new national political context did not help: an Islamist president who had recovered full executive powers from the military further widened the distance between Islamist delegates and their critics, who were now certain that the constitution would be a winner's document. Constitution-writing unavoidably became an expression of much larger political conflicts unfolding under intense time pressure. Drafters had six months to complete their work, with a due date of December 12.[39] If Jon Elster has characterized post-Communist constitution-making in Eastern Europe as rebuilding a boat in the open sea with no new timber,[40] we may liken Egypt's process to rebuilding in the open sea, with immovable ideological baggage that threatened to capsize the rickety vessel at any moment.

The CA was divided into five committees based on the sections of the 1971 text.[41] A handful of religion-centered clauses generated intense controversy in the committee drafting the constitution's first chapter, "Foundations of State and Society." Salafis pushed aggressively for revising article 2 from the 1971 constitution to omit its first two words: "Principles of Islamic Sharia are the Principal Source of Legislation," rendering specific *rulings* of shari'a as the fountainhead of legislation rather than the looser "principles." While they did not prevail and article 2 remained intact, as secular and Muslim Brother delegates favored, Salafis did get a new article placed further down in the text (art. 219), spelling out what the principles of shari'a are.[42] The new article 4 constitutionalized the status of al-Azhar, granting it consultation on all shari'a-related matters. Some secular drafters were leery of granting one state body ultimate authority over interpretation; Wahid Abdel Meguid, the assembly's spokesman and a prominent liberal, wrote that he feared a Sunni version of Iran's Guardian Council.[43] But other secular figures welcomed al-Azhar's role, preferring a friendly state institution's mediation to leaving the field open to lay Islamist preachers.[44] The state's guarantee of freedom of belief (art. 43) was restricted to the Abrahamic religions, opening the door to the denial of rights to Egypt's Baha'is, while the new article 44 prohibited insult and abuse of prophets.

Contemporaneous and subsequent accounts of constitution-drafting give the impression that the Islamist-secular divide was the only cleavage that mattered. However, drafters across the four committees jostled and bargained their way through a farrago of controversies that did not neatly align along an Islamist-secular axis. Consider this minimal list: Should new presidential elections be held after constitutional ratification? Morsi's opponents outside the assembly strenuously argued yes, while all but one member of the System of Government committee voted no.[45] Should libel be constitutionalized? Both secularists and Islamists favored this innovation; the president's outraged supporters wanted consequences for the repeated attacks on Morsi in the hostile liberal media, as did intellectuals and actors subject to constant attacks in Salafi media outlets; the outcome was article 31.[46] What should be the constitutional status of the armed forces? SCAF's two representatives lobbied successfully for two new articles: article 198 permitted military trials of civilians "for crimes that harm the Armed Forces," and article 197 established a joint civilian-military eighteen-member National Defense Council with authority over the military budget, military-related bills, and a consultative role in war-making and sending troops abroad. What should municipal governance look like? Some held fast to electing governors as the only effective means of democratic devolution, while others favored electing municipal councils to hold presidentially appointed governors to account. In the end, local councils were empowered to be "watchdog mini-parliaments"[47] with budgetary control and other prerogatives (arts. 190–92). Remarkably, one issue around which there emerged consensus was the shape of the political system. The System of Government committee, led by two non-Islamist constitutional law professors, drew up a semipresidential design highly influenced by the French Fifth Republic.[48] To break with Egypt's history of superpresidentialism while avoiding the paralysis of pure parliamentarism, executive power would be shared between a popularly elected president, who directs foreign policy and has significant domestic policymaking powers, and a prime minister designated by the president and drawn from the parliamentary majority.[49]

As delegates worked their way through these and dozens more issues, pressures from outside the deliberation chambers buffeted them from multiple directions. Powerful state interests lobbied to preserve or augment their status in the constitution, often demanding specific wording of articles and dictating where they ought to be placed in the text. Administrative court judges sent a laudatory letter to the assembly, endorsing the draft clause setting strict limits on judicial secondment to ministries, a mechanism widely used during the Mubarak regime to cultivate loyalist judges. Angry prosecutors held a four-day nationwide strike, hundreds of them massing in serried ranks outside the assembly's headquarters to protest what they feared was a downgraded status in the constitutional draft. Supreme Constitutional Court judges held a press conference to announce that they would be in permanent session until the relevant constitutional articles were amended to their satisfaction. Government auditors convened an emergency general assembly to demand constitutional wording that would empower them to be real anticorruption watchdogs.[50]

Civil society interests, already mobilized by revolution, also trained their sights on the CA. Two hundred secular intellectuals gathered in front of the assembly's headquarters to demand a "civil constitution," the word civil (*madaniyya*) having come to signify "nonreligious" in the lexicon of revolutionary politics. "We believe that public freedoms are currently threatened even more than they were during the old regime," said a prominent Nasserist journalist at the protest. Independent feminists coordinated with state feminists in the Mubarak-era National Council for Women along with irate prosecutors in a conference to decry women's 7 percent representation on the CA and the rollback of women's rights in the draft.[51] Two consecutive Friday Tahrir milyuniyyas in mid-October, timed to coincide with the end of Morsi's first hundred days, improvised a new slogan: "Bread! Freedom! The downfall of the CA!" ('Aysh!

Huriyya! Isqat al-Ta'sisiyya!). At the Friday rally of October 12, opponents and supporters of the president clashed violently in Tahrir, marking the first time since Mubarak's fall that rival factions of civilians exchanged blows and pelted one another with rocks. The CA's deliberations also drew international scrutiny. Human Rights Watch sent a letter to the drafters urging them to amend articles that conflicted with Egypt's obligations under international human rights treaties. And a prominent American columnist cast the constitution-writing process in apocalyptic terms, "If Egypt under the Muslim Brotherhood is the world's most important experiment in how Islam and democratic modernity can be reconciled, then the country's Constitution, now in its last phase of drafting, is the crux of that test."[52]

The international attention and domestic protests were sparked by one high-profile resignation from within the CA's ranks. Human rights activist Manal al-Tibi, one of the four non-Islamist women on the assembly, resigned in September, concluding, "It is very clear that the constitution is being drafted to serve the interests of people keen on creating a religious state and maintaining power."[53] Tibi's exit became the focal point around which scattered fears, animosities, and partisan interests fused into a groundswell of opposition to the CA and the Islamists perceived to control it. Former presidential contender Hamdeen Sabahy and opposition leader Mohamed ElBaradei escalated the anti-CA agitation they had begun in summer, calling on all the secular drafters to resign. Anxious that the CA would implode just as it was nearing a complete draft, the president stepped in to mediate. Over three consecutive days in November, he met one-on-one with Sabahy, ElBaradei, and former presidential contender Amr Moussa, a CA member and leader of the group in the assembly threatening a collective walkout. Morsi also sounded out a broad range of NGO and Tahrir activists, and their key demands were a less controversial constitutional text and an extension of the December 12 deadline hovering over the CA.[54]

An international crisis suddenly shifted the president's attention. Israel had embarked on a new bombing campaign of Gaza and Morsi stepped in to personally mediate. At the same time, the internal tensions of the assembly exploded to the surface. On November 18, Amr Moussa, the four representatives of Egyptian churches, erstwhile CA spokesman Wahid Abdel Meguid, and nine other non-Islamists announced their withdrawal from the assembly, decrying the "cooking" (*salq*) of the constitution.[55] The next day, Islamist and non-Islamist members of the CA held a press conference to defend the assembly's integrity and accuse their critics of bad faith. Islamist Wasat Party chairman Abul Ela Madi distributed to the press a copy of a signed collective agreement drawn up by the withdrawers and the Islamist drafters pledging to resolve the twelve most contentious constitutional articles by consensus rather than vote, and to omit altogether the highly divisive draft article 68 on equality of the sexes.[56] The president intervened again, this time in writing. On November 22, his spokesman read out a seven-point new "Constitutional Declaration" introduced by a boldly worded preamble designating the president as the protector of the January 25 revolution, tasked with "confronting with utmost power and firmness the figures of the old regime and establishing a new legitimacy, crowned with a constitution that lays the foundations for good governance." To that end, the decree resolved to:

1. Order retrials of old regime figures implicated in the killing and injury of revolutionaries.
2. Shield the president's constitutional declarations, laws, and decrees from review by any judicial body until the constitution goes into effect and a parliament is elected. All lawsuits contesting presidential actions in any court were annulled.
3. Appoint a new Prosecutor-General by the president from among members of the judiciary for a four-year term, effective immediately.
4. Extend the deadline for the Constituent Assembly by two months to February 12, 2013.
5. Prevent any judicial body from dissolving the Shura Council (upper house of parliament) or the Constituent Assembly.
6. Empower the president to take any measures to prevent dangers to the January 25th revolution or national unity, as organized by law.
7. The declaration would go into effect immediately.[57]

The omnibus decree bundled several distinct, smoldering problems that had piled up since the end of Morsi's first hundred days. Articles 1 and 3 must be seen together as a response to a court ruling acquitting all twenty-four defendants in the infamous "Battle of the Camel," when pro-Mubarak armed men on horses and camels charged into Tahrir on February 2, 2011, to dislodge the Tahrir encampment. The acquittals brought back onto the national agenda the unreformed general prosecution and its bungling of cases for the trials of Mubarak party officials and policemen, leading to a spate of acquittals due to insufficient evidence. The decisions to remove the prosecutor-general and order retrials were responses to a major popular demand.[58] Article 4 was similarly a concession to the liberal and leftist activists Morsi had sounded out about their concerns on the constitution, slowing the clock to give constitution drafters more time to resolve their differences. Articles 2 and 5 were motivated by the fear that had gripped the government from Day 1 that the Supreme Constitutional Court would dissolve the two remaining elected bodies as they had dissolved the lower house of parliament on June 14, a fear nourished by the knowledge that the SCC was reviewing multiple lawsuits against both the CA and parliament's upper house, and had withdrawn its sole representative on the CA even before it had its first meeting.[59]

The decree was an odd amalgam of political intervention and emergency enabling act, authorizing the executive to suspend certain normal operations of government to counter a public danger. Normally, a constitution spells out the conditions under which the executive proposes and the legislature approves time-limited emergency measures. Here, Morsi was self-enabling to shield the constitution-in-process and parliament's upper house from being torpedoed by a court order, a reflection of the abnormal situation he found himself in, holding executive and legislative power because of a judicial decision that shuttered parliament's lower house and now seemed poised to do the same to the Constituent Assembly. However, rather than explain the predicament and build public support and understanding for the exceptional measures, Morsi's spokesman stiffly read out the decree-law on state television from behind a podium; then regular programming resumed, leaving the field open to others to construct its meaning.

**EGYPT'S NEW PHARAOH**

Minutes after the decree was broadcast, Mohamed ElBaradei dashed off a tweet: "Morsi today usurped all state powers and appointed himself Egypt's new pharaoh." Hours later, he was at a boisterous press conference of party leaders where a Nasserist politician angrily read out a manifesto that Morsi had fused legislative, executive, and judicial powers in his hands; ElBaradei, Moussa, and Sabahy raised their linked arms in a victory pose for the cameras. For the second time in 2012, Egyptian politics plunged into a fortnight of continuous public meetings, demonstrations and counterdemonstrations, emergency general assemblies, denunciations on opinion pages and late-night television talk shows, and a scramble by the administration to contain an outcry that it did not foresee. The day after the decree, crowds made a beeline for the Ittihadiyya presidential palace in East Cairo, chanting "Yasqut Yasqut Morsi Mubarak!" (Down, down with Morsi Mubarak!). FJP offices were ransacked in several provincial capitals and the Suez office was torched. In Damanhour, one protester was killed in three days of street battles between the president's partisans and opponents.[60] Judges across different courts and political positions closed ranks in institutional outrage; "executive authority is of a lower rank than judicial authority," sniffed an anti-Mubarak judge.[61] The Judges' Club once again became the locus of antiexecutive mobilization, helmed by Mubarak loyalist Ahmed El-Zend, who led the club's coordination of a general strike by judges and prosecutors. Then 158 diplomats submitted a letter of protest to the foreign minister, refusing to defend the president's decree abroad and imploring him to "maintain the neutral nationalist line of the Ministry and refrain from politicizing it."[62] Eight more drafters withdrew from the Constituent Assembly, bringing the total number to twenty-four departures. Rights groups lodged a petition challenging Morsi's act before the administrative courts, rubbishing it as "a collection of tyrannical orders." The April 6th youth movement abandoned the president, apologizing to the public for urging it to vote for him five months earlier.[63]

Disarray reigned inside Ittihadiyya. The president's seventeen-member advisory team gathered in an urgent meeting to discover that none of them had been consulted about the decree; two immediately announced their resignations, joined by one of the president's four assistants, Coptic intellectual Samir Morqos. The justice minister and his brother the vice president (both leaders of the judicial independence movement) shuttled behind the scenes to manage the uproar among their former colleagues. Morsi's legal advisor, administrative judge Muhamad Fu'ad Gadallah, who had helped draft the decree, insisted that the controversial article 2 was temporary, then impugned the motives of the opposition: "It seems that the forces who want to pounce on power, dreaming of holding new presidential elections after the constitution, want to dominate and impose their hegemony on the constitution and don't want any stability for this country."[64] The president's party members spoke of "a grand conspiracy" to oust Morsi to which the decree was a preemptive strike.⁶⁵ Since Tahrir was claimed by anti-Morsi crowds, the pro-Morsi gatherings filled the plaza outside Cairo University. It was one full week after his decree that Morsi gave an interview on state television, attempting to reframe the narrative on his emergency decree, characterizing it as "a delicate surgical procedure." Holding up a printout of the document, he told the two anchors pelting him with questions about presidential dictatorship, "I'm saying this is a very temporary decree until the Constituent Assembly completes the constitution, the people have their say, the matter returns to its rightful owners, and the president becomes the holder of only executive power."⁶⁶

Though the decree had given the Constituent Assembly two more months to complete its work, SCC judges announced that they were defying the president and reviewing the forty-five lawsuits against the CA on December 2 as planned. That led the CA to ignore the grant of extra time and begin final article-by-article voting on the draft, to head off the scuttling of all their work by the politicized court. With twenty-four alternate members filling in for those who had withdrawn, the CA voted on and passed all 234 articles of the draft in a seventeen-hour marathon session that ended on November 30.⁶⁷ The vote prompted international censure, with the UN High Commissioner for Human Rights urging Morsi to retract his decree and reorder the Constituent Assembly for "adequate representation of the full political spectrum."⁶⁸ Tahrir Square made the same demand, with Moussa, ElBaradei, Sabahy, and other party heads addressing the crowds and ruling out any negotiations until the decree's retraction. With the constitution now complete, another ticking clock took over: the fifteen days to put it to a public referendum. The government was intent on moving ahead with the poll on December 15; the opposition demanded a reconstituted assembly to replace what they called an "illegitimate and unrepresentative" body.

The geography of protests and counterprotests reflected the institutional standoff. The president's partisans gathered at the SCC courthouse to shout slogans against the judges on the day they were reviewing the lawsuits, prompting them to suspend their work in outrage at the intimidation. Two days later, anti-Morsi protesters gathered outside Ittihadiyya and set up tents for a sit-in, covering the palace walls with anti-Morsi graffiti. In the morning, the president's motorcade was greeted with chants of "Irhal! Irhal!" and "Yasqut Yasqut Hukm al-Murshid!" With protesters on the verge of storming the palace, the president was quickly ferried out of the building and to his home in New Cairo twelve miles away.[69] In what has come to be called the Ittihadiyya events, outraged partisans of the president descended on the palace on December 5, violently tore up the tents and pamphlets of the opposition, and a night of partisan fighting ensued, with combatants using rocks, birdshot, and firebombs, leading to ten deaths and hundreds of injuries.[70] Police officers said they had instructions from their minister not to intervene. The commander of the Presidential Guard, the division of the armed forces tasked with protecting the president, also admitted his own inaction, telling a reporter, "The armed forces, and the presidential guard at their head, will not be a tool to repress protestors." MB and FJP partisans set up a makeshift detention center where they beat and mistreated 49 anti-Morsi protesters, before handing them over to the local police station.[71]

A new round of intense conflict began, with a president abandoned by military and police yet responsible for the consequences of their inaction, and an emboldened opposition that successfully framed the conflict as a battle between dictatorship and democratic resistance. The opposition held a press conference to declare that Morsi was "leading the country into civil war and has lost the moral legitimacy to govern," as Nasserist leader Hamdeen Sabahy said.[72] Four more of Morsi's advisers publicly resigned in protest at the killings, and intellectual Rafiq Habib, the Muslim Brothers' most prominent Christian member, announced his withdrawal from politics and return to scholarship. Twenty-eight FJP offices were ransacked or torched countrywide, including the main Cairo headquarters. Hundreds of protesters massed outside Morsi's private residence in Sharqiyya, leading to violent clashes with police and twenty injuries.[73] At the Red Card milyuniyya on December 7, large crowds again gathered outside the palace, calling on Morsi to resign by presenting him with soccer red cards expelling him from the field of play, and spray-painting "Irhal!" on the palace walls. The medium of political exchange turned from partisan polemics to Manichaean vitriol. Opposition leaders branded themselves the National Salvation Front. A loudspeaker on the pro-Morsi side of the Ittihadiyya clashes exhorted, "This is not a fight for President Morsi, we are fighting for God's law against the secularists and liberals."[74]

Sixteen days after he had issued it, the president rescinded his decree but refused to call off the referendum or overhaul the constitution, prompting a liberal opposition leader to declare this "an act of war" against Egyptians.[75] At this point, the military moved from the sidelines to the center of the political arena, where it was to remain. At a white tablecloth banquet for top police and military generals, Defense Minister Abdel Fattah al-Sisi invited the president, prime minister, opposition leaders, judges, and activists to a mediation meeting the next day under his auspices. Then he clasped the interior minister's hand and raised it in a triumphal pose, both grinning and vowing that police and army were *'Id Wahda* (one hand).[76] Upon hearing of this, the presidency swiftly canceled the meeting. With the military short-circuited in its bid to play the arbiter, the two sides braced for a mutual test of strength in the referendum. The government banked on its superior voter mobilization capacity and conviction that the opposition did not encompass the country; "we will prove that the opposition is not the whole people," vowed an FJP official.[77] The opposition alternately called for a boycott and a "No" vote, confident that the political turmoil and discrediting of the president at home and abroad would depress turnout and further undermine his rule. Bolstering this perception was the continued disintegration of Morsi's team. His own vice president, Mahmoud Mekky, suddenly resigned on December 22, issuing a terse statement saying that his judicial temperament was unsuited to political work.[78]

The voters delivered an ambiguous verdict. Sixty-four percent approved the charter, a sizable and unexpected majority, enabling the government to claim endorsement of its firm stance and to move ahead with general elections in two months to finally restore the legislative power. But as the anti-Morsi camp was quick to highlight, only 33 percent of voters turned out, compared to the 41 percent in the March 2011 referendum, allowing the opposition to credibly claim that its negative campaign worked to produce the second-lowest turnout in the revolution's free polls.[79] What's more, in three provinces, the vote against the constitution exceeded the "Yes" vote. In Cairo, Menoufiyya, and Gharbiyya, respectively 57, 51, and 52 percent voted "No"; in Port Said, the constitution squeaked by with 51 to 49 percent. Such significant enclaves of resistance contradicted the FJP's claim that the opposition had no presence outside the capital. As he observed the political conflict, Palestinian intellectual Azmi Bishara, one of the most astute analysts of the Arab uprisings, had a pointed message for the Morsi government and the MB: "If I were them I'd be grateful about scraping through this test ... what they got isn't a constitutional majority but a partisan one. Again, I invite them to separate the two."[80]

As the revolution's second anniversary approached, a new bipolar alignment organized national politics. On one side stood the Morsi government and its shrunken pool of exhausted allies; on the other, an antigovernment, anti–Muslim Brother coalition of Morsi's rivals in the presidential race; principled anti-Islamists among both revolutionary groupings and the Mubarak state elite, especially judges; erstwhile constitution drafters embittered by their experience with the Islamists on the Constituent Assembly; media personalities hostile to the president from Day 1; and disenchanted voters who had cast a vote for Morsi not out of conviction but to prevent the presidency from falling into the hands of the Mubarak state. The glue binding this heterogeneous assemblage was a common conviction that Morsi was a stand-in for his parent organization's hunger for absolute power. The slogan "Yasqut Yasqut Hukm al-Murshid!" (Down, down with the General Guide's rule!) spewed hostility, to be sure, but it also expressed outrage at the unclear lines of authority between the president and his party. If the Egyptian revolution was a demand for clear lines of accountability between rulers and ruled, Morsi's partisan background undermined his claim to be answerable to all Egyptians. Egypt's first democratically elected civilian president was also the first party-based politician to attain the post, running up against the entrenched authoritarian tradition of antipartisan bureaucratic-military authority claiming to hover above divisive party politics.

## I HOLD MORSI RESPONSIBLE

The president began the new year resolved to focus on economic policy, securing international financing, and broadening domestic revenue sources. Negotiations over an impending $4.8 billion loan from the IMF had been delayed by the December turmoil, and the Ittihadiyya clashes had cost one million tourists during the New Year's high season.[81] A depreciation of the Egyptian pound to its lowest level since 2004 exacerbated energy and water price rises and augured similar hikes in food prices. The IMF loan was the necessary seal of approval for the government's economic reform program, itself dependent on ameliorating the public security deficit. A limited cabinet reshuffle on January 6 brought in ten new ministers, including three from the MB, increasing the total MB presence on the cabinet to eight out of thirty-seven ministers (21.6 percent). Attention focused on the interior, finance, and supply ministries as most relevant for the international loan. The supply minister was a young MB engineering professor tasked with restructuring food and fuel subsidies, but the new interior minister Mohamed Ibrahim was a consummate insider of the unreconstructed Mubarak police hierarchy, as was his predecessor. Instead of a return to security, however, the new minister and his policies spurred the wave of violence in Cairo and several provinces with which we began the chapter. By mid-February, the toll stood at sixty dead, 2,000 injured, 966 arrested, and forty-eight public and private buildings attacked.[82] To appreciate the political significance of this toll for the Morsi government, we must pause to untangle the distinct dynamics jumbled under the umbrella word "violence," beginning with the focal event.

The partisan clashes outside Ittihadiyya palace on December 5 were interpreted through partisan lenses. The president's supporters came away convinced that police inaction was part of a broader Mubarak state conspiracy to bring down Morsi, and that self-reliance was the only way to protect the president and FJP headquarters. The president's opponents saw the rise of dangerous "Ikhwan militias" acting as a government paramilitary force against any opposition demonstration, to hasten the Muslim Brothers' takeover of the country. On the revolution's second anniversary, a new actor stepped into the fray. The black-clothed, black-masked youths of the Revolutionary Black Bloc vowed to defend against police attacks on protesters and what they called the MB's "military wing." Borrowing the antiestablishment style and tactics of antiglobalization protesters in Seattle and Genoa, the Egyptian masked men did not disavow violence, claiming responsibility for the torching of several MB headquarters.[83] As the government was reckoning with this new development in protest dynamics, and the MB perceiving it as a new tentacle in the conspiracy against them, the new interior minister's get-tough approach antagonized not only established opposition, the Black Bloc, and the MB (for continuously failing to protect their offices), but domestic and international human rights groups, parliamentarians, media outlets, and ordinary citizens in the provinces for whom police brutality signified a double indignity: general degradation and abuse, and Cairo's imperiousness and neglect.

This all redounded to the president's discredit. Protest fatalities individually and in the aggregate were immediately pinned on Morsi. When a thirty-five-year-old Mansoura resident was crushed beneath an armored police truck, opposition NSF members traveled to the province to front a protest procession, chanting, "Yasqut yasqut Mohamed Morsi!" and "al-Shaʿb Yurid Isqat al-Nizam!"

(The people want to bring down the regime!). When media circulated a video of a forty-eight-year-old man being beaten, dragged, and disrobed by riot police near Ittihadiyya palace, activists tweeted "Morsi is divested of his legitimacy." The culture minister resigned in disgust. Mohamed ElBaradei demanded a new unity government, and Salafi and Wasat lawmakers in the Shura Council echoed his demand, declaiming, "This government has done a great deal of harm and is poised to cause more disaster and chaos." When a March court ruling eventually confirmed the initial twenty-one death sentences but acquitted seven police officers implicated in the stadium disaster, Port Said residents launched a civil disobedience campaign, shutting down schools, factories, the provincial government headquarters, and the railway line. The mother of a twenty-three-year-old man shot in the head by police during the January 26 clashes grieved, "Who bears responsibility for the blood of my son? God is my only agent. I hold Morsi, the minister of the interior and the director of security responsible for the death of my son."[84]

Incensed at being the target of popular anger, policemen and officers in a third of Egyptian provinces held a four-day strike, refusing to protect the president's residence in Sharqiyya and claiming that they were being used as pawns in the partisan battle between the president and his opponents. Ironically, human rights activists shared the police view, claiming that Morsi was instrumentalizing the police in his quest for total power.[85] The president became the lightning rod for the master problem that had triggered the revolution and propelled so much of its politics: people's relationship with the police. At this juncture, a highly sensitive document landed on the president's desk requiring immediate action. As one of his very first acts in office, Morsi had formed a fact-finding commission to investigate the repeated mass killings of protesters from the initial protest of January 25, 2011, up to his swearing-in on June 30, 2012. The commission compiled a thorough report, shedding light on one of the most chilling aspects of the revolution: the more than a thousand persons who went missing during the Eighteen Days, some turning up later in morgues. Unsurprisingly, the report implicated the police, but it also confirmed for the first time the armed forces' role in the disappearance, torture, and killings of protesters, recommending that senior army leaders be investigated for issuing the orders. Relying on the military for public order given the strike by police, and already menaced by the defense minister's bid to act as a "mediator" between political factions, Morsi could not confront the military about its rights violations. He shelved the report that he had commissioned, earning the enmity of human rights advocates and families of the disappeared, who accused the president of complicity in the state's mass killing of civilians.

By spring 2013, influential commentators and the opposition spoke of a country adrift, mismanaged, and in danger of a complete breakdown of public order. Crime and vigilantism received much media attention, and a new petition drive began calling on Defense Minister Abdel Fattah al-Sisi to step in and lead the country until new elections for presidency and parliament.[86] "Egypt now is like a ship with an official captain and crew, but the captain is not in control, the crew does not follow his commands, the ship has no direction, and no one cares about the passengers," rued former Social Democratic MP Ziad Bahaa-Eldin.[87] Polls revealed this mood to be widely shared, but its political effects were not as clear-cut. A Pew survey conducted in March found that only 30 percent of respondents thought the country was headed in the right direction, down from 65 percent in 2011. But Morsi edged his opponents in favorable ratings, with 53 percent compared to Sabahy's 48 percent and ElBaradei's 40 percent, and the FJP received 52 percent compared to the NSF's 45 percent. Another barometer a month later echoed the national state of polarization. In the closely watched national student union elections, the post of president went to the candidate representing secular parties by a vote of 24 to 22 for his MB rival, and the vice presidency went to the MB candidate, with 24 votes to his rival's 21.[88]

## A NEW JUDICIAL SLAP IN THE FACE

Next to the problem of restoring public order, perhaps the biggest challenge for the president that spring was his appointment of a new prosecutor-general (PG) as part of his November 22 act. The appointment fused the various flashpoints of judicial resistance to the president into a single, sustained bloc of opposition, now including hundreds of prosecutors. The conflict soon metastasized into a battle between judges and prosecutors as one camp, the upper house of parliament and the president's parent organization in a rival camp, and Morsi caught in the middle, expending endless hours in harried mediation between the judicial and legislative branches of the state.

The root of the issue was that judges and prosecutors believed the president had no authority to dismiss a sitting PG and appoint a replacement.[89] Another layer was Morsi's particular selection: he had replaced the Mubarak-appointed Abdel Meguid Mahmoud with Tal'at Abdallah, a second-rank judge from the 2006 judicial independence movement. The deep divide between judges that had reared its head in 2006 now resumed in a volatile new context where the protagonists had switched places. Reformist judges and a new Islamist president were in government, and the Mubarak-era judicial corps were still in their posts, determined to fend off any threatening change. On December 17, hundreds of prosecutors besieged Abdallah's office for ten hours, vowing a nationwide strike if he did not resign. Encircled by hostile prosecutors and public defenders after police had withdrawn, Abdallah handwrote his resignation as the condition for safely exiting the building; prosecutors cheered and applauded that they had restored "the prestige of the judiciary" (Haybat al-Qada'). Five days later, the chief justice of the Cassation Court reinstated Abdallah, invalidating his resignation produced under duress. But then an appeals court annulled the presidential decree appointing Abdallah, deeming it a violation of judicial independence. "A New Judicial Slap in the Face of the President," a major and increasingly antigovernment daily gleefully headlined.[90] The president and the new PG refused to back down, waiting for a definitive decision by the apex Cassation Court.

At that point, and without coordinating with the president, the MB and FJP decided to push for a confrontation with the judges in the streets and in the Shura Council, the upper house they dominated that held legislative power pro tempore until the seating of a new parliament. Convinced of a widening judicial-political conspiracy against them powered by ancien régime brains and brawn, the FJP organized a very large Friday milyuniyya outside the High Court on April 19.[91] Under a huge banner proclaiming a "Purge of the Judiciary" (Tatheer al-Qada'), orderly rows of protesters demanded revolutionary tribunals for Mubarak and his officials; the resignation of Morsi's justice minister; and a new bill to lower judges' retirement age from seventy to sixty. A few days later, FJP and Wasat legislators began discussion of the bill, over the heated objections of secular and Salafi legislators who correctly pointed out that the Shura Council had no constitutional authority to propose bills.

Lowering the mandatory retirement age to sixty had been a cardinal demand of reformist judges before and after 2011, but its adoption by the president's party was seen as a cynical ploy to purge three thousand judges (one quarter of the corps) and replace them with younger MB loyalists. The battle over the PG now turned into an existential fight over the integrity of the judicial branch. The president promptly lost the two prominent judges in his administration; Justice Minister Ahmed Mekky and chief legal advisor Muhamad Fu'ad Gadallah resigned in outrage at the MB/FJP attack.[92] Egypt's highest judges on the Supreme Judicial Council met with the president to express alarm at his partisans' demonstration. FJP legislators framed the crisis as a corrupt judicial establishment fearful of losing its perch. Judges countered with a large demonstration on the High Court steps, instead framing the crisis as thuggish Islamists' rampage against established state institutions. After six weeks of continuous conflict, the president finally put an end to the legislative-judicial tit-for-tat on June 4, prevailing on the Shura Council to shelve the bill pending consensus talks.[93]

The furor caused enormous complications for the president, shrinking his circle of advisers, undermining negotiations with opposition leaders over an impending cabinet reshuffle (conducted by one of his few remaining advisers, political scientist Pakinam al-Sharqawy), and bringing out into the open disputes between Morsi and his party. Mekky and Gadallah's departures were in part responses to sharp differences between the two men and the president's FJP advisers on the PG crisis and other gathering threats.[94] The opposition's mainstay—that Morsi was nothing but a tool of the MB—ignores the real differences that had developed between the organizational leadership's vision, and the man who was, after all, their second choice for president. Beginning with the November 22 decree, MB leaders freely expressed frustration with the president and what they perceived as his inept advising team, telegraphing their displeasure at being frozen out of key presidential deliberations.[95] Similarly, FJP leaders were now openly defying the president, organizing the April 19 demonstration against his own justice minister and proclaiming that he had no authority to tell a legislature to shelve any bill.[96] First the judges, and now his own party, were contesting Morsi's use of presidential authority.

## MUTINY

As he was navigating the new rifts with his party, the president also had to tend to suddenly assertive generals. At an emergency April 11 meeting with SCAF that looked more like a summons by the generals, the president had to reassure them that he stood firm against what the generals complained was a defamation

FIGURE 10. President Mohamed Morsi meets with SCAF, April 11, 2013; handout of the presidency.

campaign against them by MB members.[97] The real agenda of the meeting was to reclaim foreign relations as the military's reserved domain, putting a stop to Morsi's energetic foreign policy. In the new year, he had undertaken several bold departures from Mubarak-era foreign policy, inaugurating charter flights between Cairo and Tehran, making off-the-cuff conciliatory remarks about the disputed Halayeb Triangle with Sudan, and signing off on a new property ownership regime in Sinai permitting non-Egyptians to own land in the area on ninety-nine-year leases. But the centerpiece was a Suez Canal logistics megaproject that Morsi had traveled to China to drum up investment for, appointing an MB advisor to the Transport Ministry helming the project. In statements to national television after the meeting with SCAF, a diminished and shaken-looking president stood encircled by two dozen generals in full dress uniform. And he spoke second, after Defense Minister Abdel Fattah al-Sisi.[98]

In the days and weeks after the meeting, Morsi's initiatives were methodically reversed. The Cairo-Tehran flights were canceled indefinitely. Defense Minister Sisi dispatched his chief of staff back to Sudan to reiterate Egypt's uncompromising position on the border region. Sisi had already overruled the

Sinai land ownership decision in December, issuing a decree banning property ownership in "strategic areas," including the Red Sea islands of Tiran and Sanafir.[99] And control over the Suez Canal project was wrested back from the president; a military spokesman told an English-language newspaper, "The military will remain the major partner and key player in decision-making when it comes to Suez Canal and Sinai affairs."[100]

The military did not retreat after the April 11 meeting. Sisi embarked on a busy schedule of appearances before military and civilian audiences, always with journalists in tow. He hosted the US secretary of defense at a high-profile visit on April 24. After that visit, the US ambassador sent an encrypted email to the White House indicating that a coup was a likelihood in a few months.[101] But to the Egyptian public, the military continued to send ambiguous messages. In mid-May, before an audience of military brass and film stars, Sisi warned of "the extreme danger of once again summoning the army to political life." Ruling party politicians interpreted it as upholding the legitimacy of the elected government, and NSF politicians read it as affirming the role of the army as guardian, if not as government.[102]

By the first days of June, several currents flowed into a miasma of repudiating the government and rubbishing every action of the president. A new Cairo-based petition drive gained much traction and excited media attention. Called "Tamarrud," or Mutiny, the youth-led campaign asked citizens to sign a statement "withdrawing confidence from the 'Ikhwan regime'" and calling for early presidential elections. The petition read in part, "Since the coming to power of Mohamed Morsi al-Ayyat, the ordinary citizen feels that no goal of the revolution has been achieved, which were bread, freedom, social justice, and national independence. Morsi has failed in realizing them all." The campaign's three youth leaders were not known faces in the activist youth milieu that had flourished since 2011. As emerged two months later, they were bankrolled by a UAE slush fund controlled by Egyptian intelligence. Spokesman Mahmoud Badr presented the Tamarrud initiative as activating the silent majority that was ostensibly against Morsi. "If 13 million voted for Mohamed Morsi during last June's presidential elections, there are tens of millions who are against him. Our mission is to make their voices heard."[103] Tamarrud quickly gained the endorsement of the NSF, April 6th, and various luminaries in Egypt's political and cultural spheres; celebrities and regular citizens posted photos and videos of themselves signing the petition as an act of urgent civic duty and sound political judgment. The initiative tapped into a storied political tradition of collecting signatures as a form of public demand-making. The process had been popularized by ElBaradei when he allied with the MB in autumn 2010 to pressure Hosni Mubarak for political reforms, but it reached even further back, to the 1919 mass petition drive deputizing nationalist leader Saad Zaghlul to negotiate Egypt's independence from British rule. Tamarrud, however, was the first time a petition drive called on a democratically elected president to abdicate.

The campaign coordinated the scattered calls for early presidential elections that had been percolating on the margins since the revolution's second anniversary. Badr and his confreres held biweekly press conferences to report progress on their target goal of 15 million signatures, although no one outside of the campaign was given access to the petitions to verify their number. On June 10, Badr announced that the goal was in sight and offered a roadmap for mass demonstrations to converge on Ittihadiyya palace on June 30, the first anniversary of Morsi's swearing-in. In tandem, Hamdeen Sabahy's Popular Current party outlined a post-Morsi plan for a three-man directory to steer the country for an interim six months until the convoking of elections: the chief justice of the Supreme Constitutional Court; the minister of defense; and an independent public figure.[104]

By that point, the government was encircled from multiple directions. Intellectuals and members of the film industry were occupying the Ministry of Culture, blocking Morsi's new minister from accessing his office on the grounds of defending Egypt's identity from "the Brotherhoodization of the State" (Akhwanat al-Dawla). The day after the president announced a gubernatorial reshuffle on June 16, protesters locked the MB governors out of their offices in two provinces, set up protest encampments in two others, besieged the residence of one governor and torched his car, and burned the MB headquarters in Tanta.[105] Suddenly and inexplicably, the Presidential Election Commission (PEC) reconstituted itself to review Ahmed Shafiq's challenge to the 2012 presidential election result, violating its own bylaws that its decisions were final.[106] Mothers of the revolution's martyrs in their mourning black gathered outside Morsi's private residence in New Cairo, chanting, "There is no God but God! Mohamed Morsi is the enemy of God!"[107]

The state's coercive institutions openly invited people to the streets, using the press to relay their messages. The interior minister volunteered that some of his officers had signed Tamarrud petitions and informed the public that police forces would not be present at the site of any demonstrations, nor would they protect any political party offices. On June 26, military tanks and armored vehicles began deploying around vital installations and public buildings across the country. Unidentified police sources said that on June 30, police officers would wear t-shirts emblazoned with "We are with you" on the front and "We are with the people" on the back. Unnamed military sources told reporters, "The armed forces have not gone into the streets to protect the regime of President Mohamed Morsi, as some claim, but to protect the Egyptian people and its facilities, in addition to protecting peaceful demonstrators from any targeting by armed militias attempting to abort the June 30 demonstrations." The commander of the presidential guard, General Mohamed Zaki, indicated that all roads leading to the presidential palace would be open; "no elements from the guard will be outside the palace, our mission is restricted to securing the palace from the inside."[108] Coptic Pope Tawadros II and the Grand Imam of al-Azhar both declined the president's appeal for support, issuing separate statements of tacit support for the June 30 demonstrations.[109]

## SEEKING A COUP

Five weeks after Tamarrud's eruption on the scene, MB leaders recognized the threat and began preparing. To gainsay Tamarrud's intangible numbers with manifest bodies, a massive pro-Morsi rally of 100,000 gathered outside Rabʻa al-ʻAdawiyya mosque in East Cairo on June 21, the same site of December displays of support after the Ittihadiyya clashes. A defiant crowd and speakers decried the violence breaking out against MB headquarters and governors along with the incipient threat of removing Morsi by force. A twenty-two-year-old protester said, "There are people seeking a coup against the lawful order. Dr. Morsi won in free and fair elections like any state in the world."[110] Speaking before a military audience two days later on June 23, Defense Minister Sisi announced that the armed forces were breaking their silence to prevent civil strife, issuing a one-week ultimatum for "all political groups to develop consensus and reconciliation." This time there was less ambiguity about the armed forces' posture; the military cast itself as the ultimate arbiter between warring civilian factions, not a division of government under a civilian president's command. Behind the scenes, Sisi was in regular contact with friendly jurists to discuss "constitutionally correct" scenarios for military intervention.[111] In anticipation of the mass gathering outside the presidential palace on June 30, the commander of the presidential guard advised Morsi and his core group of advisers to relocate to a secure crisis management location on the grounds of the Republican Guard club a few miles away. It was there that Morsi prepared for his address to the nation on June 26, promising a balance sheet of his first year in office.

Speaking to a packed conference hall with members of his cabinet, legislators, and party leaders in the front rows and cheering partisans in the back (the NSF refused to attend), the president spoke for over two-and-a-half hours that stretched past midnight, alternating between reading a sober presidential script and digressing into folksy banter. Morsi acknowledged his mistakes and then went on the offensive, naming names after a year of vague allusions to shadowy networks. He criticized prominent secular leaders and NSF politicians for refusing offers to serve on his first cabinet; identified ancien régime bosses and media personalities who stoked the continual political violence on the streets; taunted Ahmed Shafiq to return from the UAE and face trial on corruption charges; and lambasted Mubarak crony businessmen who still controlled media outlets that "spewed poison" about his administration. He announced a reconciliation commission and a committee to amend the most controversial clauses of the 2012 constitution. To his partisans, it was a strong speech, projecting steadfastness in the face of mounting threats. To his opponents, it was a rambling address that further demonstrated his unfitness for office. Prominent Nasserist commentator Mohamed Hasanein Haykal continued his month-long derision campaign against Morsi on a television interview program, dismissing him as an unpresidential, hidebound party leader incapable of managing the Egyptian state. The nonagenarian enthused that he mentored Tamarrud and saw it as the future.[112]

The Morsi government was taken aback by the scale of the crowds that turned out on June 30, making for two destinations: Tahrir Square and the Ittihadiyya palace. Police and military sources were quick to disseminate crowd numbers of 15 and 17 million countrywide to foreign and local media; "it is the biggest protest in Egypt's history," proclaimed a military official. Independent analysts put the numbers at 1 to 2 million.[113] The military offered movie director Khaled Youssef a helicopter to capture aerial footage of the crowds; he panned over the Tahrir and Ittihadiyya crowds in majestic extreme wide shot, falsely conveying the Rab'a sit-in where pro-Morsi protesters had decided to camp out since June 28 as part of the anti-Morsi outpouring. Police officers in their summer white uniforms joined the crowds in holding up red cards against Morsi. Hundreds of protesters demonstrated outside the president's private residence, the neighborhood filling up with honking cars and flag-waving passengers demanding that Morsi step down. NSF leaders fronted a march to Tahrir from Mostafa Mahmoud Square, holding up signs that read, "Raise your voice a bit louder, tomorrow will be here without Ikhwan!" The MB headquarters were again burned and looted overnight, part of a wave of violence that killed sixteen and injured 780.

On July 1, four non-MB cabinet ministers tendered their resignations and five more were in the process. In the afternoon, as MB leaders were being placed on security watch-lists, Defense Minister Sisi delivered another ultimatum giving "political forces" forty-eight hours to meet the people's demands or the army would impose its own roadmap. The NSF and the anti-Morsi crowds hailed the announcement; some of the president's supporters in Rab'a donned white burial shrouds, as had Tahrir protesters during the Eighteen Days, signaling their readiness to perish for the cause. The president and his team weighed their options, including calling a public referendum on whether the president should resign or finish out his term. But a military source spelled out the president's options as seen by the military: announce early presidential elections in the new year, or refuse and SCAF will make the announcement.[114]

From a makeshift studio in the crisis management location, on July 2 the embattled president delivered his refusal to abdicate. Standing behind a lectern, he recalled his oath before the Tahrir crowds on June 29, 2012, to protect the revolution. Underscoring his constitutional obligation, he vowed not to yield the legitimacy of his elected office, even at the cost of his own life. Pounding the podium, he thundered, "I want to protect the children, and the girls, who will be the mothers of the future, and will tell their children that their fathers and grandfathers were men! Men who never accepted the counsel of the degraded ones!" Under Sisi's leadership, SCAF convened in permanent session. Late the next evening of July 3, as security forces were arresting three dozen senior MB leaders and Islamist television hosts, Sisi stood at a lectern, flanked on both sides by seated military generals and prominent civilians: Mohamed ElBaradei, the Coptic Patriarch and Shaykh al-Azhar, Tamarrud's Mahmoud Badr, a Salafi leader, and the lone woman, former assistant to the president Sakina Fuad. The careful framing sought to project an image of inclusive national reconciliation that a divisive Islamist president had failed to achieve, not a naked military putsch. The defense minister announced the suspension of the constitution, appointment of the SCC chief justice as acting president, naming of a new interim government, drafting of a new constitution, then new legislative and presidential elections.

On July 5, when the commander of the presidential guard, General Mohamed Zaki, appeared with soldiers to forcibly transport Mohamed Morsi to detention in an Alexandria naval base, Morsi told him, "You'll be tried for this, ya Mohamed."[115]

\* \* \*

The Morsi presidency has been told as a story of the hubris of power, or inept leadership, or a futile attempt at civilian rule in a political system run by the military since 1952. The account presented here does not start with the president and his ideological disposition, nor with immovable structures, but a reconstruction of the elements of an unstable power distribution. Extracting these elements, we see their family resemblance to other instances of first-time executives who were outsiders in one way or another, to wit: hostility from entrenched state interests and their foreign patrons; cascading demands for goods and accountability from newly empowered publics; upkeep of fractious positive coalitions; management of powerful negative coalitions; navigating tensions with party and base; all while maintaining a dense schedule of politico-economic diplomatic outreach. The demands and pressures of the situation are not of equal magnitude and do not present themselves in helpful linear fashion, so the probability of error, miscalculation, mishap, and escalation is likely to be high. When conspiracy is added to the mix, by definition an ingredient in coup situations, the precarious executive's decision-making is bound to be fraught with high risks and uncertain returns. Seen from this level of abstraction, variables such as the leader's ideological commitment and personal leadership traits recede in importance or, more precisely, are rearranged relative to the other, more salient features of the situation.

The other deposed executives mentioned at the beginning of this chapter had wildly different ideological commitments, leadership skills, and structural constraints, but they were all felled by a constellation of forces that proved stronger than what they themselves could muster. Venezuela's Romulo Gallegos was a former mayor and leader of a national social democratic party in a new democracy. Mohammad Mossadegh was a fixture of the ruling elite and a committed constitutionalist in a relatively new but foreign-backed monarchy. Salvador Allende was both a Marxist and "the consummate political insider, who had been everything in Chilean politics—deputy, senator, minister, party head, Senate president."[116] He operated in a famously consolidated, consensual democracy. Mohamed Morsi was an Islamist organization man, a former parliamentarian and party leader in an Egyptian political system that was reliably authoritarian for thirty years and then suddenly in wild flux between authoritarianism and democratization. Cutting across ideology, leadership traits, and regime type, these men faced similar situations that trumped individual attributes. Leon Trotsky vividly captured the overwhelming power of crisis situations:

> Similar (of course, far from identical) irritations in similar conditions call out similar reflexes; the more powerful the irritation, the sooner it overcomes personal peculiarities. To a tickle, people react differently, but to a redhot iron alike. As a steam-hammer converts a sphere and a cube alike into sheet metal, so under the blow of too great and inexorable events resistances are smashed and the boundaries of "individuality" are lost.[117]

I would characterize the civilian president's predicament as a catch-22. To implement change he needed power. When he attempted to build that power, he was blocked by hostile state fiefdoms claiming ultimate authority and branded a dictator by an uncompromising opposition. As he counter-acted and maneuvered, obstruction and attack intensified, leading to sinking popularity and abandonment by enraged allies and expectant publics at the moment when he most needed their support. To the military and judicial claims of sovereignty he asserted a counterclaim of authority based in a higher power, the will of voters, even as those voters withdrew their support or disengaged from the debilitating fights or agreed with the opposition that Morsi was the aggressor. This set of interactions could have continued and taken on new forms and articulations, especially with the imminent election of a new parliament that the courts were obstructing,[118] but conspiratorial action and force terminated the political struggle within peak state institutions.

That Morsi was an Islamist president only heightened the antipathy of the Mubarak state's guardians, men in the military, judicial, policing, and diplomatic corps with a built-up sense of mission and an aversion to civilian outsiders. The implication is that any civilian president of any ideological hue would have faced similar obstruction. Had any of the other presidential contenders—such as Hamdeen Sabahy or Abdel Moneim Aboul Fotouh or Khaled Ali (but not career diplomat Amr Moussa)—won the presidency, the commanding heights of the Egyptian state would have resisted him similarly, especially if he had attempted to assert his authority in the manner of Morsi. But these bureaucratic factions could not act alone to depose the president in a sudden, secretive putsch. For them, the revolutionary situation was both constraint and opportunity. Acting alone against the president would have drawn international condemnation, but acting in concert with civilian opposition lent the mantle of popular approbation. The partisan political elites embittered by their loss in the presidential election or their experience with the Muslim Brothers during constitution-writing were only too willing to cast their lot with the generals. The National Salvation Front was a hodgepodge of ideologies, leadership styles, and political experiences, but it embodied the political class that was very much a creation of Mubarak-era politics, men who were caught between intense aspirations for national leadership but weak ties to broad constituencies. Their great fear was that they had no future in an Islamist-dominated polity; their hope was that the generals, chastened by their experience of governing in 2011–12, would oust the unfit Islamist and hand power to them.

It is a measure of the ambiguity of relative power during the revolutionary situation that NSF politicians believed military intervention would be a neutral arbiter between civilians and not seek to rule directly. Especially for runner-up presidential contenders such as Hamdeen Sabahy and Amr Moussa, with a demonstrated capacity to win popular support, they could not abide the verdict at the polls in 2012 and agitated for a re-do. In that sense, such ambiguity also exposes the many tenuous filaments of Egypt's first democracy. Some civilian political forces were more willing to prolong military tutelage of the political process than face their civilian opponents directly in unfettered competition.

Then there is the force of public opinion that all political contenders wooed and sought to mold. Mohamed Morsi faced a more potent form of the popular rage that SCAF contended with in 2011. There is indeed a certain homology between the master slogan of 2011, "Yasqut Yasqut Hukm al-'Askar," and "Yasqut Yasqut Hukm al-Murshid," the linchpin chant during Morsi's year in office. Both evince a startlingly rapid desacralization of governing authority, driven by an uncompromising thrust against continued state abuses and misrule. And yet there is an irreducible difference. As the rump of Mubarak's regime, public disaffection with the generals was an extension of antipathy to the autocrat. The discontent with Morsi had a different source. Made president by freely cast votes, Morsi faced the bitter charge that he had violated a trust. The depth of public disappointment in a new government born in a revolutionary situation can be immense, since, to use Peter Amann's words, "the fact that this government is their own personal creation deprives it of the *mystique* of impersonal power in which an established government is clothed."[119] Morsi stood accused of betraying revolutionary ideals, failing to end decades-long abuses not of his own making, and, when he attempted to build his capacity to govern, replicating the autocratic ways of his predecessor. These are the sentiments that state actors and politicians stoked and steered, but did not create, in the making of Egypt's very public coup by acclamation.

*Chapter 6*

# STATE PRESTIGE
هيبة الدولة

> Nobody could possibly underestimate the state-generating and state-strengthening functions of revolutions.
>
> —Eric Hobsbawm, "Revolution"

THE THIRD ANNIVERSARY OF THE REVOLUTION ON JANUARY 25, 2014, was a joyous national celebration in Tahrir Squares across the country that was nearly wrecked by a baleful minority. But the deployment of paratroopers in Chinook helicopters as well as plainclothes and uniformed police officers with canines, all under the personal direction of Defense Minister Abdel Fattah al-Sisi, thwarted nefarious attempts at sabotage.[1] This was the message disseminated by government media organs and erstwhile independent newspapers, a narrative of national concord threatened by a revanchist internal enemy. One week before the anniversary, government officials laid the groundwork, inviting the public to the streets as they had on June 30, 2013. "I reiterate my call to the Egyptian people," exhorted Interior Minister Mohamed Ibrahim. "You have to take to the streets on Saturday to celebrate the revolution's anniversary because we've discovered Muslim Brotherhood plots that seek to spread chaos."[2] In the event, the Cairo governor held a celebration for families of prominent 2011 martyrs, unveiling new street signs bearing their names. In most provincial capitals, government headquarters that had been targets of crowd anger in 2011 were now given over to military bands and flag-waving throngs. Amid a brass band playing patriotic songs, the governor of Gharbiyya cut the ribbon for a memorial to the revolution's martyrs, including police and army personnel along with civilians.[3]

Tahrir Square was the epicenter of a state-led carnival. Police manned all entrances to the square, admitting only Sisi supporters. Men and women wore Sisi face masks and held up large cloth banners and posters bearing his face. Many also held up uniform red posters with the tag "No to Terrorism" in English. Vendors sold balloons, helicopters dropped flags, and Tannoura folk dancers twirled their colorful skirts. A bridal couple in full finery was serenaded by a crowd holding up large photos of the defense and interior ministers. If in 2011 various musicians energized and entertained protesters, now a single stage blared *Teslam al-Ayyadi* ("Grateful to You"), the anthem dedicated to the armed forces by a cast of pop singers in the wake of President Mohamed Morsi's ouster on July 3, 2013.

Blocks away from Tahrir in Tal'at Harb Square, secular youth groups attempting autonomous celebrations of the revolution were teargassed and charged by armored police vehicles. In the teeming east Cairo district of Matariyya, a large procession of male and female supporters of the former president marched briskly down the central thoroughfare, some holding up both hands in the four-fingered salute that had become their icon of resistance, others carrying large yellow flags imprinted with the hand symbol. It was their thirty-first week of continuous protests since first assembling in Rab'a Square on June 28, 2013, to support their embattled president. To evade overwhelming police violence, they had adapted their protest repertoire, shifting from large Tahrir-like encampments to speed-walking marches down narrow residential lanes and back streets. Many of the processions were nocturnal, to reduce the risk of being gunned down. But the January 25 processions were in the full light of day, and police set upon the Matariyya procession with tear gas and live rounds, killing thirty. By the end of the day, government officials announced more than a thousand arrests countrywide, sixty-four killed, and hundreds injured.[4]

Three days later on January 28, 2014, the anniversary of 2011's Friday of Rage, the deposed president appeared at one of his many criminal trials to face a bevy of charges: ordering the unlawful detention of protesters outside Ittihadiyya palace in December 2012; conspiring with Hamas and Hizbullah to break out of his [illegal] prison detention on January 29, 2011; passing on state secrets to

Qatar; and insulting the judiciary. Morsi and fellow MB leaders appeared in a soundproof glass cage, short-circuiting their attempt to use the trial as a pulpit to address public opinion. When the judge turned on the microphone so that the former president could answer his questions, Morsi repudiated the unconstitutional nature of the court and his lack of access to a lawyer. "You talk too much, Mohamed Morsi," said Judge Shaʿban al-Shamy. "My name is President Mohamed Morsi." "You are defendant Mohamed Morsi."[5]

## HAYBAT AL-DAWLA

The military's keen interest in casting itself as the revolution's guardian in 2014 was nothing new. What was new was the swagger of the police as coguardians and the embodiment of the military in a single heroic leader rather than a collegium of generals. In 2011, SCAF had pushed the idea of an unbreakable bond between the army and the people, in which the latter commanded and a faithful armed forces executed their wishes. By the third anniversary of the revolution, that narrative had been reconstructed to make room for the police. Now the armed forces and police, led by a valiant warrior, protected the nation from a murderous and depraved internal enemy, while the people amassed and acclaimed in gratitude. In this framing, people, police, and army were an organic unity, but sovereignty clearly lay with the army.

This chapter shows how Egypt's revolutionary situation terminated in a nonrevolutionary outcome, with the military rump of the Mubarak regime reconquering the state and building a new counterrevolutionary order. It circles back to the three political arenas identified in chapter 2, tracing how the state-led counterrevolutionary project systematically repressed protests, hollowed out elections, and subordinated courts. Its central argument is that the counterrevolution is not a return to the Mubarak order, a dialing back of the clock to the political world of 2010 with a powerful presidency skillfully managing an array of parliamentary and extraparliamentary opposition. In this it runs against the grain of multiple scholarly assessments (and even more journalistic accounts) that see authoritarian restoration as precisely what happened. Whether coding Egypt's a "revolution" or a "democratic transition," these scholars agree that it "failed," nesting this common assessment within different conceptual frameworks.[6] Developing the argument that "success" and "failure" oddly conflate prorevolution aspirations with outcomes, and in any case telling us very little about the workings of the Sisi regime, the chapter reasons that the counterrevolution is neither an upgraded version of Mubarakism nor the direct negation of revolution but a surprising blend of familiar autocratic modes of rule and new administrative and ideological arrangements. Counterrevolutionary thought and practice brought together repressive laws and policing techniques, unprecedented state violence, internal state reorganization, war-making in Sinai, a regimen of economic austerity, an unambiguous regional alliance between Egypt, Saudi Arabia, the UAE, and Israel, and a bespoke ideology. The ideational component was itself an amalgam of prerevolutionary Arab authoritarian political thought and new ideas developed dialectically in confrontation with the revolutionary situation.

Capturing this complex of ideas, tactics, and alliances, haybat al-dawla (state prestige) was the justifying doctrine of counterrevolution. A murky concept floating in the lexicon of conservative Arab political thought, it was dusted off and filled out by entrenched state elites when they found themselves under threat for the first time from both parliamentary and extraparliamentary opposition currents. We saw in chapter 2 how haybat al-dawla was invoked by Algerian incumbent elites and their intellectual allies in the immediate wake of that country's 1989–92 opening, followed by repression of its Islamist movement. It resurfaced again in 2011 across the Arab press, as entrenched autocrats were deposed or challenged as never before by insurgent mass protests and diverse forms of political opposition. At its core, the concept connotes a Hegelian state standing above and steering society toward economic development and cultural modernization, and it cultivates a posture of reverence toward the state: "the people must have access to the majesty of the state, their hearts filled with its love and sublimity," wrote an establishment columnist in 2011.[7] In this mystifying conception, the 2011 uprisings are framed as a catastrophic assault by the forces of extremism, partisan divisiveness, and territorial disintegration. As the political scientist and former Gamal Mubarak publicist Muhammad Safieddine Kharbush argued, the January 25 revolution was not an attempt at regime change but "a tightly organized plan to destroy the pillars of the state that Egyptians have struggled to build since 1805 with Muhammad Ali Pasha."[8] Restoring state prestige became the master frame of the counterrevolution, meant as a reimposition of the awe, obedience, and fear of a mystified state—a state wrested back from the clutches of the Muslim Brothers, now recast as a transnational Islamist movement and the progenitor of al-Qaʿida and Daesh.

Haybat al-dawla is a mirror image of Eric Hobsbawm's reminder that revolutions are not simply rhetorical or metaphorical tropes but concrete historical processes that lead to expanded state capacity. Egypt's counterrevolution can be thought of in the same terms, as a process and project that is equally state-generating and expanding, if only as a reaction to the perceived breakdown of the standing and "prestige" of the state during the revolutionary upheaval. The haybat al-dawla umbrella also has the advantage of bringing together what are often analytically segregated as state "strategies" and state "ideologies," showing the coconstruction of policies and ideas, defined as "meaning work—the struggle over the production of mobilizing and countermobilizing ideas and meanings."[9] By substituting the concept of framing for ideology, the chapter underscores the observable, contested, interactive work of meaning-making, eschewing the psychologizing, individualizing tendencies of the term "attitudes" and the totalizing connotations of opaque "ideology."

### THE PEOPLE DEMANDED AND THE ARMY RESPONDED

The counterrevolution was not implemented in one stroke as a coherent blueprint immediately after the military deposed Morsi on July 3, 2013. Even after the arrest of the president, his advisers, and top MB leaders, it was still uncertain who would rule Egypt next. In Sisi's televised announcement on July 3, he outlined a "roadmap" that suspended the 2012 constitution, appointed the chief justice of the Supreme Constitutional Court as acting president, and called for new presidential elections. Days later, several prominent and respected figures were appointed to the interim cabinet, including Mohamed ElBaradei as vice president, Hazem Beblawi as prime minister, Ziad Bahaa-Eldin as deputy prime minister, and anti-Mubarak trade unionist Kamal Abu Eita as labor minister, bolstering the probability of a credible transition to civilian rule, albeit excluding the Muslim Brothers. However, the countrywide protest marches by Morsi's supporters and the enlargement of their encampments at Rabʿa and al-Nahda Squares demonstrated that resistance to the military-backed government could sustain itself over time and spread to new locales. An escalating sense of crisis prevailed, pulling in US, EU, and African Union mediation efforts.

A month after the July 3 coup, Egypt was visibly split between two claims grounded in popular sovereignty and manifested in rival encampments in the capital: Morsi's supporters built an elaborate infrastructure of resistance in Rab'a and al-Nahda Squares to the east and west of Tahrir, claiming the constitutional legitimacy of the first democratically elected president. Morsi's critics held Tahrir Square, framing their claim in terms of a rival "popular legitimacy" ( *shar'iyya sha'biyya*), the mass demonstrations on June 30 demanding that Morsi step down and accede to early elections. The situation was rife with two layers of uncertainty: which camp would prevail? And who would arbitrate the "real" meaning of such a highly indeterminate concept as popular sovereignty, one that could connote both citizens as voters, as the pro-Morsi camp meant, and citizens as crowds filling streets, as the anti-Morsi camp insisted? More questions abounded: If new presidential elections were held, would the military go back to their barracks? Would the constitution be revised or rewritten de novo, and by whom? If the generals did not wish to rule directly, would they revisit their plan on the eve of Morsi's election, fencing off key policy arenas from democratic control while engineering the election of a pliable civilian as a figurehead president? The definitive answer arrived in the midst of the state-scripted commemorations of the revolution's third anniversary in January 2014. SCAF convened and announced that it was unanimously delegating Defense Minister Sisi to run for the presidency. The intense and ceaseless power struggle unleashed on February 11, 2011, with Mubarak's abdication ended thirty-five months later on January 27, 2014, with the certainty that a Mubarak-era military general would assume the presidency in elections that no one believed would be free or fair. A revolutionary situation had terminated in a nonrevolutionary outcome.

The counterrevolutionary realignment was completed in the crucial seven months between Morsi's ouster on July 3, 2013, and SCAF's announcement on January 27, 2014. Two seemingly contradictory ideological and material mechanisms went hand-in-hand. There was the framing of June 30 as a massive second revolution, reenacting the January 25 revolution's script of an autonomous popular revolt against a reviled dictatorship resolved by the army's decisive intervention on the side of the people. Military propagandists revised the opening of the revolution's master slogan, "The People Want [to Bring Down the Regime]," as an appeal to the military; a cover story in a special issue of a defense ministry glossy proclaimed, "The People Wanted and the Army Responded."[10] A similar sleight was at work during the June 30 anti-Morsi protests, overwriting and not simply appropriating January 25. An unidentified military source dubbed it "the biggest protest in Egypt's history," a claim widely repeated thereafter without independent corroboration.[11] The claim that June 30 surpassed January 25 was twined with the anti-MB framing that had developed during Morsi's year in office into a master narrative of a nation united against the usurpation of power by a malignant Islamist minority. Counternarratives or doubts about this construction of reality were ridiculed and suppressed. When youth activists calling themselves the "Third Square" attempted to carve out an urban space that was at once antimilitary and anti-MB, Tamarrud spokesmen and pro-Sisi media outlets scorned them as divisive dreamers.[12]

The material component was the use of overwhelming force to crush the Muslim Brothers' manifest resistance. The first mass killing came on July 8, when Morsi's partisans attempted to establish a sit-in across from the Republican Guard headquarters where they believed the former president was detained; ninety-three unarmed civilians and two security personnel were killed in a dawn raid. On July 27, 108 Morsi supporters were gunned down at the Tomb of the Unknown Soldier as they attempted to march from the Rab'a camp to a bridge leading to downtown.[13] Facing no real sanction for the killings, the military and its civilian cabinet felt emboldened to disband the sit-ins. They acted with urgency, as US, EU, and African Union mediators shuttling between imprisoned MB leaders and the interim government felt that they were making good progress toward a post-Morsi political settlement. And leaders of the Rab'a protest camp were effectively reaching out to the foreign press corps, organizing tours of the camp for journalists and garnering sympathy as victims of state violence. In mid-July, a broad range of progovernment media outlets launched a concerted campaign to evoke public revulsion at the sit-ins and short-circuit any sentiments of solidarity.[14] From Sisi down to the most marginal television presenter, the sit-ins were depicted as an armed zone of danger and defilement held by a foreign-inspired organization holding entire neighborhoods hostage. In his first interview after ousting Morsi, Sisi said of the MB, "The idea that gathers them together is not nationalism, it's not patriotism, it is not a sense of a country."[15] Columnists and television anchors spoke of the sit-ins as riven with contagious diseases and filled with hapless followers paid or coerced by ruthless leaders to remain in the camp.¹⁶ Xenophobia and misogyny were mixed in the claim that special tents were set aside in the camps for conscripted MB women and Syrian refugee women to engage in *jihad al-nikah* (sexual jihad), providing comfort to their warring men.¹⁷ Intellectuals and leaders of professional unions called on the police and army to break up the "huge terrorist pit." Even as the international mediators felt close to a settlement, Prime Minister Beblawi met with National Salvation Front leaders to assure them that the decision to disband the sit-ins was final and awaiting implementation.¹⁸

Shortly after 6 a.m. on the morning of August 14, security forces began their assaults on Rabʻa and al-Nahda Squares, lobbing tear gas canisters into the sit-ins for some minutes, then advancing with bulldozers, armored personnel carriers, and helicopters. Gunmen in the APCs and snipers on rooftops and in helicopters fired vast quantities of birdshot and live ammunition; ambulances were prevented from accessing the grounds to evacuate the injured. The twelve-hour assault on the much larger Rabʻa camp, 85,000 protesters at capacity, ended with the burning of the central stage, field hospital, and the eponymous mosque. Pro-Morsi protest camps in eleven other provinces were simultaneously evicted. To prevent people from traveling to Cairo and swelling protest marches against the dispersals, the country's railways were shut down for an unprecedented fifteen days starting on August 14, exceeding the Mubarak regime's suspension of the rail network for nine out of the Eighteen Days in 2011. During and after the dispersals, crowds in eight provinces attacked at least forty-two churches and scores of other Christian religious institutions. Based on a year-long investigation, Human Rights Watch recorded at least 817 deaths at Rabʻa and eighty-seven at al-Nahda, including women and children, calling it "one of the world's largest killings of demonstrators in a single day in recent history." The central Zeinhom morgue was overwhelmed, operating round the clock from August 14 to August 16. Corpses were lined up on the pavement outside the building, surrounded by blocks of ice brought by family members and neighborhood volunteers to slow decomposition. Inside, arguments broke out between relatives and forensic examiners who were writing "suicide" and "car accident" as the cause of death on the certificates; relatives wanted "martyrs of the dispersal" as the cause of death. An ambulance operator delivering four unidentified bodies said, "in Egypt now, we have queues of the dead longer than bread queues."¹⁹

The Rabʻa and Nahda dispersals were not the last instances of state-led mass killings (see Table 7), but they did put an end to a signature protest tactic of the revolutionary situation: occupying and holding public space for days on end as a mode of pressure on governing authorities. We have seen uses of this tactic by various groups, beginning with the January 28–February 11, 2011, encampment in Tahrir Square; Qena residents' protest camp outside the provincial government building in April 2011; anti-Morsi protesters' setting up of tents outside Ittihadiyya palace in December 2012; and Morsi supporters' forty-seven-day occupation of Rabʻa from June 28 to August 13, 2013.[20] If a revolutionary situation is by definition an interregnum of contested sovereignty, then capturing and holding territory is a basic means of forwarding a claim to sovereignty, a facet underlined by theorists of sovereignty from very different traditions. "The problem of sovereignty is closely tied to the establishment of boundaries," reflects historian James Sheehan. "Boundaries measure how far a sovereign's power extends, and also, by definition, where it stops." Writing of colonial occupations, philosopher Achille Mbembe theorizes that "space was therefore the raw material of sovereignty and the violence it carried with it. Sovereignty meant occupation."[21] Though developed for contexts of interstate competition and conquest, this connection between sovereignty and territory helps make sense of the high-stakes conflicts over public spaces that coursed throughout the revolutionary situation. For state power holders beating back domestic challengers, control over streets and squares is a basic manifestation of sovereignty, to the point of killing to reclaim turf. Against the familiar "romance of sovereignty" as autonomy and self-institution, Mbembe excavates a counterconception of sovereignty as the right to kill:

> The ultimate expression of sovereignty resides, to a large degree, in the power and the capacity to dictate who may live and who must die. Hence, to kill or to allow to live constitute the limits of sovereignty, its fundamental attributes.[22]

Asked about the mass killings at Rabʻa two years later, Sisi justified his actions in terms of the exigency of killing, repeating his refrain that the army's actions averted even greater deaths from an imminent civil war:

> Had the army not intervened, hundreds of thousands, if not millions, would have died.... The number of victims at Rabaa could have been 10 times higher if the people had stormed the square. And the Egyptians were prepared to do that.[23]

TABLE 7. Protester Fatalities from Security Forces' Use of Force, 2011–2015.*

| Date | Event(s) | Civilian Fatalities |
| --- | --- | --- |
| January 25–February 11, 2011 | The Eighteen Days, nationwide | 1,022 |
| October 9, 2011 | Maspero Demonstration, Cairo | 27 |
| November 19–22, 2011 | Mohamed Mahmoud Street Protests, Cairo | 61 |
| December 16, 2011 | Sit-in at Cabinet Headquarters, Cairo | 26 |
| February 3–7, 2012 | Protests at Interior Ministry, Cairo | 22 |
| April 28–May 4, 2012 | Sit-in near Defense Ministry, Cairo | 15 |
| January 25, 2013 | Second Anniversary of January 25, 2011, Protest | 26 |
| January 26–27, 2013 | Port Said Demonstrations | 49 |
| July 5, 2013 | Anticoup Protests in Alexandria, and Cairo | 36 |
| July 8, 2013 | Sit-in at Republican Guard Headquarters, Cairo | 93 |
| July 27, 2013 | Anticoup March near Manassa Memorial, Cairo | 108 |
| August 14, 2013 | Sit-ins at Rab'a, Nahda, and other sites | 1,104 |
| August 16, 2013 | Anticoup Protests around Ramses Square, Cairo, and other locations | 294 |
| August 18, 2013 | Gassing of Detainees in a Police Van, Cairo | 37 |
| October 6, 2013 | Pro-Morsi Marches | 62 |
| January 25, 2014 | Third Anniversary of January 25, 2011, Protest | 64 |
| January 25, 2015 | Fourth Anniversary January 25, 2011, Protest | 20 |

*Source:* Wikithawra (https://wikithawra.wordpress.com/), Amnesty International, and Human Rights Watch reports.

*This table includes the use of force by both police personnel and military divisions, but does not include other forms of collective violence during the same period, principally communal and/or sectarian clashes; soccer brawls such as that in Port Said stadium on February 1, 2012; multiple forms of violence in Sinai; attacks on political party headquarters such as the fatalities that occurred outside the Muslim Brothers' headquarters on June 30, 2013; and partisan fighting such as the December 5, 2012, clashes outside the Ittihadiyya palace. However, it ought to be noted that the inaction or collusion of police and/or security forces was an enabling condition in the outbreak of these forms of violence among civilians.

The interim government swiftly whitewashed the charred walls of Rabʿa mosque, cleared away the debris from the assault, and repaved surrounding roads. In November, they erected a memorial at the center of the roundabout, two angular arms representing the army and police, cradling an orb representing the people.[24] In Tahrir Square, another memorial commemorated "the martyrs of the two revolutions of January 25 and June 30," Prime Minister Hazem Beblawi said.[25] A few hours after Beblawi led the dedication ceremony in November 2013, activists entered Tahrir for the first time since July 2013 and vandalized the structure, spray-painting slogans against the military, fulul, and Muslim Brothers.

## INVIOLABLE SPACES

Protests were not extinguished after the Rabʿa and al-Nahda killings but instead took on new forms and locations, prompting new initiatives from the government to maintain unwavering control over public spaces. Neil Ketchley has analyzed how the Muslim Brothers altered their anticoup resistance to evade further state violence, adopting five kinetic tactics and experimenting with early morning and late-night protests.[26] This chapter widens the lens to survey other protest forms and participants, then turns to the politics of elections and courts after the termination of the revolutionary situation to examine how political interaction in those arenas was repressed at the same time as its form was appropriated.

With the start of the academic year in fall 2013, university campuses became hotbeds of anticoup resistance. Coalescing nationally as "Students Against the Coup," Islamist students organized near-daily confrontational protests that targeted campus security and occupied administrative buildings. When pro–June 30 counterprotesters petered out after the first two weeks of the term, the interim government ordered police forces to deploy at twenty-two public universities, the first time they had set foot on campuses since January 2011. University presidents were empowered to summarily expel students with no appeals process. By the end of the academic year 2013–14, 998 students had been arrested, eighteen killed by police use of birdshot and live ammunition, and hundreds expelled or suspended.[27] The start of the next academic year (2014–15) was pushed back to give time for police and university administrations to implement preemptive measures. A private security firm was hired to install metal detectors and search students at the gates of fifteen public universities; surveillance cameras and concrete barriers were erected around administrative buildings. University presidents were empowered to expel faculty members who participated in pro-Morsi protests, and a presidential decree expanded military jurisdiction over universities, paving the way for military trials of student activists.[28] Although protests continued and students at al-Azhar and Cairo Universities gave chase to the hired security guards, by 2016, sixty-five students had been referred to military tribunals and three more had been killed.[29]

Outside the campuses too, controlling the streets could not be sustained by filling them with the fading anti-Morsi protests, so police applied new tactics of preemption. The interior minister was frank in describing one such method. "Every Friday no less than 500 to 600 get arrested . . . at the beginning, we used to wait for the demonstration to turn violent, but now we confront them once they congregate. When we confront them, there are some that run, but, whoever we can grab, we detain." In the three weeks leading up to the third anniversary of the revolution, police made 703 arrests and killed twenty-seven.[30]

The state's administrative machinery was activated to supply longer-term solutions. In the first piece of legislation on rights and freedoms after the coup, acting president Adli Mansour issued Law 107/2013 in November 2013, regulating public meetings and demonstrations. Ironically, it had first been introduced as a bill in February 2013 by the Morsi government in the wake of the mass demonstrations in the canal cities, but it was quickly retracted after an opposition outcry. The new act replaced a 1923 law issued in the aftermath of Egypt's first mass rising in 1919 against British rule. The 2013 law encoded police mastery over public space, requiring their permission for all demonstrations and public meetings of more than ten people, including electoral gatherings. Protest organizers are obliged to notify the district police station three days in advance of an action, may be turned down with no reasons given, and may be imprisoned for two to five years and fined in the event that a demonstration "breaches public order."[31] Placing the 1923 and 2013 laws side by side, what is striking is how the new rendition, twice as long as the old, carefully itemizes and prohibits the protest practices developed by Egyptians over the span of ninety years:

- Organizing processions to and from places of worship (punishable by one year in prison), the itinerary widely used throughout the revolutionary situation, especially the common sense understanding of Friday prayers as muster points for subsequent demonstrations.

- Using explosives, fireworks, or flares (punishable by seven years' imprisonment) and wearing masks (punishable by up to one year), the signature protest performances of soccer Ultras, student activists, the Black Bloc, and residents' burning of police stations during the Eighteen Days.
- Blocking highways and railways (punishable by two-to-five years' imprisonment), the escalatory tactic used by a wide range of interest groups as a form of "collective bargaining by riot," as Eric Hobsbawm called this form of direct action.
- Trespassing an "inviolable space" in front of official buildings to be demarcated by governors and police chiefs (punishable by one year in prison), the ubiquitous tactic used by protean crowds camping out in front of parliament, the presidential palace, the Maspero radio and television building, courthouse steps, ministries, provincial government headquarters, and the Tahrir Mugamma' complex before, during, and immediately after the revolutionary situation.[32]

The law is a mirror image of Egyptians' repertoire of transgressive contention, recalling Charles Tilly's insight about the spatial dimension of contentious politics, "the co-evolution of spatially organized policing with prevailing routines of popular politics."[33] Over time, as groups of Egyptians claimed bits of the built environment to press their demands on public authorities, prompting more groups to do the same, a symbolic geography of claim-making emerged, establishing shared understandings of certain itineraries and locales. Police were ever-present in this collective repertoire-making, hemming in protesters, channeling them out, or dispersing them by force. The coup was an opportunity not only to crush the Muslim Brothers but to evict transgressive encroachment on space altogether in a counterrevolutionary project of territorial reclamation.

The architects of counterrevolution may have replaced a colonial-era act with a new demonstrations law, but they resuscitated an even older colonial decree on public assembly (*tagamhur*) that has been the bedrock of Egypt's authoritarian policing for more than a century. After the outbreak of World War I, Law 10/1914 was issued on the direct order of British occupation authorities "to silence both the Egyptian political elite and ordinary people and give police greater control over dispersing crowds."[34] Defining assembly as any gathering of five people that "endangers public peace" through a set of exceedingly broad acts (committing a crime, obstructing the law, influencing the authorities, using force), the law sets a penalty of up to twenty years' imprisonment for offenders.[35] In effect, it renders it a conspiracy to gather in public. Law 10/1914 is the basis of all the trials of former president Morsi's supporters for the Rabʿa sit-in and protests against its dispersal. And *both* the demonstrations law and the assembly law are the basis of the trial and incarceration of Egypt's most- and least-known activists since the Rabʿa dispersal.[36] Alexandrian labor lawyer Mahienour al-Masry served two years for violating the 2013 protest law; April 6th founders Ahmed Maher and Mohamed Adel served three years (and three additional years of probation) for both assembly and participating in an authorized demonstration in November 2013; Kifaya youth activist Ahmed Douma is serving fifteen years for participating in the 2011 cabinet headquarters sit-in; blogger-activist Alaa Abdel Fattah served five years (and is still serving five additional years of probation) for participating in an unauthorized demonstration in November 2013; fourteen female members of the Muslim Brothers, "the 7 a.m. girls," were sentenced to eleven years each for forming a silent human chain on Alexandria's Corniche in the early morning, visualizing their anticoup message to passing motorists;[37] sixty-four al-Azhar University students were sentenced to terms ranging from one to seven years for clashes with security forces on their campus.[38] These are only the most publicized handful of cases; between November 2013 and September 2016, a documentation initiative counted 37,059 instances of arrests or detention for public gatherings, out of which 14,613 were referred to trial.[39]

## COME ON, SISI, I WANT YOU TO BE MY PRESIDENT!

Just as the postcoup authorities sought to empty the streets of self-organized protesters and fill them with their own insignia and loyalist crowds, so were elections emptied of their meaning as a competitive method for filling offices. During the revolutionary situation, Egyptians experimented for the first time with competitive contests for parliament and presidency, as we saw in chapter 4. While many voters were unhappy with the choices on offer, especially in the second round of the presidential election in June 2012, there was no gainsaying the competitive and open-ended nature of the contest. After the coup, elections lost the element of choice but did not revert to Mubarak-era contests. They turned into a form of politics that was rare under the Mubarak regime: government-orchestrated "prescribed performances."[40]

An early glimpse of this came in the first poll after the coup, the January 2014 referendum on a new constitution. Compared to the intense wrangling over process and product that dominated constitutional politics throughout 2012, postcoup constitution-drafting was a decorous affair. A committee of ten jurists drafted amendments to the 2012 document and passed them on to a committee of fifty to finalize; both committees were handpicked by acting president Adli Mansour, who had been installed by the military.[41] Unsurprisingly, the committee of fifty included no supporters of the Morsi administration; it was chaired by Amr Moussa of the anti-Morsi NSF and included various other anti–Muslim Brother public figures and representatives of state institutions. The two Islamists were a member of the Salafi Nur party that cheered the coup and an ex-Muslim Brother.[42] For weeks leading up to the referendum, public spaces were awash in "Yes" posters, and activists who tried to urge a "No" vote were arrested and faced charges of "the use of force or terrorism."[43] State officials and allied media outlets framed the referendum as a battle against terrorism, vowing that the Muslim Brothers' call for a boycott would "be confronted by a level of force and severity that has not been seen before."[44] In some polling stations, women queued up to vote held flags and identical posters of the defense minister with the taglines "We will fight terrorism to the death" and "The army, police, and people are as one." When the results were announced a few days later, they were heralded as a fresh start of a new era that needed to be crowned with new leadership. Tahrir Square was made accessible to dozens of cheerleaders who chanted, "Come on Sisi! I want you to be my president!"[45]

The 2014 referendum was hardly the only one that was less about constitutional content than the charged political context in which it occurred. The

TABLE 8. Results of Three Constitutional Referenda, 2011–2014.

|  | Yes | No | Turnout |
| --- | --- | --- | --- |
| March 2011 | 77.3% | 22.7% | 41.2% |
| December 2012 | 63.8% | 36.2% | 33% |
| January 2014 | 98.1% | 1.9% | 38.6% |

*Sources:* Higher Judicial Commission, https://referendum2011.elections.eg/homepage/2011-03-10-13-20-00/84-slideshow/158-2011-03-20-19-09-58.html; Supreme Election Commission, https://referendum2012.elections.eg/results/referendum-results; https://referendum2014.elections.eg/results/referendum-results.

provisions of the 2011 and 2012 referenda were similarly eclipsed by the political battles waged around them. In all three polls, the governing authorities were quick to disseminate their interpretation of the plebiscite as an expression of public confidence in their leadership and a manifestation of their oppositions' marginality. The difference is that the January 2014 referendum was accompanied by state repression and lethal use of force against the opposition. In addition to arresting the activists urging a "No" vote before the referendum, during the two days of polling police killed nine protesters and arrested 444.[46]

"Voting need not mean electing." Adam Przeworski's arresting reminder helps make sense of what appears a farcical charade of Abdel Fattah al-Sisi's election as president a few months after the referendum.[47] If the casting of ballots was not about voters choosing a president, that is, an act of popular authorization to exercise power for a set period of time, what did it mean? It harks back to what voting used to be before the advent of competitive or even semicompetitive elections: a spectacle of acclamation by grateful subjects for a leader who is depicted as the possessor of extraordinary qualities. In his portrait of nondemocratic charismatic authority, Max Weber underlined the crucial role of the ruled in validating the claim to charismatic legitimacy. The basis of the claim is:

> The conception that it is the duty of those subject to charismatic authority to recognize its genuineness and to act accordingly. Psychologically this recognition is a matter of complete personal devotion to the possessor of the quality, arising out of enthusiasm, or of despair and hope.[48]

In the variant of charismatic authority that he called plebiscitary democracy, Weber pointed out that "it is characteristic of the Führerdemokratie that there should in general be a highly emotional type of devotion to and trust in the leader."[49] The vote becomes the act of recognition that the leader is exceptional and has the complete devotion of the voter.

In the lead-up to election day, Sisi and the state he controlled intensified the image-making campaign begun in summer 2013, marketing the defense minister as a valiant, patriotic general who acted resolutely to defend his country from a dangerous internal menace. A catastrophizing frame was necessary to drown out the oppositional counterframe: that he had seized power by force from a democratically elected civilian and used state violence to crush resistance. Sisi was deracinated from his previous relationships—defense minister in a civilian cabinet, youngest member of the SCAF collegium—and put forward as a sui generis natural leader whose only bond was with an abstract and unitary people. His campaign videos and posters presented him "as a familiar, yet transcendent, figure," as Mohammed El-Nawawy and Mohamad Hamas ElMasry analyzed, "the posters showed Al-Sisi as 'one of us' but, at the same time, a true representative of Egypt capable of guiding the nation through a difficult period."[50] Political parties and groups endorsing Sisi cited a Middle East region wracked with wars and conspiracies that he was uniquely capable of navigating as a nonideological military manager and state insider. To the editor of a major progovernment daily, Sisi confessed his exceptional powers. "I am one of those with a long history of visions, though I've stopped talking about this for the past eight years." He related one dream where he was speaking to President Sadat and both shared that they had foreknowledge they would become presidents.[51]

To offset the leader's qualities was the sole competitor in the race: the maverick Nasserist parliamentarian Hamdeen Sabahy, whose 2010 election battle opened chapter 2 and who went on to become the dark horse in the first round of the 2012 presidential race, coming in third place after Mohamed Morsi and Ahmed Shafiq; he then served in the troika of NSF leaders that spearheaded the anti-Morsi coalition in 2012–13. Out of conviction or coercion, Sabahy was pressed into service as a foil to Sisi, though he said he was running to bring the revolution to the seat of power.[52] Instantiating Weber's idea that it is followers' duty to hail the leader, state organs and allied media used many means to get people into polling stations. Civil servants were given the first day off of the two-day voting period, then election commissioners made an unprecedented last-minute decision to extend voting for a third day when turnout was still sparse; election officials threatened fines for those who failed to vote; public transport was made gratis in Cairo, major shopping malls closed early, and vehicles with loudspeakers roamed the streets exhorting people to head to the polls.

The significance of Sabahy's role became clear in the tally of election returns. In province after province, including Sabahy's home province of Kafr al-Shaykh and those he carried in the 2012 election, Sisi trounced his presumptive challenger, receiving a minimum 90 percent of the vote in each district.[53] Sabahy's standing as a credible politician whose stature was confirmed in the 2012 contest made Sisi's overweening popular support appear all the more authentic. The turnout result hewed closely to the 2012 figure, 46 percent, compared to the 46.4 percent of the first round in 2012. Sisi won with what was announced as 97 percent of the vote to Sabahy's 3 percent. The dominant visual motif in coverage of the voting process was voters' joy, expressed through dancing outside polling stations and kissing posters of Sisi. At the press conference where election commissioners announced the results, loyalist journalists chanted "Sisi" and took over the podium, dancing to pro-army songs.[54] The plebiscitary result and the performances of enthusiasm communicated the bond between people and leader, the marginality of the prorevolution contingent represented by Sabahy, and the futility of the protest-based resistance to such a popular new order. The meaning of elections had changed from a barometer of political divisions and preferences (recall the five-way division of the first-round vote in 2012) to a national festival of acclamation.

The fate of legislative and subnational elections under the Sisi regime extended the leader-centered logic. One of Sisi's first decrees as president was to close off another space of free elections, namely faculty election of university presidents and deans that had been a major gain of the 2011 revolution. And when parliamentary elections occurred in fall 2015, they were a far cry from the NDP-opposition and intra-NDP contestation of the Mubarak years, to say nothing of the first free and competitive vote of 2011–12. Closer to a loyalist rally, the election's purpose was to seat a reliable adjunct to executive dominance in the form of a parliament. Instead of a state party as the organizational vehicle, the General Intelligence Service and Sisi's Military Intelligence division coengineered the process and outcome. Journalist Hossam Bahgat has shown how General Intelligence sponsored a slate called "For the Love of Egypt" that became known as "Sisi's list" and included in its fold the Wafd and Free Egyptians Party that supported the coup. Military Intelligence created a youth party (*Mustaqbal Watan* or Nation's Future) supporting the president and headed by a twenty-four-year-old college student who was too young himself to contest the election; it quickly attracted the sons of former NDP members and big businessmen eager for proximity to Sisi.[55] The Salafi Nur party that had supported the coup and won 25 percent of the seats in the 2011–12 election was allowed only eleven seats. The resulting legislature was a rubber stamp; out of the 341 executive decrees passed since 2013 and put to parliament for approval in its first session, all but one (the civil service law discussed below) were passed without question. In its second and third sessions, the laws passed by the legislature that originated in the executive branch were 76 percent and 89 percent of its total output, respectively.[56]

The second presidential election in 2018 retained the plebiscitary character to signal popular adulation of the unrivaled leader, but it took place in a more challenging environment. Intervening events between 2014 and 2018 had punctured Sisi's manufactured mystique. Several large protests across the country were triggered by the government's investment and austerity policies, particularly the government's signing of a $12 billion loan agreement with the IMF in 2016 that devalued the currency by half, reduced food and fuel subsidies, and implemented a range of new taxes. Several provinces witnessed protests against bread shortages; metro riders gathered on platforms and within metro carriages to agitate against tripled fare hikes; and one person was killed as residents of the Nile island of Warraq resisted security forces attempting to evict them and make way for luxury developments to be constructed by the armed forces' engineering arm.[57] Even before the IMF agreement, civil servants had organized a series of large protests in 2015 against a Sisi decree activating the civil service bill that had been quickly shelved by the Nazif government in the Eighteen Days in 2011. The law instituted performance reviews and gave managers wider latitude in determining promotions, which functionaries argued meant easier dismissals and shrinking benefits. As the civil servants protested, the police gradually corralled them into ever-smaller spaces and finally herded them into a park walled off from public view, a case study of how the 2013 demonstrations law's spatial control techniques worked to blunt the impact of even ostensibly nonpolitical protests.[58]

While the socioeconomic conflicts animating these protests recall the Mubarak era, when similar actions occurred daily in streets and public spaces, the difference is how harshly these protests were policed and their participants apprehended, and how they fed into a current of discontent with Sisi as the 2018 election cycle neared. The trigger for that discontent was his fateful foreign policy decision transferring sovereignty over the two Red Sea islands of Tiran and Sanafir to Saudi Arabia, the Sisi regime's principal diplomatic and economic patron. Opposition to the move was immediate and unexpectedly grew into the most significant domestic challenge to Sisi, damaging his carefully cultivated image as the only leader capable of preserving Egypt's territorial integrity. The next section on law and courts examines the Tiran and Sanafir controversy in more detail since court rulings played a central role in its unfolding; here its significance is what it meant for the presidential election in

2018. What Sisi had successfully blocked since the 2013 coup materialized after the islands' handover: the emergence of credible challengers who attempted to run against him, presenting themselves as more trustworthy protectors of Egypt's sovereignty.

The most serious challengers were three military men who sought to capitalize on the brewing opposition within the ranks to Sisi's transfer of the islands.[59] An unknown army colonel named Ahmed Qunsuwa announced his intention to run in a video statement that boldly criticized the human rights abuses and unilateral decision-making of the Sisi regime.[60] He was then tried before a military tribunal and sentenced to six years in prison. Ahmed Shafiq, Mubarak's last prime minister who narrowly lost to Mohamed Morsi in the 2012 election, emerged from his Dubai exile and fixated on the lack of tangible economic improvements as his plank. Left unchecked, Shafiq could have rallied the cross-class, anti-MB constituency that supported him in 2012 and appealed to those disenchanted with Sisi's unfulfilled promises. In short order, the UAE authorities deported Shafiq to Cairo, where he was whisked away by security agents at the airport and kept incommunicado until he announced the withdrawal of his candidacy on Twitter.

Sami Anan was Sisi's senior colleague in SCAF and had been retired by President Mohamed Morsi in August 2012. He reemerged with a prepared video statement broadcast by al-Jazeera in which he explicitly mentioned Sisi's inability to improve living conditions, eradicate terrorism, or protect Egypt's territory and natural resources as his rationale for running. Promising a pluralistic political order, restoration of rights and liberties, and a civilian-military partnership, he announced two prominent civilians as his vice presidential running mates, a political scientist and the former top government auditor (and Morsi appointee) that Sisi had sacked in 2016.[61] Such messaging addressed the segment of both the domestic public and foreign patrons who may have been receptive to a new civilian-military ruling group after losing confidence in exclusive military rule and its paltry returns under Sisi. Soon after his video aired, Anan was arrested and held in a military prison. The former auditor, Hisham Geneina, was assaulted by armed men and then sentenced to five years in prison by a military court for "publishing false information harmful to national security." The trial and conviction came after Geneina had made the explosive announcement that Anan possessed videotapes of SCAF meetings from autumn 2011 that exposed the role of military intelligence in the mass murder of unarmed protesters, when Sisi was the chief of military intelligence.

Three civilian critics and would-be contenders posed less of a challenge but gave voice to wider grumblings; they were pressured to withdraw their candidacies or were placed in jail. A poet/songwriter who authored a cutting satire of the president was charged with lèse-majesté and sentenced by a military court to three years in prison.[62] Buffeted by these unexpected challenges and prevented by austerity measures from pursuing expansionary fiscal policies, Sisi reached for the other fount of plebiscitary rulership: glory in war.[63] Three weeks before the election, the armed forces announced the launch of "Comprehensive Military Operation Sinai 2018" to crush the Islamic State affiliate in the peninsula, an assault involving army, navy, air force, border patrol, and police forces that Sisi vowed would eliminate the insurgency within three months. The insurgency was not terminated, but the operation entailed the most intense wave of home demolitions since 2014. With war-making against what state propagandists called "black terrorism" as the election's propellant, conscripting an opponent to run against Sisi was an eleventh-hour afterthought. The politician eventually selected was unknown to the public and a Sisi supporter.[64] The parliamentary youth organ *Mustaqbal Watan* was conscripted to get voters to the polls by hook or by crook, and Sisi exhorted that it was important to head to the polls even if one chose "No."[65] The result of 97 percent approval was identical to the 2014 election, with a lower turnout of 41 percent.[66]

Compared to 2014, the unforgiving circumstances accompanying the 2018 elections point to the diminishing returns of plebiscitary rituals, but they also highlight a deeper difficulty faced by Sisi in opting for the trappings of charismatic authority. Maintaining and consolidating the loyalty of followers hinges on victory in war, material improvements for the citizenry, or prestige on the international stage. Unable to deliver any of these desiderata, Sisi's approach was to build a highly personalized regime that delivered benefits of loyalty only to the indispensable few. A raft of laws and regulations steadily expanded the military establishment's privileges, immunities, and profit-making opportunities. In addition to infrastructure megaprojects that army companies would build and major new weapons imports, new decrees expanded military jurisdiction over public properties; allowed military, police, and intelligence services to establish security firms; and authorized the military agency that controls the sale of land to form companies with both domestic and foreign businesses.⁶⁷ The armed forces even got their own act of indemnity; Law 161/2018 shielded senior military commanders from prosecution for acts of violence committed between July 3, 2013, and January 2016. Symbolic details were not overlooked. In August 2013, a new decree changed the armed forces' oath from swearing loyalty to the president to "executing the orders of my leadership," formalizing SCAF's desire since 2011 to be beyond the reach of any civilian institution.

### EVERYTHING, THERE IS PUNISHMENT IN IT

Perhaps no arena better illustrates Hobsbawm's epigraph of revolutions as "state-generating" than that of law and courts. The counterrevolutionary work of producing new laws, instilling new understandings, and applying new intensities of state violence to eliminate political opponents was facilitated in large part by the courts. Far-reaching changes in the criminal law and the procedures and creation of exceptional courts have enabled a staggering roster of repression. Between 2014 and 2019, civilian and military courts handed down more than 1,891 death sentences and executed at least 174 persons. At least 1,700 people were subjected to enforced disappearances. Between 2013 and 2016, 534 persons died in custody. To house the tens of thousands of detained and convicted, sixteen new prisons were built between 2013 and 2016.

Under President Sisi, prisoners are held in inhuman conditions, subjected to prolonged solitary confinement which in some cases amounts to torture, and overcrowding is acute. The vast majority of the victims are supporters of the Morsi government, but anti-Morsi activists and journalists doing their work have been imprisoned, as well as untold numbers of uncommitted people who happened to get in the way of police sweeps. A fifteen-year-old bystander in Damietta who was picked up by police in a random roundup after a protest and sentenced to three years' imprisonment by a military court wrote to his mother, "I'll be standing, bending my legs, I have to take permission from the person who's older than me to stretch them. Everything, there is punishment in it."⁶⁸

The abuses committed by the legal and penal systems are enabled by a body of "state protective" decrees and legislation grafted on to Egypt's copious existing penal provisions; the 1914 Assembly Law discussed above is but one instance. In his magisterial work on the many facets of legal repression, Otto Kirchheimer traces the history of state protection enactments as a mirror of power holders' relations with their populations, from the Roman res publica to post–World War II Eastern and Western Europe. In the 1950s, legislative innovations sought "to protect the political order from any intellectual, propagandist, and especially organizing activity directed ultimately toward revolution."[69] The legal philosophy of Egypt's counterrevolutionary order evinces a similar zeal to inflate the concept of subversion so as to capture even seemingly trifling acts such as satirical online speech or private meetings of handfuls of dissidents that the Mubarak regime did not target. The notion of state protective legislation helps us see how restoring haybat al-dawla is an overwhelmingly although not wholly penal endeavor: "Because the substance of authority is under constant attack, its purveyor must watch closely the protection of its institutions and adornments."[70] A torrent of state protective decrees and laws have been passed from the days immediately after the coup and up to the present, hence the centrality of a rubber-stamp parliament; new laws establish strict administrative control over demonstrations, NGOs, trade unions, universities, all forms of media, and information technology. Amendments to the Code of Criminal Procedure and rules of appeal before the apex Cassation Court have further eroded the rights of the accused relative to the prosecuting machinery of the state.

This makes it reasonable to think of judges as the penultimate link in a chain of repression that starts with police officers arresting and torturing dissidents and bystanders; prosecutors pressing charges authored by police detectives; judges rendering summary sentences; and jailers overseeing degrading confinement conditions. As in other counterrevolutionary episodes, the police and judiciary seem to be a single apparatus, the former working to nip resistance in the bud and the latter punishing it after the fact.[71] The increasing odds of detention, even for nonpolitical citizens, prompted cause lawyer Haytham Mohamadein to author a step-by-step guide on navigating Egypt's penal process, titled *Make Yourself at Home, It's Your Prison*.[72] However, imagining a monolithic judiciary quickly falling in line with the new laws ignores a more checkered reality. To carry out legal repression on a counterrevolutionary scale, work had to be done to ensure judges' cooperation, bypassing the refractory ones, purging the open dissenters, and promoting the amenable.[73] The sprawling, institutionally diverse nature of Egypt's judiciary was as much an obstacle as a resource for counterrevolutionary power holders, requiring constant improvisation and workarounds to achieve the government's goals.

Criminal court judges began the resistance. In the autumn of 2013, when anticoup protests on and off campuses showed no signs of fading after the Rabʻa massacre, prosecutors began referring hundreds of protesters and MB leaders to criminal courts, only to have judges repeatedly recuse themselves from the politically motivated trials. The solution was to identify cooperative judges and assign them the task. In December 2013, one day after the cabinet decreed the Muslim Brothers a terrorist organization, the Justice Ministry announced the creation of eight specialized chambers within criminal courts, "the terrorism circuits" (*dawa'ir al-irhab*), presided over by twenty-four judges that would convene in two fortified police institutions.[74] It is these chambers that have handled the notorious mass trials of MB leaders, members, and followers. Some high-profile cases include:

- In March and April 2014, a Minya circuit imposed 1,212 death sentences in two cases involving attacks on police stations; these were later reduced to 220 while sentencing 495 other defendants to life in prison.
- In February 2015, a Giza circuit handed down death sentences for 183 defendants in the case of storming a police station in the Kerdasa neighborhood that killed eleven police officers and two civilians.
- In May 2015, a Cairo circuit sentenced to death former president Mohamed Morsi and 105 others, including senior MB leaders, for allegedly orchestrating mass prison breaks in January 2011 with the aid of Hamas and Hizbullah fighters.
- In September 2018, in the mass trial of 739 persons for participating in the Rabʻa sit-in, a Giza circuit sentenced seventy-five people to death, forty-seven to twenty-five years' imprisonment, and 612 to prison terms ranging from five to fifteen years. Among this latter group are twenty-two children, one son of former president Morsi, and photojournalist Shawkan.[75]

Judges in these courts often barred defense lawyers or refused them access to case files; reviewed no evidence, or considered only evidence provided by National Security officers; did not attempt to establish individual responsibility or even links to the purported events; and did not act on defendants' reports of forced confessions obtained through torture. They made little effort to disguise the bureaucratic nature of their work as an instrument of administrative authority in judicial form. However, since these courts are part of the criminal justice system and subject to Cassation Court review, defendants and their lawyers used multiple tactics to contest their dysfunction. Defense lawyers submitted sixteen motions for judges' recusal, citing their ideological hostility to defendants; four of the requests were granted and their cases assigned to new judges.[76] Lawyers have appealed verdicts to the apex Cassation Court, which has sided with defendants and repeatedly ordered retrials, including in the Minya, Kerdasa, and jailbreak cases, but has also upheld other convictions. Still, to close off this viable channel of appeal, in 2017 parliament passed amendments to the Code of Criminal Procedure reducing appeal opportunities and the retrial of whole cases.[77]

More new laws activated exceptional courts to circumvent the thrusts and counterthrusts of the ordinary judiciary and loosened the definition of terrorism to give even more scope to police and prosecutors. Four months after becoming president, Sisi decreed a Law on Protecting Public Properties (Law 136/2014) that expanded military jurisdiction over highways, universities, railroads, and bridges, opening the way for the military trials of civilians, which had peaked in 2011 but momentarily ceased during Mohamed Morsi's year in office. In its first two years of operation, the law enabled the military trial of 7,420 civilians, and in 2016 was extended for five more years.[78] A 2015 Counterterrorism Law punished a dozen different acts with the death penalty and inflated the definition of terrorism to cover acts of civil disobedience such as sit-ins or blocking roads.[79] In 2017, after suicide bombings of two churches, Sisi declared a state of emergency that automatically brought into force Emergency State Security Courts. Judges on these courts are appointed by the president and verdicts cannot be appealed in any way except by presidential amendment. The prime minister then decreed that all crimes under protest, assembly, labor, and terrorism laws would henceforth fall under the sole jurisdiction of the emergency courts.

If severe punishment and deterrence were the purpose of these measures, pedagogy was the point of the cases against the MB leadership. Quintessential political show trials, these were televised spectacles that sought to instill in the public again and again fear and revulsion toward the Muslim Brothers and gratitude to the military for delivering the country from their evil. Placing Muslim Brothers in the dock as foreign-aided internal enemies is as old as Egypt's republic,[80] but a new narrative was fashioned after 2013 anathematizing them as a fundamentally un-Egyptian threat to the state and nation. In this sense, the endless trials of MB leaders did the same reality-construction work as the media campaign that preceded the Rabʿa massacre and the Bonapartist aura contrived for Sisi. When seen together, the charges against Morsi in the six separate cases against him tell an official story of an experienced political operative who first abetted the chaos of the revolution by co-organizing a jailbreak with foreign fighters and then seized the presidency and used it as a beachhead to pass on state secrets to foreign powers, torture his opponents, and insult judges.[81] The indictment's distortion of actual events (such as the December 2012 Ittihadiyya clashes) is characteristic of show trials, which "use actual events as a small peg, at best, on which to hang an all-inclusive educational tale."[82] That tale could only be told if Morsi and other MB leaders could not use the trial as a forum to tell their own story. They were placed in soundproof cages during trial sessions, went for months at a time without seeing their lawyers, and were consistently addressed with contempt by judges.

Of course, the story that the government wished to tell was about more than the Muslim Brothers. During a December 2018 trial session of the jailbreak case, a smartly dressed and lucid Hosni Mubarak walked into the courtroom, protectively flanked by his two sons and solicitously addressed by the judge. Sitting on a plush leather chair while Morsi sat on a bench in the cage, Mubarak testified that on January 29, 2011, his director of intelligence, Omar Suleiman, informed him that eight hundred Hamas and Hizbullah fighters had breached Egypt's eastern border through the Gaza tunnels, attacked Wadi al-Natroun prison and looted its weapons depot, freed Morsi and other MB leaders detained in the prison, and then all headed to Tahrir Square where they sniped at protesters from atop surrounding buildings.[83] The idea that the Tahrir Square encampment was a foreign conspiracy to bring down the state emerged forcefully during the Eighteen Days but was laughed off after February 11, 2011. By 2018, paying homage to the January 25 revolution had been dropped from official discourse, and revolution-as-conspiracy had become the master frame. The purpose of the trials was to instill this idea. "The morality play, after serving the political needs of the day, will survive mainly as a testimony to its initiators' own frame of mind," Kirchheimer wrote.[84]

On one level, the jailbreak tale is an attempt to establish an official story of one of the most mysterious events of the Eighteen Days: how 23,000 prisoners were able to escape from several jails on January 29, 2011.[85] The rival popular understanding is that prison wardens let out the convicts, to sow mass fear and turn public opinion against the anti-Mubarak Tahrir protests. More abstractly, the story distills state elites' view of the popular uprising as a massive breach in the fortress of the state, an injury to its majesty (lèse-majesté). It brings into force the counterconcept of revolution as an act of high treason, government overthrow being the ultimate offense against the sovereign power. It remains a mystery what effects the show trials had on the uncommitted public. Newspapers covered the proceedings and talk show hosts brought in retired military generals to further mold perceptions of the court drama. In his last court appearance on June 17, 2019, former president Morsi continued to insist on his status as the legitimate president and demanded a special tribunal. He collapsed in the cage and passed away shortly thereafter.

The authorities acted with dispatch to preempt any public reaction. The prosecutor-general pronounced a heart attack as the cause of death, and security officials supervised the burial before dawn on June 18, with only immediate family present. They defied Morsi's wish to be buried in the family plot in Sharqiyya, insisting that he be interred in a Cairo cemetery alongside other MB leaders. Police armored vehicles and agents fanned throughout his hometown of El-'Adwa to prevent bereavement processions or condolence gatherings. Intelligence agents sent all private and government-owned newspapers the same forty-two-word death notice and instructed them to place it on an inside page. The notice made no reference to Morsi as the former president. Moncef Marzouki, the human rights activist who became Tunisia's first president after Ben Ali's fall, eulogized Morsi on his Facebook page, seeing his death in custody as "forever a testament to the fortitude of the man, his courage, his humanity, holding fast to his values and positions to the last breath."[86]

### EGYPT IS NOT FOR SALE

As they had in the Mubarak era and during the revolutionary situation, the administrative courts were still willing to strike down arbitrary acts of the postcoup government in defense of individual rights and public liberties. They reinstated expelled university students, upheld civil servants' right to strike, and ordered unemployment compensation for dismissed employees.[87] It was these courts' high-stakes challenge to Sisi's treaty-making that set them apart from the terrorism circuits and the exceptional courts, unwittingly facilitating the broadest domestic challenge to his rule. In April 2016, Egypt-Saudi relations were recemented with a series of agreements signed by King Salman bin Abdulaziz and Sisi in Cairo. The Saudi monarch, along with the ruling families of the United Arab Emirates and Kuwait, were the Sisi regime's chief patrons, supporting it with $23 billion since the 2013 coup and pledging an additional $16 billion in 2016 for a joint investment fund. In exchange, Sisi transferred sovereignty over the two disputed Red Sea islands of Tiran and Sanafir to the Saudi kingdom in what was formally called a maritime border demarcation agreement.

The uninhabited islands were not known to many Egyptians, but they had played a central role in the country's history of war with Israel. After Egypt's defeat in the 1967 Six-Day War, Israel had occupied the islands until 1982, returning them along with Sinai under the terms of the 1979 Peace Treaty. The treaty committed Egypt to guarantee free passage to Israeli shipping through the Straits of Tiran, at the mouth of which sat Tiran and Sanafir. Weeks before the transfer to Saudi Arabia, the Israeli government consented to the transfer; the kingdom would take over Egypt's commitment to guarantee Israeli passage through the straits and maintain a multinational peacekeeping force on Tiran.[88] The deal crystallized the regional realignment induced by the Arab uprisings, bringing together postcoup Egypt, Israel, Saudi Arabia, and the UAE in a concert of economic and military cooperation against Iran's influence in Syria and Iraq, on the one hand, and the Turkey-Qatar alliance that had backed the Morsi government, on the other.[89]

For many Egyptians, the deal was a humiliating giveaway in return for Gulf funding of Sisi's rule. Days after the transfer announcement, the largest street protests since 2013 broke out in downtown Cairo, university campuses, and some provincial capitals, with protesters reviving 2011's master chant as "'Aysh! Hurriya! El-Guzur di Masriyya!" (Bread! Freedom! These islands are Egyptian!). All of the major political and youth factions that Sisi had repressed and the politicians he had silenced came together in a campaign called "Egypt Is Not for Sale," with the conspicuous exception of the Muslim Brothers, who agitated against the transfer separately. All vowed to overturn Sisi's decision and set the Sinai Liberation Day holiday on April 25 as a day of protest. But in the days leading up to April 25 and for weeks thereafter, police arrested more than a thousand activists in their homes and on the streets.[90] Government publicists rushed to confirm the islands were Saudi territory that the kingdom had entrusted to

Egypt in 1950 and was now simply reclaiming. Cause lawyers and activists led by Khaled Ali, the youngest presidential candidate in 2012, began to assemble a case against Sisi's transfer for Majlis al-Dawla (the administrative courts), an initiative that took on the character of a crowd-sourced fact-finding commission. A heap of government publications, historical atlases, cadastral surveys, nineteenth-century manuscripts, military maps, and other original documents were delivered to Ali's law office by concerned citizens, researchers, and high-placed bureaucrats to bolster the case for Egypt's suzerainty over the islands.[91]

In June, the Court of the Administrative Judiciary was persuaded by the documents and ruled against the transfer, citing article 151 of the constitution as placing an absolute prohibition on territorial concessions.[92] The court's certification shifted the framing of the controversy from a feeble opposition howling against a fait accompli to an embarrassing international problem for the government and a minor crisis in Egypt-Saudi relations. Saudi Arabia halted its subsidized oil shipments to Egypt and made its displeasure known about its errant client's other policy lapses.[93] Pro-Sisi government media retorted with strong-worded criticisms of the Saudis' haughtiness; by that point, Egypt's debt to the Gulf states exceeded the total it owed to international financial institutions or any other state.[94] While Sisi's publicists were chest-beating, government lawyers quickly appealed the ruling before the Supreme Administrative Court (SAC), hoping for more circumspection from appellate judges aware of the international ramifications for Egypt and Sisi personally. In January 2017, in a courtroom packed with activists and television cameras, the panel of four senior judges upheld the lower court ruling. Amid cheers and tears of joy, Khaled Ali was lifted onto supporters' shoulders for a celebratory rally and media interviews in the street outside Majlis al-Dawla. Per the 2013 demonstrations law, the courthouse steps that activists had made into a favorite protest site since the 2000s were now inviolable space.

The day after the court decision, a pro-Sisi editorialist mused, "Now there is a new political reality. If the government insists on transferring the islands to Saudi Arabia by any means, the cost will be its legitimacy."[95] But a treaty confirming the regional counterrevolutionary order was not about to be repealed by an Egyptian High Court ruling. The government put into motion its plan for an end to the crisis. It obtained a ruling from a nonspecialized lower court that SAC had no jurisdiction to rule on treaty-making, then worked on threatening and cajoling refractory members of parliament to ratify the demarcation agreement into law.[96] On June 14, as security forces broke up protests and arrested more opposition figures, parliament voted by a show of hands to approve the deal; but then a hundred opposing deputies disrupted the proceedings and chanted "Masriyya! Masriyya!" Ten days later, Sisi signed the agreement into law. It remained to tie the legal loose ends of the controversy. Resorting to a time-tested workaround perfected by Mubarak's legal officers to deal with inconvenient SAC decisions, the government referred the nonspecialized lower court ruling and the SAC ruling to the Supreme Constitutional Court. The SCC was the only court with the competence to review conflicting court rulings issued by different courts. Whenever the SAC issued a ruling that went against government interests on a hot-button issue, the government would produce a rival ruling from the nonspecialized Court of Urgent Matters, then present both rulings to the SCC for a final, congenial disposition. On Tiran and Sanafir, the SCC handed down its final decision on March 3, 2018, three weeks ahead of Sisi's reelection. It ruled that only parliament and not Majlis al-Dawla had the prerogative to review international agreements.[97]

What is the significance of the Tiran and Sanafir contention? Its beginnings looked much like the lead-up to the January 25 day of action in 2011. Disparate groups from across the political spectrum found common cause in the highly charged matter of territorial integrity. After three years of silencing and repression, the reenergized protests demonstrated that Sisi had not decisively incapacitated public opposition, nor delivered the material welfare that might win him a genuine, broad loyalist base that he could lean on in times of trouble. The treaty induced the most visible split among the top generals since their coming together as SCAF in 2011. At the peak of the controversy, Sami Anan wrote on his Facebook page what amounted to an announcement of his presidential intentions: "It's not important now to prove that Tiran and Sanafir are Egyptian, that's not in doubt. What's doubtful is the Egyptian identity of those who oppose the Egyptianness of the islands." Differences over Tiran and Sanafir reportedly lay behind Sisi's dismissal of his top two loyalists, the minister of defense and the army chief of staff.[98] In sum, cause lawyers' activation of the administrative courts dragged out what was intended as a cordial international agreement into an acrimonious yearlong imbroglio that stripped Sisi of his self-styled standing as an irreproachable nationalist.

Yet he succeeded in turning the treaty into law before it could become the trigger for a mass movement against him. Prosecutors used the repressive new laws to charge nearly six hundred protesters, and the terrorism circuits sentenced scores of them to years behind bars.[99] Through intimidation and coercion, Sisi eliminated from the field all those who sought to leverage the controversy to run against him in the 2018 elections. Then he moved to establish greater control over the judiciary, using parliament to pass a law in 2017 that achieved what Nasser, Sadat, and Mubarak had struggled to do: control top judicial appointments. Echoing Sisi's control over universities, Law 13/2017 granted the president the power to appoint the chief justices of the two apex courts, overturning the strong norm of judicial self-selection based on seniority that had developed since the founding of the courts in 1931 and 1946.[100] Then, in 2019, to short-circuit challenges to its constitutionality, the law was grafted onto the constitution in a referendum (along with several other amendments) that passed with an announced turnout of 44 percent and 88.8 percent approval.

What Sisi could not achieve in the 2014 constitution he was able to attain with the 2019 amendments, a package of provisions that consolidated the sprawling powers of Egypt's state in the militarized executive. The changes expanded presidential and military power and diminished judicial controls, codifying a personalized executive unchecked by any force of law or public opinion (save perhaps for his foreign creditors). They extended the president's tenure from four to six years, adding a special provision enabling Sisi to run for a third term in 2024 and thus remain in office until 2030. They constitutionalized the president's power to appoint chief justices, including the third apex Supreme Constitutional Court. They methodically abridged all three functions of Majlis al-Dawla. Article 190 stripped the administrative courts of the exclusive right to offer authoritative legal opinions to high executive officials (president and ministers); dropped the requirement that the courts vet government-issued legislation; and limited court review of all public contracts, restricting it to certain categories to be determined by law. Finally, the amendments elevated the armed forces to protectors of the constitution, democracy, and the civil foundation of the state. In an Orwellian construction, article 200 also designated the armed forces as "protectors of the gains of the people and the rights and liberties of individuals," the latter a usurpation of Majlis al-Dawla's self-definition.[101]

What is at issue with the Tiran and Sanafir controversy is not whether it constituted a defeat or victory for Sisi, since it was both in succession. He parlayed what started as the largest domestic challenge to his standing into an opportunity to extend his personal rule, by codifying executive and military dominance in the constitution. From the perspective of this book, what matters is how the episode conformed to a robust pattern in Egypt's politics before, during, and after the revolutionary situation, where political struggles are conducted through juridical forms. After two decades of articulation, the phenomenon has the quality of a script. It starts with a government decision, its opponents, and a judicial arbiter rendering an unpredictable judgment. From that basic trilateral relation ramify many more actors and controversies: media organs; protesters, police, and prosecutors; other courts; parliamentary deputies, government and opposition; government lawyers and publicists; if the government decision concerns foreign relations, the officials and publicists of a foreign government enter the controversy; and, not least, there is domestic and international public opinion, the real target of the claimants' litigation. The unpredictability of how the court will rule drives the process, given administrative judges' resistance to complete integration with government objectives. This in turn stems not from judges' personal ideologies but from their adversarial institutional position as final inspectors of the legality of executive acts. It is that wedge between the executive and judicial domains of the Egyptian state that litigating citizens have seized and tried to deepen, in the process developing a form of doing politics by judicial means.

Of course, when activists and regular citizens pull judges into political controversies, whether high affairs of state such as Tiran and Sanafir and the 2008 sale of natural gas to Israel or seemingly lowly matters of municipal garbage collection, they hope for rulings that invalidate government acts. But even when a court rules for the government, there is the channel for appeal. For the cause lawyers and opposition activists' ultimate goal is disruption, to create a controversy, to slow down official decision-making processes and bring them into the light so that a public opinion can take shape and people can see how they are being governed. A competitive media helps them in this airing, motivated by its own interests in boosting circulation or grinding the axes of its tycoon owners. One way to see these dynamics is in the terms coined by political theorist

Norberto Bobbio, who defines political rule as a long history of invisible power, the *arcana imperii*, the "need to make major political decisions in secret, far from the public's indiscreet eyes."[102] From this vantage, the nub of administrative litigation is purposeful, organized indiscretion, ensnaring power holders in judicially mediated disputes contrived expressly to unmask the *arcana imperii*. The manifesto of the *"Egypt Is Not for Sale"* campaign made its claim in these terms, denouncing the obscurity of the border demarcation negotiations "and the norm of ignoring the Egyptian people and continuously excluding them from the decision-making process."[103] Reestablishing the secrecy and sanctity of government acts is the purpose of the 2019 constitutional changes shielding certain public contracts from judicial scrutiny. Coupled with a 2014 law prohibiting third parties from challenging public contracts before the administrative courts, closing off an avenue to airing corrupt land and privatization deals that activists in the Mubarak years had carved out, the Sisi regime's rule changes seek to block citizens' use of juridical means to attain political ends.[104] To the extent that they terminate this mode of political struggle, they will have succeeded.

\* \* \*

Counterrevolution is a creative endeavor. It chases out the practices and collective understandings of the revolutionary interregnum with its own counter ideas and institutions. To be sure, a state-led counterrevolution such as Egypt's has a great deal of antirevolution in it, using the maximal legal and coercive apparatus of the state to liquidate opposition. But it is more ambitious than routine state repression. It seeks to overwrite the parenthesis of the revolution and to recode the Mubarak era before it, eliminating the subcultures of opposition that had developed under the Mubarak regime as a harmful and unnecessary obstruction to smooth ruler-ruled relations. In elections, the revolutionary practice of marking a ballot paper with multiple choices to decide who governs was replaced with marching to the polls as an act of gratitude for decisions made elsewhere. Courts as a forum for establishing facts and rights were countered with courts as instruments of prosecutorial calumniation, platforms from which to air the official *thèse du complot* of the revolution as a foreign-aided conspiracy to bring down the Egyptian state with the help of MB fifth columnists. Protests were first met with countercrowds hailing the leader, then when that became unsustainable, policemen plucked activists from their homes and pedestrians off the streets before the first chants could be shouted; "now we confront them once they congregate," as the interior minister said.

To the extent that Hosni Mubarak's regime developed a doctrine of rule, it was that Mubarak's sage and steady leadership was to be continued and modernized by his reform-minded son, a former banker fluent in the workings of international finance. Sisi's governing ideology is couched in catastrophic terms, as a rescue mission from a near-fatal breakdown of the state that had brought out all that is dangerous and uncouth in Egyptian society. Religious fanatics infiltrated the state; "these people believe they are martyrs who will go to paradise when they die," he told German journalists. Women shamelessly camped out with men in Tahrir Square; he admitted that military doctors had conducted forced pelvic exams on female protesters, to "protect the army against potential allegations of rape." Insolence toward revered institutions was rampant; "I will not allow you to use that word again, the proper term is the military institution," he scolded journalist Ibrahim 'Issa for uttering the revolutionary commonsense word 'askar to refer to the military. Unseemly public controversies erupted over high matters of state; "Please let us not talk about this matter again," he said about the Tiran and Sanafir agreement.[105] More than an offended patriarchal sensibility, what underlies these phrases is a Hobbesian conception of communal life, that Egyptians are naturally inclined to baseness and violence if not held in thrall by a secure and transcendent state. The revolution was a calamity that unleashed these forces of disorder, "and now we're picking up the pieces," Sisi said in an extended interview days before the 2018 elections.[106]

Having survived the trauma, state managers constructed fortifications of protective legislation, acclamatory elections, and penal colonies, driven by an acute awareness of future threats. What appears as paranoia or overkill in the state's pursuit of dissent is endemic to the military/police fixation on anticipating future harms and planning for their prevention. Unlike elected governments that are legitimized by their origins, as Alain Rouquié observes, "military regimes are only really legitimized by their future."[107] No longer fighting interstate wars, the Egyptian military turned its combat energies to the internal unrest and mayhem that civilians called a revolution. The work of the counterrevolution is to rhetorically recode revolution-era political struggles as "disorder" and materially establish every possible safeguard to prevent its recurrence. "The conservative tone of military thought on civil contention or riot, for example, comes from

FIGURE 11. Funeral procession for former president Hosni Mubarak, February 2020. Khaled Desouki/AFP via Getty Images. Reprinted with permission.

surrounding contentiousness with visions of doom," noted Arthur Stinchcombe in an insightful obiter dictum.[108] If the Mubarak regime had evolved from the preemption to the management of citizens' collective action, the Sisi regime now obsessively acts first before action gets off the ground, convinced that any small protest, individual act of dissent, or legal challenge will escalate in unpredictable ways into turmoil of national proportions. The 2019 constitutional amendments can be read in this light, as a permanent anticipatory posture, ever ready for a host of possible scenarios. Rolling back judicial autonomy and jurisdiction fills in loopholes from underneath which future challenges may slip through. Inscribing the armed forces as arbiters of the meaning of the constitution, democracy, and the civil state works as a catch-all shield against possible futures, should others emerge and claim the mantle to those lofty aspirations. Appropriating the institutional ethos of protecting individual rights from the judiciary endows the military with full discretion to define what individual rights and liberties are.

Initially circumspect about invoking the Mubarak regime, the counterrevolutionary order reembraced Hosni Mubarak after he was cleared by an appeals court in 2017 of any responsibility for the killing of protesters during the Eighteen Days. When he died in 2020, the state ordered three days of national mourning and organized a full-honors military funeral, with cannon fire and a horse-drawn carriage carrying his coffin. Fronted by Abdel Fattah al-Sisi, Mubarak's sons, and the former acting president appointed by the military after the July 3, 2013, coup, a cortege of top state officials marched to a military-owned mosque for the funeral service. Observing the state pomp, one would hardly know that Mubarak had been toppled by a national uprising. The funeral displayed an uninterrupted lineage of state prestige.

*Conclusion*

# BREAD AND FREEDOM
عيش و حرية

> The business conducted by government is the public business of the realm and of everyone in it rather than the patrimony of any privileged individual or family.
> —Jeremy Waldron, "Accountability and Insolence"

AT THE END OF 2010, HOSNI MUBARAK CONTROLLED ONE OF THE most resilient authoritarian regimes in the world. When Tunisian president Zine al-Abidine Ben Ali fled his country on January 14, 2011, after a month-long popular revolt, no one seriously projected a similar fate for the powerful Egyptian president-for-life. Just under a month later, Mubarak was toppled by a popular uprising-cum-coup; his top military generals capitalized on the opportunity to edge aside their commander and his dynastic succession plans and put themselves in charge. They expertly exploited divisions within the fractious opposition to enervate the Islamist and secular politicians and inexperienced youth activists who had come together to unseat Mubarak. They allowed a presidential election that an Islamist politician narrowly won. But his divisive rule and executive overreach spurred a mass movement calling for his ouster one year into his term. On July 3, 2013, the generals stepped in again, removing the new president and crushing his political organization. This time, they did not attempt to rule from behind a civilian facade but placed one of their own in the presidency and returned Egypt to military dictatorship. The uprising ended in tragic failure.

This book has tunneled underneath this standard retrospective account of the most eventful juncture in Egypt's contemporary political history, ruffling its cool compression, raising questions suppressed by its linear logic, and resurfacing events it has redacted to arrive at its conclusions. If the uprising boils down to a story of shrewd military generals seizing a historic opportunity to put themselves in charge, why did they take such a circuitous path that involved law as much as force? Why did they allow free elections to a parliament and presidency that they then overturned? How was the civilian opposition "weak," if it had united to topple Hosni Mubarak? And how did it then unite again against the first elected president that many of them had grudgingly voted for? Why did courts and judges figure so prominently in revolutionary politics? Is it not possible that things turned out as they did not because of the incompetence of the civilians and the strategic deception of the generals, but because far more than two or three stylized antagonists were pulled into the fray of revolutionary politics, and their interactions made a large difference to the outcome?

This book has taken uncertainty, which nearly every study on Egypt's uprising mentions in passing, and placed it at the center of the analysis as its foundational framework, taking seriously what political interaction looks like in the midst of so many intersecting, opaque, and confounding circumstances. It has waded through a great number of events to construct an analytical narrative, not of everything that happened or all the twists and turns, but of those big and small events that bore on the mainline struggle to rearrange power within the state, and between state organs and various interest groups. It has attempted "to account for the kind of volatility that seems to be characteristic of the processes of regime transformation," as Adam Przeworski observed during an earlier epoch of political upheaval, "in which alliances are extremely shaky and particular groups and pivotal individuals at times shift their positions by 180 degrees."[1] By temporally tracing dynamic trajectories rather than fixating on causes and consequences, I have moved closer to the historical traditions of studying revolutionary upheaval and further away from causal social science frameworks that select one or two decisive factors that are argued to produce outcomes.

I have no quarrel with the judgment that the uprising is a failure, if by that is meant the historiographical invitation to explain what happened, though "defeat" would be the more precise term.[2] As the Sudanese protesters who brought down the thirty-year reign of Omar al-Bashir chanted in April 2019, "Either Victory or Egypt!" The problem with "failure" is when it slips into claims of futility, the favorite intellectual weapon of conservatives ever ready to diminish challenges to the status quo, especially their bugbear of revolutions. Albert Hirschman has already memorably unmasked this sort of argument and its "insulting character, by the contemptuous rebuff it opposes to any suggestion that the social world might be open to progressive change."[3]

Chapter 1 noted that state power changed hands three times during the revolutionary situation: from Mubarak to the military generals in February 2011; from the generals to president Mohamed Morsi in 2012; and the final seizure of power by the military with its removal of Morsi on July 3, 2013. In the course of the analysis, five more dates assumed significance (see table 9), revealing that state power was not a prized single bloc to be captured in one stroke but instead comprised of the distinct components of legislative and executive powers, with judicial powers acting as decisive arbiters. The seating of parliament on January 23, 2012, and its assumption of legislative powers proved unexpectedly disruptive, leading to a confrontation with SCAF over appointing a new government and an intraparliamentary battle over the constitution. Five months into its existence, a Supreme Constitutional Court ruling dissolved the legislature. The second date was June 17, 2012; in what amounted to a second coup, SCAF quickly reseized the vacated parliament's legislative power and claimed for itself presidential prerogatives and final say over constitution-making. Thus when he was sworn in as president two weeks later, Mohamed Morsi was widely perceived as a "president without power."[4] However, two months later, on August 12, Morsi upended expectations with a presidential countercoup, reshuffling SCAF's leadership, seizing legislative power, and appointing the youngest SCAF member, Abdel Fattah al-Sisi, as defense minister. Three months later on November 22, 2012, Morsi confronted the courts. To preempt impending court rulings to dissolve the elected constituent assembly, Morsi issued an emergency powers decree shielding the assembly and his decisions from judicial annulment until the assembly's constitution was put to a referendum. Swift, broad-based opposition forced him to rescind the decree two weeks later.

The many other events analyzed throughout these pages all radiate from or impinge upon these transfers. Indeed, their listing in a table belies the fact that these dates were not scheduled calendar events but outcomes of unremitting struggles over the core powers of lawmaking and executive actions, some of

TABLE 9. Transfers of Power during the Revolutionary Situation, 2011–2013.

| | |
|---|---|
| February 11–13, 2011 | SCAF seizes executive and legislative power after resignation of Hosni Mubarak |
| January 23, 2012 | Parliament assumes legislative powers |
| June 14–17, 2012 | Parliament dissolved by court order, SCAF seizes legislative and some executive powers |
| June 30, 2012 | SCAF turns over truncated executive powers to President Mohamed Morsi |
| August 12, 2012 | Mohamed Morsi wrests executive powers from SCAF and seizes legislative powers |
| November 22, 2012 | Mohamed Morsi assumes emergency powers |
| December 8, 2012 | Mohamed Morsi rescinds emergency powers |
| July 3, 2013 | Defense Minister Abdel Fattah al-Sisi ousts President Mohamed Morsi, appoints Judge Adli Mansour as acting president |

which were resolved by judicial powers. Various courts repeatedly intervened to block the new elected institutions' exercise of lawmaking and executive prerogatives. An administrative court annulled the new parliament's most significant act: the selection of one hundred delegates to the Constituent Assembly (CA). The Supreme Constitutional Court (SCC) invalidated the hastily passed lustration law and then parliament as a whole. It then invalidated the second CA formed by parliament, even though it had already produced a constitution that was ratified in a referendum, in what Nimer Sultany terms a form of "retroactive delegitimation."[5] Under the regime of Abdel Fattah al-Sisi, the administrative courts continued to issue troublesome rulings in response to opposition lawsuits, especially against Sisi's controversial handover of Red Sea islands to Saudi Arabia. To seal off this dangerous opening to opposition litigation, in 2019 Sisi introduced an amendment to the constitution limiting administrative courts' jurisdiction over public contracts. As the late Ellis Goldberg aptly remarked, "Unlike any other similar upheaval in the previous two centuries, the Egyptian revolution was one in which legality and the interpretive decisions of the country's highest judges played a dominant role in its outcome."[6]

By definition, revolutions are about control over states. The causes-and-consequences sociological tradition is all about how state structures break down and then get reconstructed under new management. The concept of a revolutionary situation focuses on the intervening power struggle, after the initial breakdown but before the consolidation of a new arrangement. It makes visible a truth so basic that it goes unmentioned: state institutions possess multiple powers. Hence, the struggle will be a multilateral affair, with many actors within and outside of state institutions vying over authorities and jurisdictions. When the unexpected 2011 uprising vacated the supreme office in the republican authoritarian state, the presidency, a hectic scramble ensued within the executive as agencies and personnel experienced rapid shifts in status and disruption of routines. As Ivan Ermakoff characterizes the posture of actors during these general processes of transition, "Some are on the move: they experience the conjuncture as an opportunity to advance their own interests. Others are under challenge: they believe that their interests are jeopardized."[7] The military generals who rapidly constituted themselves as the Supreme Council of the Armed Forces did so out of both opportunity and jeopardy. The threat was that the momentum of the popular revolt would reach into the exclusive preserves of the state and eventually target them and other state aristocrats. The opportunity was to set the agenda of political reconstruction and define the limits of the possible. The challenge was to reduce rates of change within state organs and between state agencies and social forces.

Indeed, we saw how one of the generals' main problems was controlling the churning within the civil service, as humble functionaries seized the opportunity of national political turmoil to agitate against degrading work conditions and the petty tyrannies of bureaucratic bosses. Similarly, from the moment Mubarak was toppled, low-ranking policemen engaged in demonstrations and strikes. As with their civilian counterparts, patrolmen and police superintendents acted collectively against what they decried as their impossible situation: following the orders of superiors and becoming reviled targets of popular wrath and revenge; or refusing orders and being subjected to military tribunals and other stiff disciplinary measures. It was partly due to this disarray in the police hierarchy that the military took on direct policing functions in the months following February 2011, evicting squatters from vacant housing units and prosecuting thousands of civilians before military tribunals for petty and property crimes.[8] The uprising generated disobedience toward constituted authority by those within the state as well as those outside it.

The biggest disruption to the state was the incursion of new social forces into its political institutions, the Islamist and secular political parties that populated parliament in a surge unseen since the 1940s, and the Islamist political party leader who was elected president. The incipient democratization of an authoritarian state has become rather routinized in the literature on democratic transitions, so that we forget how threatening, and revolutionary, fledgling democracy is. Historical sociologist Michael Mann recovers that sense of precarity in his description of how nineteenth-century European states, essentially elite holdings, came under assault through contested elections. "Civil society also becomes far more politicized than in the past, sending out diverse raiding parties—pressure groups and political parties—into the various places of the state, as well as outflanking it transnationally."[9] States became cohabited by monarchies, the military, bureaucrats, and political parties, institutionalizing new social conflicts.

In Egypt, the first freely elected parliament and presidency were so fleeting, crisis-filled, and controversial that they are not remembered at all (parliament), or only primarily as an object lesson in Islamist autocracy (president). My reconstruction casts doubt on these judgments, drawing attention to the destabilizing effects of new entrants into exclusive institutions. Not only did existing elites—military generals, judges, diplomats, police chiefs, ministers—resent having to cohabit the state and take orders from elected civilians, those civilians wasted no time in launching confrontations with entrenched officeholders to assert their authority. This did not make for cordial relations. The new parties were vulnerable to the accusation leveled at every parvenu: seeking to impose their will by force. The elected president's attempts to counteract the blockage of his policies was widely framed as a power grab. Ideologues of the ancien régime, as well as intellectuals disenchanted with the endless maneuvers of party and bureaucratic politics, activated implicit yet embedded conceptions of state neutrality, premised on the superiority of ostensibly nonpolitical state managers over divisive and incompetent political party leaders. Juan Linz memorably captured the resurgence of this worldview in the turbulence of new democracies, a *ressentiment* politics that poses a serious problem for newly elected leaders. "Certain sectors of society, particularly army officers, civil servants, and sometimes intellectual leaders, feel a stronger identification with the state or the nation than with a particular regime and reject in principle the partisan identification of the state."[10]

Similarly, Adam Przeworski described the shock experienced by state managers at the advent of even timid democratization. "For authoritarian bureaucrats, the introduction of democracy constitutes an ideological defeat, a collapse of their very vision of a world that can be rationally commanded to one's will. Uncertainty is what they abhor ideologically, psychologically, and politically."[11] When a military general gathered journalists as parliamentary elections were underway in late 2011 to inform them that parliament would not be controlling the government or the constituent process, he was retracing a long line of authoritarian state elites determined not to devolve power to civilians.

The counterrevolutionary state's haybat al-dawla doctrine is the apogee of this weltanschauung, this vision of a world without contending interests or multiple solutions to pressing problems: a world where major public policies, domestic and foreign, are a matter of the *arcana imperii*, not public controversy or deliberation. It preaches instead a metaphysical conception of the state as an integrated unity, rising above the divisions and parochial identities of fractious civil society to lead the nation. In Egypt and the Arab world more broadly, this conflict between democratic publicity and statist prerogative is invariably cast in terms of the Islamist-secular divide; Islamists want to Islamize society and "take over" the state to realize their vision, and secularists want to modernize state and society and protect them from Islamist obscurantism. The implication of my discussion here is that, had the Islamists espoused a different ideology, say socialism, or liberalism, or communism, as elected civilians they would have faced the same hostility from nonpartisan, but not nonpolitical, state elites. The social locations of the insurgent forces and the incumbents is what drives the conflict, not a free-floating ideational contest. Elected state institutions with a new social basis, particularly a legislature, threatened the cozy comity of military, diplomatic, and intelligence enclaves of the state, long accustomed to being well beyond public scrutiny and responsible only to their peers and superiors. In Arab politics, these untouchable state departments even have a matter-of-fact appellation: "sovereign ministries" (*wizaraat al-siyada*).

Decisions by the third state authority were decisive in this battle between the elected and unelected institutions. Court rulings overturned acts of the legislature and eventually nullified the institution itself. But since courts do not act alone, we ought to write back into the narrative the role of litigants, mobilizing the courts as a weapon to weigh in on the central constitutional conflicts. In Egypt, judicial action took three forms: rulings by administrative courts, rulings by the Supreme Constitutional Court (SCC), and the concerted activism of the national association of judges, the Judges' Club. These were the very same forms that had developed during the Mubarak years. Legal contention became one of the three main arenas of political sparring between government and opposition. During the revolutionary situation, the movers and targets of judicial action switched sides. Pre-2011, the dissident-controlled Judges' Club and oppositional litigants resorted to both kinds of courts to contest the policies of the Mubarak regime. From 2011 to 2013, litigants challenged the majority-controlled elected state institutions, as did the Judges' Club, wrested from the dissidents by Mubarakists and turned into a main platform for antiparliamentary and anti-Morsi agitation. Under the Sisi regime, the Judges' Club became a main government ally (its head was appointed justice minister), as did the SCC, leaving administrative courts as the sole institutional avenue of challenging the regime.

The one thing that can be said about all this complexity is that courts remained a viable channel for dissent across regime types; under Mubarak, citizen activists resorted to courts to expose his unaccountable policies, and in the interregnum they mobilized the courts to check the majoritarian legislature. Consistent with courts' basic role as countermajoritarian institutions, Egypt's courts proved an attractive avenue for weak actors under different kinds of state power configurations. Hence the gravity of the Sisi regime's attempt to end this role with the 2019 constitutional amendments, reversing a three-decade-long trend of growing popularity and visibility of judicial power, what Enid Hill pinpointed many years ago as "the present political struggle to wrest control over law-making from the Executive."[12] The extreme and unprecedented centralization of public powers in the executive under Sisi is a direct response to the fragmentation of state powers opened up by the revolutionary situation. The 2011 uprising unmade one power balance (monarchical presidency, subordinate parliament, resistant judiciary), opening the way to a triennium of contested sovereignty that terminated in a durable new distribution (supreme presidency, presidential offshoot in parliamentary form, disempowered judiciary). A revolutionary situation, a nonrevolutionary outcome.

\* \* \*

If the politics of the uprising is a story about entrenched bureaucratic elites defeating civilian democratic forces, it manifestly is also about bitterly divided and mutually antagonistic civilians. This book's pages can be read as a series of ramifying cleavages that kept splintering the original anti-Mubarak coalition. The schisms were so serious, and the initiatives of bridge-building so tenuous, that twenty-eight months after Mubarak's fall, most civilian factions had realigned with their erstwhile enemies, fulul politicians and Mubarakist judges, against the isolated Muslim Brother president, organizing mass protests demanding early presidential elections to eject him from office. The military used the June 30, 2013, demonstrations to strike three days later, arresting and imprisoning the president and suspending the constitution. It is this aspect of fatal divisions that has received the most attention and chagrin of commentators from a range of backgrounds. Khalil al-Anani finds that "secular, liberal, Islamist, and leftist forces all failed astonishingly in making the compromises and concessions required in any democratic transition." The Palestinian scholar-activist Azmi Bishara, one of the most knowledgeable and incisive observers of the Arab uprisings, argued that, "the decisive factor, in my view, is the inability of the pro-revolution forces to agree on democratic principles and impose them as a united front on the ancien regime." The late Alfred Stepan wrote that the "intensive negotiations among leading secularists and leading Islamists to overcome mutual fears of the sort we have documented for Tunisia, never really occurred in Egypt."[13] All identify the absence of the hard work of political communication and bargaining as the Achilles' heel preventing the civilians from closing ranks, ultimately enabling the military to exploit their divisions and terminate the democratic experiment.

These authors do not probe why the civilian forces failed to do this work, even though there was hardly a shortage of political conferences in the years 2011–13. They argue by assertion, taking it as self-evident that a coalescence of civilian forces would have formed a formidable barricade against the generals' designs for a tutelary role in the fledgling democracy. This goads us to think more deeply about why political factions that had developed a persuasive framing of the Mubarak regime as corrupt and inept, and built constituencies of public support for their argument, could not sustain their cooperation after Mubarak fell, not only parting ways but some actively constructing a coup coalition that helped build sizable public support for the military takeover of July 3, 2013. The issue boils down to not why Islamists en bloc split with secularists en bloc; neither camp acted coherently. But why did virtually all political forces, including Salafis, turn against the Muslim Brothers? Why was the MB abandoned, bereft of allies, hemorrhaging electoral support in major urban centers, its offices and cadres repeatedly violently attacked during Morsi's last months in office, and without much public sympathy or concern even after their ejection from power and the mass killings of their supporters by security forces in 2013?

The conventional answer is that the Muslim Brothers brought this on themselves. Their domination of parliament, the constituent process, then the presidency showed their true colors; their ejection from power was comeuppance for their intolerable political hubris. This is an emotionally satisfying tale, resurrecting the idea developed after Algeria's 1991 election that Islamists would only concede "one man, one vote, one time," instrumentalizing democracy to establish their dictatorship. An explanation stressing the primacy of politics sees it differently, surfacing details that make it even more of a puzzle why an unbridgeable rift developed between the largest civilian political organization and its fellow travelers.

Though the March 19, 2011, referendum is remembered as the turning point that fractured the anti-Mubarak coalition, because the 77 percent public approval rating for the electoral transition path is read as "the rise of the Islamists," an all-party coalescence against the military occurred several more times during the revolutionary situation. In November 2011, a Tahrir Square milyuniyya forced the military generals to backtrack on their desire to stay in power for two more years until they secured the constitution they wanted. Liberal and Nasserist parties contested the general elections on the MB's slate. In the first month of parliament's life in 2012, the Port Said stadium disaster and US NGO crisis acted as bonding events, bringing together Salafi, MB, and secular deputies in a coalition of outrage against SCAF and its Ganzouri cabinet. Untold numbers of political activists and ordinary citizens made an agonizing choice to vote for Mohamed Morsi, to avert the worse outcome of Ahmed Shafiq becoming president. Days before he was sworn in as president, Mohamed Morsi convened with two dozen leaders of secular parties and youth groups at the Fairmont Meeting, to promise that he would appoint a coalition cabinet not led by an MB figure.[14]

Why were these rapprochements not sufficient to build a robust front against the ancien régime? Why could they not withstand intervening events that consistently broke down emergent cooperative relations and turned them into collisions? Here we can look more closely at the damaging legacies of the Mubarak regime and civilian actors' diverging assessments of how best to organize the transition. Underlying those varied assessments are the multiple layers of differences that ultimately kept the civilians fragmented. First among them is a major philosophical distinction that transcends Egypt's fractious civilians and cuts through the theory and practice of democracy. The MB and its political wing, the FJP, adhered to a majoritarian conception of democracy. As the plurality party certified through honest elections, MB leaders believed that they should be allowed to lead and get things done, with some inclusion of other parties based on their relative electoral weight, but as junior partners rather than equals. Power in this view amounts to rotation of power, not power-sharing arrangements, and the ultimate test of parties' viability is the verdict at the polls.

This is an uncontroversial view among plurality and majority parties in consolidated majoritarian democracies, but it resonates differently in first-time democracies, injecting a damaging strain of paternalism. MB leaders routinely and unself-consciously spoke of other political forces as novices, presenting themselves as elder statesmen exerting a moderating influence on the turbulence of revolutionary politics.[15] An observation by two political scientists in the immediate wake of postcommunism in Hungary illuminates the point. Describing reform Communists' "postpaternalism" toward other parties, László Bruszt and David Stark identify their "latent image that among the equal participants there was an older brother with maturity and experience who could be called on in the most difficult times to lead the younger siblings through the dense forest of extrication from authoritarianism."[16] Relying on their real credentials as the Mubarak regime's most organized opposition, the Muslim Brothers distractedly tolerated but did not take into account other civilian factions.

This enraged the other civilians, and not only the secular among them. From the very beginning, the Salafis, who came in second place in the general elections, maintained an independent line from the MB, bristling at the latter's condescension and assumption that it was the natural leader of the Islamist political space. The MB and Salafis are routinely lumped together, along with the Wasat and Gama'a Islamiyya, as a coherent camp of "Islamists," but this book has insisted on distinguishing between them to better understand the dynamics of intra-Islamist and intracivilian conflict and cooperation. Salafi and MB candidates competed fiercely during general elections; the Salafis refused to join the FJP's parliamentary battle against the Ganzouri government, did not endorse Mohamed Morsi in the first round of the presidential elections, and broke with Morsi when they deemed his offer of a single cabinet post an insult. *Al-Nur*, the largest Salafi party, backed the July 3 coup, its secretary-general among the civilian and religious figures surrounding Abdel Fattah al-Sisi as he announced the coup on television. In the constitution-drafting deliberations, the Salafis sometimes sided with the MB and other times with their adversaries, and postcoup, they continue to vocally support the Sisi regime.

Parties on the left and liberal spectrum embraced a different vision of democracy, one that has come to be known as the consociational model, advocating a system of power-sharing and mutual vetoes among a greater number of parties.[17] The core value of consociationalism is inclusion of a larger range of interests, to prevent disenfranchisement of minority voices, even at the cost of slowing down political reconstruction and risking recurrent logjams. Although the consociational model was developed to organize politics in ethnically and religiously heterogeneous societies and may seem oddly invoked for largely homogeneous Egypt, its underlying logic is apposite: postconflict management in societies divided along various lines of cleavage. The unexpected breakdown of an authoritarian regime and ensuing deep divisions among the democratic opposition renders the consociational formula relevant and attractive for political rebuilding. When fashioning a new political order, inclusion and deliberation are of the utmost importance, both as a matter of righting historic wrongs of political repression and as pragmatic insurance against spoilers who would sooner wreck the proceedings than accede to an ornamental role on the margins.[18]

The contending philosophies of majoritarian and consociational forms of democratic rule came to a head in spring 2012 when constitution-making got underway. The fierce debates over how to select the Constituent Assembly (CA) mirrored the difference in democratic conceptions: majoritarians believed that only duly elected parliamentarians had the right to select constitution-drafters, without externally imposed "binding principles" or any other supralegislative devices. Consociationalists insisted that constitution-making should not be reduced to electoral weightings and must include sectors and voices without a parliamentary presence but significant social weight and claims for recognition, principally women, young people, industrial and clerical workers, and Egypt's minority communities (Coptic and other Christian denominations, Baha'is, Nubians, and Bedouins). As the rights lawyer Gamal Eid exhorted the majoritarians,

"A constitution is not like an election outcome that pleases some and angers others," urging a more expansive conception of constitution-writing as inclusive citizenship. What made this division a true conundrum is that both camps were very recent legatees of a history of political exclusion. Both MB majoritarians and minoritarians were systematically repressed under authoritarianism. If anything, the MB felt a special sense of grievance as the chief bearer of the state's draconian legal and material repression. They heard talk of binding principles and social inclusion as highfalutin smokescreens to keep them away from what they had earned, fair and square. Consociationalists feared decades of political irrelevance and extinction if they conceded the procedural understanding of democracy as the aggregation of votes, thereby substituting authoritarian repression for the tyranny of the majority.

Certainly, this is not only about rival democratic theories but also contending interests. Civilian factions occupying different locations in the political field embraced the view of democracy that suited their interests. Electorally confident Muslim Brothers cast the ballot box as the ultimate arbiter of democratic legitimacy, and electorally marginal parties invoked the more abstract of the democratic virtues, inclusion and equity. We might expect the majoritarians to win, or constitution-making to turn into a forum for hashing out the parties' differences, through hard bargaining and perhaps distilling shared principles while deferring the deal-breaking intractable problems. In other words, what the political scientists al-Anani, Bishara, and Stepan demand for a successful transition. Neither transpired. Instead, when MPs elected a Constituent Assembly with a 64 percent Islamist majority, secular delegates walked out and leveraged the media to decry Islamist majoritarianism, and political activists outside parliament went to administrative court to challenge the CA composition. When the court agreed with them and invalidated the CA, it was widely seen as a rebuke to Islamists and vindication of the consociationalists' argument of a bullying majority.

This had two lasting consequences for the course of revolutionary politics: individual actors had discovered a form of veto power through strategic litigation, an existing political weapon honed by opponents of Mubarakist authoritarianism that could now be leveraged to check the majority. And minority parties and politicians found another unexpected political resource: walking away from their Islamist coparliamentarians and taking their case to the print and television media in Egypt and abroad, crafting a persuasive narrative of a constituent process hijacked by Islamists to impose their new religious dictatorship. As scholars of Eastern European constitutional politics have found, "the party who can afford to walk away from the bargaining table has an advantage."[19] To the puzzle of why contending civilians failed to engage in the hard work of mutual accommodation, this suggests a surprising answer: minority actors found other effective means of dealing with a dismissive majority than the tough slog of negotiations. They pulled in third parties, courts, and media, to pressure the majority to change its behavior. But rather than compelling the majority to submit to real compromises, this only intensified its sense of being besieged by a minority-court-media alliance. The outcome was that already tenuous mechanisms of negotiation were even further eroded, as each party went its own way. The Islamists ignored the secular minority and moved frenetically to present the constitution to their only recognized arbiters, voters in a referendum, and the secular parties took to the courts and media (a court of public opinion) as their preferred arbiters. The institutional structure of Egypt's politics worked against compromise, giving the contenders viable alternative options of getting their way. When the 2012 constitutional referendum was approved by voters, the rivals emphasized selective bits of the reality. The MB triumphantly pointed to the 64 percent public approval rate, and their opponents retorted that only 33 percent of voters turned out, the lowest in the revolution's elections.

\* \* \*

This then is a story about the contention over political power and authority between partisan and institutional actors, insurgents and incumbents, street-level bureaucrats and apex judges, millions of regular citizens who refused to be ruled in the old manner, and millions of other citizens who reckoned that the known is less bad than the unknown. The premise throughout has been that a revolutionary situation is an extraordinary version of routine political contention, not a transcendent condition impervious to politics; it is "simply the maximum moment of conflicts which endure long before and long after the transfer of power."[20] The victorious state with its counterrevolutionary doctrine stands as a monument to the grand unresolved conflict that launched the revolutionary-democratic breakthrough and endures in the present: how to rule Egypt without the Egyptians.

The concept of the revolutionary situation appealed to me because it captured the reciprocal relationship between unstable power arrangements and contests over supreme authority that dominated the years 2011 to 2013. It holds together within one frame the seemingly contradictory combination of institutional politics with transgressive mass action, political violence and political argument, democratic aspirations and revolutionary modes of action. But it is not the only label in existence for such varieties of politics. The disciplines of political sociology and political science have a family of cognate terms for moments of peak political conflict: constitutional crises; critical junctures; civil wars; first democracies. An antique umbrella term is "interregnum," denoting a vacancy leading to a period of provisional government.[21] Interregnum may be the grandparent of the modern political science concept of "transition," which, in its early formulation, did not assume a telos of democracy. In their classic statement, Guillermo O'Donnell and Philippe Schmitter called this variant of transition "confusion," namely, "the rotation in power of successive governments which fail to provide any enduring or predictable solution to the problem of institutionalizing political power."[22] An apt description of Egypt's interregnum.

The social sciences are ambivalent about such episodes of momentous political confusion, seeing them as forbiddingly chaotic and ultimately evanescent, without scrutable legacies or tangible lessons. Studying fluid conjunctures is "something like retrieving spilled mercury," in the vivid expression of two historians of 1917 Russia, "just as one is about to get an analytical grasp on events, their form shifts and they skitter from reach, changing size and shape even as they continue to remain the same elemental material."[23] O'Donnell and Schmitter addressed the same problem of "undetermined" social change. In a playful, serious passage, they counseled social scientists on what a theory of political flux needs to account for:

> Such a theory would have to include elements of accident and unpredictability, of crucial decisions taken in a hurry with very inadequate information, of actors facing irresolvable ethical dilemmas and ideological confusions, of dramatic turning points reached without an understanding of their future significance. In other words, it would have to be a theory of "abnormality," in which the unexpected and the possible are as important as the usual and the probable. Moreover, the actors' perception of this very abnormality surrounding regime

change is itself a factor affecting its eventual outcome. Compared to periods of "order" which characterize the high point of authoritarian rule, the uncertainty and indirection implied in movements away from such a state create the impression of "disorder."[24]

In lieu of a theory of abnormality, I have opted for an anatomy of disorder, disentangling the mad jumble of events and rearranging them in temporal order to understand their interrelations. That clarified a point so basic it borders on the jejune. So much of Egypt's interregnum can be explained by the continuous movement of many collectivities into and out of episodes of contention. Focusing on only the "major players" leads to a strange rendition of what happened, an image of sparring actors on a stage directly beholding one another on one or two issues without mediation, their interaction resolving in an immediate end-result. The two- or three-player assumption not only brackets how other actors are pulled in and drop out, it downplays as ambient noise so much of what goes into the production of outcomes: mechanisms of escalation, the twining of once-distinct issues, the making and unmaking of provisional coalitions, the changing goals of actors, object shift, and the interconnection between simultaneous events.[25]

Does this have any relevance to politics in more normal times? What might be some implications for politics more generally from junctures where volatility is the central feature of political life? Risking a foray into the obvious, Egypt's revolutionary situation makes visible familiar building blocks of political mobilization that may be taken for granted as they hum in the background of routine politics. Here I focus on just three: institutions, arguments, and time. One of the most striking features of Egypt's revolutionary politics is how contending forces built up different types of political resources in their quest for influence and recognition. To speak of institutions as resources sounds jarring in light of influential institutionalist approaches that emphasize institutions as constraints on actors' strategies. Historical institutionalists point to the strong status quo bias built into political institutions ("institutional stickiness"), and rational choice institutionalists define them as focal points facilitating coordination that actors are loath to abandon.[26] Both conceive of them as resistant to change, and both would likely interpret Egypt's nonrevolutionary outcome as an illustration of this postulate; the enormous investment in and sheer inertia of long-standing authoritarian structures defeated new political forces' attempts to alter political relations. As Paul Pierson summarizes the logic, "actors find that the dead weight of previous institutional choices often seriously limits their room to maneuver."[27]

Conceiving of institutions as resources redirects attention from the outcome to the struggle, starting with the contending actors and their goals and temporally tracing the dynamics of their interactions. When it comes to a contest over state institutions, it shows the lengths to which insurgent and incumbent actors will go to acquire or maintain the use of public powers. José María Maravall and Adam Przeworski recover the primacy of politics in the development of institutions and their interrelations, pointing out that when state institutions confront one another, it is because they are populated by persons using institutional prerogatives and political forces seeking to instrumentalize those prerogatives. "Those who have the votes use the legislature, those who have laws on their side use courts, those who have access use the bureaucracy."[28] This explains why actors who seem all-powerful from one vantage, say MB majoritarians who command votes, were weakened and ultimately defeated, their institutions blocked by political rivals mobilizing the courts, and military and civil bureaucrats employing their coercive and administrative prerogatives. The fact that there are different currencies of institutional politics available to different actors also demystifies how it is that electoral lightweights, or seemingly weak actors, are able to activate the courts to counteract majoritarian legislatures, unelected autocratic executives, and democratically elected executives. The general insight is the multiplicity of institutional powers within a polity, sometimes referred to as the presence of "veto players" with formal or informal powers to block others' initiatives.[29]

In contrast to the depoliticizing thrust of structural-functional accounts of institutions as fulfilling system needs, or path-dependent "lock-in" models stressing their imperviousness to change, the conflict-centric approach suggested here presents a parallax view of institutions as both objects of and terrains of battle involving a shifting set of contending parties. This highlights how ambiguous it is to render judgment about institutional change versus continuity. "What may look like institutional continuity in a formal sense may disguise very considerable changes in institutional functioning."[30] The judgment that the Sisi regime represents a continuity of durable pre-2011 authoritarianism occludes the different workings and institutional configurations of two different authoritarian regimes. Indeed, I have argued that the Mubarak regime itself was the product of a twenty-year evolutionary dialectic that produced stability through constant alterations in mechanisms of rule. Ultimately, the different depictions of institutional politics during both revolutionary and routine epochs comes down to a difference in how the analyst defines change. Change as wholesale renovation will not deem significant many of the regime dynamics discussed here, since they all took place within what such an analysis might consider a uniform authoritarian context. By contrast, my close-up view punctures the seemingly placid surface of institutional continuity to reveal the roiling interactions underneath, in line with a methodological dictum articulated by historical anthropologist Eric Wolf. "Whenever possible we should try to identify the social agents who install and defend institutions and who organize coherence, for whom and against whom."[31] Even when focusing only on the problem of institutional continuity, explaining how the actors populating these institutions do their work of status quo reinforcement is a more powerful alternative than assuming impersonal forces of institutional resilience. "Change and stability are two sides of the same coin."[32]

It can hardly be news that persuasive arguments are an important resource in political struggles. A revolutionary conjuncture merely throws into bold relief the collective, competitive construction of claims and counterclaims that is part and parcel of all political interaction. The field of relational sociology has done the most to explain "meaning work," the interactive construction of compelling ideas to organize experience and compel action, what Robert Benford and David Snow call "framing processes" that go beyond the aggregation of individual attitudes.[33] As with Wolf's antireifying stance toward institutions, relational sociologists tunnel underneath the apparent coherence of cultural ideas to investigate how specific social agents fashion palpable ideas that gain traction and shape public perceptions, in agonistic interaction with competing ideas and counterframes. From this perspective, the occupation of Tahrir Square during the Eighteen Days takes on a new significance. Rather than a utopian enclave of confessional harmony and gender equality, it was a hard-won political space for the collective work of diagnostic framing (the misrule of the Mubarak regime), prognostic framing (We won't leave, he must go), and action mobilization (the banner articulating demands; see fig. 1).[34] The frame of the people as sovereign that emerged out of this meaning construction compelled the military to intervene on the eighteenth day, under its own conception of sovereignty.

"Unexpected events do not produce their own interpretations," Ivan Ermakoff points out. "They call for them."[35] Just as the uprising opened a new juncture of altered relations within state organs and between them and multiple social groups, it created a space for competitive definitions of the situation. The fight over whether to call the uprising a transition or a revolution did not concern only academics, it was a live issue for every new and old political actor, since the answer affected their prospects in the emergent order; "we should expect actors who have a stake in the outcome to struggle to impose their definition of the situation."[36] As the actor with the most to lose from a revolutionary and radical democratic definition of the situation, the military council lost no time in imposing its interpretive frame. It worked to limit civilian political forces' sense of power to control the future and re-create laws by swiftly seizing legislative and executive powers after Mubarak's deposition and casting the military as the savior of the nation.[37] This meaning work was not fashioned out of whole cloth but invoked extant constitutional texts and built-up reserves of deference to the armed forces. Nor was the power to construct compelling arguments monopolized by the "big players." For much of 2011, the Revolution Youth Coalition (RYC) and Maspero Youth Union commanded real political standing. Within Egypt and abroad, they represented the popular moral authority of Tahrir, and they shaped public perceptions of other political actors, such as the negative framing of the Muslim Brothers as calculating, self-interested politicians with no fidelity to the revolution.

A conjuncture of contestation over state powers helps us see in real time the building of arguments for rightful authority that may have no occasion to surface in routine politics. Recalling Sidney Tarrow's definition of revolutionary situations as "passages through openly contested sovereignty," we come close to the root of why a revolutionary interregnum is unstable and seemingly chaotic. For a claim to sovereignty is not only a bid for authority, it is an argument about political paramountcy, or ultimate power. Inherent in the concept is a range of meanings that have rendered it analytically baffling but historically a potent weapon wielded by very different kinds of claimants. Sovereignty can be attributed to several entities concurrently (the people, the state, certain institutions within a state); it can be cast as a mystical foundation of authority outside of politics, or a set of specific powers (making and unmaking laws, declaring war and peace, adjudicating litigation). The doctrine of popular sovereignty alone has a double meaning, what Bernard Yack calls "the people's two bodies":

> Alongside an image of the people who actually participate in political institutions, it constructs another image of the people as a prepolitical community that establishes institutions and has the final say on their legitimacy.[38]

Hence conceptual historians' counsel that claims of sovereignty be conceived as an "argumentative resource," and that in fact was how the concept was wielded in Egypt's political battles.[39]

The Tahrir Square occupation claimed superior power over the constituted Mubarak autocracy, and, after Mubarak fell, the milyuniyyas cast themselves as embodiments of popular sovereignty. SCAF too justified its claim to rule in terms of popular sovereignty, casting the armed forces as an incarnation of a mystical people and explicitly claiming constituent power. Administrative and constitutional court judges claimed sovereignty over parliament and guardianship over the constitution. The gathering opposition against Morsi in spring 2013 saw the people's two bodies in direct confrontation: President Morsi and his supporters maintained that democratically elected institutions are sovereign and cannot be undone on a whim. Their adversaries acted in the name of an extralegal, unscheduled popular power with authority to unmake and remake the elected institutions. The warring parties announced their positions in the same terms of sovereignty, "the master concept of legal and political philosophy," not because they were protophilosophers but because they had to justify their claims to authority against persuasive counterclaims.[40] Haybat al-dawla puts an end to this riot of competing supremacy claims, gathering up sovereignties in a unitary conception of the state to suppress the diversity of their manifestations.

Time as a political resource is so deeply submerged in political interaction that it does bear explicit articulation. Examined closely, the structuring and distribution of time consumes the efforts of contending parties in a range of political settings, from agenda control in the relatively ritualized arena of legislative politics to controlling rapid rates of change that Arthur Stinchcombe identified as the main characteristic of political revolutions.[41] Aside from the fact that "interregnum" and "revolutionary situation" are by definition temporal concepts, control over political time emerged as a major object of contention in this environment of continuous volatility. As George Wallis sketched in a brief and suggestive piece, groups' awareness of living through a time of transition leads to an escalation in the perceived stakes of politics. "Control *now* will become immeasurably more important than the illusionary hope of another turn at the wheel of power."[42] The time-perspectives of Egypt's actors, or their "chronopolitics," compelled them to act quickly to secure advantages or simply remain viable politically, in the face of an undefined future. So much is unsurprising; these are O'Donnell and Schmitter's "crucial decisions taken in a hurry," of which the revolutionary situation abounds. Yet time did not move only in the direction of acceleration. Weak parties leveraged court decisions and media publicity for dilatory ends, blocking the initiatives of their majoritarian opponents and crafting interpretive frames that cast them as sinister forces. After all, as Ermakoff concludes, "In a conflict situation, power amounts to the ability to incapacitate an opponent."[43]

So much of the confusion of Egypt's revolutionary situation dissipates if we peer through the prism of chronopolitics. Fears of the future drove the military generals to maintain exclusive agenda-setting power in the early weeks of the transition, setting a brisk timeline of elections and ignoring alternative proposals for more deliberation and civilian comanagement of the transition. "I need more time" was a widespread sentiment then, as a leaflet from Tahrir Square had it. When the generals realized that *they* needed more than six months' time to craft their status in the new order, they changed the timetable to remain in power until 2013. But the November 2011 milyuniyyas forced them to backtrack and set a date for presidential elections in 2012. Their menacing signals about controlling constitution-writing hung over parliamentarians like a sword of Damocles, forcing them to hurriedly complete within weeks what the interim constitution granted them six months to deliberate, selecting the hundred constitution-writers in a frenetic rush. When President Morsi decreed more time for the second Constituent Assembly to hash out its differences and bring back boycotters, he was ignored by the assembly and branded a dictator by his opponents, an interpretive frame that drove mass demands for early presidential elections that the military instrumentalized to carry out its coup.

But why did the military opt to extinguish democracy altogether instead of transfer power to Morsi's opponents, as the latter had hoped, carving out for the armed forces a comfortably insulated role as kingmaker? A hypothesis is that, based on their experience of direct rule in 2011, the generals looked at the future and saw only threats, an erosion of their primacy, and the takeover of political space by a chaotic scenario of pluralist politics. An unpredictable, evolving set of parliamentarians, ministers, media moguls, cause lawyers, community activists, trade unionists, and a slew of other political creations would take the reins, vie over the framing of public issues, build constituencies, craft public policies, clash and collaborate in patterns that would shift Egypt's politics from limited to out-of-control pluralism. Perhaps they feared that even limited democratic competition would eventually lead to a coalition for civilian control, and, worse, demands for accountability for the military's human rights abuses. The military acted with dispatch to preempt this kind of political temporality, the time of democratic consolidation.

\* \* \*

No one knows who made up the slogan "Bread, Freedom, Social Justice" ('Aysh, Huriyya, 'Adala Igtima'iyya), or its Tunisian homologue, "Work, Freedom, National Dignity" (Shughl, Huriyya, Karama Wataniyya).[44] As with so much else in the Arab uprisings, these were crowd-sourced arguments, articulating the refusal to be ruled in the old manner and the right to possess the means of a decent life. They are the counterframes to postcolonial governing elites' constructions of reality over a sixty-year span. In the 1950s and 1960s, the so-called social contract was that states would provide a dignified standard of living but with limited political freedom. Freedom was cast as divisive and dangerous, weakening the home front in the struggle against Israel and neo-imperialism. After peace with Israel and the reorientation to the West, there was neither bread nor freedom, as increasingly dynastic states captured the proceeds from privatization and instituted new forms of political repression to deal with rising opposition. Bread and freedom communicate a vision of collective life unhampered by false choices between survival and dignity, spurning the bureaucratic auditing mindset that segregates the "economic" from the "political," domestic politics from foreign relations. Confronting the corrosion of the republican idea into dynastic forms, bread and freedom rubbishes modern presidential monarchism with a fresh restatement of republicanism, "that the business conducted by government is the public business of the realm and of everyone in it," writes

Jeremy Waldron, "rather than the patrimony of any privileged individual or family."⁴⁵

* * *

Days after Hosni Mubarak's fall, former Soviet leader Mikhail Gorbachev wrote one of the most insightful reflections on what had just occurred, at a time when both mindless celebration and reflexive foreboding filled the airwaves. "Power without accountability cannot last," he reflected. "This is what hundreds of thousands of Egyptian citizens, whose faces we've seen on television, stated loud and clear." He framed the uprising as bringing Egypt to a historic crossroads, branching to either fake or genuine democracy. "The second alternative is daunting. It means ensuring that there is a real opposition, and knowing that a real opposition will come to power sooner or later. Then abuses will come to light, the networks of corruption leading to the top will be broken, and someone must be held accountable for all that."⁴⁶ Reading these words ten years on, it is possible to rue what happened as a tragedy or offer the counterfact that unaccountable power is what in fact endures. I cannot help reading them as a piercing reminder of how enormously difficult it is to fashion democratic accountability. That word has grown dull from overuse, folded into the sanitized lexicon of international organizations and their good-governance-speak. But when we think about political relationships, democratic accountability entails a stark inversion, "the idea that political authority is the creation of those subject to it," as Jean Hampton skillfully condensed.⁴⁷ The nub of democracy flies in the face of constituted power relations with the force of history and custom behind them.

Jeremy Waldron helps refresh our understanding of just what is involved in building democracy.

> Democratic accountability purports to confer authority on those who are otherwise powerless over those who are already well endowed with power. It takes those who have the wherewithal to protect themselves and seeks to make them vulnerable to the verdicts and assessments of those who are, factually speaking, among the least powerful members of society. This vulnerability of the powerful at the hands of the powerless does not come into existence by magic. It has to be constructed, and unless something is done to sustain it, it will not last.⁴⁸

During the 2011–13 triennium, the powerful were vulnerable in a way they had never before experienced, exposed to the heterogeneous demands and brash self-confidence of communities and groups that did not need to read political philosophy to understand that they were remaking the structures of authority governing their lives. Fear Us, O Government, they said. The powerful were vulnerable, but they were not prostrate. "Anything we say about accountability is said also in the presence of strong doctrines of political authority and political obligation. The point of these doctrines is to emphasize and explain what people owe to their governments, not vice versa."[49] It is a truism that one of the most striking effects of revolution is the consolidation of antirevolutionary thought and practice into a coherent form, gathered up from its scattered and inchoate presence in the various corners of a polity.

And so the hidden thesis of this book is that the triennium I have called a revolutionary situation reminds us just how formidable it is to construct democratic accountability from scratch: because of the fierce reactions and ample resources of the powerful, the ambivalence of fence-sitters, the fickleness of the uncommitted, the *desencanto* of true believers, the dissension among reasonable people confronted with wrenching dilemmas of political reconstruction under unbearable time constraints. Perhaps this is why one historian judged democracy "one of humanity's most precious political creations."[50]

Egypt's interregnum illuminates the entanglement of revolution and democracy, the inversions, leveling, and reinversions that unfold when a polity's power relations come undone. As with all manifold social reality, the scale of this happening exceeds the bounds of any single analytical abstraction. It is a protean episode, a memory, a cautionary tale, a resonance, a taboo, a reference point, a confounding human political experience.

*Acknowledgments*

MY EARLIEST MEMORY OF IMMERSIVE SOCIAL RESEARCH WAS READING bad photocopies of dense, tiny print on the hacienda system, for a report in junior high school. I lost all sense of space and time as I read; illustrations of small bent workers tilling the fields made me wonder how it was possible to subjugate so many laborers. Naturally, these thoughts did not make it into the report. They had nothing to do with the assignment, and I had no clue how and to whom I could express them. As I grew older, the gap between what I loved in social studies and what I was expected to produce got worse and worse. I dealt with it by sometimes smuggling my real interests into college and graduate school papers, but mostly by suppressing them as idiosyncratic musings.

Charles Tilly was the first authority figure to see the tension and mercilessly bring it to light. In one of his characteristic crack-of-dawn emails delivering feedback on written work, he began, "Your proposal has no chance of passing the Dissertation Proposal Review Committee. Here are your bad ideas." He itemized these in a bullet-point list, then pointed out, "There is a good idea flapping around in the eaves," and tersely sketched what it would take to rescue it. After the shock and tears, I spent an entire summer rewriting a twelve-page proposal. In the fugitive years thereafter, until his death in April 2008, Chuck sent me many more cutting, edifying responses to written work. One favorite said, "Democracy does not come about because people demand it, here is my chapter on Ireland." Another email had just one word, "Courage!" I never got a chance to directly thank Chuck for encouraging my independence but demanding that I make it cogent to others. This book owes much to his uncompromising instruction and his vitality of spirit. I will never get over the grief of him not witnessing Egypt's revolution—or stop daydreaming about the three points of feedback he'd write on this analysis.

I will always be grateful to Lisa Anderson for her care and support from the very beginning. Ira Katznelson models the kind of social science that embraces, not flattens, the complexity of the world. I thank him for being the kind of teacher/reader who pays equal attention to micro diction and macro structure, who delivers feedback that motivates you, and who makes you laugh at your own ridiculousness.

Readers of this book's initial conception offered an uplifting blend of focused criticism and enthusiasm. Heartfelt thanks to Evelyn Alsultany, Karen Barkey, George Gavrilis, Ellis Goldberg, Ira Katznelson, Arang Keshavarzian, Tamir Moustafa, Eyal Press, Aziz Rana, Joshua Stacher, Elizabeth Thompson, and Chris Toensing. David Larsen, Mitra Rastegar, Dina Siddiqi, and Peter Valenti offered their undivided attention and sharp questions on the material that became chapter 5.

A special thanks to al-Ustaz, Chris Toensing, for giving me a first platform, polishing my prose for years, telling the funniest Egypt (and DC) fieldwork stories, and plugging away at the world-historical comparative ethnographic genealogical taxonomy of *koshari* joints.

For both their attention to details and engagement with the main claims and structure, I am very grateful to the manuscript reviewers for Stanford University Press. Their concrete suggestions were a most helpful guide in the revision process. I'm grateful to everyone at the press who worked on making the manuscript into a book, and to Susan Olin, for her extraordinary, tireless copyediting and edifying comments. Kate Wahl has an amazing capacity to hold together the insane number of tasks required to fashion a manuscript. I especially thank her for her stimulating ideas about the book's organization, her caution about adverbs, and her reminder to trust the reader. My thanks to Joel Beinin for his support, and especially for prompting me to clarify my attitude to theory. To my schoolmate Laleh Khalili, whose lifelong love of research reminds me of Chuck, much gratitude for her enthusiasm and support.

Though this is not an interview-based study, so much of my understanding of Egypt's politics was shaped through discussions with some of its most insightful analysts and dedicated principals. I acknowledge with much gratitude Khaled Ali, Mohamed Ahmed Atteya, Zakariyya Abdel Aziz, the late Atef al-Banna, Tareq al-Bishri, Hisham al-Bastawisi, Kamal Abu Eita, Adel Farghali, Abdel Moneim Aboul Fotouh, Hossam al-Ghiryani, Essam al-Islamboly, Mahmoud al-Khodeiry, Abul Ela Madi, Ahmed Mekky, Mamdouh Nakhla, Hamdi Yassin Okasha, Farouq Abdel Qader, Hamdeen Sabahy, the late Sayed Sadeq and Mohamed Sayed Said, Atef Said, Abdel Ghaffar Shukr, and Noha al-Zainy. All sat down with me for hours when I showed up at their offices and living rooms, not quite unannounced but certainly unvetted. They shared their knowledge and experiences, modified my questions, and gave me otherwise inaccessible documents. In this vein, I must also thank Mr. Sami Abdalla, the longtime secretary of the First Circuit of the Court of Administrative Justice, who trusted me to carry out of his office for photocopying, unaccompanied, his precious copy of a landmark ruling in Majlis al-Dawla's history.

I met other members of Egypt's political and legal class who were hostile, dismissive, and supercilious. I acknowledge them for how much they indirectly taught me about the stakes of change.

So much of the material of this book relies on the work of dozens of journalists, famous and obscure, partisan and professionalized. They painstakingly recorded Egypt's revolutionary situation plus the thirty years of contentious politics that preceded it. I know only a handful of them, but I am deeply grateful to them all for writing luminous first drafts of Egypt's political history, enabling me to compose a second draft.

These mentions of interlocutors in Egypt do not do justice to the thousands of little interactions and observations that feed into one's understanding of a place in time. As other researchers know well, so much of what shapes the final version of a work goes unmentioned and unrecorded. A sentiment that haunted me throughout the writing of this book is how much was left out, how much eluded me, how imperfectly concepts represent social relationships. I acknowledge that here simply to register the perplexity that has always attracted me to social research.

George Gavrilis and Arang Keshavarzian worked on the guts of the whole manuscript with a selflessness and hilarious sense of humor that perhaps only old school bonds can explain. Dedicated social scientists and talented teachers, they are the most endearing fellow travelers I could have asked for. George's capacity to see the whole and pinpoint unevenness and infelicities helped enormously with revision. Arang read countless memos, raised counterpoints, nixed the inside-baseball, banned organic metaphors, and discussed more Egyptian politics and relational social science than anyone should have to endure.

Just after the first draft was completed, as I was about to send it to him, Ellis Goldberg passed away, without giving me a chance to say goodbye. So many of the ideas and sources I engage with here I discussed endlessly with Ellis, who was by turns extremely kind and caring, unyielding, and had a depth of intellect and love for Egypt that still fills me with awe. He insisted that I make clear where my account differs from alternatives, and that this is my construction and not "what really happened." I don't think I can fully convey in words my gratitude and sense of loss.

All of my readers instructed and encouraged me, but I alone am responsible for errors, omissions, and misinterpretations.

I am grateful to the Carnegie Corporation of New York for a grant supporting a project then entitled "Petition and Protest in Authoritarian Egypt." The work for that project mutated and was eventually distilled into chapter 2 of this book. For one year, I made use of a wonderful public resource: the New York Public Library's charming Frederick Lewis Allen Room. The nooks and crannies of Burke and Butler Libraries were the most wonderful havens, thanks to the kindness and professionalism of their staff.

I thank several dear friends and colleagues who sustained me with friendship and support: Harlem flâneur Hisham Aidi, for his incomparable sense of humor. *Vecinos* Roosevelt Montas, Deborah Martinsen, and Elina Yuffa, who welcomed me back into the Contemporary Civilization classroom, where I regained the love of teaching. Rebecca Jane Stanton, in whose library company I composed the zero drafts. Mandy McClure, whose sparkling intellect and conversations in 2011 helped me make sense of that extraordinary year. Dina Ramadan, for wide-ranging discussions of the aftermath. Michelle Woodward, for her much-appreciated advice in the final stage. Benefo Ofosu-Benefo for a last-minute lifesaver. And Wiebke Denecke, for sending me a lantern to illuminate the path.

As I neared the end, my high school history teachers appeared insistently in my memory. I realized that they were the ones who introduced me to some of the problems and heuristics I revisit here. Ms. Sylvia Gordon taught us synoptic thinking, making us write out a list on facing pages of the elements of Bismarck's *kulturkampf* and antisocialist laws. Mr. David Evans was the first to put a chronology in my hands, making me see causal complexity for the first time. Ms. Wendy Aldous whizzed around the room as she unfolded maps and recounted the lineaments of the Haitian Revolution; I'll never forget her exaggerated British pronunciation of Toussaint "L'Ouverturrrre." Ms. Jane Kaminski had us calculate the length of the Strait of Gibraltar, an assignment we all got wrong.

Ron Kassimir was one of my favorite teachers in college, infecting us all with his enthusiasm for African politics. He introduced me to the fascinating world of bottom-up constitution-writing and Ngũgĩ wa Thiong'o, both of which fed this work via winding tributaries.

The love and ribbing of friends and family propelled me to overcome self-estrangement and embark on the kind of book I want to write. Since UNIS days, Mireille Abelin, Evelyn Alsultany, Elif Bali, and Nina Demeksa have been the most wondrous life companions, the kind of people who impart the breadth and generosity of humanity. I can't imagine trudging the path of learning without the grace and fortitude of Evelyn Alsultany. Ev is that rarity who excels at the modern trivium of teaching, research, and service; talking with her about all three is a continuous education. For years, the Bali-Hollands (Elif, Fred, Kaan, Kaya) indulged my talk about the manuscript over lovely dinners, the way one indulges a child's narrative of their imaginary friend. When he was all of five or six, Kaan insisted, "You *have* to write your book in Arabic!"

The endless wisecracking of Antonio Borrelli and the Novembres (Thomas, Aura, Jasmine, Stella) wiped away the mental strain, as did little Uly's face. The Brollosy clan's love and bemusement offered the best kind of perspective—thank you so much Khalo, Ellen, Lu, Dooma, Gina, and Jon.

My sisters Noha and Amira cared about this book only to the extent that it gave them ammunition. They regularly asked the worst question ("so when are you gonna be done?") and laughed at my protestations. But they felt sorry for me and bought me nice commodities (and helped extricate me from a yucky situation), so they are hereby thanked for their irreverence and lack of respect. I also thank Noha for making the mockup for map 2. Thanks, TamTam, for acknowledging how awful it is to write a book, and Dalia for the best visual diversion and thoughtful curations. And to wonderful Ramy, thank you for listening to me talk about the book without smirking.

The only times I felt an overweening tug away from research was when Ali, Zacky, Sherif, and a little cherub named Farris arrived. Time with them, real and virtual, is an ineffable experience.

Latifa Abdel Meguid El-Brollosy and Sayed El-Ghobashy model two symbiotic stances toward life: an unflinching gaze at its realities, and a "spatial awareness" that things can always be otherwise. They embody autonomy in all its shades, long before I encountered it in books, and they lovingly aid and abet my stubbornness. When I think about my parents, words dissolve and I can only reach for the aphorism of al-Niffari: the more expansive the range of vision, the more compressed the expression.

## Abbreviations and Glossary

| | |
|---|---|
| 'Askar | Derogatory term for "military," used to denounce military rule |
| 'Aysh, Huriyya, 'Adala Igtima'iyya | A major slogan from the uprising's first eighteen days, "Bread, Freedom, Social Justice" |
| al-Barlaman | Parliament, also a metonym for formal institutional politics |
| CA | Constituent Assembly |
| Dustur | Constitution; also the name of a liberal political party |
| FJP | Freedom and Justice Party, the parliamentary wing of the MB |
| Fulul | Remnant, a derogatory term referring to an official or associate of the Mubarak regime |
| Haybat al-Dawla | State prestige, a doctrine that the state is owed reverence |
| al-Ikhwan al-Muslimun | Muslim Brothers (also MB below) |
| Karama | Dignity; also the name of a Nasserist political party |

| | |
|---|---|
| *Kifaya* | Anti-Mubarak campaign (est. 2004) agitating against the president and the political grooming of his son, Gamal |
| *Majlis al-Dawla* | Administrative courts with the power to review executive acts |
| MB | Muslim Brothers |
| *al-Midan* | The Square, also a metonym for crowds' pressure on governing authorities |
| *Milyuniyya* | Mass demonstration in Tahrir Square, typically on Fridays |
| MP | Member of Parliament |
| NDP | National Democratic Party |
| NSF | National Salvation Front |
| PEC | Presidential Election Commission |
| RYC | Revolution Youth Coalition |
| SAC | Supreme Administrative Court |
| *Salafis* | Islamist revivalist movements countering both the MB and secular groupings |
| SCAF | Supreme Council of the Armed Forces |
| SCC | Supreme Constitutional Court |
| SDP | Social Democratic Party |
| *Al-Sha'b Yurid Isqat al-Nizam* | A major slogan originating in Tunisia, "The People Want the Downfall of the Regime" |
| SSI | State Security Investigations |
| *Thawra* | Revolution; also the name of a liberal political party (Ghad al-Thawra) |

# Notes

**PROLOGUE**

1. Abdel Nasser Laouini is a cause lawyer who defended in court leaders of the 2008 protests against nepotism in Tunisia's Gafsa mining basin; he also participated in the lawyers' demonstration in Tunis during the uprising. The video of his cri de coeur is at https://youtu.be/OKKvc4sxwfw. "Ben Ali *harab*!" translates to "Ben Ali has fled!"

2. Roger Owen, *The Rise and Fall of Arab Presidents for Life* (Cambridge, MA: Harvard University Press, 2012), 172.

3. *Al-Shurouq*, January 15, 2011.

4. "One people against the emergency" and "Khaled Said, martyr of the emergency" were the banners held up by Alexandria protesters. *Al-Shurouq*, June 26, 2010.

5. Associated Press, "Thousands of Egyptians Protest What They Call Police Torture," June 25, 2010.

6. Fahmi Howeidy, "Jadal al-Ḥadath al-Tunisi wa Ajrasihi," *Al-Shurouq*, January 25, 2011.

7. "Tunisia Echoes in the Arab Street," *Al-Ahram Weekly*, January 20–26, 2011.

8. A transcript of the January 25 interview is printed in *Al-Misri al-Yawm*, January 27, 2011.

9. "Ta'jil tarh qanun al-wazifa al-'amma bi-sabab ahdath Tunis," *Al-Shurouq*, January 19, 2011; "Al-ukuma Tastajib li Malib al-Muhtajjin," *Al-Misri al-Yawm*, January 21, 2011.

10. On January 25, 1952, colonial British forces massacred fifty nationalist policemen in Ismailia, leading to large anticolonial demonstrations in Cairo. See Nancy Reynolds, *A City Consumed: Urban Commerce, the Cairo Fire, and the Politics of Decolonization in Egypt* (Palo Alto, CA: Stanford University Press, 2012).

11. Intelligence agents threatened the Muslim Brothers' leadership with arrest if they officially endorsed the protest action. "Al-Ikhwan Yusharikun bi Muzaharat al-Yawm," *Al-Shurouq*, January 25, 2011.

12. Sarah Carr, "Stories from the Day of Anger," *Egypt Independent*, January 26, 2011.

13. "Usrat Awwal Shahid bi-l Suez Tattahim al-Amn," *Al-Shurouq*, January 27, 2011.

14. "Masirat bil Alaf fi Shawari' al-Iskandariyya," *Al-Shurouq*, January 26, 2011; "15 Mu'taqal wa 15 Musab fi Muzaharat Balteem," *Al-Shurouq*, January 27, 2011; "Isabat Baligha li Ra'is Mabaheth al-Mahalla ," *Al-Shurouq*, January 26, 2011.

15. Reuters, "US Urges Restraint in Egypt," January 25, 2011.

16. Unnamed police officer's testimony published in *Al-Misri al-Yawm*, March 12, 2011.

17. *Al-Misri al-Yawm*, January 27, 2011.

18. These scenes are recorded at https://www.youtube.com/watch?v=g58Sl_4GNoE.

19. Police said ten thousand demonstrators turned out in Tahrir Square and "no more than several thousand total" in the provinces, while organizers said one hundred thousand participated overall. The number of arrests ranged from five hundred to a thousand and injuries were estimated at three thousand. "Time for Action," *Al-Ahram Weekly*, January 27–February 2, 2011.

20. *Al-Misri al-Yawm*, January 28, 2011.

21. A capsule history of Sinai residents' protests and police response is in "Istinfar Amni bi Shamal Sina," *Al-Shurouq*, September 30, 2009.

22. "Mutazahirun Yaghliqun al-Tariq al-Dawli fi Sina," *Al-Shurouq*, January 26, 2011; "Ishtibakat bi-l Rusas al-Hayy wa-l RPG," *Al-Shurouq*, January 28, 2011.

23. Four days prior to the Day of Wrath, displaced local workers assaulted Thai laborers and attempted to set fire to the truck transporting them; *Al-Shurouq*, January 23, 2011. On the 2009 assassination of Police General Ibrahim Abdel Ma'boud, see "Tashyee' Janazat Liwa al-Suez," *Al-Shurouq*, September 11, 2009.

24. "Al-Suez Nuskha Misriyya min Sidi Bouzid," *Al-Shurouq*, January 27, 2011; "Tajaddud al-Muzaharat fi Madinat al-Suez," *Al-Misri al-Yawm*, January 28, 2011; "Tazahur

al-Mi'at bil Suez lil Solb ," *Al-Misri al-Yawm*, January 28, 2011; Reuters, "Could Suez Be Egypt's Sidi Bouzid?" January 27, 2011.

25. Statement by the EU High Representative Catherine Ashton on the events in Egypt, Brussels, January 27, 2011 (A 032/11); https://www.consilium.europa.eu/uedocs/cms_data/docs/pressdata/EN/foraff/118963.pdf.

26. "Hamlat I'tiqalat Ghayr Masbuqa," *Al-Shurouq*, January 29, 2011.

27. "Egypt Cuts off Most Internet and Cell Service," *New York Times*, January 28, 2011; "Nashitun Aqbat Yandamun li Jum'at al-Shuhada' *Al-Shurouq*, January 28, 2011; "Awqaf al-Daqahliyya: Khutbat al-Jum'a 'an Hubb al-Watan," *Al-Shurouq*, January 28, 2011; "Al-Televizion Yanqil al-Jum'a min Masjidihi," *Al-Shurouq*, January 29, 2011.

28. These scenes are captured by Mohammed Ahmad, "Bidayat Jum'at al-Ghadab min Masjid al-Qa'id Ibrahim bi-l Iskandariyya," February 14, 2011, https://youtu.be/LU6fVJn9fY4, https://youtu.be/tarWjuhZPWA; abdelhamidsaber, "Jum'at al-Ghadab—al-Iskandariyya—al-Qa'id Ibrahim," February 14, 2011, https://youtu.be/g7Je_EMcXz8.

29. "'Ashar Alaf fi al-Zaqaziq Yahtajun," *Al-Misri al-Yawm*, January 29, 2011; "Min al-Ahali ila al-Shurṭa," *Al-Shurouq*, January 30, 2011.

30. Hatem Rushdy, ed., *18 Days in Tahrir: Stories from Egypt's Revolution* (Hong Kong: Haven Books Limited, 2011), 94.

31. "Al-Misri al-Yawm Tanshur Tafasil Ittisalat Shurtat ," *Al-Misri al-Yawm*, March 15, 2011. The police's director of telecommunications later testified in court that he had destroyed the recordings between field commanders in Cairo, and he confirmed what protesters had seen: police commandeering ambulances to transport reinforcements of weapons and ammunitions. "Awwal Shahed li Saleh Mubarak," *Al-Misri al-Yawm*, September 6, 2011.

32. "Li-l Dhikra al-Khalida: Jum'at al-Ghadab Sa'a bi-Sa'a," *Al-Shurouq*, January 31, 2011.

33. "28 Yanayir 2011: Khiṭab Mubarak al-Awwal Athna' al-Thawra," Dhakirat Maspero, December 8, 2015, https://youtu.be/L6rMTbxEXvU.

34. "Remarks by the President on the Situation in Egypt," The White House, Office of the Press Secretary, January 28, 2011. https://obamawhitehouse.archives.gov/the-press-office/2011/01/28/remarks-president-situation-egypt.

35. "Egyptians Wonder What's Next," *New York Times*, January 29, 2011.

36. She was one of thirty-four killed in her neighborhood. "Mawkib al-Shuhada'," *Al-Shurouq*, February 12, 2011.

37. "Al-Jaysh Yusaytir 'ala al-Dakhliyya," *Al-Shurouq*, January 31, 2011.

38. "Idarat Harb fi Qasr al-'Ayni," *Al-Shurouq*, January 31, 2011.

39. "Fighter Jets Used to Intimidate Egyptian Protesters," CBS, "Face the Nation," January 30, 2011; https://www.youtube.com/watch?v=cmRGF_G5oi8.

40. Jack Goldstone and Charles Tilly, "Threat (and Opportunity): Popular Action and State Response in the Dynamics of Contentious Action," in *Silence and Voice in the Study of Contentious Politics*, ed. Ronald Aminzade et al. (New York: Cambridge University Press, 2001), 188.

41. Ursula Lindsey, "Revolution and Counter-Revolution in the Egyptian Media," *Middle East Report Online*, February 15, 2011; https://merip.org/2011/02/revolution-and-counter-revolution-in-the-egyptian-media/.

42. Gwen Ackerman, "Netanyahu Concerned Islamists May Exploit Egyptian 'Chaos,'" *Bloomberg News*, January 31, 2011.

43. "Atfal 'ala Khatt al-Thawra," *Al-Shurouq*, February 1, 2011.

44. "Updates on Day 8 of Protest in Egypt," *New York Times*, February 1, 2011.

45. "Obama Urges Faster Shift of Power in Egypt," *New York Times*, February 1, 2011.

46. Partido Lakas ng Masa (PLM, Party of the Labouring Masses), "In Solidarity with the People of Egypt, Tunisia, and the Middle East," January 29, 2011.

47. "Remarks by the President on the Situation in Egypt," The White House, Office of the Press Secretary, February 1, 2011. https://obamawhitehouse.archives.gov/the-press-office/2011/02/01/remarks-president-situation-egypt.

48. *Al-Ahram*, February 3, 2011.

49. "Muzaharat Madfu'at al-Ajr," *Al-Shurouq*, February 3, 2011; "Mubarak's Allies and Foes Clash," *New York Times*, February 2, 2011.

50. Beltagui recounted the incident in his court testimony on the Battle of the Camel criminal case in 2012, "Al-Yawm: Sima' Shahadat Ahmad Shafiq wa-l Liwa' al-Roueiny fi Mawqi'at al-Jamal," *Al-Shurouq*, June 14, 2012.

51. It later emerged that the horse- and camel-drivers worked in the tourist economy in the Nazlet al-Saman district of the Giza pyramids area. Chris Hondros's remarks in "Chris Hondros on the Madness in Tahrir Square," *Reading the Pictures*, February 3, 2011; https://www.readingthepictures.org/2011/02/chris-hondros-on-the-madness-in-tahrir-square/.

52. Wikithawra, "Hasr Qatla al-Thaman 'Ashar Yawm al-Ula min al-Thawra Tafsiliyyan," October 23, 2013, https://wikithawra.wordpress.com/2013/10/23/25jan18days casualities/.

53. Observers hailed this as an unprecedented show of communal harmony, but as with the Tahrir sit-in itself, it was but a visible national echo of invisible local precedents. In 2007, Qursaya islanders demonstrating against eviction and Shibeen al-Kom textile workers on strike protected each others' prayers from impending police violence. "Al-Amn Yuhaddid bi Fadd I'tisam," *Al-Dustur*, February 7, 2007; "Al-Muslimun fi Himayat al-Masihiyyin," *Al-Badeel*, December 1, 2007.

54. Patrick Kingsley, "Abdel Fatah al-Sisi: Behind the Public Face of Egypt's Soon-to-be President," *Guardian*, May 22, 2014.

55. Anthony Shadid, "Egypt's Leaders Seek to Project an Air of Normalcy," *New York Times*, February 7, 2011.

56. Associated Press, "Mideast Allies: 'US Go Easy on Egypt,'" February 9, 2011.

57. Human Rights Watch, "Egypt: Statements from Protesters Detained by Army," February 8, 2011.

58. A later fact-finding commission established by President Mohamed Morsi in 2012 confirmed the involvement of military personnel in the abduction and torture of protesters and furnished more details. "Egypt's Army Took Part in Torture and Killings during Revolution, Report Shows," *Guardian*, April 10, 2013.

59. Human Rights Watch, "Egypt: Statements from Protesters Detained by Army," February 8, 2011.

60. Pew Research Center, "Events in Egypt Trigger Record Coverage," February 5, 2011.

61. "Leaders without Disciples," *Al-Ahram Weekly*, February 10–16, 2011.

62. A photo of the wedding appears on the front page of *Al-Misri-al-Yawm*, February 10, 2011.

63. "Thalath Alaf Muwatin Bur Sa'idi," *Al-Misri-al-Yawm*, February 10, 2011.

64. "Tawasul al-Muzaharat al-Mutaliba bi-Rahil Mubarak fi-l Muhafazat," *Al-Misri-al-Yawm*, February 10, 2011; "Labor Actions across Egypt Lend Momentum to Anti-Mubarak Protests," *New York Times*, February 10, 2011.

65. "Updates on Day 17 of Egypt Protests," *New York Times*, February 10, 2011.

66. "Egypt Protests, Thursday 10 February," *Guardian News Blog*.

67. "Nasibuhu min al-dawla," *Al-Shurouq*, February 12, 2011. The final tally of 841 martyrs from the Eighteen Days is tabulated by name, age, date, cause, and location of death in *Daw' fi Darb al-Hurriya* (Light on the Path to Freedom) (Cairo: Arab Network for Human Rights Information, 2012). Profiles of some of the fallen are in Denis

Dailleux, Abdellah Taïa, Mahmoud Farag, *Égypte, les martyrs de la revolution* (Marseille: Bec en l'air, 2014).

68. Etman recounted this in an April 2011 television interview, available at https://youtu.be/fK-qfRKu5Kg. Footage of Etman inside the newsroom as the videotape is being broadcast can be seen at https://youtu.be/KPp0BlY4QqY.

## CHAPTER 1

1. One study found that out of 303 dictators between 1946 and 2008, only thirty-two were removed by a popular uprising but another thirty stepped down under public pressure to democratize. Milan Svolik, *The Politics of Authoritarian Rule* (New York: Cambridge University Press, 2012), 4.

2. Robert Springborg, "Protest against a Hybrid State: Words without Meaning?," in *Political and Social Protest in Egypt*, ed. Nicholas Hopkins (Cairo: American University in Cairo Press, 2009), 6–18.

3. "It would be a great political stroke if the El-Azhar University could be removed from Cairo to Mecca or Medina," recommended the Norwegian Consul in Cairo on April 7, 1919. "I am moreover of opinion that such a measure would not be unpopular with the Moslem world as a whole, and it would certainly enhance the prestige of the King of the Hedjaz." F.O. 407/184 (*Further Correspondence Respecting the Affairs of Egypt and the Soudan, January to June 1919*).

4. Noah Feldman, *The Arab Winter: A Tragedy* (Princeton, NJ: Princeton University Press, 2020); Amr Hamzawy, "The Tragedy of Egypt's Stolen Revolution," *Al-Jazeera*, January 25, 2017, https://www.aljazeera.com/indepth/features/2017/01/tragedy-egypt-stolen-revolution-170125062306232.html; Tariq Ramadan, "The Revolution in Egypt Turns from Tragedy to Farce," ABC Religion and Ethics, July 10, 2013, https://www.abc.net.au/religion/the-revolution-in-egypt-turns-from-tragedy-to-farce/10099752; "Egypt's Tragedy," *Economist*, July 6, 2013; Mohamed El-Bendary, *The Egyptian Revolution: From Hope to Despair* (New York: Algora Publishing, 2013).

5. Amy Hawthorne and Andrew Miller, eds., "Why Did Egyptian Democratization Fail? Fourteen Experts Respond," Project on Middle East Democracy (POMED), January 2020.

6. Slavoj Žižek, "For Egypt, This Is the Miracle of Tahrir Square," *Guardian*, February 10, 2011.

7. Samuel Huntington, "Democracy's Third Wave," *Journal of Democracy* 2, no. 2 (Spring 1991): 12–34. Michael Hardt and Antonio Negri, "Arabs Are Democracy's New Pioneers," *Guardian*, February 24, 2011.

8. Hardt and Negri, "Arabs are Democracy's New Pioneers."

9. Daron Acemoglu and James A. Robinson, *Why Nations Fail: The Origins of Power, Prosperity, and Poverty* (New York: Crown Publishers, 2012), 2.

10. Judith Butler, *Notes toward a Performative Theory of Assembly* (Cambridge, MA: Harvard University Press, 2015), 89.

11. Tom Eley, "Protests, Teacher Walkouts Mount in Wisconsin," World Socialist Web Site, February 19 2011, https://www.wsws.org/en/articles/2011/02/wisc-f19.html.

12. *Inter alia*, see Mona Prince, *Revolution Is My Name: An Egyptian Woman's Diary from Eighteen Days in Tahrir* (Cairo: American University in Cairo Press, 2015); Wael Ghonim, *Revolution 2.0: The Power of the People Is Greater Than the People in Power: A Memoir* (New York: Houghton Mifflin Harcourt, 2012); Hatem Rushdy, ed., *18 Days in Tahrir: Stories from Egypt's Revolution* (Hong Kong: Haven Books Limited, 2011); Karima Khalil, *Messages from Tahrir: Signs from Egypt's Revolution* (Cairo: American University in Cairo Press, 2011); Tatiana Philiptchenko, *Fearless: Egyptian Women of the Revolution* (Montreal: Megapress Images, 2013); James Dorsey, *The Turbulent World of Middle East Soccer* (New York: Oxford University Press, 2016).

13. David Kirkpatrick, "Wired and Shrewd, Young Egyptians Guide Revolt," *New York Times*, February 9, 2011.

14. *Time*, February 28, 2011. Rabab El-Mahdi critiqued this framing at the time, challenging the "new imaginary homogeneous construct called "youth"; "Orientalising the Egyptian Uprising," *Jadaliyya*, April 11, 2011.

15. Jeffrey Alexander, *Performative Revolution in Egypt: An Essay in Cultural Power* (London: Bloomsbury, 2011), 32.

16. Slavoj Žižek, *The Year of Dreaming Dangerously* (London: Verso, 2012), 74.

17. Ashraf Khalil, "The Fading of Tahrir Square," *Foreign Affairs*, July 3, 2012.

18. I borrow the term from historian Christopher Clark's study of World War I. Challenging the logic of such accounts, Clark writes: "A further drawback of prosecutorial narratives is that they narrow the field of vision by focusing on the political temperament and initiatives of one particular state rather than on multilateral processes of interaction" (*The Sleepwalkers: How Europe Went to War in 1914* [New York: HarperCollins, 2013], 560).

19. Mohammad Fadel, "Egyptian Revolutionaries' Unrealistic Expectations," in *Egypt beyond Tahrir Square*, ed. Bessma Momani and Eid Mohamed (Bloomington: Indiana University Press, 2016), 28–40; Ashraf El-Sherif, "The Egyptian Muslim Brotherhood's Failures" (Washington, DC: Carnegie Endowment for International Peace, July 2014).

20. Abdeslam Maghraoui, "Egypt's Failed Transition to Democracy: Was Political Culture a Major Factor?" *E-International Relations*, April 29, 2014. https://www.e-ir.info/2014/04/29/egypts-failed-transition-to-democracy-was-political-culture-a-major-factor/.

21. Gilbert Achcar, *Morbid Symptoms: Relapse in the Arab Uprising* (Palo Alto, CA: Stanford University Press, 2016), 10–11, and "The Egyptian Counterrevolution: An Interview with Sameh Naguib," *Jacobin*, March 11, 2016. https://www.jacobinmag.com/author/sameh-naguib.

22. Brookings Institution, "An Interview with Amr Darrag," February 8, 2017; https://youtu.be/yzCNPSUf3xI. He specified the security, judicial, media, and military sectors as the areas that the Morsi government ought to have targeted with revolutionary measures.

23. International Crisis Group, "Popular Protest in North Africa and the Middle East (IV): Tunisia's Way," *Middle East/North Africa Report*, no. 106 (April 28, 2011).

24. James B. Rule, *Theories of Civil Violence* (Berkeley: University of California Press, 1988), 279.

25. Asef Bayat, *Revolutions without Revolutionaries: Making Sense of the Arab Spring* (Redwood City, CA: Stanford University Press, 2017), 209; Jason Brownlee, Tarek Masoud, and Andrew Reynolds, *The Arab Spring: Pathways of Repression and Reform* (New York: Oxford University Press, 2015); Amy Austin Holmes, *Coups and Revolutions: Mass Mobilization, the Egyptian Military, and the United States from Mubarak to Sisi* (New York: Oxford University Press, 2019); Saïd Amir Arjomand, "The Arab Revolution of 2011 and Its Counterrevolutions in Comparative Perspective," in Saïd Amir Arjomand, ed., *The Arab Revolution of 2011: A Comparative Perspective* (Albany, NY: The State University of New York Press, 2015), 9–51.

26. Rod Aya, *Rethinking Revolutions and Collective Violence: Studies on Concept, Theory, and Method* (Amsterdam: Het Spinhuis, 1990), 20.

27. Saïd Amir Arjomand, "Iran's Islamic Revolution in Comparative Perspective," *World Politics* 38, no. 3 (April 1986): 404.

28. John Dunn, "Revolution," in *Political Innovation and Conceptual Change*, ed. Terence Ball, James Far, and Russell Hanson (Cambridge: Cambridge University Press, 1989), 333–56; Mary Ashburn Miller, *A Natural History of Revolution: Violence and Nature in the French Revolutionary Imagination, 1789–1794* (Ithaca, NY: Cornell University Press, 2011); Keith Michael Baker and Dan Edelstein, eds., *Scripting Revolution: A Historical Approach to the Comparative Study of Revolutions* (Palo Alto, CA: Stanford

University Press, 2015); Saïd Amir Arjomand, *Revolution: Structure and Meaning in World History* (Chicago: University of Chicago Press, 2019).

29. Alexander J. Motyl, "Concepts and Skocpol: Ambiguity and Vagueness in the Study of Revolution," *Journal of Theoretical Politics* 4, no. 1 (1992): 93–112, 108.

30. Eric Hobsbawm, "Revolution," in *Revolution in History*, ed. Roy Porter et al. (Cambridge: Cambridge University Press, 1986), 19.

31. Charles Tilly, *European Revolutions, 1492–1992* (Oxford: Blackwell Publishers, 1993), 12; Charles Tilly, "To Explain Political Processes," *American Journal of Sociology* 100, no. 6 (May 1995): 1594–1610.

32. This last example comes from Peter Amann, who proposes more forms of irrepressible "power blocs," including paramilitary formations such as the Nazi *Sturmabteilung* (S.A.); "inspired improvisations" such as the 1905 soviets; a spontaneous *jacquerie*; a bureaucracy systematically sabotaging the policies of its government; or a national army that has escaped civilian tutelage. See Peter Amann, "Revolution: A Redefinition," *Political Science Quarterly* 77, no. 1 (March 1962): 36–53.

33. Jeff Goodwin, *No Other Way Out: States and Revolutionary Movements, 1945–1991* (Cambridge: Cambridge University Press, 2001), 40; Theda Skocpol, *States and Social Revolutions: A Comparative Analysis of France, Russia, China* (Cambridge: Cambridge University Press, 1979).

34. Charles Kurzman, "The Arab Spring Uncoiled," *Mobilization* 17, no. 4 (2012): 377–90; Charles Kurzman, "Can Understanding Undermine Explanation? The Confused Experience of Revolution," *Philosophy of the Social Sciences* 34, no. 3 (2004): 328–51.

35. For studies that center the emotions of the revolution's participants, their accelerated sense of time, and their special rhetorics, see, inter alia, Wendy Pearlman, "Emotions and the Microfoundations of the Arab Uprisings," *Perspectives on Politics* 11, no. 2 (2013): 387–409; Samia Mehrez, ed., *Translating Egypt's Revolution: The Language of Tahrir* (Cairo: American University in Cairo Press, 2012); Donatella della Porta, *Where Did the Revolution Go? Contentious Politics and the Quality of Democracy* (New York: Cambridge University Press, 2016), 259–310.

36. Louis O. Mink, "The Autonomy of Historical Understanding" (1966), in *Historical Understanding*, ed. Brian Fay, Eugene O. Golob, and Richard T. Vann (Ithaca, NY: Cornell University Press, 1987), 82.

37. Mink, "Autonomy," 84. Historian Clayton Roberts calls this "colligation" (*The Logic of Historical Explanation* [University Park, PA: Pennsylvania State University Press, 1996], 16).

38. I borrow reliving the chaos "as it really was" from Amann, "Revolution: A Redefinition," 36.

39. As the authors of the Dynamics of Contention research program write, "We treat social interaction, social ties, communication, and conversation, not merely as expressions of structure, rationality, consciousness, or culture but as active sites of creation and change" (Doug McAdam, Sidney Tarrow, Charles Tilly, *Dynamics of Contention* [Cambridge: Cambridge University Press, 2004], 22). Ivan Ermakoff spells out the most important implication of the interactionist ontology: actors' changing locations and goals. "As they react to moves, countermoves, claims and challenges by competitors, opponents, or allies, individual and collective actors take stances that can lead them far away from their initial stand—stances in other words that neither they nor external observers would have anticipated given the dispositions at play. From this perspective, strategic interactions acquire a logic of their own which cannot be reduced to pre-existing structural conditions" (Ermakoff, "Theory of Practice, Rational Choice, and Historical Change," *Theory and Society* 39 [2010]: 547).

40. Sidney Tarrow, *Strangers at the Gates: Movements and States in Contentious Politics* (New York: Cambridge University Press, 2012), 129.

41. Charles Tilly, *From Mobilization to Revolution* (Reading, MA: Addison Wesley, 1978), 44.

## CHAPTER 2

1. The fishermen made their living by going out to sea for a fortnight at a time, subsisting on unleavened bread prepared from subsidized flour rations distributed directly to households.

2. Amal Kandeel, "Egypt at a Crossroads," *Middle East Policy* 18, no. 2 (2011): 37–45; Zeynep Tufekci, *Twitter and Tear Gas: The Power and Fragility of Networked Protest* (New Haven, CT: Yale University Press, 2017), 13; Jeroen Gunning and Ilan Zvi Baron, *Why Occupy a Square? People, Protests, and Movements in the Egyptian Revolution* (London: Hurst, 2013), 94, 95.

3. The definition is Charles Tilly's in *Trust and Rule* (New York: Cambridge University Press, 2005), 4. Public politics is distinguished from routine political interactions such as census taking, tax collection, military service, and the internal organizational activity of political actors that go on most of the time without public collective claim-making (5).

4. Timur Kuran, "Now out of Never: The Element of Surprise in the East European Revolution of 1989," *World Politics* 44 (October 1991): 7–48.

5. Clement Henry Moore, "Authoritarian Politics in Unincorporated Society: The Case of Nasser's Egypt," *Comparative Politics* 6, no. 2 (January 1974): 193–218; Robert Bianchi, *Unruly Corporatism: Associational Life in Twentieth-Century Egypt* (New York: Oxford University Press, 1989), 6; Robert Springborg, "Protest against a Hybrid State: Words without Meaning?," in *Political and Social Protest in Egypt*, ed. Nicholas Hopkins (Cairo: American University of Cairo Press, 2009), 6–18; Holger Albrecht, *Raging against the Machine: Political Opposition under Authoritarianism in Egypt* (Syracuse, NY: Syracuse University Press, 2013), 23–37.

6. Juan Linz, "Opposition in and under an Authoritarian Regime: The Case of Spain," in *Regimes and Oppositions*, ed. Robert Dahl (New Haven, CT: Yale University Press, 1973), 188.

7. Linz, "Opposition," 188–89.

8. Charles Tilly, *Contentious Performances* (New York: Cambridge University Press, 2008), 149.

9. On the regimen of prescribed performances set up by Hafez al-Assad, see Lisa Wedeen, *Ambiguities of Domination: Politics, Rhetoric, and Symbols in Contemporary Syria* (Chicago: University of Chicago Press, 1999). On Tunisia, see Beatrice Hibou, *The Force of Obedience: The Political Economy of Repression in Tunisia* (Cambridge, MA: Polity Press, 2011).

10. The changing dynamics of the NDP are analyzed in Jason Brownlee, *Authoritarianism in an Age of Democratization* (Cambridge: Cambridge University Press, 2007); Lisa Blaydes, *Elections and Distributive Politics in Mubarak's Egypt* (Cambridge: Cambridge University Press, 2010); and Joshua Stacher, *Adaptable Autocrats: Regime Power in Egypt and Syria* (Palo Alto, CA: Stanford University Press, 2012).

11. Andreas Schedler, *The Politics of Uncertainty: Sustaining and Subverting Electoral Authoritarianism* (New York: Oxford University Press, 2013), 148.

12. Prior to Mubarak's shift to multicandidate presidential elections in May 2005, presidential selection in Egypt was based on the nomination of one candidate by a two-thirds majority of parliament that was then put to a public referendum.

13. Erika Post, "Egypt's Elections," *Middle East Report* (July/August 1987): 17–22.

14. The opposition boycotted the intervening 1990 general elections to protest the lack of judicial supervision that would ensure a marginally clean poll.

15. Samer Soliman, *The Autumn of Dictatorship: Fiscal Crisis and Political Change in Egypt under Mubarak* (Palo Alto, CA: Stanford University Press, 2011), 55.

16. Figures are for the years 1992–97, compared to 120 deaths in political violence between 1970 and 1989. See Mohammed Hafez and Quintan Wiktorowicz, "Violence as Contention in the Egyptian Islamic Movement," in Quintan Wiktorowicz, ed., *Islamic Activism: A Social Movement Theory Approach* (Bloomington: Indiana University Press, 2003), 71.

17. The speech was delivered by State Department official Edward Djerejian six months after the Algerian coup, in June 1992 at Meridian House in Washington, DC. In his memoir, Djerejian implies that the "one person, one vote" phrase was not a commentary on the Algerian election, but he does not elaborate. Edward P. Djerejian, *Danger and Opportunity: An American Ambassador's Journey through the Middle East* (New York: Simon and Schuster, 2008), 22. Oddly, while Djerejian devotes one chapter to discussing it, the speech's full text is not included in his memoir. The full text is in the minutes of US House of Representatives, "Extended Remarks, June 25, 1992." https://www.govinfo.gov/content/pkg/GPO-CRECB-1992-pt12/pdf/GPO-CRECB-1992-pt12-1-3.pdf.

18. Yusuf al-Qaʿid, "Lan Nuddahi bi-l Jazaʾir min Ajl al-Dimuqratiyya," *Al-Musawwar*, July 2, 1993.

19. Fatality and injury figures from the first independent election monitoring report issued by a collection of six NGOs. *Taqrir al-Lajna al-Wataniyya al-Misriyya li-Mutabaʿat al-Intikhabat al-Barlamaniyya, 1995* (Cairo: Markaz Ibn Khaldun lil-Dirasat al-Inmaʾiyya, 1995), 62. The number of candidates is in *Contours et détours du politique en Egypte: Les élections législatives de 1995*, ed. Sandrine Gamblin (Cairo: CEDEJ; Paris: L'Harmattan, 1997), 29.

20. On the Egyptian business elites' links to state officials, see John Sfakianakis, "The Whales of the Nile: Networks, Businessmen, and Bureaucrats during the Era of Privatization in Egypt," in *Networks of Privilege in the Middle East: The Politics of Economic Reform Revisited*, ed. Steven Heydemann (New York: Palgrave Macmillan, 2004), 77–100.

21. Amy Dockser Marcus, "In Mideast, Leaders' Offspring Emerge as Top Advocates of Economic Reform," *Wall Street Journal*, October 2, 1997.

22. Robert Springborg, "Egypt," in *Legislative Politics in the Arab World: The Resurgence of Democratic Institutions*, ed. Abdo I. Baaklini, Guilain Denoeux, and Robert Springborg (Boulder, CO: Lynne Rienner Publishers, 1999), 238.

23. Amr Hashem and Noha El-Mikawy, "Business Parliamentarians as Locomotives of Information and Production of Knowledge," in *Institutional Reform and Economic Development in Egypt*, ed. Noha El-Mikawy and Heba Handoussa (Cairo: American University in Cairo Press, 2002), 49–60. This study of businessmen's behavior in the 1995 parliament finds that they neither acted as a bloc to represent private sector interests nor activated instruments of oversight or legislation.

24. *Al-Ahali*, May 21, 1997, and June 25, 1997.

25. *Al-Ahali*, July 9, 1997.

26. The "intifada" moniker is by the leftist party weekly *Al-Ahali*. For details and specific locations of peasant disobedience, see *Al-Ahali* issues of July 2, July 9, September 24, October 8, and October 22, 1997. Aggregate casualty figure in Douglas Jehl, "Egypt's Farmers Resist End of Freeze on Rents," *New York Times*, December 27, 1997. For a fuller account of the tenants' uprising, see Reem Saad, "State, Landlord, Parliament and Peasant: The Story of the 1992 Tenancy Law in Egypt," in *Agriculture in Egypt from Pharaonic to Modern Times*, ed. Alan Bowman and Eugene Rogan, Proceedings of the British Academy (Oxford: Oxford University Press, 1999), 96:387–404. On peasant collective action in 1919, see Ellis Goldberg, "Peasants in Revolt—Egypt 1919," *International Journal of Middle East Studies* 24, no. 2 (1992): 261–80.

27. *Al-Ahram*, March 6, 2000, and April 18, 2000. The articles in this flagship government-controlled daily are often verbatim transcriptions of police and prosecution accounts.

28. *Al-Wafd*, March 12, 2000; *Al-Ahram*, March 12, 2000; *Al-Usbu'*, March 13, 2000.

29. Eric Hobsbawm, "The Machine Breakers," *Past and Present* 1 (February 1952): 59.

30. *Al-Wafd*, September 26, 2001.

31. These events are reported in *Al-Ahrar*, January 25, 2004; *Al-Ahali*, August 4, 2004; and *Al-Dustur*, November 20, 2007, respectively.

32. *Al-Wafd*, October 6, 2001, *Al-Usbu'*, October 15, 2001.

33. *Al-Ahrar*, February 8, 2003.

34. The account of this episode is culled from *Al-Ahali*, December 8, 2004; *Watani*, December 12, 2004; and *Al-Ahram Weekly*, 16–22 December 2004.

35. For more on the shift in Coptic politics, see Samer Soliman, "The Radical Turn of Coptic Activism: Path to Democracy or to Sectarian Politics?," in *Political and Social Protest in Egypt*, ed. Nicholas Hopkins (Cairo: American University in Cairo Press, 2009), 135–54; Mariz Tadros, "Vicissitudes in the Entente between the Coptic Orthodox

Church and the State in Egypt," *International Journal of Middle East Studies* 41, no. 2 (2009): 269–87.

36. E. P. Thompson, "The Patricians and the Plebs," in E. P. Thompson, *Customs in Common: Studies in Traditional Popular Culture* (New York: New Press, 1993), 72.

37. For examples of mass protest in the wake of the Second Intifada in 2000, see *Al-Ahali*, October 18, 2000. For protests at the 2002 reinvasion of the West Bank, "The Street Reacts to Operation Defensive Shield: Snapshots from the Middle East," *Journal of Palestine Studies* 31 (Summer 2002): 44–65. See also Marc Lynch, *Voices of the New Arab Public: Iraq, al-Jazeera, and Middle East Politics Today* (New York: Columbia University Press, 2006).

38. An informative play-by-play of the police-protester negotiations during this protest is in Khaled Dawoud, "Message to 'The Castle,'" *Al-Ahram Weekly*, September 13–19, 2001.

39. Khaled Dawoud, "A Message to Sharon—from Egypt," *Al-Ahram Weekly*, July 5–11, 2001.

40. "Effigy Burning Ban," *Al-Ahram Weekly*, May 9–15, 2002.

41. *Al-Ahram Weekly*, May 2–8, 2002.

42. Amira Howeidy, "Solidarity," *Al-Ahram Weekly*, April 4–10, 2002.

43. Political scientist and NDP publicist Gehad Auda made this case in a book titled *Gamal Mubarak: Tajdid al-Libiraliya al-Wataniya* (Cairo: Dar al-Hurriyya, 2004).

44. *Al-Ahram Weekly*, March 27–April 2, 2003.

45. A detailed account of the March 20–21 crackdown is in Human Rights Watch, "Egypt: Security Forces' Abuse of Anti-War Demonstrators," November 2003.

46. Tamir Moustafa, "Protests Hint at New Chapter in Egyptian Politics," *Middle East Report Online*, April 9, 2004. https://merip.org/2004/04/protests-hint-at-new-chapter-in-egyptian-politics/.

47. "Liman Yaqulun bi-intiha' Zaman al-'Ummal, al-'Ummal Yasrukhun: Nahnu Huna," *al-Tagammu'*, January 1, 2005.

48. Joel Beinin, *Justice for All: The Struggle for Worker Rights in Egypt* (Washington, DC: Solidarity Center, 2010), 14.

49. Joel Beinin, "Workers' Struggles under 'Socialism' and Neoliberalism," in *Egypt: The Moment of Change*, ed. Rabab El-Mahdi and Philip Marfleet (London: Zed Books, 2009), 68–86.

50. *Al-Musawwar*, December 29, 2006.

51. Beinin, "Workers' Struggles," 80.

52. *Al-Akhbar*, February 13, 2007.

53. Nazih Ayubi was one of the first to draw attention to widening income differentials between the "core" and the "periphery" of the Egyptian bureaucracy ("Government and the State in Egypt Today," in *Egypt under Mubarak*, ed. Charles Tripp and Roger Owen [New York: Routledge, 1989], 11). One of the few serious sociological studies of the internal structure and politics of Egypt's bureaucracy (employer of 5.7 million civil servants) is Abdel Khaleq Farouq, *Judhur al-Fasad al-Idari fi Misr* (Cairo: Dar al-Shurouq, 2008).

54. As pointed out by Jean Lachapelle, "Lessons from Egypt's Tax Collectors," *Middle East Report* 264 (Fall 2012).

55. *Nahdet Misr*, December 10, 2007.

56. Taking the tax collectors as their inspiration, three other groups formed independent unions in 2009–2010. Dina Bishara, *Contesting Authoritarianism: Labor Challenges to the State in Egypt* (New York: Cambridge University Press, 2018), 129.

57. Abbas al-Tarabili, *Al-Wafd*, July 12, 2007.

58. Michael Slackman, "Egypt Concedes to Resistance and Backs Off a Privatization Drive," *New York Times*, June 28, 2010.

59. L. Neville Brown and John S. Bell, *French Administrative Law*, 5th ed. (London: Oxford University Press, 1998), 50.

60. Achille Mestre, *Droit Administratif*, quoted in Michael J. Remington, "The Tribunaux Administratifs: Protectors of the French Citizen," *Tulane Law Review* 51, no. 1 (1976–77): 33–94.

61. Law professor Hossam Eissa hailed the decision in the festschrift *Tareq Al-Bishri: al-Qadi al-Mufakkir*, ed. Ibrahim al-Bayoumi Ghanem (Cairo: Dar al-Shurouq, 1999), 31.

62. *Al-Wafd*, March 20, 1992, and December 1, 1992.

63. *Al-Ahali*, June 5, 1996.

64. Coverage of Nakhla's lawsuits in *Al-Ahali*, January 17, 1996; August 28, 1996; October 23, 1996; February 18, 1998.

65. *Al-Ahali*, September 11, 1996.

66. Figures are for the First Circuit of the Court of Administrative Justice, which reviews citizens' lawsuits against the administration; civil servants' suits against their superiors are handled by separate administrative tribunals. Data made available to the author by Judge Adel Farghali, president of the Court of the Administrative Justice in 2010.

67. An article on the Society of Friends of the Environment's successful litigation concerning polluted Lake Maryut is headlined, "Administrative Court Ruling Reveals Intentional Destruction of the Lake," *Al-Araby*, June 2, 2002.

68. *Al-Ahali*, June 20, 2001.

69. *Al-Ahali*, October 13, 1999, and December 6, 2000.

70. Dena Rashed, "Mess over Garbage," *Al-Ahram Weekly*, December 16–22, 2004. Ten years later in 2014, the government acknowledged the failure of the corporatized waste collection scheme and began integrating *zabbaleen* into a formal structure. Patrick Kingsley, "Waste Not: Egypt's Refuse Collectors Regain Role at Heart of Cairo Society," *Guardian*, March 27, 2014.

71. Mona El-Naggar, "Court in Egypt Annuls Deal with Israel on Gas Supply," *New York Times*, November 18, 2008.

72. Abdel Razzaq Ahmad al-Sanhuri and Ahmad Hishmat Abu Stait, *Usul al-Qanun aw al-Madkhal li-Dirasat al-Qanun* (Cairo: Matb'at Lajnat al-Ta'lif wal Tarjama wal Nashr, 1950), 267.

73. Michael Herzfeld, *The Social Production of Indifference: Exploring the Symbolic Roots of Western Bureaucracy* (Chicago: University of Chicago Press, 1993), 122.

74. Timothy Mitchell, *Carbon Democracy: Political Power in the Age of Oil* (London: Verso, 2011), 9.

75. *Al-Ahram Weekly*, December 16–22, 2004. For Kifaya's founding statement and roots in Palestine solidarity activism of 2000–2003, see Rabab El-Mahdi, "Enough! Egypt's Quest for Democracy," *Comparative Political Studies* 42, no. 8 (2009): 1011–39; and Albrecht, *Raging against the Machine*, chap. 3.

76. For more on this decision, see Tamir Moustafa, *The Struggle for Constitutional Power: Law, Politics, and Economic Development in Egypt* (New York: Cambridge University Press, 2007), chap. 6.

77. Human Rights Watch, "From Plebiscite to Contest? Egypt's Presidential Election," September 2, 2005.

78. Zainy's testimony is in "al-Misri al-Yawm Tanshur Shahadat Mustashara Sharikat fi-l Ishraf 'ala al-Intikhabat fi Damanhour," *Al-Misri al-Yawm*, November 24, 2005.

79. *Al-Ahram Weekly*, March 31–April 6, 2005.

80. International Republican Institute, Final Report, "2005 Presidential Election Assessment in Egypt, August 15–September 9, 2005," (Washington, DC: International Republican Institute, 2005).

81. Joel Beinin and Marie Duboc, "A Workers' Social Movement on the Margin of the Global Neoliberal Order, Egypt 2004–2012," in *Social Movements, Mobilization, and Contestation in the Middle East and North Africa*, ed. Joel Beinin and Frederic Vairel (Palo Alto, CA: Stanford University Press, 2013), 210.

82. "All Rise for the Judges of Egypt," *Christian Science Monitor*, May 16, 2006.

83. Mohamed Sayed Said, "A Political Analysis of the Egyptian Judges' Revolt," *Judges and Political Reform in Egypt*, ed. Nathalie Bernard-Maugiron (Cairo: American University in Cairo Press, 2008), 19–26.

84. Mohamed Basal, "Majlis al-Dawla . . . al-Batal al-Ladhi Hakama Misr 'Am 2010," *Al-Shurouq*, December 31, 2010.

85. Beinin and Duboc, "Workers' Social Movement," 221.

86. *Al-Ahram Weekly*, May 15–21, 2008.

87. Doug McAdam, Sidney Tarrow, and Charles Tilly, *Dynamics of Contention* (Cambridge: Cambridge University Press, 2001), 157.

88. In 2009, the dissident judges narrowly lost the Judges' Club internal election by 329 votes to a government loyalist faction.

89. McAdam, Tarrow, Tilly, *Dynamics of Contention*, 147.

90. Linz, "Opposition," 253.

91. Robert Dix, "Why Revolutions Succeed and Fail," *Polity* 16, no. 3 (1984): 423–46, 443.

## CHAPTER 3

1. "Al-Jaysh Yahmi al-Mutazahirin," *Al-Shurouq*, March 6, 2011.

2. Amira Howeidy, "The Night State Security Fell," *Al-Ahram Weekly*, March 10–16, 2011.

3. Reuters, "Egypt Dissolves Hated Internal Security Force," March 15, 2011. Glimpses into the content of the files are in Mohamed Abdel-Baky, "Tip of the Iceberg," *Al-Ahram Weekly*, March 10–16, 2011.

4. "Midan al-Tahrir al-ladhi intaqal illa kulliyat al-i'lam," *Al-Shurouq*, March 19, 2011; "Mi'at al-tullab yuwasilun i'tisamihim," *Al-Shurouq*, March 23, 2011.

5. "Ihalet asatidhat sahafat i'lam al-Qahira," *Al-Shurouq*, March 25, 2011; "University Backtracks," *Al-Ahram Weekly*, May 26–June 1, 2011.

6. Background on the political economy of Qena before the appointment of its first and second Coptic governors is in Samer Soliman, *The Autumn of Dictatorship: Fiscal*

*Crisis and Political Change in Egypt under Mubarak* (Palo Alto, CA: Stanford University Press, 2011), 90–95.

7. Footage of the protest and chants can be viewed at Sahifat Akhbar Qena al-Iliktruniyya, "Muzaharat Sha'b Qena Rafdan li-Ta'yin Mikhail Muhafizan Laha," April 15, 2011; https://youtu.be/jzLAhoNz1pw.

8. Ahmed Zaki Osman, "Qena Protests Reflect Sectarian Tensions, Marginalization," *Egypt Independent*, April 18, 2011.

9. "Mutazahiru Qena," *Al-Shurouq*, April 21, 2011. Sectarian tensions had flared during the previous governor's tenure, and he was perceived as doing nothing after an attack on a church in 2010 that killed seven. See Egyptian Initiative for Personal Rights (EIPR), *Naga Hammadi: Witness to the Strife, Fact-Finding Mission Report*, January 21, 2010. After the church attack, Coptic cause lawyer Mamdouh Nakhla (see chap. 2) filed an unsuccessful lawsuit demanding the governor's dismissal. "Al-Qada' Ghayr Mukhtas bi Ilgha' Qararat Ta'yeen al-Muhafizin," *Al-Shurouq*, January 21, 2011.

10. "Shabab al-Thawra Ya'rid Mubadara," *Al-Shurouq*, April 23, 2011; Osman, "Qena Protests."

11. "Infiraj Azmat Qena," *Al-Shurouq*, April 26, 2011. For two informed interpretations of the Qena protests, see Muhammad Abul Fadl, "Fitnat Qena Qabaliyya wa Laysat Ta'ifiyya," *Al-Shurouq*, April 23, 2011, and Sameh Fawzy, "Nazra Mukhtalifa l-Intifadat Qena," *Al-Shurouq*, April 23, 2011.

12. Charles Tilly, "Political Identities," in *Challenging Authority: The Historical Study of Contentious Politics*, ed. Michael Hanagan, Leslie Page Moch, and Wayne te Brake (Minneapolis: University of Minnesota Press, 1998), 3–16.

13. Vladimir Lenin, "The Collapse of the Second International," 1915, in Vladimir Lenin, *Lenin Collected Works* (Moscow: Progress Publishers, 1974), 21:205–59; Marxists Internet Archive: https://www.marxists.org/archive/lenin/works/1915/csi/.

14. Vladimir Lenin, "The Dual Power," *Pravda*, April 9, 1917, in Lenin, *Lenin Collected Works* (Moscow: Progress Publishers, 1964), 24:38–41; Marxists Internet Archive: https://www.marxists.org/archive/lenin/works/1917/apr/09.htm.

15. Leon Trotsky, *History of the Russian Revolution* (Chicago: Haymarket Books, 2008), 150. The interchangeability between government and sovereignty is intentional. Trotsky used the capacious Russian concept *vlast*, a term that bundles together the many shades of wielding and exercising power, including authority, governance, control, dominion, and sovereignty.

16. James Sheehan, "The Problem of Sovereignty in European History," *American Historical Review* (February 2006): 1–15, 3.

17. Charles Tilly, *From Mobilization to Revolution* (Reading, MA: Addison-Wesley, 1978), 192.

18. Arthur Stinchcombe, "Ending Revolutions and Building New Governments," *Annual Review of Political Science* 2 (1999): 49–73, 51.

19. Richard Stites, *Revolutionary Dreams: Utopian Vision and Experimental Life* (New York: Oxford University Press, 1989), 3.

20. "I'tilaf Shabab al-Thawra Yutalib bi Dustur Mu'aqqat," *Al-Shurouq*, February 15, 2011.

21. Jayson Casper, "Mapping the Coptic Movements: Coptic Activism in a Revolutionary Setting," *Arab West Report*, May 15, 2013.

22. "Tsunami thawrat sughra yahtaj al-muhafazat," *Al-Shurouq*, February 14, 2011; Matt Bradley and David Luhnow, "Egyptians Take on 'Mini-Mubaraks'" *Wall Street Journal*, March 10, 2011; "Al-Thawra tasil lil-niqabat al-mihaniyya," *Al-Shurouq*, February 14, 2011.

23. Egyptian Center for Economic and Social Rights, "Al-'Ummal wal Thawra al-Misriyya—Ru'ya Huquqiyya," February 16, 2011.

24. "Milyuniyya Jadida al-Jum'a," *Al-Shurouq*, February 14, 2011.

25. "Essam Sharaf Ra'is al-Wuzara min al-Tahrir," *Al-Misri al-Yawm*, March 5, 2011.

26. Thomas Sélégny, "Suez's Culture of Resistance, Its Causes and Its Future" (master's thesis, Leiden University, 2015).

27. Asya El-Meehy, "Egypt's Popular Committees: From Moment of Madness to NGO Dilemmas," *Middle East Report* 265 (2012): 29–33. See also Hatem Hassan, "Extraordinary Politics of Ordinary People: Explaining the Microdynamics of Popular Committees in Revolutionary Cairo," *International Sociology* 30 (2015): 383–400.

28. "Hareeq fi Ahad al-Adriha bil Menoufiyya," *Al-Shurouq*, March 27, 2011. On the tensions between Sufis and Salafis, see Injy El-Kashef, "The Shrine Affair," *Al-Ahram Weekly*, April 7–13, 2011.

29. A description and accompanying photo is in "Thawrat al-Alwan bi Furshat Shabab Bani Suef," *Al-Shurouq*, March 26, 2011, 16.

30. "We make our spaces/spatialities in the process of constructing our various identities." Doreen Massey, "Thinking Radical Democracy Spatially," *Environment and Planning D: Society and Space* 13 (1995): 283–88.

31. Kristen Chick, "In Egypt's Tahrir Square, Women Attacked at Rally on International Women's Day," *Christian Science Monitor*, March 8, 2011.

32. "Al-Salafiyyun Yatazaharun amam al-Katedra'iyya," *Al-Shurouq*, April 30, 2011.

33. "Istishhad al-Katedra'iyya Yantahi Doon Sidamat," *Al-Shurouq*, May 7, 2011.

34. SCAF membership changed every six months based on promotions and transfers within the armed forces. "Al-Shurouq Tanshur Tashkil wa Ikhtisasat al-Majlis al-'Ala li-l-Quwwat al-Musallaha," *Al-Shurouq*, February 12, 2011.

35. Hosni Mubarak's distancing of the military from political life, partly by expanding their economic holdings as a privileged caste, is explained in Robert Springborg, *Mubarak's Egypt: Fragmentation of the Political Order* (Boulder, CO: Westview Press, 1989); Imad Harb, "The Egyptian Military in Politics: Disengagement or Accommodation?" *Middle East Journal* 57, no. 2 (2003): 269–90; and Dina Rashed, "The Egyptian Military and the Presidency: Continuity and Change," in *Egypt beyond Tahrir Square*, ed. Bessma Momani and Eid Mohamed (Bloomington: Indiana University Press, 2016), 133–50.

36. Yezid Sayigh, *Above the State: The Officers' Republic in Egypt* (Washington, DC: Carnegie Endowment for International Peace, 2012), 18.

37. The White House, Office of the Press Secretary, "Remarks by the President on Egypt," February 11, 2011, https://obamawhitehouse.archives.gov/the-press-office/2011/02/11/remarks-president-egypt.

38. Atef Said, "The Paradox of Transition to 'Democracy' under Military Rule," *Social Research* 79, no. 2 (2012): 397–434, 411.

39. The definitive account of the military's economic holdings and activities is Yezid Sayigh, *Owners of the Republic: An Anatomy of Egypt's Military Economy* (Washington, DC: Carnegie Endowment for International Peace, 2019). For representations of the army in popular culture, see Dalia Said Mostafa, *The Egyptian Military in Popular Culture: Context and Critique* (London: Palgrave Macmillan, 2017).

40. The term "reserve domains" comes from J. Samuel Valenzuela, "Democratic Consolidation in Post-Transitional Settings: Notion, Process, and Facilitating Conditions," Working Paper #150, Helen Kellogg Institute for International Studies (December 1990).

41. "The Supreme Council will not field a candidate from one of their own," an unnamed military official told a reporter in Washington, DC. Elisabeth Bumiller, "Pentagon Places Its Bet on a General in Egypt," *New York Times*, March 11, 2011.

42. David Kirkpatrick, "Egypt Army Sets 6-Month Blueprint, but Future Role Is Unclear," *New York Times*, February 14, 2011.

43. Anthony Shadid, "Egyptian Military Dissolves Parliament," *New York Times*, February 13, 2011.

44. Clement M. Henry and Robert Springborg, "A Tunisian Solution for Egypt's Military: Why Egypt's Military Will Not be Able to Govern," *Foreign Affairs*, February 21, 2011.

45. Stinchcombe, "Ending Revolutions," 54.

46. Moataz Abdel Fattah, "Al-Jaysh lam Yujhidd al-Thawra," *Al-Shurouq*, April 2, 2011.

47. The interview is available at Dreamstvchannel, "Al-'Ashera Mas'an Mona al-Shazly Thalatha min Qiyadat al-Majlis al-'Ala li-l Quwwat al-Musallaha," February 22, 2011; https://youtu.be/fCBi-HDRYLw. An unnamed American official in continuous communication with SCAF during the Eighteen Days said that this was his keen advice to the generals. "We just kept repeating the mantra, 'Don't break the bond you have with your own people.'" David Sanger, "When Militaries Decide," *New York Times*, February 19, 2011.

48. Sherif Younis has dissected the military-led republican regime's founding myth of a metaphysical "people" in whose name Nasser and his fellow colonels claimed the right to rule (*Nida' al-Sha'b: Tarikh Naqdi li-l Idiulujiyya al-Nasiriyya* [Cairo: Dar al-Shurouq, 2012], 95–111). Azmi Bishara has aptly observed that "the military easily transcends the idea of serving the unified nation to claiming to embody the nation and its will, considering itself the real nation in its pure form, undistorted by sectional interests" (*Thawrat Misr* [Doha: al-Markaz al-Arabi li-l Abhath wa Dirasat al-Siyasat, 2016], 2:59).

49. "Kayf Yara al-Majlis al-'Ala Ma Jara wa ma Yajri," *Al-Shurouq*, February 16, 2011, emphasis added.

50. Dreamstvchannel, "Al-'Ashera Masa'an Mona al-Shazly."

51. "Umana' wa Afrad al-Shurta Yatazaharun fi Sitt Muhafazat," *Al-Misri-al-Yawm*, March 23, 2011; "Izalat 2,844 Halat Ta'adi 'Ala Amlak al-Dawla," *Al-Shurouq*, February 26, 2011; "Ra'is al-Qada' al-'Askari: Waqf Ihalat al-Madaniyyin ila al-Mahakim al-Askariyya ma' Intiha' al-Tawari,'" *Al-Misri-al-Yawm*, September 6, 2011; Liam Stack, "You Should Thank God You're Not Inside: The Expansion of Military Trials in Post-Revolutionary Egypt" (master's thesis, New York University, 2012). Decree-Law 10/2011 (March 10, 2011) stiffened penalties for disturbing the peace, including resisting authorities, and Decree-Law 11/2011 (March 22, 2011) added the death penalty for the rape of females and imprisonment for morally defined crimes committed in public such as debauchery (*fisq*).

52. The five-member panel was appointed by Ahmed Shafiq as a concession to the protest movement during the Eighteen Days. The committee continued work after Shafiq's dismissal and released its findings in April. "Mulakhas al-Taqrir al-Niha'i li Lajnat al-Tahqiq wa Taqassy al-Haqa'iq bi-Sha'n al-Ahdath allaty Wakibat Thawrat 25 Yanayir 2011"; https://manshurat.org/node/13539.

53. Walter Armbrust, *Martyrs and Tricksters: An Ethnography of the Egyptian Revolution* (Princeton, NJ: Princeton University Press, 2019), 57, and chaps. 3–4.

54. In April 2011, the Cairo Court of Urgent Matters ordered the removal of the Mubarak family's name from all public institutions, but this was later suspended by its appeals court.

55. "699 min Usar al-Shuhada' wa 3124 Musaban Sarafu al-Ta'widat," *Al-Shurouq* January 20, 2012.

56. Amnesty International, "Egypt: Protect Families of Those Killed in Protests from Intimidation," February 25, 2011; "Al-Tibb al-Shar'i: Shuhada' al-Thawra bi-l Daqahliyya Laqu Masra'ihim bi-l Rusas al-Hayy," *Al-Misri al-Yawm*, February 26, 2011; "Lijan Sha'biyya li Ta'min Muhakamat Dubat al-Iskandariyya," *Al-Shurouq*, April 16, 2011.

57. This was the third forcible disbandment of protesters' encampments in Tahrir Square. On March 9, soldiers and plainclothes armed men attacked protesters, detaining 173 men and seventeen women in military prisons and subjecting the latter to forced pelvic exams that military officials called "virginity tests." On April 9, two protesters were killed and seventy-one were injured by soldiers using live ammunition to break up a sit-in.

58. Anthony Shadid, "At Mubarak Trial, Stark Image of Humbled Power," *New York Times*, August 4, 2011.

59. How and why SCAF selected these eight men for the expert panel is one of the many unexplained pivotal decisions of the revolutionary situation. Three members of the panel at the time and after the fact publicly and separately gave the same reason for Sobhi Saleh's selection: his demonstrated legal expertise. For the panel members' comments on Saleh, see David Kirkpatrick and Kareem Fahim, "In Egypt, A Panel of Jurists Is Given the Task of Revising the Country's Constitution," *New York Times*, February 16, 2011; "Al-Mustashar Hatem Bagato Muqarrir Lajnat al-Ta'dilat al-Dusturiyya: Al-Ta'dilat Sat'udi Hatman li-Taghyir Dusturi Shamil," *Al-Misri al-Yawm*, March 18, 2011; Tareq al-Bishri, *Min Awraq Thawrat 25 Yanayir* (Cairo: Dar al-Shurouq, 2012), 40–41. Criticism of the exclusion of youth and women is in Nawal El Saadawi, "Shortcomings of the New Constitution Committee," *Ahram Online*, February 21, 2011; http://english.ahram.org.eg/News/6129.aspx.

60. The thesis of a deal between SCAF and the Muslim Brothers was a widespread belief among many political factions. An example may be found in a Tahrir Square leaflet titled "Gornal," February 25, 2011. Tahrir Square Collection, UCLA Library International Digital Ephemera Project (IDEP); https://idep.library.ucla.edu/search#!/document/edu.ucla.library.dep.tahrir:155. The General Guide of the Muslim Brothers denied that such a deal had been struck in "Murshid al-Ikhwan: La Safqaat Ma' al-Jaysh," *Al-Ahram*, April 13, 2011.

61. For discussion of the panel's rule changes that were not welcomed, see Nathan Brown and Michele Dunne, "Egypt's Draft Constitutional Amendments Answer Some Questions and Raise Others" (Washington, DC: Carnegie Endowment for International Peace, March 1, 2011); https://carnegieendowment.org/2011/03/01/egypt-s-draft-constitutional-amendments-answer-some-questions-and-raise-others-pub-42817.

62. Legislative involvement in constitution-making is an international norm, but the two common pathways are direct elections to a new legislature that simultaneously serves as a constituent assembly (the model adopted by Tunisia in 2011), or a separate constituent assembly elected by a direct popular vote. The Bishri panel's rationale for their composite choice was that indirect elections would guard against constitution-drafting turning into a popularity contest. See the interview with Bishri in Amira Howeidy, "Between Two Constitutions," *Al-Ahram Weekly*, March 10–16, 2011.

63. For one of the most cogent summations of the counterproposals, see Hasan Nafa', "Limadha Yata'yyan Rafd al-Ta'dilat al-Dusturiyya al-Muqtaraha," *Al-Misri al-Yawm*, March 13, 2011.

64. The Popular Democracy Movement (under construction), "La Lil Ta'dilat al-Dusturiyya al-Mu'adiya lil-Thawra," March 7, 2011. Tahrir Square Collection, UCLA Library International Digital Ephemera Project (IDEP); https://idep.library.ucla.edu/search#!/document/edu.ucla.library.dep.tahrir:186.

65. The Popular Campaign Against Constitutional Amendments, "As'ela 'Ala Balena wa Shaghla Fikrina," March 2011. Tahrir Square Collection, UCLA Library International Digital Ephemera Project (IDEP); https://idep.library.ucla.edu/search#!/document/edu.ucla.library.dep.tahrir:269.

66. Khaled Tallima, quoted in Sarah Eissa, "Their Eyes on the Future," *Al-Ahram Weekly*, March 17–23, 2011.

67. Amira Howeidy, "Between Two Constitutions," *Al-Ahram Weekly*, March 10–16, 2011.

68. 6aprilorg1, "Vote NO," March 17, 2011; https://youtu.be/IB_7MH9C9Kc; "Mawjat Rafd Jadida li-l Ta'dilat al-Dusturiyya," *Al-Shurouq*, March 16, 2011.

69. "Mu'tamar al-Ikhwan al-Sikandari Yuhadhir min Makhatir Rafd al-Ta'dilat al-Dusturiyya," *Al-Shurouq*, March 16, 2011.

70. "Lafitat Wajib Shar'i Tuthir Ghadab al-Muwatinin min al-Ikhwan," *Al-Shurouq*, March 16, 2011.

71. Michael Slackman, "Islamist Group Is Rising Force in a New Egypt," *New York Times*, March 25, 2011.

72. The remarks of preacher Mohamed Hussein Yaqub can be viewed at mansoura2010, "Ghazwat al-Sanadiq," March 22, 2011; https://youtu.be/tnOxAQGFSHU. The remarks of SCAF general Mamdouh Shahin on a television talk show can be viewed at boty82, "Baladna Bil Masri: al-Istifta' kan 'ala Shar'iyyat al-Jaysh," May 15, 2011; https://youtu.be/IjU5sQoZQPU. Two of the most insightful contemporaneous analyses that disaggregate the two vote clusters are 'Ammar Ali Hasan, "Ma'rakat al-Istifta' Hasamha al-Din wa-l Tabaqa wa-l Mustawa al-Ta'limi," *Al-Misri al-Yawm*, March 26, 2011; Ellis Goldberg, "A Closer Look at the Referendum Results: District by District," April 8, 2011, Nisr al-Nasr blog, http://nisralnasr.blogspot.com/2011/04/closer-look-at-referendum-results.html.

73. Nimer Sultany, *Law and Revolution: Legitimacy and Constitutionalism after the Arab Spring* (Oxford: Oxford University Press, 2018), 248. Analysis of the March 30 Declaration's added provisions is in Kristen Stilt, "The End of 'One Hand': The Egyptian Constitutional Declaration and the Rift between the 'People' and the Supreme Council of the Armed Forces," *Yearbook of Islamic and Middle Eastern Law* 16 (2010–11): 43–52.

74. Talal Asad, "Fear and the Ruptured State: Reflections on Egypt after Mubarak," *Social Research* 79 (Summer 2012): 271–89, 274. An overview of the pervasive political fears that accompanied the referendum are in Amr al-Shobaky, "Takhawwufat al-Misriyyin," *Al-Misri al-Yawm*, March 7, 2011.

75. Nathan Brown uses the phrase to describe SCAF's machinations in the March 30 Declaration, whereas I use it to characterize the Bishri panel's most consequential decision (Brown, "Landmines in Egypt's Constitutional Roadmap" [Washington, DC: Carnegie Endowment for International Peace, December 7, 2011]).

76. For the parallel stream in new associational life, independent trade unions, see Nadine Abdalla, "The Labor Movement in the Face of Transition," in *Egypt's Revolutions: Politics, Religion, and Social Movements*, ed. Bernard Rougier and Stéphane Lacroix (New York: Palgrave Macmillan, 2016), 197–211. On international support for the new union federations and their eventual fracturing, see Ian Hartshorn, *Labor Politics*

*in North Africa: After the Uprisings in Egypt and Tunisia* (New York: Cambridge University Press, 2019), 80–93.

77. Mohamed Abdel-Baky, "Liberal Uncertainty," *Al-Ahram Weekly*, May 5–11, 2011.

78. The party's formation was marked by uncharacteristically open feuds that were concealed from the public before 2011. See Amani Maged, "Not without Squabble," *Al-Ahram Weekly*, May 5–11, 2011. A thorough account of the three main factions within the Muslim Brothers that had crystallized around a disputed internal election in 2009 is in Carrie Rosefsky Wickham, *The Muslim Brotherhood: Evolution of an Islamist Movement* (Princeton, NJ: Princeton University Press, 2013).

79. Ashraf El-Sherif, "Egypt's Salafists at a Crossroads" (Washington, DC: Carnegie Endowment for International Peace, April 29, 2015). A more sharply radical, antiestablishment agglomeration of Salafis coalesced around the charismatic maverick preacher Shaykh Hazem Salah Abu Ismail, becoming energetic foot soldiers in his presidential campaign, discussed in chap. 4. See Stéphane Lacroix and Ahmed Zaghloul Shalata, "The Rise of Revolutionary Salafism in Post-Mubarak Egypt," in *Egypt's Revolutions: Politics, Religion, and Social Movements*, ed. Bernard Rougier and Stéphane Lacroix (New York: Palgrave Macmillan, 2016), 163–78.

80. Arthur Stinchcombe, "Social Structure and Organizations," in *Handbook of Organizations*, ed. James March (Chicago: Rand McNally, 1965), 142–93, 148.

81. As Stéphane Lacroix observes, "Although this is impossible to prove, a widespread belief is that generous donations from associations and individuals in the Gulf may have helped provide the Da'wa [Salafi religious movement] with the financial means to grow" ("Egypt's Pragmatic Salafis: The Politics of Hizb al-Nour" [Washington, DC: Carnegie Endowment for International Peace, November 2016], 5).

82. For example, the FJP, Salafi parties, and Wasat contested the elections separately; the FJP was in alliance with the Nasserist Karama and the liberal Ghad parties. The hybrid electoral system under which the elections were held is explained in International Foundation for Electoral Systems (IFES), "Elections in Egypt: The Electoral Framework in Egypt's Continuing Transition, February 2011–September 2013," October 11, 2013. For more on the volatile dynamics of the four electoral alliances, see Nate Wright, "Egypt's Intense Election Eve," *Middle East Report*, November 10, 2011; Hesham Sallam, ed., *Egypt's Parliamentary Elections, 2011–2012: A Critical Guide to a Changing Political Arena* (Fairfax, VA: Tadween Publishing, 2013).

83. Pew Research Center, "Egyptians Embrace Revolt Leaders, Religious Parties and Military, as Well," Global Attitudes Project, April 25, 2011. The second poll by the

International Republican Institute is cited in Ellen Lust and David Waldner, "Parties in Transitional Democracies: Authoritarian Legacies and Post-Authoritarian Challenges in the Middle East and North Africa," in *Parties, Movements, and Democracy in the Developing World*, ed. Nancy Bermeo and Deborah Yashar (New York: Cambridge University Press, 2016), 157–89, 172.

84. Basem Adel, *Sina'at al-Ahzab fi Misr Ba'd 25 Yanayir* (Cairo: Al-Masriyya li-l Nashr wal Tawzi', 2011). The Sultan-Hamzawy debate can be viewed at Bridges Foundation, "Al-Munazara al-Kubra hawl Mustaqbal Misr bayn Hamzawy wa Sultan," April 21, 2011; https://youtu.be/yCd_iglXmgo.

85. "Khamsat Alaaf min al-Qiwa al-Siyasiyya Yusharikun fi Mu'tamar Misr al-Awal," *Al-Misri al-Yawm*, May 8, 2011.

86. "National Council Document: The Declaration of the Principles of the Egyptian Constitution after the January 25, 2011 Revolution," included with a collection of two other documents and with an introduction by Tahany El Gebaly, "Constitutional Principles: Documents on Post-Revolution Egypt," *Alif: Journal of Comparative Poetics*, no. 32 (2012): 228–53, 239.

87. The thinking was that the generals had to know "who they were handing power to and on what basis. That was the point." David Kirkpatrick, "Judge Helped Egypt's Military to Cement Power," *New York Times*, July 4, 2012.

88. Guillermo O'Donnell and Philippe Schmitter, *Transitions from Authoritarian Rule: Tentative Conclusions about Uncertain Democracies* (Baltimore: Johns Hopkins University Press, 1986), 31.

89. An insightful analysis of the contest over the "civil state" is in Clément Steuer, "The Role of Elections: The Recomposition of the Party System and the Hierarchization of Political Issues," in *Egypt's Revolutions: Politics, Religion, and Social Movements*, ed. Bernard Rougier and Stéphane Lacroix (London: Palgrave Macmillan, 2016), 81–99.

90. Lally Weymouth, "Egyptian Generals Speak about Revolution, Elections," *Washington Post*, May 18, 2011.

91. Hesham Sallam, "Striking Back at Egyptian Workers," *Middle East Report* 259 (2011): 20–25.

92. I compiled the protest events from the two most-read privately owned dailies, *Al-Misri Al-Yawm* and *Al-Shurouq*, both of which had on-the-ground correspondents in every province and copiously covered protests before and after 2011. For the annual tally of protests from 1998 to 2010, see Joel Beinin and Marie Duboc, "A Workers' Social Movement on the Margin of the Global Neoliberal Order, Egypt 2004–2012," in

*Social Movements, Mobilization, and Contestation in the Middle East and North Africa*, ed. Joel Beinin and Frédéric Vairel, 2nd ed. (Palo Alto, CA: Stanford University Press, 2013), 205–27.

93. "Ahali Helwan Yutalibun b-Istifta'," *Al-Shurouq*, April 16, 2011; "Muzaharat Ghadiba dedd Ilgha' Muhafazatayy Helwan wa Sitat Uktubar," *Al-Shurouq*, April 17, 2011.

94. Guillermo O'Donnell, *Bureaucratic Authoritarianism: Argentina, 1966–1973, in Comparative Perspective* (Berkeley: University of California Press, 1988), 26.

95. O'Donnell, *Bureaucratic Authoritarianism*, 25–26.

96. Joel Beinin, *The Rise of Egypt's Workers* (Washington, DC: Carnegie Endowment for International Peace, 2012), 14.

97. Abdel Khaleq Farouq, *Iqtisadiyyat al-Ujur wa-l Murattabat fi Misr* (Cairo: Maktabat al-Shurouq al-Dawliyya, 2012), 92, 170.

98. "Al-Thawra Asqatat Sinario al-Tawrith wa-l Hukuma Tuttabiquhu," *Al-Misri al-Yawm*, February 21, 2011.

99. Robert Fishman, "Democratic Practice after the Revolution: The Case of Portugal and Beyond," *Politics and Society* 39, no. 2 (2011): 233–67.

100. Decree-Law 45/2011 amended the Code of Military Justice 25/1966 to grant exclusive jurisdiction to military prosecutors to investigate the finances of military personnel. This came in response to lawyers and activists flooding the Ministry of Justice's Office of Illicit Gain with petitions demanding investigation into ancien régime officials' embezzlement. The quote is from an unnamed military official in David Kirkpatrick, "Egyptian Military Warns the Media to Censor Criticism," *New York Times*, June 1, 2011. The military council was meticulous about tracking direct criticism in the media. In a lecture to 1,500 handpicked youth, SCAF general Mohamed al-Assar complained, "In a single week, from 21 to 27 May, we noted 23 talk shows in which there were 82 personal attacks on members of SCAF." Galal Nassar, "Army Battles Conspiracy Theories," *Al-Ahram Weekly*, June 9–15, 2011.

101. Amnesty International, "Egypt: A Year After 'Virginity Tests,' Women Victims of Army Violence Still Seek Justice," March 9, 2012. https://www.amnesty.org/en/latest/news/2012/03/egypt-year-after-virginity-tests-women-victims-army-violence-still-seek-justice/.

102. Mostafa Ali, "Egypt Teachers Strike for the First Time since 1951," *Ahram Online*, September 19, 2011 http://english.ahram.org.eg/News/21568.aspx; "Idrab Shamil bi-l Naql al-'Am," *Al-Misri al-Yawm*, September 26, 2011; Mostafa Ali, "Postal Workers Strike across Egypt for Pay Raise," *Ahram Online*, September 4, 2011 http://english.ahram.org

.eg/News/20297.aspx; Reuters, "Cairo Air Traffic Controller Go-Slow Protest Ends," October 7, 2011; "Al-Dakhiliyya Tuhasir al-Dakhiliyya," *Al-Misri al-Yawm*, October 26, 2011.

103. David Kirkpatrick, "Egypt Military Moves to Cement a Muscular Role in Government," *New York Times*, July 17, 2011.

104. David Kirkpatrick, "Egypt's Military Expands Power, Raising Alarms," *New York Times*, October 14, 2011.

105. Human Rights Watch, "Egypt: Don't Cover up Military Killing of Copt Protesters," October 25, 2011. The independent database Wikithawra indicates a final tally of twenty-seven fatalities. Wikithawra, "Hasr Qatla 'Ahd al-Majlis al-'Askari"; https://wikithawra.wordpress.com/2013/09/24/scafcasualities/. The chain of events leading up to the mass demonstration is in Mariz Tadros, "Egypt's Bloody Sunday," *Middle East Report Online*, October 13, 2011; https://merip.org/2011/10/egypts-bloody-sunday/.

106. Dreamstvchannel, "al-'Ashera Mas'an Mona al-Shazly Hiwar Khas ma' Mumathilin li-l-Majlis al-'Askari," October 20, 2011; https://youtu.be/Un-jnb0OBfs.

107. An English translation of the document is available at http://constitutionnet.org/vl/item/egypt-draft-declaration-fundamental-principles-new-egyptian-state-november-2011-english.

108. Muslim Brothers' statement in "al-Ikhwan Tusharik fi-l Milyuniyya," *Al-Misri al-Yawm*, November 17, 2011; Al-Masry, quoted in "Thalath 'Ashar I'tilafan wa Haraka fi-l Iskandariyya Ta'lin Musharakatiha fi-l Milyuniyya," *Al-Misri al-Yawm*, November 17, 2011.

109. Amnesty International, "Agents of Repression: Egypt's Police and the Case for Reform" (2012), 7. The fatality figure is from Wikithawra, "Hasr Qatla 'Ahd al-Majlis al-'Askari." The injuries are reported in the National Council of Human Rights (NCHR) Fact-Finding Report, "Nata'ij A'mal Lajnat Taqasi al-Haqa'iq fi Ahdath al-'Unf fi Misr fi Shahray November wa December 2011," n.d.; https://manshurat.org/node/13397.

110. Lucie Ryzova, "The Battle of Muhammad Mahmoud Street in Cairo: The Politics and Poetics of Urban Violence in Revolutionary Time," *Past and Present* 247 (May 2020): 273–317, 275.

111. Sameh Naguib of the Revolutionary Socialists, also quoted in chap. 1, characterized the MB's role as "a classical betrayal by a reformist, non-revolutionary movement," in "The Egyptian Counterrevolution: An Interview with Sameh Naguib," *Jacobin*, March 11, 2016; https://www.jacobinmag.com/author/sameh-naguib. For the multiple, contested narratives of Mohamed Mahmoud, including the state's story, see Manar Hazzaa, "Narratives and Evidence: Struggles over Mohamed Mahmoud" (master's thesis, American University in Cairo, 2016).

112. Radio Horytna, "Khitab al-Mushir al-Awwal," November 22, 2011; https://youtu.be/I_u9ddvbv9I.

113. The White House, Office of the Press Secretary, "Statement by the Press Secretary on Recent Developments in Egypt," November 25, 2011; https://obamawhitehouse.archives.gov/the-press-office/2011/11/25/statement-press-secretary-recent-developments-egypt.

114. Voting was staggered over three phases to ensure full judicial supervision at every polling station. More information on election rules and logistics is in "Final Report of the Carter Center Mission to Witness the 2011–2012 Parliamentary Elections in Egypt," the Carter Center, 2012.

115. As the New York Times correspondent in attendance speculated, "the generals have expected that the threat of an Islamist takeover at the polls might now give Washington pause." David Kirkpatrick, "Military Flexes Its Muscles as Islamists Gain in Egypt," *New York Times*, December 8, 2011.

116. Kirkpatrick, "Military Flexes Its Muscles."

117. Guillermo O'Donnell and Philippe Schmitter remind us of the precarity of constitutions in the tumultuous politics of transitions. "Rules at some point may be packaged together into a single handbook—the constitution—but informal arrangements and norms of prudence are likely to supplement it (and occasionally to circumvent it)" (*Transitions from Authoritarian Rule*, 78).

118. The fatality figure is from Wikithawra, "Hasr Qatla 'Ahd al-Majlis al-'Askari," and the injuries from the National Council of Human Rights (NCHR) Fact-Finding Report.

119. Hillary Rodham Clinton, quoted in David Kirkpatrick, "Mass March by Cairo Women in Protest over Abuse by Soldiers," *New York Times*, December 20, 2011.

120. Nina Gronlykke Mollerup and Sherief Gaber, "Making Media Public: On Revolutionary Street Screenings in Egypt," *International Journal of Communication* 9 (2015): 2903–21.

121. The poll surveyed 1,077 adults in face-to-face interviews between December 16–23, 2011. Ahmed Younis and Mohamed Younis, "Egyptians Expect Military to Hand Power to Elected Government," *Gallup News*, January 25, 2012.

122. Anthony Shadid, "The Old Order Stifles the Birth of a New Egypt," *New York Times*, November 23, 2011.

123. Alain Rouquié, "Demilitarization and the Institutionalization of Military-dominated Polities in Latin America," in *Transitions from Authoritarian Rule: Comparative*

*Perspectives*, ed. Guillermo O'Donnell, Philippe Schmitter, and Laurence Whitehead (Baltimore, MD: Johns Hopkins University Press, 1986), 108–36, 127.

## CHAPTER 4

1. "A'la Nisbat Mushahada li-Ula "Mubarayyat" al-Barlaman," *Al-Shurouq*, January 25, 2012.

2. The session can be viewed at SotelSha3b, "Hilf al-Yamin al-Dusturi li-A'da' Majlis al-Sha'b," January 23, 2012; https://youtu.be/SmpFZ6PoliA.

3. Mona Anis, "Marginalia: Remembrance of Things Past," *Al-Ahram Weekly*, January 26–February 1, 2012.

4. "Lafetat al-Tahrir . . . Dahk wa Jadd wa 'Askar," *Al-Shurouq*, January 27, 2012. On slogans, see "Hitafat al-Thawra Tulakhis Matalibiha," *Al-Shurouq*, January 27, 2012. "Al-Sawaysa Rafadu al-Ihtifal li'an al-Thawra lam Tantahi," *Al-Misri al-Yawm*, January 26, 2012.

5. Jack Shenker, "Egyptian Parliament Sworn in under Heavy Weight of Expectation," *Guardian*, January 23, 2012.

6. Turnout figures were announced separately for each of the election's three staggered phases; phase 1 turnout was 62 percent, phase 2, 66 percent, and phase 3, 62 percent. Amr Hashem Rabi', "Nata'ij al-Intikhabat al-Barlamaniyya, 2011/2012," in *Intikhabat Majlis al-Sha'b 2011/2012*, ed. Amr Hashem Rabi' (Cairo: Markaz al-Ahram li-l Dirasat al-Siyasiyya wa-l Istratijiyya, 2012), 364.

7. Human Rights Watch, *The Road Ahead: A Human Rights Agenda for Egypt's New Parliament* (New York: Human Rights Watch, 2012).

8. "Coptic Christian Group Sends Letter to Islamist-Parliament Majority," *Ahram Online*, January 22, 2012; http://english.ahram.org.eg/News/32369.aspx.

9. Guillermo O'Donnell and Philippe Schmitter, *Transitions from Authoritarian Rule: Tentative Conclusions about Uncertain Democracies* (Baltimore: Johns Hopkins University Press, 1986), 57. For this argument applied to Egypt's elections, see Neil Ketchley, *Egypt in a Time of Revolution: Contentious Politics and the Arab Spring* (New York: Cambridge University Press, 2017), chap. 4; Joshua Stacher, *Watermelon Democracy: Egypt's Turbulent Transition* (Syracuse, NY: Syracuse University Press, 2020).

10. Sidney Tarrow, *Strangers at the Gates: Movements and States in Contentious Politics* (Cambridge: Cambridge University Press, 2012), 129.

11. Nathan Brown, "Why Are So Many Upset about al-Azhar?" Atlantic Council, January 30, 2012; https://www.atlanticcouncil.org/blogs/menasource/why-are-so-many

-upset-about-alazhar/; "Al-'Askari wa-l Sha'b Wajhan li-Wajh," *Al-Shurouq*, February 1, 2012; "Al-Mutanafasun al-Murtaqabun li-l Ri'asa Yajtami'un 'ala Naqd al-'Askari," *Al-Shurouq*, February 1, 2012.

12. This is not to say that the election was exemplary; campaigning on election days, complexity of the ballot, and chaos at counting centers were some of the major problems. See the Electoral Institute for Sustainable Democracy in Africa (EISA), "Election Witnessing Mission Report, Egypt: The People's Assembly and Shura Council Elections" (Johannesburg: EISA, 2012); the Carter Center, "Final Report of the Carter Center Mission to Witness the 2011–2012 Parliamentary Elections in Egypt" (Atlanta: Carter Center, 2012).

13. Clément Steuer, "The Role of Elections: The Recomposition of the Party System and the Hierarchization of Political Issues," in *Egypt's Revolutions: Politics, Religion, and Social Movements*, ed. Bernard Rougier and Stéphane Lacroix (New York: Palgrave Macmillan, 2016), 81–99, 89.

14. Muhammad Ali Abu Reyda, "Al-Tarkiba al-Siyasiyya wa-l Ijtima'iyya li-'Ada' Majlis al-Sha'b 2011/2012," in *Intikhabat Majlis al-Sha'b 2011/2012*, ed. Amr Hashem Rabi' (Cairo: Markaz al-Ahram l-il Dirasat al-Siyasiyya wa-l Istratijiyya, 2012), 403–43.

15. Carrie Rosefsky Wickham, *Mobilizing Islam: Religion, Activism, and Political Change in Egypt* (New York: Columbia University Press, 2002); Mona El-Ghobashy, "The Metamorphosis of the Egyptian Muslim Brothers," *International Journal of Middle East Studies* 37, no. 3 (August 2005): 373–95; Samer Shehata and Joshua Stacher, "The Brotherhood Goes to Parliament," *Middle East Report* 240 (Fall 2006): 32–39.

16. Ellis Goldberg, "Cairo: Elections and Other Issues," Nisralnasr Weblog, December 26, 2011; http://nisralnasr.blogspot.com/2011/12/cairo-elections-and-other-issues.html.

17. Egyptian Initiative for Personal Rights (EIPR), "Witness Accounts around the Port Said Tragedy," press release, February 2, 2012.

18. Shaimaa Fayed, Tom Perry, "Egyptians Incensed after 74 Die in Soccer Tragedy," Reuters, February 1, 2012.

19. The session can be viewed at SotelSha3b, "Al-Jalsa al-Tari'a li-Majlis al-Sha'b bi-sha'n Ahdath Bur Sa'id al-Damiya," February 2, 2012; https://youtu.be/puf5rUmT90I.

20. In 2015, soccer star Mohamed Salah paid tribute to the victims by wearing the number 74 shirt for Fiorentina in a Europa League semifinal.

21. I have not been able to locate the full-text version of the report. Extracts from the document are published in *Al-Misri al-Yawm*, February 13, 2012, 5.

22. Gamal Essam El Din, "Parliamentary Backbiting," *Al-Ahram Weekly*, February 16–22, 2012. The parliamentary session can be viewed at SotelSha3b, "Jalsat Munaqashat Taqrir Lajnat Taqassi Haqa'iq Ahdath Bur Sa'id," February 13, 2012; https://youtu.be/WGoyuzzEc3k.

23. Steven Lee Myers and David Kirkpatrick, "As Tensions Rise, Egypt Bars Exit of Six Americans," *New York Times*, January 27, 2012; Cheryl Pellerin, "Dempsey Addresses Concerns with Egyptian Military Leaders," *American Forces Press Service*, February 12, 2012.

24. Tamim Elyan, "Egypt MPs Move to Withdraw Confidence from Government," Reuters, March 11, 2012. The session can be viewed at SotelSha3b, "Al-Jalsa al-Sabahiya li-Munaqashat Qadiyat al-Tamwil al-Ajnabi," March 11, 2012; https://youtube/DEMWBOrcsFs.

25. "Sidam Jadid Bayna al-Sha'b wa-l Hukuma," *Al-Misri al-Yawm*, March 22, 2012.

26. Gamal Essam El-Din, "Letting Off Steam," *Al-Ahram Weekly*, March 15–21, 2012.

27. Nathan J. Brown and Kristen Stilt, "A Haphazard Constitutional Compromise" (Washington, DC: Carnegie Endowment for International Peace, April 11, 2011).

28. "SCAF Presides over Diminished Role," *Al-Ahram Weekly*, March 15–21, 2012.

29. For instance, some US Congressmen took offense at the comments coming out of the March 11 parliamentary debate urging a complete rejection of all US aid. "The Parliament has said some things that are very chilling," said Senator Lindsey Graham (R-SC). "We're not going to throw good money after bad." Steven Lee Myers, "Despite Rights Concerns, US Plans to Resume Aid to Egypt," *New York Times*, March 16, 2012.

30. However, parliament still faced the formidable tasks of making its operations transparent to the public and building its legislative capacity after decades of subordination to the presidency. For an informative workshop discussion of these and other issues, see Middle East and North Africa Programme, *Egypt's New Parliamentary Politics* (London: Chatham House, March 2012).

31. Ziad Bahaa-Eldin, "Hal Nahnu Mutajjihun li-Azma Dusturiyya?" *Al-Shurouq*, March 13, 2012.

32. "Huquqiyyun Yataqabbalun al-'Aza' fi-l Dustur al-Qadim," *Al-Shurouq*, March 26, 2012.

33. "Ta'alu Naktub Dusturna," n.d., document on file with author.

34. Jeremy Waldron, "Constitutionalism: A Skeptical View" in Jeremy Waldron, *Political Political Theory* (Cambridge, MA: Harvard University Press, 2016), 43.

35. Nada al-Kholi, "Alaa Abdel Fattah Yarwi li-l Shurouq," *Al-Shurouq*, December 27, 2011.

36. Jon Elster, "Legislatures as Constituent Assemblies," in *The Least Examined Branch: The Role of Legislatures in the Constitutional State*, ed. Richard Bauman and Tsvi Kahana (New York: Cambridge University Press, 2009), 181–97, 185.

37. Reuters photo by Amr Abdallah Dalsh, March 24, 2012; "Al-Alaaf Yakhrujun fi Masirat ila Qa'at al-Mu'tamarat I'tiradan 'ala al-Tashkil," *Al-Misri al-Yawm*, March 25, 2012.

38. Other details from the meeting, including disputes over who should oversee the vote count, are in "Azma fi-l Barlaman Bisabab Saytarat al-Ikhwan wa-l Salafiyin 'ala Ta'sisiyyat al-Dustur," *Al-Misri al-Yawm*, March 25, 2012. Out of 678 electors, there were 535 valid votes out of 589 cast. The high percentage of rejected ballots, 9 percent, may be a further indication of the disorganized nature of the voting process.

39. Ziad Bahaa-Eldin, "Haynama Tasbah al-Muqata'a Daruriyya," *Al-Shurouq*, March 27, 2012.

40. Gamal Essam El-Din, "A 'Stillborn' Assembly," *Al-Ahram Weekly*, April 5–11, 2012.

41. "Al-Katatni Ra'isan li Ta'sisiyya illa Rub'," *Al-Shurouq*, March 29, 2012.

42. "Mawjat al-Ghadab Did Ta'sisiyyat al-Islamiyeen Tatasa'ad," *Al-Shurouq*, April 1, 2012.

43. Ziad Bahaa-Eldin, "Bada'il al-Khuruj min Ma'zaq Kitabat al-Dustur," *Al-Shurouq*, April 3, 2012.

44. Arato's judgment is puzzling because he also acknowledges the role of the military. "With respect to the most important actor in Egypt, all we can say is that the Tunisian military was perhaps too weak to intervene, while the SCAF was too strong to stop itself from continually trying to steer the process." Andrew Arato, *The Adventures of the Constituent Power: Beyond Revolutions?* (New York: Cambridge University Press, 2017), 360.

45. Adam Przeworski, "Democracy as a Contingent Outcome of Conflicts," in *Constitutionalism and Democracy*, ed. Jon Elster and Rune Slagstad (Cambridge: Cambridge University Press, 1988), 59–80, 65.

46. "Al-Qada' Yujhid Ta'sisiyyat al-Dustur," *Al-Shurouq*, April 11, 2012.

47. Emad Eddin Hussein, "Masdar Mas'ul: Hukm Butlan Ta'sisiyyat al-Dustur Makhraj Mantiqi li-l Azma," *Al-Shurouq*, April 11, 2012.

48. See the full-page coverage of the controversy in *Al-Shurouq*, May 1, 2012, 5.

49. For a brief overview, see Mona El-Ghobashy, "Dissidence and Deference among Egyptian Judges," *Middle East Report* 279 (Summer 2016).

50. "Mansour Hasan Yughadir Maʿrakat al-Riʾasa," *Al-Shurouq*, March 26, 2012.

51. "Sabahy: Saʾ Uharib al-Faqr wa-l Fasad wa-l Bitala Qabl Israʾil," *Al-Shurouq*, March 26, 2012.

52. Khalil El-Anani deconstructs Abu Ismail's brand of "revolutionary Salafism" in "The Sheikh President," *Al-Ahram Weekly*, April 25–May 1, 2012. See also Stéphane Lacroix and Ahmed Zaghloul Shalata, "The Rise of Revolutionary Salafism in Post-Mubarak Egypt," in *Egypt's Revolutions: Politics, Religion, and Social Movements*, ed. Bernard Rougier and Stéphane Lacroix (New York: Palgrave Macmillan, 2016), 163–78.

53. Sarah Mourad, "Moussa Still Leads Presidential Race at 30 Percent," *Ahram Online*, April 9, 2012; http://english.ahram.org.eg/NewsWorldCup/2018/38890.aspx.

54. "Mawjat al-Ghadab Did Taʾsisiyyat al-Islamiyeen Tatasaʿad," *Al-Shurouq*, April 1, 2012.

55. Ian Black, "Muslim Brotherhood Bid for Presidency Raises the Stakes in Egyptian Elections," *Guardian*, April 2, 2012; "Al-Shater Murashah al-Ikhwan fi-l Sibaq al-Riʾasi bi-ʿAfw min al-ʿAskari," *Al-Shurouq*, April 1, 2012; Fahmi Howeidy, "Waqaʿu fi-l Fakh," *Al-Shurouq*, April 2, 2012; Mohamed Mahdi Akef, quoted in "Al-Gazzar: Al-Ikhwan Qad Tass-hab Tarshih al-Shater Idha Shakkalat al-Aghlabiyya Hukuma Jadida," *Al-Shurouq*, April 3, 2012. This article illustrates the confusion within the group in the early days after the decision, with one member stating it was a bargaining chip to compel SCAF to let parliament form a coalition cabinet, and a spokesman hastening to contradict him and affirm that the decision was final.

56. The three Islamist contenders were Abu Ismail, Aboul Fotouh, and the niche campaign by the Islamist attorney Mohamed Selim al-Awwa.

57. Even before Mubarak's ouster, the group took to influential international outlets to signal its self-restraint. See Essam al-Errian, "What the Muslim Brothers Want," *New York Times*, February 10, 2011.

58. Yasser El-Shimy, "The Muslim Brotherhood," in *Egypt after the Spring: Revolt and Reaction*, ed. Emile Hokayem and Hebatalla Taha (New York: Routledge, 2016), 75–104, 80; Carrie Rosefsky Wickham, *The Muslim Brotherhood: Evolution of an Islamist Movement* (Princeton, NJ: Princeton University Press, 2015), 248.

59. O'Donnell and Schmitter, *Transitions from Authoritarian Rule*, 5.

60. "Bayan min al-Ikhwan Hawl al-Muʿawwaqat alati Taʿtarid Taslim al-Sulta," March 24, 2012; https://www.ikhwanonline.com/article/104341.

61. One newspaper account, based on an unnamed MB source, says that a meeting took place on March 24 between SCAF generals, Prime Minister Ganzouri, and MB leaders Khairat al-Shater and Mohamed Morsi to convey the threat in person, and that the MB's March 24 statement was the response to that meeting. "Al-Ikhwan wa-l 'Askar 'ala Hafat al-Siddam," *Al-Shurouq*, March 26, 2012.

62. The SCAF statement was disseminated by the state news agency and is reprinted in "In Sunday Statement, SCAF Hits Back at Brotherhood Criticisms," *Ahram Online*, March 25, 2012; http://english.ahram.org.eg/News/37691.aspx. For reactions to the dueling statements among non-Islamist party leaders and activists, see Dina Ezzat, "Not Yet Divorce," *Al-Ahram Weekly* March 29–April 4, 2012; "Shabab al-Thawra: Al-Khilaf bayn al-Jama'a wa-l Majlis Mu'aqqat," *Al-Misri al-Yawm*, March 27, 2012.

63. Matt Bradley, "U.S., Egypt Look to Settle Nerves over Aid, Trial," *Wall Street Journal*, February 21, 2012; Senate Republican Conference, Floor Updates, Brown-OH, Hutchison, McCain, Hoeven, Blumenthal, March 1, 2012; https://www.republican.senate.gov/public/index.cfm/floor-updates?ID=cf673b42-92a1-4570-8f2f-6a6a853ad555. As Nathan Brown quipped of the MB, "At this point, the movement seems to have picked a fight with everybody except the US Department of State and Senator John McCain" ("Egypt's Muddy Waters," *National Interest*, April 4, 2012).

64. David Kirkpatrick, "In Egyptian Hard-Liners' Surge, New Worries for the Muslim Brotherhood," *New York Times*, April 2, 2012.

65. "Al-Barlaman Yahrim Fulul Nizam Mubarak min al-Tarashuh li-l Ri'asa," *Al-Misri al-Yawm*, April 13, 2012.

66. Khodeiry's intervention is available at https://youtu.be/rCjkgOfu4fY.

67. Liberal politician Ayman Nour, Mubarak's sole challenger in the 2005 elections, was disqualified for the same reason as Al-Shater, but news of his removal was overshadowed by the three more prominent candidates. "Bi-l Watha'iq: Qararat al-'Ulya li-l Ri'asa Bistib'ad al-Murashahin al-'Ashara," *Al-Misri al-Yawm*, April 16, 2012.

68. "Siyasiyyun: Istib'ad al-Murashahin Qarar Siyasi bi-Ghita' Qanuni," *Al-Misri al-Yawm*, April 16, 2012.

69. Kareem Fahim and Mayy El Sheikh, "Generals in Egypt Deny Role in Clashes," *New York Times*, May 4, 2012.

70. Khaled Dawoud, "The Last Stretch," *Al-Ahram Weekly*, May 17–23, 2012.

71. Shibley Telhami, "What Do Egyptians Want? Key Findings from the Egyptian Public Opinion Poll," Brookings Institution, May 21, 2012; https://www.brookings.edu/

research/what-do-egyptians-want-key-findings-from-the-egyptian-public-opinion-poll/.

72. The law also required presiding judges to provide candidate agents with signed official copies of the count. "Al-Barlaman Yuwafiq 'ala Ta'dil Qanun Intikhabat al-Ri'asa," *Al-Misri al-Yawm*, February 28, 2012.

73. A compilation of revealing voter reflections is in Dina Ezzat, "Countdown to the Unknown," *Al-Ahram Weekly*, June 14–20, 2012, and Amira Howeidy, "A Third-Way?," *Al-Ahram Weekly*, June 14–20, 2012.

74. Translated bits of the ruling and analysis are in the IFES Briefing Paper, "Elections in Egypt: Implications of Recent Court Decisions," August 2012. The SCC ruling followed an unprecedented fast-track sequence, with judges hearing arguments, issuing their decision, and printing it in the official gazette in barely half a day.

75. The text of Article 60 B1 of the addendum reads: "If the president, the head of SCAF, the prime minister, the Supreme Council of the Judiciary, or a fifth of the constituent assembly find that the new constitution contains an article or more which conflict with the revolution's goals and its main principles or which conflict with any principle agreed upon in all of Egypt's former constitutions, any of the aforementioned bodies may demand that the constituent assembly revise this specific article within 15 days. Should the constituent assembly object to revising the contentious article, the article will be referred to the Supreme Constitutional Court, which will then be obliged to give its verdict within seven days. The SCC's decision is final and will be published in the official gazette within three days of the date of issuance." The full addendum in English is in IFES Briefing Paper, "Elections in Egypt: Implications of Recent Court Decisions."

76. "Al-Nur: La Natawaqa' Lujju' al-Askari ila Khiyar Shamshun," *Al-Shurouq*, March 27, 2012.

77. The first thirty minutes of the press conference containing Shahin's remarks are available at https://youtu.be/M8oln32KzRQ.

78. Carrie Rosefsky Wickham witnessed the run-off vote and count and relates her observations in her *Muslim Brotherhood: Evolution of an Islamist Movement*, 262–64.

79. "Tafasil Ijtima' al-Sa'at al-Khams Bayn Mursi wa-l Qiwa al-Wataniyya," *Al-Shurouq*, June 23, 2012.

80. 6aprilmans, "As'ab Thalath Daqa'if fi Tarikh Misr," June 25, 2012, https://youtu.be/5P99d1zFERI; Evan Hill, "Tahrir Square Reacts to Morsi's Victory," June 24, 2012, https://youtu.be/h7grlfgoK2s.

81. That founding elections create legitimate power but not automatically social support is underlined by László Bruszt and David Stark, "Remaking the Political Field in Hungary: From the Politics of Confrontation to the Politics of Competition," in *Eastern Europe in Revolution*, ed. Ivo Banac (Ithaca, NY: Cornell University Press, 1992), 13–55, 53.

82. A breakdown of the electoral geography in the revolution's four polls is in Jeff Martini and Stephen Worman, "Voting Patterns of Post-Mubarak Egypt," (Santa Monica, CA: Rand Corporation, 2013).

83. "Egypt: Final Round of the Presidential Elections in Photographs," *GlobalVoices*, June 18, 2012; https://globalvoices.org/2012/06/18/egypt-final-round-of-the-presidential-elections-in-photographs/#.

84. Ikhwanweb, "President Mohamed Morsi's Speech in Tahrir Square, Friday June 29, 2012"; http://www.ikhwanweb.com/article.php?id=30153.

85. David Kirkpatrick, "Power Struggle Begins as Egypt's President Is Formally Sworn In," *New York Times*, July 1, 2012.

86. Edmund Blair, "Tables Turn as Egypt's Islamist President Sworn In," Reuters, June 30, 2012; "Misr Tuwada' Situn 'Aman Min al-Hukm al-'Askari," *Al-Misri al-Yawm*, July 1, 2012.

87. Przeworski, "Democracy as a Contingent Outcome of Conflicts," 62.

## CHAPTER 5

1. "Al-Ultras Yuzhir al-'Ayn al-Hamra," *Al-Misri al-Yawm*, January 24, 2013.

2. "Al-Ghadibun Yaqta'un Harakat al-Qitarat," *Al-Shurouq*, January 26, 2013; "Al-Muhafazat Tantafidd," *Al-Misri al-Yawm*, January 26, 2013); "Al-Baradei wa Sabahy wa Hamzawy wa Ghoneim Yaqudun Masirat Mostafa Mahmoud," *Al-Shurouq*, January 26, 2013; "Min Imbaba 'ila Morsi," *Al-Shurouq*, January 26, 2013; "Al-Black Blok Azalu Hawajiz Maspero," *Al-Shurouq*, January 26, 2013; El-Nadeem Centre for Rehabilitation of Victims of Violence and Torture, "Sexual Assault and Rape in Tahrir Square and Its Vicinity: A Compendium of Sources 2011–2013" (February 2013).

3. Amnesty International Press Release, "Egypt: Uprising Commemoration Unleashes Death and Destruction," January 28, 2013.

4. David Kirkpatrick, "Morsi Declares Emergency Rule in 3 Egypt Cities," *New York Times*, January 28, 2013.

5. "Ethnan wa Sab'un Sa'a min 'Uzlat al-Madina al-Basila," *Al-Shurouq*, January 29, 2013.

6. Bernard Rougier and Stéphane Lacroix, "Introduction: Egypt in Revolution," in *Egypt's Revolutions: Politics, Religion, and Social Movements*, ed. Bernard Rougier and Stéphane Lacroix (Basingstoke: Palgrave Macmillan, 2016), 9. The "beginning of the end" comment is also Rougier and Lacroix's phrase, 9.

7. Jason Brownlee, Tarek Masoud, and Andrew Reynolds, *The Arab Spring: Pathways of Repression and Reform* (New York: Oxford University Press, 2015), 122.

8. Patrick Haenni, "The Reasons for the Muslim Brotherhood's Failure in Power," in *Egypt's Revolutions: Politics, Religion, and Social Movements*, ed. Bernard Rougier and Stéphane Lacroix (Basingstoke: Palgrave Macmillan, 2016), 36

9. Daniela Pioppi, "Playing with Fire: The Muslim Brotherhood and the Egyptian Leviathan," *International Spectator* 48, no. 4 (December 2013): 51–68 (quote on 63–64).

10. John D. Martz, *Acción Democrática: Evolution of a Modern Political Party in Venezuela* (Princeton, NJ: Princeton University Press, 1966); Ervand Abrahamian, *The Coup: 1953, the CIA, and the Roots of Modern U.S.-Iranian Relations* (New York: New Press, 2013); Peter Kornbluh, *The Pinochet File: A Declassifijied Dossier on Atrocity and Accountability* (New York: New Press, 2013).

11. The General Guide is elected by an absolute majority of the political organization's legislative body (the Shura Council), from a list of candidates nominated by the group's executive council (the Guidance Bureau). Mona El-Ghobashy, "The Metamorphosis of the Egyptian Muslim Brothers," *International Journal of Middle East Studies* 37 (August 2005): 377.

12. Peter Amann, "Revolution: A Redefinition," *Political Science Quarterly* 77 (March 1962): 40.

13. The poll of 1,074 adults was conducted on April 8–15. See Mohamed Younis, "Egyptians to Government: Focus on Jobs," *Gallup News*, July 16, 2012; https://news.gallup.com/poll/155732/egyptians-government-focus-jobs.aspx.

14. Mohamed Younis and Ahmed Younis, "Support for Islamists Declines as Egypt's Election Nears," *Gallup News*, May 18, 2012.

15. Sharif Abdel Kouddous, "In Egypt, A President without Power," *Nation*, June 20, 2012.

16. Reem Leila, "Too Many Complaints," *Al-Ahram Weekly*, July 12–18, 2012; "Bilsiwar: Al-Muwatinun 'ala Bab al-Ra'is Raghm Diwan al-Mazalim," *Al-Misri al-Yawm*, July 9, 2012.

17. Dina Zayed, "Morsi Meter" Tries to Keep Egypt Leader on Toes," Reuters, August 2, 2012; Tom Perry, "Egypt's Morsi Dogged by Own Promises in First 100 Days," Reuters, October 5, 2012.

18. Reem Leila, "Back from Sudan," *Al-Ahram Weekly*, July 19–25, 2012.

19. Gamal Essam El-Din, "Inching Towards a Showdown?," *Al-Ahram Weekly*, July 12–18, 2012.

20. "Gamal Eid: Qarar Mursi b-ilgha' Hal Majlis al-Sha'b Darbat Mu'allim," *Al-Misri al-Yawm*, July 8, 2012; https://www.almasryalyoum.com/news/details/196610.

21. Kareem Fahim and Mayy El Sheikh, "Egypt President Orders Return of Parliament," *New York Times*, July 9, 2012.

22. Khaled Dawoud, "Turned Down," *Al-Ahram Weekly*, July 12–18, 2012.

23. Gamal Essam El-Din, "Inching Towards a Showdown?"

24. Gamal Essam El-Din, "Old Loyalties Die Hard," *Al-Ahram Weekly*, July 19–25, 2012.

25. Wafdist Mounir Fakhri Abdel Nour declined to continue as tourism minister, and Social Democratic MP Ziad Bahaa-Eldin declined an unspecified post.

26. "I'tiqal Khamsin bi-Asyut," *Al-Shurouq*, January 28, 2011.

27. The Salafi Nur Party was the first loud critic of the cabinet, turning down the offer of a lone portfolio (Environment) as an "insult." "Al-Salafiyyun: Awwal Khusum Qandil wa Hukumatihi," *Al-Shurouq*, August 3, 2012. For a debate aired on *Al-Jazeera* on August 5, 2012 between a supporter and critic of the Qandil cabinet, see http://www.aljazeera.net/home/Getpage/0353e88a-286d-4266-82c6-6094179ea26d/a3398c65-26de-4631-ac81-87be73310505. For a critique of the president's failure to explain his cabinet choices to public opinion, see Mustafa Kamel al-Sayyed, "Hukumat al-Duktur Mursi: Ma'ayir al-Taqwim," *Al-Shurouq*, August 6, 2012.

28. The Fairmont Meeting is discussed in chapter 4. For an explanation of the decision to part ways with Morsi by a leading member at the meeting, see Hamdi Qandil, "An'i Ilaykum al-Sharaka ma'a al-Ri'asa," *Al-Misri al-Yawm*, August 6, 2012.

29. "Fariq Morsi al-Ri'asi Islami 'illa Qalilan," *Al-Shurouq*, August 28, 2012. Among the seventeen were former presidential candidate Mohamed Saleem al-Awwa, poet Farouq Guweida, FJP leaders Essam al-Eryan and Rafiq Habib, and journalists Ayman al-Sayyad, Emad Eddin Hussein, Amr al-Leithy, and Sakina Fuad.

30. An informative account of the negotiated reshuffle is in Edmund Blair, "Breaking Free, Egypt's President Mursi Removes Generals," Reuters, August 12, 2012.

31. "The most important political skill is remembering your ultimate objectives, while biding your time until some passing event creates an opening for getting what you want." Gwynne Dyer, "Civilians Sweep Up in Egypt," *Japan Times*, August 16, 2012.

32. Quoted in Edmund Blair, "Breaking Free."

33. Gamal Essam El-Din, "Consecrating the Pharaoh," *Al-Ahram Weekly*, August, 16–22, 2012.

34. "Mursi: La Misas bi-Ayy Ha'ya Qada'iyya," *Al-Misri al-Yawm*, August 17, 2012.

35. Ziad al-Ulaimy, "Asbaht al-Mas'ul al-Wahid," *Al-Misri al-Yawm*, August 17, 2012.

36. "Morsi Approval Rating at 78 percent after 100 days: Basseera," *Ahram Online*, October 2, 2012, http://english.ahram.org.eg/News/55230.aspx; "Al-Misri al-Yawm Tanshur Nata'ij Istitla' Basseera," *Al-Misri al-Yawm*, October 10, 2012; Salma Shukrallah, "Morsi's First 100 Days: The Balance Sheet," *Ahram Online*, October 8, 2012, http://english.ahram.org.eg/News/54962.aspx.

37. *Time*, December 10, 2012.

38. Sixty non-Islamist MPs boycotted the parliamentary election of the new CA, and the sole representative of the Supreme Constitutional Court on the assembly withdrew before it convened its first meeting. A full-page list of the new constituent assembly members is in "Ha'ula' Yaktubun Dustur Misr al-Thawra," *Al-Shurouq*, June 14, 2012, 5. Gamal Essam El-Din, "Divisions Hit Constituent Assembly," *Ahram Weekly*, June 14–20, 2012.

39. The six-month timeframe was in the original March 19, 2011, referendum on the transition roadmap and had remained untouched in the subsequent battles between SCAF, secular factions, and Islamist factions over constitution-first or elections-first. Morsi left the six-month timeframe intact in his August 12 decree wresting executive power from the generals.

40. Jon Elster, "Constitution-Making in Eastern Europe: Rebuilding the Boat in the Open Sea," *Public Administration* 71 (Spring/Summer 1993): 169–217.

41. The committees were: Foundations of State and Society; Rights, Obligations, and Public Liberties; System of Government and Public Powers; and a committee working on a new fourth chapter, Independent Bodies and Regulatory Agencies. The fifth committee was tasked with receiving citizens' proposals and conducting public outreach. The CA's bylaws also stipulated that articles would be approved by consensus and, failing that, a two-stage voting process requiring 67 percent and then 57 percent approval. Constitutional amendment required a two-thirds majority in each legislative chamber, followed by a public referendum.

42. "The principles of Islamic Sharia include general evidence, foundational rules, rules of jurisprudence, and credible sources accepted in Sunni doctrines and by the larger community." An edifying explanation of article 219's genesis is in Clark Lombardi and Nathan Brown, "Islam in Egypt's New Constitution," *Foreign Policy*, December 13, 2012.

43. Wahid Abdel Meguid, *Azmat Dustur 2012: Tawthiq wa Tahlil: Shahada min Dakhil al-Jam'iyya al-Ta'sisiyya* (Cairo: n.p., 2013), 85.

44. Nathan Brown explains how secular forces began cleaving to al-Azhar in 2011 in "Contention in Religion and State in Postrevolutionary Egypt," *Social Research* 79 (Summer 2012): 531–50.

45. "Nizam al-Hukm b-il Ta'sisiyya Tuwafiq 'ala Mawwad Intiqaliyya," *Al-Misri al-Yawm*, September 21, 2012.

46. "Dignity is the right of every human being, safeguarded by the State. Insulting or showing contempt toward any human being shall be prohibited." For a glimpse into the Muslim Brothers' advocacy of this article, see Gamal Essam El-Din, "Disputes Plague the Draft Constitution," *Al-Ahram Weekly*, September 6–12, 2012.

47. Gamal Essam El-Din, "Constitutional Challenges Ahead," *Al-Ahram Weekly*, August 30–September 5, 2012.

48. The professors were Gamal Gibril and Atef al-Banna. The latter also served on the February 2011 panel of jurists that drew up the original constitutional amendments that were then folded into the March 30 interim constitution.

49. The polemics surrounding the CA drowned out reasoned article-by-article analysis. For exceptions, see Tareq al-Bishri, "Mulahazat Hawla Musawwadat al-Dustur," *Al-Shurouq*, November 9 and 10, 2012; Tareq al-Bishri, "An Mashru' al-Dustur Atahaddath," *Al-Shurouq*, December 5, 2012; Ellis Goldberg, "Drafting a Constitution: Part I of II," *Nisralnasr Blog*, October 24, 2012, http://nisralnasr.blogspot.com/2012/10/drafting-constitution-part-i-of-ii.html, and Ellis Goldberg, "Drafting a Constitution: Part II," *Nisralnasr Blog*, November 2, 2012, http://nisralnasr.blogspot.com/2012/11/drafting-constitution-part-ii.html; Holger Albrecht, "Unbalancing Power in Egypt's Constitution," *Foreign Policy*, January 31, 2013, https://foreignpolicy.com/2013/01/31/unbalancing-power-in-egypts-constitution/.

50. "Nass Khitabat Qudat Majlis al-Dawla," *Al-Misri al-Yawm*, October 7, 2012; "A'da' al-Niyaba al-Idariyya Yuwasilun Idrabihim," *Al-Misri al-Yawm*, October 11, 2012; Mona El-Nahhas, "How Will It End?" *Al-Ahram Weekly*, October 25–November 1, 2012; "Awal Jam'iyya 'Umumiyya Tar'ia li-A'da' al-Markazi lil-Muhasabat," *Al-Misri al-Yawm*, November 2, 2012.

51. Inter alia, critics pointed to the removal of the constitutional article upholding gender equality; the draft constitution's consistently paternalistic tone toward women; and failure to design an electoral system that bolsters women's participation. See the position paper by the women's rights group Nazra for Feminist Studies, "Waraqat Mawqif li-Nazra li-l Dirasat al-Nisawiyya min Musawwadat al-Dustur al-Niha'iyya," December 4, 2012, http://www.nazra.org/node/170.

52. Ahmed Morsy, "The Writers' Revolution," *Al-Ahram Weekly*, September 6–12, 2012; Reem Leila, "Moving Backwards," *Al-Ahram Weekly*, October 25–November 1, 2012;

Khaled Dawoud, "A Change in Chants," *Al-Ahram Weekly*, October 25–November 1, 2012; Human Rights Watch, "Letter to Members of the Egyptian Constituent Assembly," October 8, 2012; Roger Cohen, "Shariah's Limits," *New York Times*, October 18, 2012.

53. Khaled Dawoud, "Defending Freedoms," *Al-Ahram Weekly*, September 27–October 3, 2012.

54. An informative roundup of their views, as well as the arguments of those who declined to meet with Morsi, is in Dina Ezzat, "Too Much Talk," *Al-Ahram Weekly*, November 15–21, 2012.

55. Their decision was prompted by chairman Ghiryani's announcement of the assembly's daily work schedule before voting would begin in late November. For this schedule, see *Al-Misri al-Yawm*, November 9, 2012. For the statement of the withdrawing members and their version of events, see Wahid Abdel Meguid, *Azmat Dustur 2012*, 118–25.

56. The press conference can be viewed at https://youtu.be/aQuV8VuS76E. In his tell-all book about the assembly, erstwhile CA spokesman Wahid Abdel Meguid admits to signing this agreement but says that it was a provisional, not final, understanding (*Azmat Dustur 2012*, 90).

57. The act was accompanied by a decree-law increasing the exceptional pension for those injured by police in 2011 and 2012, reprinted in "Nass Iʿlan Mursi al-Dusturi," *Al-Shurouq*, November 23, 2012.

58. Morsi had earlier tried unsuccessfully to remove the Mubarak-appointed Prosecutor General Abdel Meguid Mahmoud. "Egypt Judges Attack Mursi Ousting of Prosecutor-General," *BBC News*, October 12, 2012.

59. "Al-Dusturiyya Tansahib li-l Marra al-Thaniya min al-Taʾsisiyya," *Al-Shurouq*, June 13, 2012.

60. "Masraʿ Shab fi Ishtibakat bi-Damanhour," *Al-Shurouq*, November 26, 2012.

61. "Quda min Tayar al-Istiqlal Yuhajimun al-Qararat," *Al-Shurouq*, November 23, 2012.

62. "Ghadab fi al-Kharijiyya bi-Sabab Taʿlimat al-Wazir," *Al-Shurouq*, November 26, 2012.

63. Constitutional law experts were divided over the decree, but all opposed article 2 shielding presidential actions from judicial review. Mona El-Nahhas, "A Controversial Declaration," *Al-Ahram Weekly*, November 29–December 5, 2012.

64. "Al-Iʿlan al-Dusturi Inʿikas li-l Irada al-Shaʿbiyya," *Al-Shurouq*, November 24, 2012.

65. "Al-Ikhwan: la Taraju' 'an Qararat al-Ra'is," *Al-Shurouq*, November 26, 2012. An extended explanation of the preemptive strike thesis was offered at the time by mainstream Islamist columnist Fahmi Howeidy, "Hal Huwwa Inqilab 'ala al-Inqilab?" *Al-Shurouq*, November 27, 2012.

66. The interview was conducted on November 29, 2012, and can be seen at https://youtu.be/xBEvgwHw3yE.

67. This final vote is often portrayed as a "hasty adoption" of the draft, when in fact it capped five months of work in both committees and intensive plenary discussions that included the departed members until they withdrew on November 18. For an account of the final voting session, see "Layla Wud'ia Fiha al-Dustur Hatta Matla' al-Fajr," *Al-Shurouq*, December 1, 2012.

68. "UN Human Rights Chief Calls on Egypt's President to Roll Back Powers of Recent Decree," *UN News*, November 30, 2012. Amnesty International criticized the constitution for failing to "provide for the supremacy of international law over national law"; Amnesty International, "Egypt's New Constitution Limits Fundamental Freedoms and Ignores the Rights of Women," November 30, 2012; https://www.amnesty.org/en/latest/news/2012/11/egypt-s-new-constitution-limits-fundamental-freedoms-and-ignores-rights-women/.

69. Charles Levinson and Sam Dagher, "Egyptians Swarm Palace in Protest," *Wall Street Journal*, December 5, 2012.

70. The medical examiner at the central Zeinhom morgue said that all seven fatalities were caused by live fire and birdshot to the upper part of the body. "Al-Niyaba Tusarrih bi Dafn Saba' Jathamin," *Al-Misri a-Yawm*, December 8, 2012. Journalists on the ground saw firearms being used by both sides, and one reporter witnessed a protester on the progovernment side collapse and die from a gunshot. "'Ashar Mashahid Tarsud Tafasil Ma'rakat al-Nar wa-l Damm," *Al-Misri a-Yawm*, December 7, 2012. Profiles of some of the dead and injured are in *Al-Shurouq*, December 7, 2012, 5.

71. "Qa'id al-Haras al-Jumhuri lil Misri al-Yawm: Lan Nakun Ada li-Qam' al-Mutazahirin," *Al-Misri al-Yawm*, December 7, 2012; Human Rights Watch, "Egypt: Investigate Brotherhood's Abuse of Protesters," December 12, 2012.

72. "Jabhat al-Inqadh Tuhammil Mursi Mas'uliyat Dima' al-Ittihadiyya," *Al-Shurouq*, December 6, 2012.

73. "Muwajahat bayn al-Amn wa-l Mutazahirin," *Al-Misri al-Yawm*, December 7, 2012; "Muwajahat bi-l Ghaz wa-l Hijara amam Manzil al-Ra'is," *Al-Shurouq*, December 8, 2012.

74. David Kirkpatrick, "Blood Is Shed as Egyptian President's Backers and Rivals Battle in Cairo," *New York Times*, December 6, 2012.

75. Reuters, "Egypt's Opposition Rejects Constitutional Referendum," December 8, 2012.

76. "Wazir al-Difaʿ Yadʿu ila Liqaʾ maʿa Qiwa al-Mujtamaʿ," *Al-Misri al-Yawm*, December 12, 2012.

77. "Istiqalat Thalatha min Mustashari Mursi," *Al-Misri al-Yawm*, December 6, 2012.

78. "Istiqalat Mahmoud Mekky min Mansib Naʾib al-Raʾis," *Al-Shurouq*, December 23, 2012.

79. The lowest turnout was 10 percent for the January–February 2012 Shura Council (upper house) elections.

80. Bishara interviewed by Amira Howeidy in "The Brotherhood Should Not Be Celebrating," *Al-Ahram Weekly*, December 27, 2012–January 2, 2013.

81. As per the minister of tourism. "Zaʿzou: Misr Khasarat Milyun Saʾih," *Al-Shurouq*, January 8, 2013.

82. The figures come from an Interior Ministry official speaking to Shura Council members, as covered by Gamal Essam El-Din, "Salafis Open Fire on Morsi," *Al-Ahram Weekly*, February 14–20, 2012, and a report by the Egyptian Organization for Human Rights, quoted in Amira Howeidy, "Blind Anger," *Al-Ahram Weekly*, February 14–20, 2012.

83. Ahmed Morsy, "Behind the Mask," *Al-Ahram Weekly*, January 31–February 6, 2013; "Kataʾib Black Bloc . . . al-Dhiraʿ al-Askariyya li-l Thuwwar," *al-Shurouq*, January 26, 2013.

84. Ahmed Morsy, "Civil Disobedience Spreads," *Al-Ahram Weekly*, March 7–13, 2013; Gamal Essam El-Din, "Salafis Open Fire on Morsi," *Al-Ahram Weekly*, February 14–20, 2012; Ahmed Morsy, "Pressure That Works," *Al-Ahram Weekly*, February 21–27, 2013.

85. Human rights activist Aida Seif el-Dawla told a journalist, "They have a choice: to remain in power supported by the people. Or remain in power supported by institutions like the police." Patrick Kingsley, "Egyptian Police Go on Strike," *Guardian*, March 10, 2013.

86. "Tawkilat al-Sisi Tatawasal bi-l Muhafazat," *Al-Misri al-Yawm*, March 6, 2013.

87. "Man Yahkum Misr Alʾan? La Ahad," *Al-Shurouq*, March 12, 2013.

88. The poll conducted face-to-face interviews with 1,000 respondents from March 3 to March 23. "Egyptians Increasingly Glum," *Pew Research Center*, May 16, 2013; "Al-Mustaqillun Yafuzun bi Mansib Raʾis Ittihad Tullab Misr," *Al-Shurouq*, April 24, 2013.

89. They cited article 67 of Law 46/1972 on the judiciary specifying that judges and prosecutors cannot be dismissed, and that only the Supreme Judicial Council (a body of senior judges) has authority over judicial appointments and promotions.

90. "Latma Qada'iyya Jadida li-l Ra'is," *Al-Misri al-Yawm*, March 28, 2013. Extracts from the ruling are in "Haythiyyat al-Isti'naf," *Al-Misri al-Yawm*, March 31, 2013.

91. The rally turned violent when Black Bloc members and Islamists exchanged rock throwing, fired birdshot, and, for the first time, threw tear gas canisters of uncertain provenance, leading to more than eighty injuries and the Black Bloc's burning of a bus belonging to the Islamists. Maggie Michael and Sarah El Deeb, "Pro- and anti-Islamist Protesters Clash in Egypt," *Associated Press*, April 19, 2013.

92. Gadallah's seven-point rationale for resigning was a grab bag of complaints about the Morsi administration. His seventh reason was opposition to resuming relations with Iran and "opening Egypt's doors to Shi'ism." See Muhamad Fu'ad Gadallah, "Istiqalat Awwal Rijal al-Ra'is," *Al-Shurouq*, April 24, 2013. Mekky's resignation is published in *Al-Shurouq*, April 22, 2013, 4.

93. Morsi's new minister for parliamentary affairs, Judge Hatem Bagato, announced the decision in a press conference. "Al-Hukuma Tu'ajjil Qanun al-Sulta al-Qada'iyya," *Al-Misri al-Yawm*, June 5, 2013.

94. Mekky earned the displeasure of FJP leaders for what they said was his sluggish response to the March signature campaign calling on Sisi to steer the country, as reported in Ahmed Eleiba, "Coup by Consent?," *Al-Ahram Weekly*, March 7–13, 2013. Morsi's adviser Gadallah cited the MB's "encroachment" on Morsi and his governance in Gadallah, "Istiqalat Awwal Rijal al-Ra'is."

95. This was reported both contemporaneously and after the fact by several credible journalists. See "Al-Ghadab min al-Ra'is Yasil Maktab Irshad al-Ikhwan," *Al-Shurouq*, November 27, 2012; David Kirkpatrick, *Into the Hands of the Soldiers* (London: Bloomsbury Circus, 2018), 178, 186, 228.

96. Both MB leaders and FJP Shura deputies were livid that the president sided with the judges, angrily asserting that Morsi had no right to tell them to shelve the bill. "Khilafat Hadda Dakhil al-Ikhwan," *Al-Misri al-Yawm*, April 30, 2013; Gamal Essam El-Din, "Judges Resist Brotherhood Intervention," *Al-Ahram Weekly*, May 2–8, 2013.

97. "Mursi: Arfud al-Isa'a li-l Quwwat al-Musallaha," *Al-Shurouq*, April 13, 2013.

98. "Al-Majlis al-'Ala li-l-Quwwat al-Musallaha—Tasreehat al-Qaada," April 11, 2013; https://youtu.be/NCfpFFblL8U.

99. Amirah Ibrahim, "No Foreign Ownership in Sinai," *Al-Ahram Weekly*, December 27, 2012–January 2, 2013. These two tiny islands that most Egyptians had never heard of would be catapulted to the center of national politics in 2016 (see chap. 6).

100. Amira Ibrahim, "Entente Cordiale," *Al-Ahram Weekly*, April 18–24, 2013. The civilian side of the government dealing with the project is explained in Ahmed Eleiba, "Project of the Century," *Al-Ahram Weekly*, May 2–8, 2013; Amira Howeidy, "Spanner in the Works," *Al-Ahram Weekly*, April 18–24, 2013; Ahmed Eleiba, "Three Corners for Morsi to Paint," *Al-Ahram Weekly*, April 11–17, 2013.

101. Kirkpatrick, *Into the Hands of the Soldiers*, 214.

102. "Al-Sisi li-l Siyasiyin: al-Jaysh Nar la Tal'abu Biha," *Al-Shurouq*, May 12, 2013; Ahmed Eleiba, "Military Messages," *Al-Ahram Weekly*, May 16–22, 2013.

103. Mohamed Abdel-Baky, "Signature Rebellion," *Al-Ahram Weekly*, May 16–22, 2013. An earlier mention of Badr in the press identified him as a member of Kifaya's youth wing, in connection with his organizing of a demonstration outside the MB's headquarters on March 22, a demonstration that capped a week of violent clashes in Cairo and around the country. "Al-Qiwa al-Thawriyya Tatawahad li-Isqat Dawlat al-Milishiyyat," *Al-Misri al-Yawm*, March 23, 2013.

104. "Al-Tayar al-Sha'bi: Taslim al-Sulta li Ra'is al-Dusturiyya al-'Ulya," *Al-Misri al-Yawm*, June 11, 2013.

105. Morsi named seventeen new governors, bringing the MB's control of governorships to thirteen out of twenty-seven. "Intifada Sha'biyya didd Muhafizi al-Ikhwan," *Al-Misri al-Yawm*, June 19, 2013.

106. The PEC took no decisions, vowing to reconvene at the end of June to hear oral arguments. "Al-'Ulya lil-Intikhabat Tatanahha," *Al-Misri al-Yawm*, June 28, 2013.

107. "Mursi Yahrab min Ummahat al-Shuhada'," *Al-Misri al-Yawm*, June 22, 2013.

108. "Wazir al-Dakhiliyya li-l Misri al-Yawm," *Al-Misri al-Yawm*, June 8, 2013; "Al-Dakhiliyya Tahtajib Yawm al-Hashd," *Al-Misri al-Yawm*, June 12, 2013; "Al-Shurta Tanhaz li-l Sha'b," *Al-Misri al-Yawm*, June 13, 2013; "Al-Jaysh Ya'ud ila al-Shari'," *Al-Misri al-Yawm*, June 27, 2013; "Qa'id al-Haras al-Jumhuri," *Al-Misri al-Yawm*, June 28, 2013.

109. Dina Ezzat, "Egypt's Morsi, Brotherhood Seek Allies," *Ahram Online*, June 19, 2013; http://english.ahram.org.eg/News/74456.aspx.

110. Tom Perry and Alastair Macdonald, "Egypt Islamists Warn Opponents with Huge Pro-Mursi rally," Reuters, June 21, 2013.

111. Perry and Macdonald, "Egypt Islamists Warn Opponents."

112. "Haykal: Khitab Mursi 'Abath wa-l-Mustaqbal Marhun bi-Tamarrud," *Al-Misri al-Yawm*, June 28, 2013.

113. "Al-Sha'b Yurid Isqat al-Ikhwan," *Al-Shurouq*, July 1, 2013; "Army Estimates 'Millions' of Protesters on Egypt's Streets," *Agence France-Press*, June 30, 2013. Joel Beinin estimated that the June 30 crowds were "at least two million," whereas Neil Ketchley assessed "a little over one million." Joel Beinin, "Egyptian Workers after June 30," *Middle East Report Online*, August 23, 2013, https://merip.org/2013/08/egyptian-workers-after-june-30/; Neil Ketchley, "How Egypt's Generals Used Street Protests to Stage a Coup," *Washington Post*, July 3, 2017, https://www.washingtonpost.com/news/monkey-cage/wp/2017/07/03/how-egypts-generals-used-street-protests-to-stage-a-coup/?utm_term=.6f9b20b5484d.

114. "Al-Shurouq Takshif Kawalis Bayyan al-Qiyada al-'Amma li-l Quwwat al-Musallaha," *Al-Shurouq*, July 2, 2013.

115. From Mohamed Morsi's court testimony at a trial session in 2014. "Jalsa Muthira fi Qadiyyat al-Takhabur," *Al-Shurouq*, December 7, 2014.

116. Peter Winn, "Salvador Allende: His Political Life—and Afterlife," *Socialism and Democracy* 19, no. 3 (2005): 129–59, 144.

117. Leon Trotsky, *History of the Russian Revolution*, as quoted in Arthur Stinchcombe, *Theoretical Methods in Social History* (New York: Academic Press, 1978), 32.

118. David Kirkpatrick, "Egypt Court Cancels Parliamentary Elections," *The New York Times*, March 7, 2013; "Egypt Court Delays Verdict on Parliamentary Elections," *Ahram Online*, April 14, 2013, http://english.ahram.org.eg/News/69182.aspx.

119. Amann, "Revolution: A Redefinition," 40.

## CHAPTER 6

1. "Al-Jaysh Yusharik bi-'Urud Jawiyya," *Al-Shurouq*, January 26, 2014.

2. Ahmed Morsy, "Planning for All Contingencies," *Al-Ahram Weekly*, January 23–29, 2014.

3. "Al-Muhafazat . . . Ta'zim Salam li-Thawrat Yanayir," *Al-Shurouq*, January 26, 2014; "Muhafazat al-Qahira Tahdi Lawhat Ma'daniyya li-Usar al-Shuhada'," *Masrawy*, January 23, 2014.

4. Amnesty International, "'The Walls of the Cell Were Smeared with Blood'—Third Anniversary of Egypt Uprising Marred by Police Brutality," February 4, 2014.

5. "Yatahadath li-l Marra al-Thaniyya: Ana al-Ra'is Mohamed Mursi," *Al-Misri al-Yawm*, January 29, 2014.

6. Nathan Brown, "Egypt's Failed Transition," *Journal of Democracy* 24 (2013): 45–58; Marcus Mietzner, "Successful and Failed Democratic Transitions from Military Rule in Majority Muslim Societies: The Cases of Indonesia and Egypt," *Contemporary Politics*

20 (2014): 435–52; Hicham Bou Nassif, "Coups and Nascent Democracies: The Military and Egypt's Failed Consolidation," *Democratization* 24, no. 1 (2017): 157–74; Sahar Aziz, "Independence without Accountability: The Judicial Paradox of Egypt's Failed Transition to Democracy," *Penn. St. Law Review* 667 (2015–16): 667–736.

7. Muhammad Rabi' Thabet, "Mafhum Haybat al-Dawla," *Al-Ahram*, September 26, 2011.

8. Muhammad Safieddine Kharbush, *Al-Tatawwur al-Siyasi fi Misr: Muhawalat Hadm al-Dawla al-Misriyya* (Cairo: Al-Markaz al-Arabi li-l Buhuth w-al-Dirasat, 2014), 100.

9. Robert D. Benford and David A. Snow, "Framing Processes and Social Movements," *Annual Review of Sociology* 26 (2000): 611–39.

10. *Al-Nasr*, no. 890 (August 2013).

11. "Army Estimates 'Millions' of Protesters on Egypt Streets," *Agence France-Presse*, June 30, 2013. Ruth Alexander, "Counting Crowds: Was Egypt's Uprising the Biggest Ever?" BBC News, July 16, 2013; https://www.bbc.com/news/magazine-23312656. Joel Beinin estimated that the June 30 crowds were "at least two million," whereas Neil Ketchley assessed "a little over one million." Joel Beinin, "Egyptian Workers after June 30," *Middle East Report Online*, August 23, 2013, https://merip.org/2013/08/egyptian-workers-after-june-30/; Neil Ketchley, "How Egypt's Generals Used Street Protests to Stage a Coup," *Washington Post*, July 3, 2017, https://www.washingtonpost.com/news/monkey-cage/wp/2017/07/03/how-egypts-generals-used-street-protests-to-stage-a-coup/?utm_term=.6f9b20b5484d.

12. Tom Finn, "Egypt's 'Third Square' Protests Reject Army, Islamists," Reuters, July 31, 2013; Dina El Khawaga, "La Waqt li-l Haqq: 'An Sun' al-Ijma' Ba'd 30 Yunyu," *Bidayat* 6 (Summer 2013): 68–72.

13. Fatality figures from Wikithawra, "Hasr Qatla 'Ahd al-Sisi wa Adli Mansour Tafsiliyyan Hata 31 Yanayir 2014," https://wikithawra.wordpress.com/2013/11/12/sisi casualities/.

14. An insightful discussion of solidarity, hostility and other sentiments by non-MB Egyptians toward the sit-in is in Yasmin Moll, "The Wretched Revolution," *Middle East Report* 273 (Winter 2014): 34–39.

15. Lally Weymouth, "Rare Interview with Egyptian Gen. Abdel Fatah al-Sissi," *Washington Post*, August 3, 2013.

16. These multiple claims are made by longtime establishment columnist Salah Montasser, "Inqaz Mu'tasimi al-Adawiyya," *Al-Ahram*, July 14, 2013. On the sit-in as a threat to public health, see also Huda Rashwan, "Mudir Al-Haq fi-l Dawa': Zuhur

Amrad al-Sadafiyya wa-l Garab wa-l Eczema wa-l Erticaria Bayn Muʻtasimi Rabʻa," *Al-Watan*, July 13, 2013.

17. The claim appears to have been first circulated by Beirut-based pan-Arab satellite station *Al-Mayadeen* about Tunisian women providing comfort to Syrian fighters and then diffused to Egypt's progovernment media. See "Baʻd Ittiham Suriyyat bi-Mumarasat Jihad al-Nikah fi Maydan Rabʻa al-Adawiyya," *Al-Hayat*, July 16, 2013.

18. Details on mediators' work toward a settlement are in David Kirkpatrick, Peter Baker, and Michael Gordon, "How a U.S. Push to Defuse Egypt Ended in Failure," *New York Times*, August 18, 2013; "al-Tahaluf al-Watani Yarfud Ziyarat Ashton," *Al-Misri al-Yawm*, July 31, 2013; "Al-Biblawi: Qarar Fadd Iʻtisamay Rabʻa wa-l Nahda Nihaʼi," *Al-Misri al-Yawm*, August 4, 2013.

19. Information on the dispersals and the church attacks is in Human Rights Watch, *All According to Plan: The Rabʻa Massacre and Mass Killings of Protesters in Egypt* (2014). A list of the eleven provinces where simultaneous dispersals were occurring is in Neil Ketchley, *Egypt in a Time of Revolution: Contentious Politics and the Arab Spring* (New York: Cambridge University Press, 2017), 130. On the railway shutdown, "Raʼis al-Markaziyya li-l Mobiʻat: Al-Hayʼa Khasarat Sittun Milyun Junaih," *Al-Misri al-Yawm*, September 1, 2013. On the Zeinhom morgue, Omar Abdel Aziz, "Mashrahat Zeinhom: Muwahiddat al-Misriyyin," *Al-Misri al-Yawm*, August 17, 2013.

20. The al-Nahda sit-in began in early July.

21. James Sheehan, "The Problem of Sovereignty in European History," *American Historical Review* 111, no. 1 (2006): 1–15, 3; Achille Mbembe, "Necropolitics," *Public Culture* 15, no. 1 (2003): 11–40, 26.

22. Mbembe, "Necropolitics," 11.

23. Dieter Bednarz and Klaus Brinkbäumer, "Extremists Offend the Image of God," *Spiegel Online*, February 9, 2015; https://www.spiegel.de/international/world/islamic-state-egyptian-president-sisi-calls-for-help-in-is-fight-a-1017434.html.

24. Kareem Fahim and Mayy El Sheikh, "Memory of a Mass Killing Becomes Another Casualty of Egyptian Protests," *New York Times*, November 14, 2013. In 2015, Rabʻa Square was renamed Midan Hisham Barakat, after the assassinated prosecutor-general whose death the government blamed on the Muslim Brothers and Hamas.

25. Mada Masr, "Tahrir Monument Met with Skepticism," November 17, 2013.

26. Ketchley, *Egypt in a Time of Revolution*, chap. 6.

27. Association for Freedom of Thought and Expression (AFTE), *Besieged Universities: A Report on the Rights and Freedoms of Students in Egyptian Universities from the*

*Academic Years 2013–2014 to 2015–2016* (Cairo: AFTE, 2017), 25–26. AFTE's count of the total number of expulsions and suspensions from 2013 to 2016 is 1,051.

28. Maggie Michael, "On Campus in Egypt, A Heavy Security Clampdown," *Associated Press*, October 8 2014.

29. AFTE, *Besieged Universities*, 24, 26.

30. Human Rights Watch, "Egypt: Activists Arrested for 'No' Campaign," January 13, 2014.

31. Article 8 also requires that demonstration organizers include in their application for a permit the location, purpose, demands, and slogans of the protest.

32. For an instructive comparison between the 2013 law and the 2012 bill proposed by the Morsi administration, see the Arabic Network for Human Rights Information's position paper on the latter, "Taqnin al-Qam' wa Takmim al-Afwah fi 'Ahd al-Ikhwan!," December 31, 2012; https://anhri.net/?p=66874.

33. Charles Tilly, "Spaces of Contention," *Mobilization* 5, no. 2 (2000): 135–59, 137.

34. Cairo Institute for Human Rights Studies, *Toward the Emancipation of Egypt: A Study on Assembly Law 10/1914* (Cairo: Cairo Institute for Human Rights Studies, 2017), 28. This study explains how, despite parliament's repeal of Law 10 in 1928, it was kept on the books by successive postindependence governments.

35. Stiffening the penalty to twenty years was the only amendment made to the five-article law, signed in December 1968 by Gamal Abdel Nasser in the wake of the largest mass protests against his rule earlier that year.

36. A list of the five most common charges leveled at protesters deriving from both laws is in Cairo Institute for Human Rights Studies, *Toward the Emancipation of Egypt*, 49.

37. The fourteen women's sentences were later commuted to one-year suspended sentences.

38. AFTE, "Bara'at 13 minhom 'Ziyada' wa Habs 64 Talib Mudad Mukhtalifa Tasil ila Saba' Sanawat fi Ahdath al-Azhar," April 29, 2015; https://afteegypt.org/media_freedom/2015/04/29/9797-afteegypt.html.

39. Daftar Ahwal, "Halat al-Qabd wa-l Istiqaf wa-l Ittiham 'ala Khalfiyyat Qanun al-Tazahur Khilal Thalath Sanawat," September 30, 2016; https://daftarahwal.com/arrests-accusations-protest-law-abstract-ar/.

40. Charles Tilly, *Regimes and Repertoires* (Chicago: University of Chicago Press, 2006), chap. 4.

41. For the committee's attempts not to appear as a rubber stamp, see Nathan J. Brown, "Egypt's Daring Constitutional Gang of 50," *Foreign Policy*, September 20, 2013.

42. Muhammad Mansour, "Members of Constitutional Committee of 50 Announced," *Egypt Independent*, September 1, 2013. For an analysis of the constitutional text, see European Parliament, Directorate-General for External Policies, "Egypt: In-Depth Analysis of the Main Elements of the New Constitution," April 2014.

43. Human Rights Watch, "Egypt: Activists Arrested for 'No' Campaign," January 13, 2014.

44. The remarks of the interior minister are cited in Human Rights Watch, "Egypt: Activists Arrested."

45. The front-page headline of the January 19 *Al-Misri al-Yawm* read, "New Constitution for a New Era." Tahrir Square chants are quoted in the lead story, "Dustur Jadid li-'Ahd Jadid," *Al-Misri al-Yawm*, January 19, 2014.

46. Tom Perry and Maggie Fick, "Egyptians Back Constitution, Opening Way to Sisi Presidential Run," Reuters, January 16, 2014.

47. Adam Przeworski, *Why Bother with Elections?* (Medford, MA: Polity Press, 2018), 7.

48. Max Weber, *Economy and Society*, vol. 1, ed. Guenther Roth and Claus Wittich (Berkeley: University of California, 1978), 242.

49. Weber, *Economy and Society*, 1:269.

50. Mohammed El-Nawawy and Mohamad Hamas ElMasry, "The Signs of a Strongman: The Semiotic and Discourse Analysis of Abdel Fattah al-Sisi's Egyptian Presidential Campaign," *International Journal of Communication* 10 (2016): 2275–96, 2290. For the campaign's appropriation of the Gamal Abdel Nasser mystique, see Gilbert Achcar, *Morbid Symptoms: Relapse in the Arab Uprising* (Palo Alto, CA: Stanford University Press, 2016), 115.

51. Osman El Sharnoubi, "Who Will Egypt's Political Groups Vote for? A Guide," *Ahram Online*, May 16, 2014. http://english.ahram.org.eg/News/101316.aspx. The off-the-record remarks were part of an interview with *Al-Misri al-Yawm* editor Yasser Rizq and were leaked in an audio recording in December 2013, five months before the election. Recording available at https://www.youtube.com/watch?v=hXshq-sADWo&hd=1.

52. Salma Shukrallah and Fouad Mansour, "Exclusive Hamdeen Sabahi Interview: The Army Should Not Be Burdened by Politics," *Ahram Online*, March 29, 2014. http://english.ahram.org.eg/News/97696.aspx.

53. "Egypt's Preliminary 2014 Presidential Election Results," *Ahram Online*, May 29. 2014; http://english.ahram.org.eg/News/102437.aspx.

54. Yasmine Saleh and Stephen Kalin, "Sisi Won 96.91 Percent in Egypt's Presidential Vote—Commission," Reuters, June 3, 2014.

55. Hossam Bahgat, "Anatomy of an Election," *Mada Masr*, March 14, 2016; for profiles of some *Mustaqbal Watan* deputies, see Ahmed A. Hameed Hussien, "Egypt's 2015 Parliamentarians—New Faces, Old Logic," *Arab Reform Initiative*, February 2016.

56. Parliament amended the salary increases in the civil service law. See Tahrir Institute for Middle East Policy, "Egypt Parliament Watch: Session One Report, January–September 2016"; Tahrir Institute for Middle East Policy, "Egypt Parliament Watch: Session Two Report, October 2016–September 2017"; Tahrir Institute for Middle East Policy, Egypt Parliament Watch: Session Two Report, October 2017–July 2018.

57. Neil Ketchley and Soraya El-Rayess, "On the Breadline in Sisi's Egypt," *Middle East Report Online*, March 29, 2017, https://merip.org/2017/03/on-the-breadline-in-sisis-egypt/; "Egypt Orders 20 More Alleged Metro Protesters Detained," Reuters, May 14, 2018; "Habs Tisʻa ʻala Dhimmat al-Tahqiqat," *Al-Misri al-Yawm*, July 18, 2017.

58. On the substance of protesters' demands, see Jano Charbel, "Workers Protest Civil Service Law in One of Biggest Street Actions Since 2013," *Mada Masr*, August 10, 2015. On how police corralled protesters, see "Security Attempts to Thwart Planned Civil Service Protest in Authorized Area," *Mada Masr*, September 12, 2015.

59. Bahey Eldin Hassan, "The High-Level Intrigue That's Overshadowing Egypt's Election," *Washington Post*, March 15, 2018. For the possible role of the Tiran and Sanafir transfer in Sisi's reshuffle of top generals, see Asmahan Soliman, "The Puzzling Dismissal of Egypt's Top Military Commander," *Mada Masr*, December 10, 2017.

60. The video can be viewed at https://youtu.be/UEIcFXToBK4.

61. Anan's video statement is available at: https://youtu.be/fT8MAs20E-A.

62. Former parliamentarian Mohamed Anwar al-Sadat withdrew after the security services blocked his campaign from holding press conferences. Rights lawyer Khaled Ali, the youngest contender on the ballot in 2012, withdrew soon after he announced his candidacy, citing arrests among his campaigners. Abdel Moneim Aboul Fotouh, the fourth vote-getter in the first round of the 2012 poll, had no interest in running for the 2018 election. Instead, he gave a series of hard-hitting interviews in London to *Al-Jazeera* in which he lambasted Sisi and called for a boycott of the poll. As soon as he returned to Cairo, he was arrested, placed on the terrorism list, had his assets confiscated, and was held in indefinite pretrial detention, where he suffered several

heart attacks. Poet Galal El Behairy was sentenced by a military court for insulting the military.

63. "He will attempt to consolidate the loyalty of those he governs either by winning glory and honor in war or by promoting their material welfare, or under certain circumstances, by attempting to combine both. Success in these will be regarded as proof of the charisma," Weber, *Economy and Society*, 1:269.

64. "Egypt's Other Candidate," *Mada Masr*, March 25, 2018.

65. "Sisi Calls for Big Turnout in Egyptian Election," Reuters, March 15, 2018.

66. Labor and student union elections later in the year were similarly uncontested. Mohamed Ashraf Abu Emaira, "Exclusion, Intimidation, and Suppression at Egypt's 2018 Student Union Elections," *Mada Masr*, January 14, 2019; Hadeer El-Mahdawy, "Avoiding the Blacklist: Egyptian Labor Elections as a Key to Investment," *Mada Masr*, August 15, 2018.

67. Shana Marshall, "The Egyptian Armed Forces and the Remaking of an Economic Empire" (Washington, DC: Carnegie Endowment for International Peace, 2015); Yezid Sayigh, "The Return of Egypt's Military Interest Groups" (Beirut: Carnegie Middle East Center, December 21, 2015); Transparency International, "The Officers' Republic: The Egyptian Military and Abuse of Power," (Transparency International, UK: March 2018); Bruce Rutherford, "Egypt's New Authoritarianism under Sisi," *Middle East Journal* 72, no. 2 (2018): 185–208.

68. Numbers for death sentences, executions, and forced disappearances are from Amnesty International, "Egypt: Gross Human Rights Violations under President al-Sisi," March 2019; number of deaths in custody are from Daftar Ahwal, "Halat al-Wafaat Dakhil Amakin al-Ihtijaz," April 30, 2016, https://daftarahwal.com/deaths-inside-detention-facilities-abstract-ar/; the new prisons are in addition to the country's forty-three prisons from before the revolution, one new prison under SCAF, and two new prisons under the Morsi government. See Arabic Network for Human Rights Information (ANHRI), "There Is Room for Everyone . . . Egypt's Prisons before and after January 25 Revolution" (2016). The letter from fifteen-year-old Seif al-Islam Osama is in Human Rights Watch, "Egypt: 7,400 Civilians Tried in Military Courts," April 13, 2016.

69. Otto Kirchheimer, *Political Justice: The Use of Legal Procedure for Political Ends* (Princeton, NJ: Princeton University Press, 1961), 41.

70. Kirchheimer, *Political Justice*, 42.

71. Howard C. Payne, *The Police State of Louis Bonaparte, 1851–1860* (Seattle: University of Washington Press, 1966), elaborates on the theory and practice of political

police, broadly defined as a preponderant executive in command of a centralized bureaucracy without legislative or judicial review.

72. Haytham Mohamadein, *Sijnak wa Matrahak: Dalil al-Qabd wa-l Tahqiq wa-l Sujun* (Cairo: Arabic Network for Human Rights Information, 2017). He was later arrested and charged with calling for the protests over the metro fare hikes in 2018.

73. Fifty-nine judges were forced into early retirement, including some who had signed a statement objecting to the coup in July 2013. Ahmed Aboulenein, "How Egypt's Crackdown on Dissent Ensnared Some of the Country's Top Judges," Reuters, October 18, 2016.

74. A list of the chambers and presiding judges is in "Bil Asma': Wazir al-'Adl Yuwafiq 'ala Tashkil Thaman Dawa'ir li-l Qada' 'ala al-Irhab," *Masrawy*, December 26, 2013. The cabinet's rationale was that the Muslim Brothers were responsible for the bombing of a police headquarters in Mansoura, for which the anti-MB militant group Ansar Bayt al-Maqdis claimed responsibility. In November 2018, one additional terrorism chamber was created, bringing the total to nine.

75. The presiding judge in this case, Hasan Farid, was the judge who presided over the ordinary criminal court that tried activist Alaa Abdel Fattah and others for protesting without a permit in November 2013.

76. "Zahirat Radd al-Mahkama Bayn Tawq Najat al-Muttaham wa Muhawalat Ta'til al-'Adala," *Sawt al-Umma*, September 20, 2018.

77. Tahrir Institute for Middle East Policy, "Egypt Parliament Watch: Session Two Report, October 2016–September 2017," 27.

78. Human Rights Watch, "Egypt: 7,400 Civilians Tried in Military Courts," April 13, 2016.

79. Human Rights Watch, "Egypt: Counterterrorism Law Erodes Basic Rights," August 19, 2015.

80. Richard P. Mitchell, *The Society of the Muslim Brothers* (New York: Oxford University Press, 1993), 153–62, includes a vivid description of MB leaders' trials by the "People's Tribunal" in 1954, where Anwar Sadat was one of the presiding officer-judges.

81. The charges were (1) ordering the unlawful detention and torture of opposition protesters at Ittihadiyya, (2) leaking classified documents about the armed forces to Qatar, (3) leading an illegal group, (4) insulting the judiciary in his June 2013 speech, (5) colluding with foreign militants to break out of Wadi al-Natroun prison and loot its weapons depot, and (6) conspiring to commit terrorist acts with foreign organizations

by sending "elements" in 2005 to military camps run by Hamas, Hizbullah, and the Iranian Revolutionary Guard Corps.

82. Kirchheimer, *Political Justice*, 46.

83. "Mubarak li-l Mahkama: 800 Musallah Ikhtaraqu al-Hudud wa Iqtahamu al-Sujun wa Atlaqu al-Nar fi-l Tahrir," *Al-Misri al-Yawm*, December 27, 2018.

84. Kirchheimer, *Political Justice*, 118.

85. The Interior Ministry announced that 23,060 convicts had escaped in January 2011; see "Al-Dakhiliyya Tuwasil al-Bahth," *Al-Misri al-Yawm*, February 13, 2011.

86. Moncef Marzouki, "Wafat al-Ra'is al-Shahid Mohamed Mursi," June 17, 2019; https://www.facebook.com/Dr.Marzouki.Moncef/posts/2430556107011594/.

87. "Cairo University Reinstates 52 Suspended Students," *Mada Masr*, July 27, 2016; Rana Mamdouh, "17 Striking Workers Acquitted as Court Demands Right to Strike Be Included in Civil Service Law," *Mada Masr*, June 17, 2017.

88. "Israel Says It Gave Written Consent to Saudi Island Transfer," *Times of Israel*, April 12, 2016.

89. Adam Hanieh explains the normalization of Israeli and Gulf relations in his *Money, Markets, and Monarchies: The Gulf Cooperation Council and the Political Economy of the Contemporary Middle East* (New York: Cambridge University Press, 2018), 251–55.

90. Human Rights Watch, "Egypt: Scores of Protesters Jailed Unjustly," May 25, 2016.

91. Khaled Ali describes the nature of the compiled historical documents and includes texts of the ensuing two administrative court decisions, as well as photos of judges, plaintiffs, and courtroom scenes in Egyptian Center for Economic and Social Rights (ECESR), *Hakamat al-Mahkama: Tiran wa Sanafir Misriyya: Al-Juz' al-Awwal, Watha'iq Qada'iyya* (Cairo: ECESR, 2017).

92. Ironically, that clause was an innovation by Sisi's handpicked committee of fifty. Acting under the nationalist fervor that claimed that former president Morsi intended to sell off state lands to Qatar, they placed the constitutional provision as a restraint on any incoming civilian president, when it was not yet certain that Sisi would claim the presidency.

93. The growing rift between Egypt and Saudi Arabia on several regional issues is explained in Sarah El Sirgany, "Islands Apart: Why the Saudi-Egypt Alliance Is on the Rocks," *World Policy Journal* 33, no. 4 (2016/2017): 89–95.

94. Hanieh, *Money, Markets, and Monarchies*, 260–61.

95. Emad al-Din Hussein, "Tiran wa Sanafir Misriyya," *Al-Shurouq*, January 17, 2017.

96. Asmahan Soliman, "Government Prepares to Hand Over Tiran and Sanafir through Parliament," *Mada Masr*, June 11, 2017.

97. Rana Mamdouh, "Supreme Constitutional Court Validates Tiran and Sanafir Treaty," *Mada Masr*, March 4, 2018. For an example of the government's strategy to evade SAC rulings under Mubarak, see "Egypt Court Halts Copt Remarriage Ruling for Now," Reuters, July 7, 2010.

98. Sami Anan, "Lays al-Muhim Al'an Ithbat Misriyyat Tiran wa Sanafir," June 12, 2017, https://www.facebook.com/SamiEnanSemiOfficial/posts/2028196254074528/; Asmahan Soliman, "The Puzzling Dismissal of Egypt's Top Military Commander," *Mada Masr*, December 10, 2017.

99. Human Rights Watch, "Egypt: Scores of Protesters Jailed Unjustly," May 25, 2016.

100. The law applies to four institutions: the two apex institutions, the Cassation Court and Supreme Administrative Court, and the quasi-judicial State Cases Authority (body of government lawyers) and the Administrative Prosecution Authority (body for investigating administrative corruption). It replaces the president's pro forma approval of the institutions' most senior candidate for the top post with a mechanism requiring that each institution submit a shortlist of three nominees from which the president selects the chief justice or authority head.

101. "Its purpose, from the beginning," wrote Enid Hill, "was 'the protection of liberties, of individual rights and of the public interest.'" Enid Hill, "Majlis al-Dawla: The Administrative Courts of Egypt and Administrative Law," in *Islam and Public Law: Classical and Contemporary Studies*, ed. Chibli Mallat (Boston: Graham and Trotman, 1993), 207–28, 208.

102. Norberto Bobbio, "The Future of Democracy," *Telos* 61 (1984): 3–16, 10.

103. "Siyasiyyun Yudashinun Hamla Sha'biyya bi-Shi'ar Misr Mish li-l Bay'," *Al-Tahrir al-Jadid*, April 22, 2016.

104. Law 32/2014. Amr Adly, "The Future of Big Business in the New Egypt" (Washington, DC: Carnegie Endowment for International Peace, November 2014).

105. Dieter Bednarz and Klaus Brinkbäumer, "Extremists Offend the Image of God," *Spiegel Online*, February 9, 2015, https://www.spiegel.de/international/world/islamic-state-egyptian-president-sisi-calls-for-help-in-is-fight-a-1017434.html; Amnesty International, "Egypt: Military Pledges to Stop Forced 'Virginity Tests,'" June 27, 2011; the May 5, 2014 interview with Ibrahim 'Issa can be seen at https://youtu.be/H

-JgDHLM8EU; Kareem Fahim, "Emerging from Shadows, Egyptian Protesters Stage Biggest Rally in Two Years," *New York Times*, April 16, 2016.

106. A transcript of the hour-long televised interview with filmmaker Sandra Nash'at, billed as "A President and a People," is at https://almanassa.co/ar/story/9600.

107. Alain Rouquié, "Demilitarization and the Institutionalization of Military-dominated Polities in Latin America," in *Transitions from Authoritarian Rule: Comparative Perspectives*, ed. Guillermo O'Donnell, Philippe Schmitter, and Laurence Whitehead (Baltimore: Johns Hopkins University Press, 1986), 110.

108. Arthur Stinchcombe, "Lustration as a Problem of the Social Basis of Constitutionalism," *Law and Social Inquiry* 20, no.1 (1995): 245–73, 252.

## CONCLUSION

1. Adam Przeworski, "Some Problems in the Study of the Transition to Democracy," in *Transitions from Authoritarian Rule: Comparative Perspectives*, ed. Guillermo O'Donnell, Philippe Schmitter, and Laurence Whitehead (Baltimore: Johns Hopkins University Press, 1986), 54. Przeworski advocates an approach that is sensitive to perceptions and expectations.

2. I have learned much about the productive use of "failure" as a heuristic from Richard J. Evans, *The Coming of the Third Reich* (New York: Penguin Books, 2003); Christopher Clark, "After 1848: The European Revolution in Government," *Transactions of the Royal Historical Society* 22, no. (2012): 171–97; Stanley Payne, *Spain's First Democracy: The Second Republic, 1931–1936* (Madison: University of Wisconsin Press, 1993); Abraham Ascher, *The Revolution of 1905: A Short History* (Stanford, CA: Stanford University Press, 2004).

3. Albert Hirschman, *The Rhetoric of Reaction: Perversity, Futility, Jeopardy* (Cambridge, MA: Harvard University Press, 1991), 72.

4. Sharif Abdel Kouddous, "In Egypt, A President without Power," *Nation*, June 20, 2012.

5. Nimer Sultany, *Law and Revolution: Legitimacy and Constitutionalism after the Arab Spring* (Oxford: Oxford University Press, 2018), 315.

6. Ellis Goldberg, "Courts and Police in Revolution," in *Egypt after the Spring: Revolt and Reaction*, ed. Emile Hokayem and Hebatalla Taha (London: Routledge, 2016), 33–51, 38.

7. Ivan Ermakoff, "Exceptional Cases: Epistemic Contributions and Normative Expectations," *European Journal of Sociology* 55 (2014): 237.

8. Yezid Sayigh discusses pressures for police reform from within and outside the police hierarchy in *Missed Opportunity: The Politics of Police Reform in Egypt and Tunisia* (Washington, DC: Carnegie Endowment for International Peace, 2015).

9. Michael Mann, *The Sources of Social Power*, vol. 2: *The Rise of Classes and Nation-States, 1760–1914* (Cambridge: Cambridge University Press, 1993), 61.

10. Juan Linz, *The Breakdown of Democratic Regimes: Crisis, Breakdown, and Reequilibration* (Baltimore: Johns Hopkins University Press, 1978), 45.

11. Adam Przeworski, "Some Problems in the Study of the Transition to Democracy," 59.

12. Enid Hill, "Majlis al-Dawla: The Administrative Courts of Egypt and Administrative Law," in *Islam and Public Law: Classical and Contemporary Studies*, ed. Chibli Mallat (Boston: Graham and Trotman, 1993), 227.

13. Khalil al-Anani, in "Why Did Egyptian Democratization Fail? Fourteen Experts Respond," ed. Amy Hawthorne and Andrew Miller (Project on Middle East Democracy [POMED], January 2020), 2; Azmi Bishara, *Thawrat Misr*, vol. 2 (Doha: Al-Markaz al-Arabi li-l Abhath wa Dirasat al-Siayasat, 2016), 19; Alfred Stepan, "Mutual Accommodation: Islamic and Secular Parties and Tunisia's Democratic Transition," in Alfred Stepan, ed., *Democratic Transition in the Muslim World: A Global Perspective* (New York: Columbia University Press, 2018), 52.

14. As chap. 5 discussed, Morsi kept this promise, appointing Hisham Qandil as prime minister, a pious, non-Islamist career deputy minister in the Irrigation Ministry, after several more high-profile secular political figures turned down Morsi's offers of the premiership. However, Qandil was deemed unsatisfactory by several of the Fairmont attendees, who broke publicly with Morsi at that point.

15. See the interviews with FJP leaders Essam el-Erian and Saad al-Katatni in David Kirkpatrick, "Islamists in Egypt Back Timing of Military Handover," *New York Times*, January 9, 2012; Leila Fadel, "Egypt's Islamist Party Backs Down from Demand to Form Government," *Washington Post*, January 9, 2012.

16. László Bruszt and David Stark, "Remaking the Political Field in Hungary: From the Politics of Confrontation to the Politics of Competition," in *Eastern Europe in Revolution*, ed. Ivo Banac (Ithaca, NY: Cornell University Press, 1992), 46. The analogy to the MB is imperfect, since their position in post-Mubarak politics is more akin to the largest opposition in postcommunist Hungarian politics, the Hungarian Democratic Forum, rather than the reform Communists. My point is not that the Muslim Brothers are analogous to the reform Communists, but that they shared a similar self-concept in relation to other political forces.

17. Arend Lijphart, *Thinking about Democracy: Power Sharing and Majority Rule in Theory and Practice* (New York: Routledge, 2008).

18. A thought-provoking critique of consociationalism as the right path for new democracies is Courtney Jung and Ian Shapiro, "South Africa's Negotiated Transition: Democracy, Opposition, and the New Constitutional Order," *Politics and Society* 23 (1995): 269–308.

19. Jon Elster, Claus Offe, and Ulrich Preuss, *Institutional Design in Post-communist Societies: Rebuilding the Ship at Sea* (Cambridge: Cambridge University Press, 1998), 78.

20. Charles Tilly, *From Mobilization to Revolution* (Reading, MA: Addison Wesley, 1978), 44.

21. This older connotation of the term is to be distinguished from the more well-known Gramscian conception of "interregnum," which I do not use, that "the crisis consists precisely in the fact that the old is dying and the new cannot be born; in this interregnum, morbid phenomena of the most varied kind come to pass" (Antonio Gramsci, *Prison Notebooks*, vol. 2: Notebook 3 [1930], ed. Joseph Buttigieg [New York: Columbia University Press, 1996], 32–33).

22. Guillermo O'Donnell and Philippe Schmitter, *Transitions from Authoritarian Rule: Tentative Conclusions about Uncertain Democracies* (Baltimore: Johns Hopkins University Press, 1986), 3.

23. Diane Koenker and William Rosenberg, "Strikes in Russia, 1917: The Impact of Revolution," in *Strikes, Wars, and Revolutions in an International Perspective: Strike Waves in the Late Nineteenth and Early Twentieth Centuries*, ed. Leopold Haimson and Charles Tilly (Cambridge: Cambridge University Press, 1989), 512.

24. O'Donnell and Schmitter, *Transitions from Authoritarian Rule*, 3–4.

25. Doug McAdam, Sidney Tarrow, and Charles Tilly define "object shift" as a change in the target of claim-making, from local officials to national institutions, or from the national state to international networks or governments; see their *Dynamics of Contention* (Cambridge: Cambridge University Press, 2011), 158–59. In the period this book studies, the most palpable object shift occurred when the new parliament was constituted and faced an avalanche of public demands, including the demand to wield both legislative and executive power in lieu of SCAF (chap. 4).

26. For an elaboration of the self-reinforcing nature of initial institutional adoption, see Paul Pierson, *Politics in Time: History, Institutions, and Social Analysis* (Princeton, NJ: Princeton University Press, 2004), 142–53.

27. Pierson, *Politics in Time*, 152.

28. José María Maravall and Adam Przeworski, introduction to *Democracy and the Rule of Law*, ed. José María Maravall and Adam Przeworski (Cambridge: Cambridge University Press, 2003), 4.

29. George Tsebelis, *Veto Players: How Political Institutions Work* (Princeton, NJ: Princeton University Press, 2002). Although developed for the relatively controlled setting of legislative politics in advanced democracies, Tsebelis extends his framework to nondemocratic regimes. He argues that "it is not true that nondemocratic systems have a single veto player" (77), an observation upheld by my reconstruction of politics during the Mubarak regime.

30. "Furthermore, because the meaning of formal rules must be interpreted, and multiple interpretations are often plausible, the substantive role of a set of rules may change even in the absence of formal revision" (Pierson, *Politics in Time*, 138).

31. Eric Wolf, *Envisioning Power: Ideologies of Dominance and Crisis* (Berkeley: University of California Press, 1999), 67.

32. Pierson, *Politics in Time*, 141–42.

33. Robert D. Benford and David A. Snow, "Framing Processes and Social Movements," *Annual Review of Sociology* 26 (2000): 611–39.

34. Benford and Snow, "Framing Processes and Social Movements," 615.

35. Ivan Ermakoff, "Theory of Practice, Rational Choice, and Historical Change," *Theory and Society* 39 (2010): 545.

36. Ermakoff, "Theory of Practice," 545–46.

37. SCAF's first proclamation on February 13, 2011, affirms that "human freedom, rule of law, values of pluralist democracy, equality, and social justice, and uprooting corruption are the foundations of any regime leading the country in the coming period." Thus appropriating the demands of the mass uprising, SCAF then cast the armed forces as the agent leading the nation to this regime, due to "its historical and constitutional responsibilities to protect the country and preserve its territory and security"; https://manshurat.org/node/4258.

38. Bernard Yack, "Popular Sovereignty and Nationalism," *Political Theory* 29, no. 4 (2001): 517–36, 519.

39. Hent Kalmo and Quentin Skinner, "Introduction: A Concept in Fragments," in *Sovereignty in Fragments: the Past, Present and Future of a Contested Concept*, ed. Hent Kalmo and Quentin Skinner (Cambridge: Cambridge University Press, 2010), 24. This paragraph is also informed by Denis Baranger, "The Apparition of Sovereignty," in *Sovereignty in Fragments*, ed. Kalmo and Skinner, 47–63; and Daniel Lee,

*Popular Sovereignty in Early Modern Constitutional Thought* (New York: Oxford University Press, 2016).

40. Hent Kalmo and Quentin Skinner, "Introduction: a concept in fragments," 24.

41. Herbert Döring, "Time as a Scarce Resource: Government Control of the Agenda," in *Parliaments and Majority Rule in Western Europe*, ed. Herbert Döring (Mannheim: Mannheim Center for European Social Research, 1995), 223–46; Arthur Stinchcombe, "Ending Revolutions and Building New Governments," *Annual Review of Political Science* 2, no. 1 (1999): 49–73.

42. George Wallis, "Chronopolitics: The Impact of Time Perspectives on the Dynamics of Change," *Social Forces* 49, no. 1 (1970): 106; emphasis in original.

43. Ivan Ermakoff, *Ruling Oneself Out: A Theory of Collective Abdications* (Durham, NC: Duke University Press, 2008), 331.

44. An illuminating discussion of the resonance of *'aysh* (bread) in Egyptian sociopolitical communication is in Nader Srage, *Misr al-Thawra wa Shi'arat Shababiha: Dirasa Lisaniyya fi 'Afwiyat al-Ta'bir* (Doha: Al-Markaz al-Arabi li-l Abhath wa Dirasat al-Siayasat, 2014), 279–92.

45. Jeremy Waldron, "Accountability and Insolence," in Jeremy Waldron, *Political Political Theory* (Cambridge, MA: Harvard University Press, 2016), 175.

46. Mikhail Gorbachev, "Egypt's Agonizing Choice," *International Herald Tribune*, February 16, 2011.

47. Jean Hampton, *Political Philosophy* (Boulder, CO: Westview Press, 1997), 34.

48. Jeremy Waldron, "Accountability and Insolence," 189.

49. Waldron, "Accountability and Insolence," 188–89.

50. Charles Tilly, *Contention and Democracy in Europe, 1650–2000* (Cambridge: Cambridge University Press, 2004), 41; Juan Linz, "Democracy's Time Constraints," *International Political Science Review* 19, no. 1 (1998): 19–37.

*Bibliography*

**ONLINE ARCHIVAL SOURCES**
Daftar Ahwal
https://daftarahwal.com/
Egyptian Press Archive of CEDEJ
http://cedej.bibalex.org/
Manshurat Qanuniyya
https://manshurat.org/
Tahrir Documents, International Digital Ephemera Project, UCLA Library
http://idep.library.ucla.edu/tahrir-square
al-Tashriʿat al-Misriyya
http://www.cc.gov.eg/Legislations/Egypt_Legislations.aspx
Wikithawra, Statistical Database of the Egyptian Revolution
https://wikithawra.wordpress.com/

**ARABIC PERIODICALS AND WEBSITES**
*Al-Ahali* (Cairo)
*Al-Ahram* (Cairo)
*Al-Ahrar* (Cairo)
*Al-Badil* (Cairo)
*Al-Dustur* (Cairo)
*Al-Hayat* (London)

*Al-Misri al-Yawm* (Cairo)
*Al-Musawwar* (Cairo)
*Al-Shurouq* (Cairo)
*Al-Tajammuʿ* (Cairo)
*Al-Wafd* (Cairo)
*Al-Watan* (Cairo)
*Al-Yawm al-Sabiʿ* (Cairo)

**ENGLISH PERIODICALS AND WEBSITES**
*Ahram Online*
*Al-Ahram Weekly*
Associated Press
*The Economist*
*Egypt Independent*
*The Guardian*
*Jacobin*
*Mada Masr*
Middle East Research and Information Project (MERIP)
*The Nation*
*The New York Times*
*Nisralnasr*
Reuters
Tahrir Institute for Middle East Policy (TIMEP)
*The Wall Street Journal*
*The Washington Post*

**SECONDARY LITERATURE**
**Books, Articles, and Reports in Arabic**
All translations and title transliterations are by the author unless otherwise indicated.

Abdel Meguid, Wahid. *Azmat Dustur 2012: Tawthiq wa Tahlil: Shahada min Dakhil al-Jamʿiyya al-Taʾsisiyya*. Cairo: n.p., 2013.

Abu Reyda, Muhammad Ali. "Al-Tarkiba al-Siyasiyya wa-l Ijtimaʿiyya li-ʿAdaʾ Majlis al-Shaʿb 2011/2012," in *Intikhabat Majlis al-Shaʿb 2011/2012*, ed. Amr Hashem Rabiʿ. Cairo: Markaz al-Ahram li-l Dirasat al-Siyasiyya wa-l Istratijiyya, 2012, 403–43.

Adel, Basem. *Sina'at al-Ahzab fi Misr Ba'd 25 Yanayir*. Cairo: Al-Masriyya li-l Nashr wa-l Tawzi', 2011.

al-Bishri, Tareq. *Min Awraq Thawrat 25 Yanayir*. Cairo: Dar al-Shurouq, 2012.

al-Sanhuri, Abdel Razzaq Ahmad, and Ahmad Hishmat Abu Stait. *Usul al-Qanun, aw al-Madkhal li-Dirasat al-Qanun*. Cairo: Matb'at Lajnat al-Ta'lif wal Tarjama wal Nashr, 1950.

Arab Network for Human Rights Information. *Daw' fi Darb al-Hurriyya*. 2012.

Auda, Gehad. *Gamal Mubarak: Tajdid al-Libiraliyya al-Wataniyya*. Cairo: Dar al-Hurriyya, 2004.

Bishara, Azmi. *Thawrat Misr*. Vol. 2. Doha: Al-Markaz al-Arabi li-l Abhath wa Dirasat al-Siyasat, 2016.

Egyptian Center for Economic and Social Rights (ECESR). *Hakamat al-Mahkama: Tiran wa Sanafir Misriyya: Al-Juz' al-Awwal, Watha'iq Qada'iyya*, 2017.

El Khawaga, Dina. "La Waqt li-l Haqq: 'An Sun' al-Ijma' Ba'd 30 Yunyu," *Bidayat* 6 (Summer 2013): 68–72.

Farouq, Abdel Khaleq. *Iqtisadiyyat al-Ujur wa-l Murattabat fi Misr*. Cairo: Maktabat al-Shurouq al-Dawliyya, 2012.

———. *Judhur al-Fasad al-Idari fi Misr*. Cairo: Dar al-Shurouq, 2008.

Ghanem, Ibrahim al-Bayoumi, ed. *Tareq Al-Bishri: Al-Qadi al-Mufakkir*. Cairo: Dar al-Shurouq, 1999.

Kharbush, Muhammad Safieddine. *Al-Tatawwur al-Siyasi fi Misr: Muhawalat Hadm al-Dawla al-Misriyya*. Cairo: Al-Markaz al-Arabi lil Buhuth wa-al-Dirasat, 2014.

Markaz Ibn Khaldun lil-Dirasat al-Inma'iyya. *Taqrir al-Lajna al-Wataniyya al-Misriyya li-Mutaba'at al-Intikhabat al-Barlamaniyya, 1995*.

Mohamadein, Haytham. *Sijnak wa Matrahak: Dalil al-Qabd wa-l Tahqiq wa-l Sujun*. Cairo: Arabic Network for Human Rights Information, 2017.

Rabi', Amr Hashem, ed. *Intikhabat Majlis al-Sha'b 2011/2012*. Cairo: Markaz al-Ahram li-l Dirasat al-Siyasiyya wa-l Istratijiyya, 2012.

Srage, Nader. *Misr al-Thawra wa Shi'arat Shababiha: Dirasa Lisaniyya fi 'Afwiyat al-Ta'bir*. Doha: Al-Markaz al-Arabi li-l Abhath wa Dirasat al-Siayasat, 2014.

Younis, Sherif. *Nida' al-Sha'b: Tarikh Naqdi li-l Idiulujiyya al-Nasiriyya*. Cairo: Dar al-Shurouq, 2012.

## Books, Articles, and Reports in English and French

Abdalla, Nadine. "The Labor Movement in the Face of Transition." In *Egypt's Revolutions: Politics, Religion, and Social Movements*, ed. Bernard Rougier and Stéphane Lacroix, 197–211. New York: Palgrave Macmillan, 2016.

Abdelrahman, Maha. *Egypt's Long Revolution: Protest Movements and Uprisings*. New York: Routledge, 2014.

Abrahamian, Ervand. *The Coup: 1953, the CIA, and the Roots of Modern U.S.-Iranian Relations*. New York: New Press, 2013.

Acemoglu, Daron, and James A. Robinson. *Why Nations Fail: The Origins of Power, Prosperity, and Poverty*. New York: Crown Publishers, 2012.

Achcar, Gilbert. *Morbid Symptoms: Relapse in the Arab Uprising*. Palo Alto, CA: Stanford University Press, 2016.

Adly, Amr. "The Future of Big Business in the New Egypt." Beirut: Carnegie Endowment for International Peace, November 2014.

Al-Anani, Khalil. "Why Did Egyptian Democratization Fail? Fourteen Experts Respond." In Amy Hawthorne and Andrew Miller, eds., Project on Middle East Democracy (POMED), January 2020.

Albrecht, Holger. *Raging against the Machine: Political Opposition under Authoritarianism in Egypt*. Syracuse, NY: Syracuse University Press, 2013.

———. "Unbalancing Power in Egypt's Constitution." *Foreign Policy*, January 31, 2013. https://foreignpolicy.com/2013/01/31/unbalancing-power-in-egypts-constitution/.

Alexander, Jeffrey. *Performative Revolution in Egypt: An Essay in Cultural Power*. London: Bloomsbury, 2011.

Amann, Peter. "Revolution: A Redefinition." *Political Science Quarterly* 77, no. 1 (1962): 36–53.

Amnesty International. "Agents of Repression: Egypt's Police and the Case for Reform," 2012.

———. "Egypt: A Year After 'Virginity Tests,' Women Victims of Army Violence Still Seek Justice," March 9, 2012.

———. "Egypt: Gross Human Rights Violations under President al-Sisi." March 2019.

———. "Egypt: Protect Families of Those Killed in Protests from Intimidation," February 25, 2011.

———. "Egypt's New Constitution Limits Freedoms and Ignores the Rights of Women," November 30, 2012.

———. "'The Walls of the Cell Were Smeared with Blood'—Third Anniversary of Egypt Uprising Marred by Police Brutality." February 4, 2014.

Arato, Andrew. *The Adventures of the Constituent Power: Beyond Revolutions?* New York: Cambridge University Press, 2017.

Arjomand, Saïd Amir. "The Arab Revolution of 2011 and Its Counterrevolutions in Comparative Perspective," in *The Arab Revolution of 2011: A Comparative Perspective*, ed. Saïd Amir Arjomand (Albany: State University of New York Press, 2015), 9–51.

———. "Iran's Islamic Revolution in Comparative Perspective," *World Politics* 38, no. 3 (April 1986), 383–414.

———. *Revolution: Structure and Meaning in World History* (Chicago: University of Chicago Press, 2019).

Armbrust, Walter. *Martyrs and Tricksters: An Ethnography of the Egyptian Revolution.* Princeton, NJ: Princeton University Press, 2019.

Asad, Talal. "Fear and the Ruptured State: Reflections on Egypt after Mubarak." *Social Research* 79 (Summer 2012): 271–89.

Ascher, Abraham. *The Revolution of 1905: A Short History.* Stanford, CA: Stanford University Press, 2004.

Association for Freedom of Thought and Expression (AFTE). "Besieged Universities: A Report on the Rights and Freedoms of Students in Egyptian Universities from the Academic Years 2013–2014 to 2015–2016." Cairo: AFTE, 2017.

Aya, Rod. *Rethinking Revolutions and Collective Violence: Studies on Concept, Theory, and Method.* Amsterdam: Het Spinhuis, 1990.

Ayubi, Nazih. "Government and the State in Egypt Today." In *Egypt under Mubarak*, ed. Charles Tripp and Roger Owen. New York: Routledge, 1989.

Aziz, Sahar. "Independence without Accountability: The Judicial Paradox of Egypt's Failed Transition to Democracy." *Penn. St. Law Review* 667 (2015–16): 667–736.

Baker, Keith Michael, and Dan Edelstein, eds. *Scripting Revolution: A Historical Approach to the Comparative Study of Revolutions.* Palo Alto, CA: Stanford University Press, 2015.

Baranger, Denis. "The Apparition of Sovereignty." In *Sovereignty in Fragments: The Past, Present and Future of a Contested Concept*, ed. Hent Kalmo and Quentin Skinner, 47–63. Cambridge: Cambridge University Press, 2010.

Bayat, Asef. *Revolution without Revolutionaries: Making Sense of the Arab Spring.* Stanford, CA: Stanford University Press, 2017.

Bednarz, Dieter, and Klaus Brinkbäumer, "Extremists Offend the Image of God." *Spiegel Online*, February 9, 2015.

Beinin, Joel. "Egyptian Workers after June 30." *Middle East Report Online*, August 23, 2013.

———. *Justice for All: The Struggle for Worker Rights in Egypt*. Washington, DC: Solidarity Center, 2010.

———. *The Rise of Egypt's Workers*. Washington, DC: Carnegie Endowment for International Peace, 2012.

———. *Workers and Thieves: Labor Movements and Popular Uprisings in Tunisia and Egypt*. Stanford, CA: Stanford University Press, 2016.

———. "Workers' Struggles under 'Socialism' and Neoliberalism." In *Egypt: The Moment of Change*, ed. Rabab El-Mahdi and Philip Marfleet, 68–86. London: Zed Books, 2009.

Beinin, Joel, and Marie Duboc. "A Workers' Social Movement on the Margin of the Global Neoliberal Order, Egypt 2004–2012." In *Social Movements, Mobilization, and Contestation in the Middle East and North Africa*, ed. Joel Beinin and Frederic Vairel, 205–27. Palo Alto, CA: Stanford University Press, 2013.

Benford, Robert D., and David A. Snow. "Framing Processes and Social Movements," *Annual Review of Sociology* 26 (2000): 611–39.

Bianchi, Robert. *Unruly Corporatism: Associational Life in Twentieth-Century Egypt*. New York: Oxford University Press, 1989.

Bishara, Dina. *Contesting Authoritarianism: Labor Challenges to the State in Egypt*. New York: Cambridge University Press, 2018.

Blaydes, Lisa. *Elections and Distributive Politics in Mubarak's Egypt*. Cambridge: Cambridge University Press, 2010.

Bloch, Marc. *The Historian's Craft*. New York: Vintage Books, 1953.

Bobbio, Norberto. "The Future of Democracy." *Telos* 61 (1984): 3–16.

Bou Nassif, Hicham. "Coups and Nascent Democracies: The Military and Egypt's Failed Consolidation." *Democratization* 24, no. 1 (2017): 157–74.

Brown, L. Neville, and John S. Bell. *French Administrative Law*. 5th ed. London: Oxford University Press, 1998.

Brown, Nathan J. "Contention in Religion and State in Postrevolutionary Egypt." *Social Research* 79, no. 2 (2012): 531–50.

———. "Egypt's Failed Transition." *Journal of Democracy* 24 (2013): 45–58.

———. "Egypt's Muddy Waters." *National Interest*, April 4, 2012.

———. "Landmines in Egypt's Constitutional Roadmap." Carnegie Endowment for International Peace, December 7, 2011.

Brown, Nathan J., and Michele Dunne. "Egypt's Draft Constitutional Amendments Answer Some Questions and Raise Others." Carnegie Endowment for International Peace, March 1, 2011.

Brown, Nathan J., and Kristen Stilt. "A Haphazard Constitutional Compromise." Carnegie Endowment for International Peace, April 11, 2011.

Brownlee, Jason. *Authoritarianism in an Age of Democratization*. Cambridge: Cambridge University Press, 2007.

Brownlee, Jason, Tarek Masoud, and Andrew Reynolds. *The Arab Spring: Pathways of Repression and Reform*. New York: Oxford University Press, 2015.

Bruszt, László, and David Stark. "Remaking the Political Field in Hungary: From the Politics of Confrontation to the Politics of Competition." In *Eastern Europe in Revolution*, ed. Ivo Banac, 13–55. Ithaca, NY: Cornell University Press, 1992.

Butler, Judith. *Notes toward a Performative Theory of Assembly*. Cambridge, MA: Harvard University Press, 2015.

Cairo Institute for Human Rights Studies (CIHRS). "Toward the Emancipation of Egypt: A Study on Assembly Law 10/1914." Cairo: CIHRS, 2017.

Carter Center. "Final Report of the Carter Center Mission to Witness the 2011–2012 Parliamentary Elections in Egypt." Atlanta: Carter Center, 2012.

Casper, Jayson. "Mapping the Coptic Movements: Coptic Activism in a Revolutionary Setting." *Arab West Report*, May 15, 2013.

Clark, Christopher. "After 1848: The European Revolution in Government," *Transactions of the Royal Historical Society* 22, no. (2012): 171–97.

———. *The Sleepwalkers: How Europe Went to War in 1914*. New York: HarperCollins, 2013.

Dailleux, Denis, Abdellah Taïa, Mahmoud Farag. *Égypte, les martyrs de la revolution*. Marseille: Bec en l'air, 2014.

Della Porta, Donatella. *Where Did the Revolution Go? Contentious Politics and the Quality of Democracy*. New York: Cambridge University Press, 2016.

Dix, Robert. "Why Revolutions Succeed and Fail." *Polity* 16, no. 3 (1984): 423–46.

Djerejian, Edward P. *Danger and Opportunity: An American Ambassador's Journey through the Middle East*. New York: Simon and Schuster, 2008.

Döring, Herbert. "Time as a Scarce Resource: Government Control of the Agenda," in *Parliaments and Majority Rule in Western Europe*, ed. Herbert Döring, 223–46. Mannheim: Mannheim Center for European Social Research, 1995.

Dorsey, James. *The Turbulent World of Middle East Soccer*. New York: Oxford University Press, 2016.

Dunn, John. "Revolution." In *Political Innovation and Conceptual Change*, ed. Terence Ball, James Farr, and Russell Hanson, 333–56. Cambridge: Cambridge University Press, 1989.

Egyptian Initiative for Personal Rights (EIPR). *Naga Hammadi: Witness to the Strife, Fact-Finding Mission Report*. January 21, 2010.

El-Bendary, Mohamed. *The Egyptian Revolution: From Hope to Despair*. New York: Algora Publishing, 2013.

Electoral Institute for Sustainable Democracy in Africa (EISA). "Election Witnessing Mission Report, Egypt: The People's Assembly and Shura Council Elections." Johannesburg: EISA, 2012.

El Gebaly, Tahany. "Constitutional Principles: Documents on Post-Revolution Egypt." *Alif: Journal of Comparative Poetics*, no. 32 (2012): 228–53.

El-Ghobashy, Mona. "Dissidence and Deference among Egyptian Judges." *Middle East Report* 279 (Summer 2016).

———. "The Metamorphosis of the Egyptian Muslim Brothers." *International Journal of Middle East Studies* 37, no. 3 (August 2005): 373–95.

El-Mahdi, Rabab. "Enough! Egypt's Quest for Democracy." *Comparative Political Studies* 42, no. 8 (2009): 1011–39.

———. "Orientalising the Egyptian Uprising." *Jadaliyya*, April 11, 2011.

El-Meehy, Asya. "Egypt's Popular Committees: From Moment of Madness to NGO Dilemmas." *Middle East Report* 265 (2012): 29–33.

El-Nawawy, Mohammed, and Mohamad Hamas ElMasry. "The Signs of a Strongman: The Semiotic and Discourse Analysis of Abdel Fattah al-Sisi's Egyptian Presidential Campaign." *International Journal of Communication* 10 (2016): 2275–96.

El-Sherif, Ashraf. "The Egyptian Muslim Brotherhood's Failures." Washington, DC: Carnegie Endowment for International Peace, July 2014.

———. "Egypt's Salafists at a Crossroads." Washington, DC: Carnegie Endowment for International Peace, April 29, 2015.

El-Shimy, Yasser. "The Muslim Brotherhood." In *Egypt after the Spring: Revolt and Reaction*, ed. Emile Hokayem and Hebatalla Taha, 75–104. New York: Routledge, 2016.

El Sirgany, Sarah. "Islands Apart: Why the Saudi-Egypt Alliance Is on the Rocks." *World Policy Journal* 33, no. 4 (2016/2017): 89–95.

Elster, Jon. "Constitution-Making in Eastern Europe: Rebuilding the Boat in the Open Sea." *Public Administration* 71, no. 1–2 (1993): 169–217.

———. "Legislatures as Constituent Assemblies." In *The Least Examined Branch: The Role of Legislatures in the Constitutional State*, ed. Richard Bauman and Tsvi Kahana, 181–97.. New York: Cambridge University Press, 2009.

———. "The Optimal Design of a Constituent Assembly." In *Collective Wisdom: Principles and Mechanisms*, ed. Helene Landemore and Jon Elster, 148–72. New York: Cambridge University Press, 2012.

Elster, Jon, Claus Offe, and Ulrich Preuss. *Institutional Design in Post-communist Societies: Rebuilding the Ship at Sea*. Cambridge: Cambridge University Press, 1998.

Ermakoff, Ivan. "Exceptional Cases: Epistemic Contributions and Normative Expectations." *European Journal of Sociology* 55 (2014): 223–43.

———. *Ruling Oneself Out: A Theory of Collective Abdications*. Durham, NC: Duke University Press, 2008.

———. "Theory of Practice, Rational Choice, and Historical Change." *Theory and Society* 39 (2010): 527–53.

European Parliament, Directorate-General for External Policies. "Egypt: In-Depth Analysis of the Main Elements of the New Constitution," April 2014.

Evans, Richard J. *The Coming of the Third Reich*. New York: Penguin Books, 2003.

Fadel, Mohammad. "Egyptian Revolutionaries' Unrealistic Expectations." In *Egypt beyond Tahrir Square*, ed. Bessma Momani and Eid Mohamed, 28–40.. Bloomington: Indiana University Press, 2016.

Feldman, Noah. *The Arab Winter: A Tragedy*. Princeton, NJ: Princeton University Press, 2020.

Fishman, Robert. "Democratic Practice after the Revolution: The Case of Portugal and Beyond." *Politics and Society* 39, no. 2 (2011): 233–67.

Gamblin, Sandrine, ed. *Contours et détours du politique en Egypte: Les élections législatives de 1995*. Cairo: CEDEJ; Paris: L'Harmattan, 1997.

Ghonim, Wael. *Revolution 2.0: The Power of the People Is Greater Than the People in Power: A Memoir*. New York: Houghton Mifflin Harcourt, 2012.

Goldberg, Ellis. "Cairo: Elections and Other Issues," December 26, 2011, *Nisr al-Nasr* blog.

———. "A Closer Look at the Referendum Results: District by District." April 8, 2011, *Nisr al-Nasr* blog.

———. "Courts and Police in Revolution." In *Egypt after the Spring: Revolt and Reaction*, ed. Emile Hokayem and Hebatalla Taha, 33–51. London: Routledge, 2016.

———. "Drafting a Constitution: Part I of II," October 24, 2012, *Nisr al-Nasr* blog.

———. "Drafting a Constitution: Part II," November 2, 2012, *Nisr al-Nasr* blog.

———. "Peasants in Revolt—Egypt 1919." *International Journal of Middle East Studies* 24, no. 2 (1992): 261–80.

Goldstone, Jack, and Charles Tilly. "Threat (and Opportunity): Popular Action and State Response in the Dynamics of Contentious Action." In *Silence and Voice in the Study of Contentious Politics*, ed. Ronald Aminzade et al. New York: Cambridge University Press, 2001.

Goodwin, Jeff. *No Other Way Out: States and Revolutionary Movements, 1945–1991*. Cambridge: Cambridge University Press, 2001.

Gramsci, Antonio. *Prison Notebooks*. Vol. 2, ed. Joseph Buttigieg. New York: Columbia University Press, 1996.

Gröndahl, Mia. *Revolution Graffiti: Street Art of the New Egypt*. Cairo: American University in Cairo Press, 2012.

Gronlykke Mollerup, Nina, and Sherief Gaber. "Making Media Public: On Revolutionary Street Screenings in Egypt." *International Journal of Communication* 9 (2015): 2903–21.

Gunning, Jeroen, and Ilan Zvi Baron. *Why Occupy a Square? People, Protests, and Movements in the Egyptian Revolution*. London: Hurst, 2013.

Haenni, Patrick. "The Reasons for the Muslim Brotherhood's Failure in Power." In *Egypt's Revolutions: Politics, Religion, and Social Movements*, ed. Bernard Rougier and Stéphane Lacroix, 19–39. Basingstoke: Palgrave Macmillan, 2016.

Hafez, Mohammed, and Quintan Wiktorowicz. "Violence as Contention in the Egyptian Islamic Movement." In *Islamic Activism: A Social Movement Theory Approach*, ed. Quintan Wiktorowicz. Bloomington: Indiana University Press, 2003.

Hampton, Jean. *Political Philosophy*. Boulder, CO: Westview Press, 1997.

Hanieh, Adam. *Money, Markets, and Monarchies: The Gulf Cooperation Council and the Political Economy of the Contemporary Middle East*. New York: Cambridge University Press, 2018.

Harb, Imad. "The Egyptian Military in Politics: Disengagement or Accommodation?" *Middle East Journal* 57, no. 2 (2003): 269–90.

Hartshorn, Ian. *Labor Politics in North Africa: After the Uprisings in Egypt and Tunisia*. New York: Cambridge University Press, 2019.

Hashem, Amr, and Noha El-Mikawy. "Business Parliamentarians as Locomotives of Information and Production of Knowledge." In *Institutional Reform and Economic*

*Development in Egypt*, ed. Noha El-Mikawy and Heba Handoussa, 49–60. Cairo: American University in Cairo Press, 2002.

Hassan, Hassan. "Extraordinary Politics of Ordinary People: Explaining the Microdynamics of Popular Committees in Revolutionary Cairo." *International Sociology* 30 (2015): 383–400.

Hazzaa, Manar. "Narratives and Evidence: Struggles over Mohamed Mahmoud." Master's thesis, American University in Cairo, 2016.

Henry, Clement M., and Robert Springborg. "A Tunisian Solution for Egypt's Military: Why Egypt's Military Will Not Be Able to Govern." *Foreign Affairs*, February 21, 2011.

Herzfeld, Michael. *The Social Production of Indifference: Exploring the Symbolic Roots of Western Bureaucracy*. Chicago: University of Chicago Press, 1993.

Hibou, Beatrice. *The Force of Obedience: The Political Economy of Repression in Tunisia*. Cambridge, MA: Polity Press, 2011.

Hill, Enid. "Majlis al-Dawla: The Administrative Courts of Egypt and Administrative Law." In *Islam and Public Law: Classical and Contemporary Studies*, ed. Chibli Mallat. Boston: Graham and Trotman, 1993.

Hirschman, Albert. *The Rhetoric of Reaction: Perversity, Futility, Jeopardy*. Cambridge, MA: Harvard University Press, 1991.

Hobsbawm, Eric. "The Machine Breakers." *Past and Present* 1 (1952): 57–70.

———. "Revolution." In *Revolution in History*, ed. Roy Porter et al., 5–46. Cambridge: Cambridge University Press, 1986.

Holmes, Amy Austin. *Coups and Revolutions: Mass Mobilization, the Egyptian Military, and the United States from Mubarak to Sisi*. New York: Oxford University Press, 2019.

Human Rights Watch. "All According to Plan: The Rab'a Massacre and Mass Killings of Protesters in Egypt." *Human Rights Watch* (August 12, 2014).

———. "Egypt: Activists Arrested for 'No' Campaign." January 13, 2014.

———. "Egypt: Don't Cover Up Military Killing of Copt Protesters." October 25, 2011.

———. "Egypt: Investigate Brotherhood's Abuse of Protesters," December 12, 2012.

———. "Egypt: Scores of Protesters Jailed Unjustly." May 25, 2016.

———. "Egypt: Security Forces' Abuse of Anti-War Demonstrators." November 2003.

———. "From Plebiscite to Contest? Egypt's Presidential Election." September 2, 2005.

———. "Letter to Members of the Egyptian Constituent Assembly." October 8, 2012.

———. *The Road Ahead: A Human Rights Agenda for Egypt's New Parliament*, January 2012.

Huntington, Samuel. "Democracy's Third Wave." *Journal of Democracy* 2, no. 2 (Spring 1991): 12–34.

International Foundation for Electoral Systems (IFES). "Elections in Egypt: The Electoral Framework in Egypt's Continuing Transition, February 2011-September 2013." October 11, 2013.

———. "Elections in Egypt: Implications of Recent Court Decisions on the Electoral Framework." August 2012.

International Republican Institute (IRI). "2005 Presidential Election Assessment in Egypt, August 15–September 9, 2005," Washington, DC: IRI, 2005.

Ivanov, Dmitry. "The 2017 Problem: A Next Revolutionary Situation." In *The Arab Revolution of 2011: A Comparative Perspective*, ed. Saïd Amir Arjomand, 251–69. Albany: State University of New York Press, 2015.

Jung, Courtney, and Ian Shapiro. "South Africa's Negotiated Transition: Democracy, Opposition, and the New Constitutional Order." *Politics and Society* 23 (1995): 269–308.

Kalmo, Hent, and Quentin Skinner. "Introduction: A Concept in Fragments." In *Sovereignty in Fragments: the Past, Present and Future of a Contested Concept*, ed. Hent Kalmo and Quentin Skinner, 1–25. Cambridge: Cambridge University Press, 2010.

Kandeel, Amal. "Egypt at a Crossroads." *Middle East Policy* 18, no. 2 (2011): 37–45.

Ketchley, Neil. *Egypt in a Time of Revolution: Contentious Politics and the Arab Spring*. New York: Cambridge University Press, 2017.

———. "How Egypt's Generals Used Street Protests to Stage a Coup." *Washington Post*, July 3, 2017.

Khalil, Karima. *Messages from Tahrir: Signs from Egypt's Revolution*. Cairo: American University in Cairo Press, 2011.

Kirchheimer, Otto. *Political Justice: The Use of Legal Procedure for Political Ends*. Princeton, NJ: Princeton University Press, 1961.

Kirkpatrick, David. *Into the Hands of the Soldiers*. London: Bloomsbury Circus, 2018.

Koenker, Diane, and William Rosenberg. "Strikes in Russia, 1917: The Impact of Revolution." In *Strikes, Wars, and Revolutions in an International Perspective: Strike Waves in the Late Nineteenth and Early Twentieth Centuries*, ed. Leopold Haimson and Charles Tilly, 512–22. Cambridge: Cambridge University Press, 1989.

Kornbluh, Peter. *The Pinochet File: A Declassified Dossier on Atrocity and Accountability*. New York: The New Press, 2013.

Kuran, Timur. "Now out of Never: The Element of Surprise in the East European Revolution of 1989." *World Politics* 44, no. 1 (1991): 7–48.

Kurzman, Charles. "The Arab Spring Uncoiled." *Mobilization* 17, no. 4 (2012): 377–90.

———. "Can Understanding Undermine Explanation? The Confused Experience of Revolution." *Philosophy of the Social Sciences* 34, no. 3 (2004): 328–51.

Lachapelle, Jean. "Lessons from Egypt's Tax Collectors." *Middle East Report* 264 (Fall 2012).

Lacroix, Stéphane. "Egypt's Pragmatic Salafis: The Politics of Hizb al-Nour." Washington, DC: Carnegie Endowment for International Peace, November 2016.

Lacroix, Stéphane, and Ahmed Zaghloul Shalata. "The Rise of Revolutionary Salafism in Post-Mubarak Egypt." In *Egypt's Revolutions: Politics, Religion, and Social Movements*, ed. Bernard Rougier and Stéphane Lacroix, 163–78. New York: Palgrave Macmillan, 2016.

Lee, Daniel. *Popular Sovereignty in Early Modern Constitutional Thought*. New York: Oxford University Press, 2016.

Lenin, Vladimir. "The Collapse of the Second International." 1915. *Lenin Collected Works*, vol. 21, 205–59. Moscow: Progress Publishers, 1974.

———. "The Dual Power." *Pravda*, April 9 1917, *Lenin Collected Works*, vol. 24, 38–41. Moscow: Progress Publishers, 1964.

Lijphart, Arend. *Thinking about Democracy: Power Sharing and Majority Rule in Theory and Practice*. New York: Routledge, 2008.

Linz, Juan. *The Breakdown of Democratic Regimes: Crisis, Breakdown, and Reequilibration*. Baltimore: Johns Hopkins University Press, 1978.

———. "Democracy's Time Constraints." *International Political Science Review* 19, no. 1 (1998): 19–37.

———. "Opposition in and under an Authoritarian Regime: The Case of Spain." In *Regimes and Oppositions*, ed. Robert Dahl, 171–259. New Haven, CT: Yale University Press, 1973.

Lombardi, Clark and Nathan Brown, "Islam in Egypt's New Constitution," *Foreign Policy*, December 13, 2012.

Lust, Ellen, and David Waldner. "Parties in Transitional Democracies: Authoritarian Legacies and Post-Authoritarian Challenges in the Middle East and North Africa." In *Parties, Movements, and Democracy in the Developing World*, ed. Nancy Bermeo and Deborah Yashar, 157–89. New York: Cambridge University Press, 2016.

Lynch, Marc. *Voices of the New Arab Public: Iraq, al-Jazeera, and Middle East Politics Today*. New York: Columbia University Press, 2006.

Maghraoui, Abdeslam. "Egypt's Failed Transition to Democracy: Was Political Culture a Major Factor?" *E-International Relations*, April 29, 2014.

Mann, Michael. *The Sources of Social Power*. Vol. 2, *The Rise of Classes and Nation-States, 1760–1914*. Cambridge: Cambridge University Press, 1993.

Maravall, José María, and Adam Przeworski. "Introduction." In *Democracy and the Rule of Law*, ed. José María Maravall and Adam Przeworski. Cambridge: Cambridge University Press, 2003.

Marshall, Shana. "The Egyptian Armed Forces and the Remaking of an Economic Empire." Washington, DC: Carnegie Endowment for International Peace, 2015.

Martini, Jeff, and Stephen Worman. "Voting Patterns of Post-Mubarak Egypt." Santa Monica, CA: Rand Corporation, 2013.

Martz, John. *Acción Democrática: Evolution of a Modern Political Party in Venezuela*. Princeton, NJ: Princeton University Press, 1966.

Massey, Doreen. "Thinking Radical Democracy Spatially." *Environment and Planning D: Society and Space* 13 (1995): 283–88.

Mbembe, Achille. "Necropolitics." *Public Culture* 15, no. 1 (2003): 11–40.

McAdam, Doug, Sidney Tarrow, and Charles Tilly. *Dynamics of Contention*. Cambridge: Cambridge University Press, 2004.

Mehrez, Samia, ed., *Translating Egypt's Revolution: The Language of Tahrir*. Cairo: American University in Cairo Press, 2012.

Middle East and North Africa Programme. *Egypt's New Parliamentary Politics*. London: Chatham House, March 2012.

Mietzner, Marcus. "Successful and Failed Democratic Transitions from Military Rule in Majority Muslim Societies: The Cases of Indonesia and Egypt." *Contemporary Politics* 20 (2014): 435–52.

Miller, Mary Ashburn. *A Natural History of Revolution: Violence and Nature in the French Revolutionary Imagination, 1789–1794*. Ithaca, NY: Cornell University Press, 2011.

Mink, Louis O. "The Autonomy of Historical Understanding." In *Historical Understanding*, ed. Brian Fay, Eugene O. Golob, and Richard T. Vann, 61–88. Ithaca, NY: Cornell University Press, 1987.

Mitchell, Richard P. *The Society of the Muslim Brothers*. New York: Oxford University Press, 1993.

Mitchell, Timothy. *Carbon Democracy: Political Power in the Age of Oil*. London: Verso, 2011.

Moll, Yasmin. "The Wretched Revolution." *Middle East Report* 273 (Winter 2014): 34–39.

Moore, Clement Henry. "Authoritarian Politics in Unincorporated Society: The Case of Nasser's Egypt." *Comparative Politics* 6, no. 2 (1974): 193–218.

Mostafa, Dalia. *The Egyptian Military in Popular Culture: Context and Critique*. London: Palgrave Macmillan, 2017.

Motyl, Alexander J. "Concepts and Skocpol: Ambiguity and Vagueness in the Study of Revolution." *Journal of Theoretical Politics* 4, no. 1 (1992): 93–112.

Moustafa, Tamir. "Protests Hint at New Chapter in Egyptian Politics." *Middle East Report Online*, April 9, 2004.

———. *The Struggle for Constitutional Power: Law, Politics, and Economic Development in Egypt*. New York: Cambridge University Press, 2007.

O'Donnell, Guillermo. *Bureaucratic Authoritarianism: Argentina, 1966–1973, in Comparative Perspective*. Berkeley: University of California Press, 1988.

O'Donnell, Guillermo, and Philippe Schmitter. *Transitions from Authoritarian Rule: Tentative Conclusions about Uncertain Democracies*. Baltimore: Johns Hopkins University Press, 1986.

Owen, Roger. "Review." *Middle East Report*, no. 161 (1991): 43–45.

———. *The Rise and Fall of Arab Presidents for Life*. Cambridge, MA: Harvard University Press, 2012.

Payne, Howard C. *The Police State of Louis Bonaparte, 1851–1860*. Seattle: University of Washington Press, 1966.

Payne, Stanley. *Spain's First Democracy: The Second Republic, 1931–1936*. Madison: University of Wisconsin Press, 1993.

Pearlman, Wendy. "Emotions and the Microfoundations of the Arab Uprisings," *Perspectives on Politics* 11, no. 2 (2013): 387–409.

Philiptchenko, Tatiana. *Fearless: Egyptian Women of the Revolution*. Montreal: Megapress Images, 2013.

Pierson, Paul. *Politics in Time: History, Institutions, and Social Analysis*. Princeton, NJ: Princeton University Press, 2004.

Pioppi, Daniela. "Playing with Fire: The Muslim Brotherhood and the Egyptian Leviathan." *International Spectator* 48, no. 4 (2013): 51–68.

Post, Erika. "Egypt's Elections." *Middle East Report* 147 (July/August 1987): 17–22.

Prince, Mona. *Revolution Is My Name: An Egyptian Woman's Diary from Eighteen Days in Tahrir*. Cairo: American University in Cairo Press, 2015.

Przeworski, Adam. "Democracy as a Contingent Outcome of Conflicts." In *Constitutionalism and Democracy*, ed. Jon Elster and Rune Slagstad. Cambridge: Cambridge University Press, 1988.

———. "Some Problems in the Study of the Transition to Democracy." In *Transitions from Authoritarian Rule: Comparative Perspectives*, ed. Guillermo O'Donnell, Philippe Schmitter, and Laurence Whitehead, 47–63. Baltimore: Johns Hopkins University Press, 1986.

———. *Why Bother with Elections?* Medford, MA: Polity Press, 2018.

Rashed, Dina. "The Egyptian Military and the Presidency: Continuity and Change." In *Egypt beyond Tahrir Square*, ed. Bessma Momani and Eid Mohamed, 133–50. Bloomington: Indiana University Press, 2016.

Remington, Michael J. "The Tribunaux Administratifs: Protectors of the French Citizen." *Tulane Law Review* 51, no. 1 (1976–1977): 33–94.

Reynolds, Nancy. *A City Consumed: Urban Commerce, the Cairo Fire, and the Politics of Decolonization in Egypt*. Palo Alto, CA: Stanford University Press, 2012.

Roberts, Clayton. *The Logic of Historical Explanation*. University Park: Pennsylvania State University Press, 1996.

Rosefsky Wickham, Carrie. *Mobilizing Islam: Religion, Activism, and Political Change in Egypt*. New York: Columbia University Press, 2002.

———. *The Muslim Brotherhood: Evolution of an Islamist Movement*. Princeton, NJ: Princeton University Press, 2015.

Rougier, Bernard, and Stéphane Lacroix. "Introduction: Egypt in Revolution." In *Egypt's Revolutions: Politics, Religion, and Social Movements*, ed. Bernard Rougier and Stéphane Lacroix, 1–15. Basingstoke: Palgrave Macmillan, 2016.

Rouquié, Alain. "Demilitarization and the Institutionalization of Military-dominated Polities in Latin America." In *Transitions from Authoritarian Rule: Comparative Perspectives*, ed. Guillermo O'Donnell, Philippe Schmitter, and Laurence Whitehead, 108–36. Baltimore: Johns Hopkins University Press, 1986.

Rule, James B. *Theories of Civil Violence*. Berkeley: University of California Press, 1988.

Rushdy, Hatem, ed., *18 Days in Tahrir: Stories from Egypt's Revolution*. Hong Kong: Haven Books Limited, 2011.

Rutherford, Bruce. "Egypt's New Authoritarianism under Sisi." *Middle East Journal* 72, no. 2 (2018): 185–208.

Ryzova, Lucie. "The Battle of Muhammad Mahmoud Street in Cairo: The Politics and Poetics of Urban Violence in Revolutionary Time." *Past and Present* 247 (May 2020): 273–317.

Saad, Reem. "State, Landlord, Parliament and Peasant: The Story of the 1992 Tenancy Law in Egypt." In *Agriculture in Egypt from Pharaonic to Modern Times*, ed. Alan

Bowman and Eugene Rogan, 387–404. Proceedings of the British Academy 96. Oxford: Oxford University Press, 1999.

Said, Atef. "The Paradox of Transition to 'Democracy' under Military Rule." *Social Research* 79, no. 2 (2012): 397–434.

Said, Mohamed Sayed. "A Political Analysis of the Egyptian Judges' Revolt." In *Judges and Political Reform in Egypt*, ed. Nathalie Bernard-Maugiron, 19–26. Cairo: American University in Cairo Press, 2008.

Sallam, Hesham, ed. *Egypt's Parliamentary Elections, 2011–2012: A Critical Guide to a Changing Political Arena*. Fairfax, VA: Tadween Publishing, 2013.

———. "Striking Back at Egyptian Workers." *Middle East Report* 259 (2011): 20–25.

Sayigh, Yezid. *Above the State: The Officers' Republic in Egypt*. Washington, DC: Carnegie Endowment for International Peace, 2012.

———. *Missed Opportunity: The Politics of Police Reform in Egypt and Tunisia*. Washington, DC: Carnegie Endowment for International Peace, 2015.

———. "Morsi and Egypt's Military." Carnegie Endowment for International Peace, January 8, 2013.

———. *Owners of the Republic: An Anatomy of Egypt's Military Economy*. Washington, DC: Carnegie Endowment for International Peace, 2019.

———. "The Return of Egypt's Military Interest Groups." Beirut: Carnegie Middle East Center, December 21, 2015.

Schedler, Andreas. *The Politics of Uncertainty: Sustaining and Subverting Electoral Authoritarianism*. New York: Oxford University Press, 2013.

Sélégny, Thomas. "Suez's Culture of Resistance, Its Causes and Its Future." Master's thesis, Leiden University, July 26, 2015.

Sfakianakis, John. "The Whales of the Nile: Networks, Businessmen, and Bureaucrats during the Era of Privatization in Egypt." In *Networks of Privilege in the Middle East: The Politics of Economic Reform Revisited*, ed. Steven Heydemann, 77–100. New York: Palgrave Macmillan, 2004.

Shapiro, Ian, and Sonu Bedi. "Introduction: Contingency's Challenge to Political Science." In *Political Contingency: Studying the Unexpected, the Accidental, and the Unforeseen*, ed. Ian Shapiro and Sonu Bedi, 1–18. New York: New York University Press, 2007.

Sheehan, James. "The Problem of Sovereignty in European History." *American Historical Review* 111, no. 1 (2006): 1–15.

Shehata, Samer and Joshua Stacher. "The Brotherhood Goes to Parliament," *Middle East Report* 240 (Fall 2006): 32–39.

Skocpol, Theda. *States and Social Revolutions: A Comparative Analysis of France, Russia, China*. Cambridge: Cambridge University Press, 1979.

Soliman, Samer. *The Autumn of Dictatorship: Fiscal Crisis and Political Change in Egypt under Mubarak*. Palo Alto, CA: Stanford University Press, 2011.

———. "The Radical Turn of Coptic Activism: Path to Democracy or to Sectarian Politics? In *Political and Social Protest in Egypt*, ed. Nicholas Hopkins, 135–54. Cairo: American University in Cairo Press, 2009.

Springborg, Robert. "Egypt." In *Legislative Politics in the Arab World: The Resurgence of Democratic Institutions*, ed. Abdo I. Baaklini, Guilain Denoeux, and Robert Springborg. Boulder, CO: Lynne Rienner Publishers, 1999.

———. *Mubarak's Egypt: Fragmentation of the Political Order*. Boulder, CO: Westview Press, 1989.

———. "Protest against a Hybrid State: Words without Meaning?" In *Political and Social Protest in Egypt*, ed. Nicholas Hopkins, 6–18. Cairo: American University of Cairo Press, 2009.

Stacher, Joshua. *Adaptable Autocrats: Regime Power in Egypt and Syria*. Palo Alto, CA: Stanford University Press, 2012.

———. *Watermelon Democracy: Egypt's Turbulent Transition*. Syracuse, NY: Syracuse University Press, 2020.

Stack, Liam. "You Should Thank God You're Not Inside: The Expansion of Military Trials in Post-Revolutionary Egypt." Master's thesis, New York University, 2012.

Stepan, Alfred. "Mutual Accommodation: Islamic and Secular Parties and Tunisia's Democratic Transition." In *Democratic Transition in the Muslim World: A Global Perspective*, ed. Alfred Stepan, 43–71. New York: Columbia University Press, 2018.

Steuer, Clément. "The Role of Elections: The Recomposition of the Party System and the Hierarchization of Political Issues." In *Egypt's Revolutions: Politics, Religion, and Social Movements*, ed. Bernard Rougier and Stéphane Lacroix, 81–99. London: Palgrave Macmillan, 2016.

Stilt, Kristen. "The End of 'One Hand': The Egyptian Constitutional Declaration and the Rift between the 'People' and the Supreme Council of the Armed Forces." *Yearbook of Islamic and Middle Eastern Law* 16 (2010–11): 43–52.

Stinchcombe, Arthur. "Ending Revolutions and Building New Governments." *Annual Review of Political Science* 2, no. 1 (1999): 49–73.

———. "Lustration as a Problem of the Social Basis of Constitutionalism." *Law and Social Inquiry* 20, no.1 (1995): 245–73.

———. "Social Structure and Organizations." in *Handbook of Organizations*, ed. James March, 142–93. Chicago: Rand McNally, 1965.

———. *Theoretical Methods in Social History.* New York: Academic Press, 1978.

Stites, Richard. *Revolutionary Dreams: Utopian Vision and Experimental Life*. New York: Oxford University Press, 1989.

Sultany, Nimer. *Law and Revolution: Legitimacy and Constitutionalism after the Arab Spring*. Oxford: Oxford University Press, 2018.

Svolik, Milan. *The Politics of Authoritarian Rule*. New York: Cambridge University Press, 2012.

Tadros, Mariz. "Egypt's Bloody Sunday." *Middle East Report*, October 13, 2011.

———. "Vicissitudes in the Entente between the Coptic Orthodox Church and the State in Egypt." *International Journal of Middle East Studies* 41, no. 2 (2009): 269–87.

Tarrow, Sidney. *Strangers at the Gates: Movements and States in Contentious Politics*. Cambridge: Cambridge University Press, 2012.

Telhami, Shibley. "What Do Egyptians Want? Key Findings from the Egyptian Public Opinion Poll." Brookings Institution, May 21, 2012.

Thompson, E. P. *Customs in Common: Studies in Traditional Popular Culture*. New York: New Press, 1993.

Tilly, Charles. *Contentious Performances*. New York: Cambridge University Press, 2008.

———. *Contention and Democracy in Europe, 1650–2000*. Cambridge: Cambridge University Press, 2004.

———. *European Revolutions, 1492–1992*. Oxford: Blackwell Publishers, 1993.

———. *From Mobilization to Revolution*. Reading, MA: Addison Wesley, 1978.

———. "Political Identities." In *Challenging Authority: The Historical Study of Contentious Politics*, ed. Michael Hanagan, Leslie Page Moch, and Wayne te Brake, 3–16. Minneapolis: University of Minnesota Press, 1998.

———. "Spaces of Contention." *Mobilization* 5, no. 2 (2000): 135–59.

———. "To Explain Political Processes." *American Journal of Sociology* 100, no. 6 (May 1995): 1594–1610.

———. *Trust and Rule*. New York: Cambridge University Press, 2005.

Transparency International. "The Officers' Republic: The Egyptian Military and Abuse of Power." March 2018.

Trotsky, Leon. *History of the Russian Revolution*. Chicago: Haymarket Books, 2008.

Tsebelis, George. *Veto Players: How Political Institutions Work*. Princeton, NJ: Princeton University Press, 2002.

Tufekci, Zeynep. *Twitter and Tear Gas: The Power and Fragility of Networked Protest.* New Haven, CT: Yale University Press, 2017.

Valenzuela, J. Samuel. "Democratic Consolidation in Post-Transitional Settings: Notion, Process, and Facilitating Conditions." Working Paper #150. Helen Kellogg Institute for International Studies, December 1990.

Waldron, Jeremy. *Political Political Theory.* Cambridge, MA: Harvard University Press, 2016.

Wallis, George. "Chronopolitics: The Impact of Time Perspectives on the Dynamics of Change." *Social Forces* 49, no. 1 (1970): 102–8.

Weber, Max. *Economy and Society.* Vol. 1, ed. Guenther Roth and Claus Wittich. Berkeley: University of California, 1978.

Wedeen, Lisa. *Ambiguities of Domination: Politics, Rhetoric, and Symbols in Contemporary Syria.* Chicago: University of Chicago Press, 1999.

Widner, Jennifer. "Constitution Writing in Post-Conflict Settings: An Overview." *William and Mary Law Review* 49, no. 4 (2008): 1513–41.

Winn, Peter. "Salvador Allende: His Political Life—and Afterlife." *Socialism and Democracy* 19, no. 3 (2005): 129–59.

Wolf, Eric. *Envisioning Power: Ideologies of Dominance and Crisis.* Berkeley: University of California Press, 1999.

Wright, Nate. "Egypt's Intense Election Eve." *Middle East Report*, November 10, 2011.

Yack, Bernard. "Popular Sovereignty and Nationalism." *Political Theory* 29, no. 4 (2001): 517–36.

Žižek, Slavoj. *The Year of Dreaming Dangerously.* London: Verso, 2012.

*Index*

Page numbers in *italics* denote photos, illustrations, or tables.

#Jan25, 4. *See also* January 25, 2011

Abdallah, Tal'at, 194
Abdel Fattah, Alaa, 142, 219, 328n75
Abdel Hadi, Aisha, 66–67
Abdel Khaleq, Gouda, 96
Abdel Meguid, Wahid, 137, 143, 181, 183, 316n55
Abdel Nasser, Gamal, 101, 150, 152, 324n35, 325n50; regime of, 53, 236, 295n48
Aboul Fotouh, Abdel Moneim, 148–50, 153, *157*, 204, 269, 326n62
Abu Ismail, Hazem Salah, 148–49, 152, 154, 299n79
Abul Matameer, 62
acclamation, 30, 96, 205, 221, 223, 239
accountability, 190; bureaucratic, 72; democratic, 264–65; of military, 263; presidential, 173, 202; security forces', 128

Acemoglu, Daron, 31
Achcar, Gilbert, 32, 325n50
al-Adli, Habib, 3–4, 20, 64, 87, 103
African Union, 174, 210, 212
*al-Ahali* (Cairo), 59, 287n26
Albrecht, Holger, 53, 315n49
Alexander, Jeffrey, 31–2
Alexandria, *x*, 97; in Eighteen Days, 7, 10, 12, 16, 18, 26; litigation in, 70–71; naval base, 202; presidential election results in, 156–57, 162; protests in, 2, 63–64, 77, 86, 90, 103, 129, *215*, 219;
Algeria, 56–57, 209, 251, 286n17
Ali, Khaled, 148, 167, 204, 234, 326n62
Allende, Salvador, 170, 203
alliance(s), 132, 209, 243, 255; electoral, 109, 111, *134*, 137, 299n82; inter-

alliance(s) (*continued*)
  national, 100; judicial-military, 140; opposition, 80, 84–85, 169; regional, 209, 233; secular-military, 125; support, 77–78; Tahrir, 9, 108, 113. *See also* "negative coalition"
Amann, Peter, 166, 171, 205, 283n32
Amcham (American Chamber of Commerce in Egypt), 58. *See also* United States
Amnesty International (AI), *215*
analytical narrative, 42
Anan, Sami, 100, 138, 163, 177, 225, 235
al-Anani, Khalil, 250, 254
anarchy, 17, 36, 92
Anis, Mona, 129
anticolonial 1919 uprising, 28
April 6 movement, 4, 80, 84, 107, 121, 152; members' imprisonment, 219; and Morsi, 178, 186, 197; and presidential election, 158, 161; public opinion of, 111; and SCAF, 118
Arato, Andrew, 145
*arcana imperii*, 238, 248
Arjomand, Saïd Amir, 34
armed forces. *See* military
arrests, mass, 8, 56, 60, 152, 207, 217, 219, 276n19
Asad, Talal, 108
al-Assad, Bashar, 58
al-Assad, Hafez, 54, 58
al-Assar, Mohamed, 101, 120, *196*, 301n100
Assembly Law (1914), 60–61, 218–19, 227. *See also* laws

association(s), 53: agricultural, 59; in Constituent Assembly, 180; laws restricting, 56; press syndicate, 5; protests in, 62–66, 79; teachers', 95. *See also* bar association; Judges' Club
Aswan, *x*, 23, 119
Asyut, *x*, 176
AUC (American University in Cairo), 5, *6*
auditors, 182
austerity, 56, 61, 148, 209, 224, 226
Austin Holmes, Amy, 34
authority, 255, 261: administrative, 229; arbitrary, 68, 114, 232; al-Azhar, 181; bureaucratic-military, 190; charismatic, 221, 226; constituted, 22, 92, 246; governing, 205, 265; judicial, 74, 186, 236, 248; military, 123, 160, 181; moral, 260; of Muslim Brothers, 152–53; of parliament, 109, 112, 120, 123, 131–32, 139–40, 146, 175, 247; of powerless, 264; of Mohamed Morsi, 169–70, 177–78, 190, 193, 195, 204; relations, 95, 114; of Shura Council, 194; state, 30, 42, 101, 115, 228; supreme/ultimate, 37, 44, 203, 256. *See also* constituent power; legitimacy; power; sovereignty; state
awe, 12, 46, 57, 210. See also *Haybat al-Dawla*; majesty, of state; prestige
Aya, Rod, 35
Ayubi, Nazih, 289n53
al-Azhar, 28, 68, 143, 181, 215n44; in Constituent Assembly, *180*; Imam of, 199, 202
al-Azhar University, 217, 219

Badr, Mahmoud, 197–98, 202, 320n103
Bahaa-Eldin, Ziad, 139, 143, 145, 193, 210, 313n25
Baha'is, 181, 253
Bahgat, Hossam, 223
Balteem, 7, 47–52, 55
Bani Suef, *x*, 26, 97, 166
ElBaradei, Mohamed, 105, 183, 193; in government, 210; opposition to Constituent Assembly, 183; opposition to Morsi, 167, 185, 187, 192, 202; opposition to Mubarak, 2, 9, 80, 84, 198
bar association, 4, 5, 64–65, 89, 143, 174
Barcelona Process, 58
bargaining, 61–2, 85, 96, 250, 254–55, 308n55; by riot, 60, 84, 218
*al-Barlaman*, 80, 133, 135, 273. *See also* parliament
al-Bashir, Omar, 244
al-Bastawisi, Hisham, 148
Battle of Mohamed Mahmoud, 121–23, 124, 136, *215*
Battle of the Camel, 18–19, 27, 136, 184, 278n50
Bayat, Asef, 34
Beblawi, Hazem, 210, 213, 216
Bedouin, 8, 253
Beheira, *x*, 62
Beinin, Joel, 66, 75, 79, 321n113
Ben Ali, Zine El Abidine, 1–2, 5, 9, 54, 242
Ben-Eliezer, Binyamin, 21
Benford, Robert, 259
Benjedid, Chadli, 56
Bianchi, Robert, 53
Biden, Joseph, 20

"binding principles." *See* essential principles
Bishara, Azmi, 189, 250, 254, 295n48
al-Bishri, Tareq, 69, 315n49; as panel chairman, 104, 106, 109
Bloch, Marc, 27, 33
blockade. *See* highway blockade
Board of Grievances, 173
Bobbio, Norberto, 238
boycott, 63–64, 74, 144–45, 158, 174, 189, 220, 285n14, 314n38
brokerage, 79
Brown, Nathan, 109, 139, 309n63
Brownlee, Jason, 34, 169
brutality. *See* police
bureaucracy: arbitrary power of, 72, 103; authority relations in, 95, 114–15; inequalities in, 67, 116–17, 289n53; mutinies in, 115; as political resource, 258; resistance to Morsi, 169–70
business: Amcham (American Chamber of Commerce in Egypt), 58; class, 66; cronies, 58; government and, 70; and Israel, 72; public, 127, 242, 263
Butler, Judith, 31

cabinet: al-Ganzouri, 123, 138, 146, 151, 251–52; interim, 210; MB presence in, 190–91; Nazif, 66, 68, 224; Qandil, 176, 332n14; reshuffle, 15, 95, 103, 190, 195; Shafiq, 96, 100, 296n52; Sharaf, 112, 122; sit-in, 123–24, 136, *215*
*caciquismo*, 32
Cairo, *x*, 86–88, *215*; Administrative Apparatus, 116; central morgue, 136, 213,

360 INDEX

Cairo (*continued*)
  323n19; downtown, 5, 6, 67, 73, 77, 115, 121, 123, 166; Greater, 45, 115, 119; grievances against, 168, 191; municipality, 8, 69; New, 188, 198; presidential election results in, 156–57, 162; referendum results in, 189; revolutionary, 97; stadium, 64, 178
Cairo University, 88, 129, 163, 187
campaign(s): anti-MB, 78–79, 212, 231; anti-Mubarak, 73–77, 157; anti-Sisi, 233, 238; for constitution, 141–42; electoral, 48–50, 139, 148–49, 158, 161, 189; proSisi, 221–22; Tamarrud, 197–98, 200
capacity-building, 84, 91
Carr, Sarah, 5
causal approaches, 41, 43, 243
cause lawyers. *See* lawyers
chants. *See* slogans
chronopolitics, 262
*Christian Science Monitor*, 77
churches, 98, 110; 'Abbasiyya cathedral 62, *81*, 98; attacks on, 119, 213, 230, 292n9; building of, 62, 70; in Constituent Assembly, 143, *180*, 183; denominations, 4; leaders, 62, 89, 173. *See also* Copts; Pope Shenouda; Pope Tawadros II
citizenship, 95, 111, 117, 140, 154, 254
civil-military relations, 46, 112–13, *118*, 140, 172, *196*. *See also* military; military trials; SCAF; Silmi document, the
civil servants, 2, 18, 28, 173; in parliament, 133; protests, 22, 67, 95, 113–17, 224, 232; SCAF decree, 102, 132; and vote bussing, 54, 222. *See also* bureaucracy; property tax collectors; strikes
civil society, 28, 78, 105, 182, 247–48
civil war, 56, 188, 214, 256
claim-making, 54, 63, 68, 218, 333n25. *See also* demand-making
cleavages, 43, 44, 158, 181, 250, 253
Clinton, Hillary, 7, 137, 165, 303n119
"collective bargaining by riot," 60, 84, 218
colligation, 283n37
configurational analysis, 42–3
confinement, 228; solitary, 227
conscripts, 5, 10, 99
consensus, 4, 127, 178, 195, 199; and constitution, 141, 145, 181, 184, 314n41
consociationalism. *See* democracy
conspiracy, 186–87, 191, 194, 202; foreign, 231, 238; public gathering as, 22, 219
Constantin, Wafaa, 62, 98. *See also* Copts
Constituent Assembly, the, 105; committee of fifty (2013), 220; composition of (2012), *180*; dissolution of, 146–47, 245; first iteration 140–47; Morsi decrees and, 177–78, 184, 244, 262; rival conceptions of, 253–55; SCAF edicts and, 120, 159; second iteration, 179–84, 186–87; voting in, 187, 314n41
constitutional amendments, *19*; under Morsi, 183, 200; under Mubarak, 55, 73, 80; rules of, 314n41; under SCAF, 100, 104–7; under Sisi, 220, 236, 245, 249
constitutionalism, 141
constitutional revolutions, 34

constituent power, 40, 44, 105, 142, 147, 160, 163–64, 261. *See also* power; sovereignty

constituent process, 35, 46, 131; MB domination of, 150, 251, 255; SCAF machinations in, 135, 140, 145, 164, 248

constitution-making. *See* constitution-writing

constitution-writing, 35, 179–84, 187, 254; anti-Islamists and, 142–43, 204; Bishri panel and, 104–5; in crisis conditions, 133, 142, 145, Islamists and, 109; Morsi and, 169, 184–87; public interest in, 142–44; as restitution, 140–41; SCAF and, 40, 109, 120, 123, 132–33, 262

contention: civil, 239; constitutional, 147; legal, 72, 249; political, 38, 44, 46, 68, 72, 255, 257, 262; popular, *82*; repertoire of, 96, 81; transgressive, 218

contentious politics, 28, 53, 218

convocation, 128

Copts, 253: cause lawyers, 69–70, 292n9; in Constituent Assembly, *180*; in Eighteen Days, 4, 9, 15, 20; in Morsi government, 176–77, 186; in parliament, 133; protests by, 61–62, 98, 119–120; in Qena, 88–90; in 2011 referendum, 107; women, 62, 98, 130. *See also* Maspero Youth Union; Pope Shenouda; Pope Tawadros II

corruption, 118, 148, 200, 238, 264, 330n100, 334n37; of leaders, *19, 20*, 83–84, 117, 195, 250. *See also* litigation; privatization

countergovernment, 39, 91–92

countermajoritarianism. *See* institutions

counterrevolution, 45, 92, 107; doctrine of, 208–9, 239–40, 248, 255; legal practices, 209, 218–19, 227–31; political fears of, 108, 154, 168; as regime, 30, 37, 208–9; as regional order, 234; as state-generating, 210; as territorial reclamation, 218. See also *Haybat al-Dawla*

coup d'état. *See* July 3, 2013

courts. *See* judiciary

crony capitalism, 53, 58

Culture Ministry, 198

curfew, 1, 12, 168

Daesh (Islamic State), 210, 226

Damietta, *x*, 11, 227

Daqahliyya, *x*, 64, 90, 144, 157, 162

Darrag, Amr, 33

death certificate, 102, 134

death sentences, 192, 227, 229, 327n68

Defense Ministry, 211–212, *215*

defilement, 26, 212

demand-making, 25, 55, 62, 118, 132, 198. *See also* claim-making

demobilization, 78, 130, 132. *See also* mobilization

democracy, 36, 44, 125, 141; and accountability, 264–65; consociational, 253–54; consolidated, 203, 263; contained, 125; infant, 125, 178, 247, 250; majoritarian, 252–54; multiparty, 28; plebiscitary, 221; and revolution, 34, 124, 247, 265; state and, 57; transition to, 34, 120, 256; tutelary, 29, 250

Democratic Alliance, *134*, 137
demonstrations. *See* protests
diarchy, 165, 178
dictatorship, 30, 120, 187–88, 203, 242, 255; Roman, 28, 100
die-in, 60
direct action, 11, 60–62, 85, 90–91, 218. *See also* disruption; disobedience
disappearances, 82, 192, 227, 327n68
disobedience, 59, 101, 192, 230, 246, 287n26
disruption, 91, 237, 246
dissent, 52, 76, 239, 240, 249; among judges, 228; within MB, 150
Dix, Robert, 84
Djerejian, Edward, 286n17
doctors, 14, 16, 24, 121, 123; military, 239
domination: governmental, 53; by MB, 150, 157, 251; by Morsi, 175; secular, 110; social, 85, 115
dual executive, 29
Duboc, Marie, 66, 75, 79
Duma (1906), 159
Dynamics of Contention, 284n39, 333n25
dynastic states, 58, 263

effigy, 7, 64
Egyptian Movement for Change, 34. *See also* Kifaya
Egyptian Popular Committee for Solidarity with the Palestinian Intifada (EPCSPI), 63–64
Eid, Gamal, 141, 175, 253–54
Eighteen Days (January 25-February 11, 2011), 4–26, 129, 201, *215*; and framing, 259; the missing in, 192; prisoner escapes, 231; railway shutdown in, 16, 213; as revolutionary situation, 93; uncertainty in, 27
elections: fatalities in, 47–48, 57; founding, 131, 133, *134*, 147, *157*, 158–60, *161*, 162–63; municipal, 78–79; plebiscitary, 219, 221–23, 224–26; semicompetitive, 55–58, 73–75, 77, 80–81, 223; student union, 88, 193; subnational, 56, 95, 223. *See also* referenda
emergency: powers, 244, *245*; state of, 4, 19, 95, 168, 230
English Revolution, 92
Ermakoff, Ivan, 246, 260, 262, 284n39
escalation, 23, 27
"essential principles," 112, 119, 253–54
European Union (EU), 9, 19, 83, 147, 179, 210, 212
extraparliamentary opposition, 51, 135, 208–9
extraparliamentary politics, 52, 77, 128, 137, 147, 163
Ezzat, Heba Raouf, 161

Facebook, 3, 17, 23, 44, 232, 235
fact-finding commissions, 102, 136–37, 192–93, 234, 279n58
faction(s), 37, *180*; bureaucratic, 204; civilian, 193, 200, 250, 252, 254; fighting of, 168, 183; of judges, 74, 291n88; in MB, 150, 299n78; revolution's, 104, 106, 108, 109, 125, 134, 144; youth, 233
farmers, 58–60, 133, 140, 173, *180*
Fairmont Meeting, 161, 176, 251

Farouq, Abdel Khaleq, 289n53
Fayoum, *x*, 23, 158
fears. *See* political fears
February 11, 2011, 25–26, 28, *29*, 39, 97, *215*; ambiguity of, 91, 93–94; power transfer, 211, *245*
Finance Ministry, 67, 116,
Fishman, Robert, 117
Foreign Ministry, 186
Forensic Medicine Authority, 102
framing, 210, 259–60, 263. *See also* media
Frankfurt Parliament (1848–1849), 159
Freedom and Justice Party (FJP), 110–11, 122, 129–30, 154–55, 170, 252, 299n82; attacks by, 188, 191; attacks on, 186, 188; in constitution-writing, 142–46, 149, 171; in government, 176, 189, 194–95; in parliament, 128, 133, *134*, 135, 138, 151–52, 174, 194; in opinion polls, 171, 193; women MPs, 127–28
French Revolution, 36, 39, 92
Führerdemokratie, 221
*fulul*, 44, 88, 106, 109, 156, 216, 250; coinage, 90–91; in parliamentary elections, 133–34; and 2011 referendum, 108

Gad, Emad, 175
Gadallah, Muhamad Fu'ad, 186, 195
Gallegos, Rómulo, 170, 203
al-Ganzouri, Kamal, 122, 136, 138, 146, 309n61. *See also* cabinet
Gaza. *See* Palestine
El Gebaly, Tahany, 112, 119
Geneina, Hisham, 225

General Guide, The, 144, 166–67, 171, 190, 297n60. *See also* Muslim Brothers
generals. *See* military; SCAF
geography: electoral, 311n82; of protests, 144, 187, 218
Gharbiyya, *x*, 157, 162, 189, 207
Ghonim, Wael, 23
Giza, *x*, 9, 24, 71, 147, 229; presidential election results in, 162
Goldberg, Ellis, 133, 245, 298n72, 315n49
Goodwin, Jeff, 41
Gorbachev, Mikhail, 264
government: abuse of power, 69; control, 54, 82, 98; control over, 131, 139, 141, 248; media, 18, 60, 206, 212, 222, 233–34; and opposition, 15, 51–52, 58, 249; party, 11, 13; and performances, 54; propaganda, 150, 231; toleration, 54, 81, 84; violence, 19, 74, 123. *See also* political violence
governors, provincial, 15, 88, 206–7; appointed by president, 56; appointed by SCAF, 96, 115; dismissal of, 136, 177; election of, 181; lawsuits against, 70, 292n9; managing protests, 48, 59–60, 67, 218; Muslim Brother members, 198–99, 320n105; protests against, 23, 26, 39, 85, 89–90, 114, 167
graffiti, 13, 28, *29*, 91, 147, 187
Graham, Lindsey, 306n29
Gramsci, Antonio, 333n21
Guardian Council (Iran), 181

Habib, Rafiq, 188
Haenni, Patrick, 170

364  INDEX

Halayeb Triangle, x, 196
Hampton, Jean, 264
Hamzawy, Amr, 112
Hardt, Michael, 31
*Haybat al-Dawla* (state prestige), 37, 46, 273; appearance of, 57; as counterrevolution doctrine, 208–10, 261; and state protective legislation, 228; as worldview, 248. *See also* counterrevolution; majesty; prestige
Helwan, 22, 115
hermeneutic study, 42
hierarchies, 117, 124
al-Hifnawy, Karima, 95
highway blockades, 48–49, 59–61, *81*, 82, 89, 218. *See also* railways
Hill, Enid, 249, 330n101
Hisham Mubarak Law Center, 141
historiography, 33, 42
Hizbullah, 207, 229, 231
Hobsbawm, Eric, 37, 60, 84, 206, 210, 218, 227
Howeidy, Amira, 22, 65, 87
Howeidy, Fahmi, 3, 87, 150
human rights, 183, 225, 263; activists, 21, 121, 174, 183, 192, 232; lawyers, 4, 20, 141, 193; organizations, 45, 83, 130, 176, 191
Human Rights Watch, 16, 183, 213, *215*
Hungary, 252

al-Ikhwan, 150, 191, 197, 201. *See also* Muslim Brothers (MB)
IMF (International Monetary Fund), 56, 169, 190, 224
incarceration, 219
inequality, 67–68, 72, 116–17
institutions: coercive, 38, 125, 199, 238; and constituent power, 160; countermajoritarian, 112, 146–47, 249; counterrevolutionary, 238–39; democratic, 56, 160; elected, 104, 165, 169, 245, 248–49, 261; financial, 234; judicial, 68, 330n100; political, 246–47, 261; religious, 68, *180*, 213; as resources, 257–59; social, 78. *See also* SSI; state
interaction, 43, 55; government-opposition, 51; political, 82; social, 284n39; strategic, 284n39; unpredictable, 75
Interior Ministry, 6, 12, 14, 103, 119, 137, *215*
international agreements, 235
international alliances, 100
international human rights organizations, 130, 191
international human rights treaties, 183
International Republican Institute (IRI), 137
international scrutiny, 9, 79, 183
International Women's Day (March 8), 97
internet, 10, 15, 18, 79
interregnum, 256, 261, 333n21
intifada, 33, 55, 60–61, 63
inversion, 12, 117, 264–65
Iraq, 22, 63–64, 67, 233
Iran, 15, 22, 39, 170, 179, 181, 233, 319n92
Iranian Revolution, 41, 179
Irrigation Ministry, 332n14
Iskandar, Amin, 138
Islamist-secularist divide, 44, 148

Ismail, Mamdouh, 128
Ismailiyya, *x*, 166–67, 168
Israel, *x*, 8, 16, 76, 83, 147–48: airstrikes, 177; blockade on Gaza, 71, 183; business interests, 58, 63–64, 72; and Gulf states, 209; and Egypt natural gas, 71, 78, 237; 1973 War, 24; 1979 Peace Treaty, 100, 263, 149; occupation of Tiran and Sanafir, 233; Oslo Accords, 58; 2002 reinvasion of West Bank, 63
*i'tisam. See* sit-in(s)
Ittihadiyya palace, 186, 192, 214; clashes, 188, 190–91, 199, 207, 215, 231, 328n81; June 30 demonstration, 198, 200–201

January 25, 2011, 3–8, 24, 30, 64, 84–85, 235; anniversaries of, 129, 166–67, 206–7; catalyst for, 102; demands of, 129; fatalities on, 7, 192, *215*; lineage of, 276n10; as metonym for revolution, 101, 184, 209, 211–12, 216, 231; organizing groups, 94–95, 106–7; as turning point, 97
January 28, 2011, 9–13, 20, 21, 23, 97, 136, 214; anniversary of, 207
al-Jazeera, 20, 225, 313n27, 326n62
Jordan, *x*, 17, 21
journalists, 20; American, 122–23; in Balteem elections, 50; and Constituent Assembly, 142–43; German, 239; imprisoned, 227; in *Kifaya*, 73; libel laws, 56; and litigation, 70, 72; as Morsi advisers, 177; and protests, 67, 88; at Rab'a sit-in, 212; Sisi loyalists, 223

Jribi, Maya, 33
Judges' Club, 5, 75, 77, 80, 174, 186, 248–49, 291n88
judiciary: and constituent power, 147, 164, 261; election oversight by, 73–74, 80, 104; Morsi and, 174–75, 178, 193–95, 204; prestige of, 73; 194; resort to, 68–73, 78, *81*, 146–47, 234, 237–38; Sisi and, 236; State Security courts, 60, 230. *See also* Judges' Club; litigation; Majlis al-Dawla; Supreme Administrative Court; Supreme Constitutional Court; Supreme Judicial Council
July 3, 2013 (coup d'état), 30, 207, 242, *245*; arrests on, 201–2, 210; civilian participation in, 202, 253
June 30, 2013, 45, 169, 198–201, 206, *215*, 250; as popular sovereignty, 211–12, 216
Justice Ministry, 176, 229, 301n100

Kafi, Ali, 57
Kafr al-Dawwar, 11, 22, 66
Kafr al-Shaykh, *x*, 156, 222
al-Katatni, Saad, 128, 143, 146
Ketchley, Neil, 216
Khalil, Ashraf, 24, 32
Kharbush, Muhammad Safieddine, 209
al-Khodeiry, Mahmoud, 153
Khomeini, Ruhollah, 39
Kifaya, 4, 73–77, *76*, 79–80, 84, 219, 320n1–3
kingmaker, 99, 263
Kirchheimer, Otto, 227–28, 231

Kuran, Timur, 52
Kurzman, Charles, 41–42
Kuwait, 21, 23, 233

Latuff, Carlos, *118*
law(s), 30, 53, *82*, 209, 223; administrative, 68–69, 78, 72; anti-strike, 116, 119; arbitration, 70; assembly, 60–61, 218–19, 227; basic, 142, 159; civil service, 22–24; constitutional, 72; counterterrorism, 230; decrees, 295n51; demonstrations, 217–19, 234; electoral, 56, 151, 155, 158–59; judiciary, 236; libel, 56; lustration, 164, 245; military, 118, 227; Ostracism, 153, 158; political party, 110; public contracts, 238; public properties, 230; tenancy, 59. *See also* Majlis al-Dawla, November 22 decree, Supreme Constitutional Court (SCC)
lawyers, 68, 301n100; and administrative litigation, 68–70, 78, 234–35, 237; cause, 52, 73, 84, 110, 129, 140, 263; defense, 69, 229–31; during Eighteen Days, 4–5, 24; government, 69, 72, 234, 237, 330n100; labor, 132; Tunisian, 275n1
Lebanon, 144
legitimacy, 96, 123, 184, 234; charismatic, 221; constitutional, 211; democratic, 40, 254; electoral, 162, 197, 201; institutional, 261; of Morsi, 188, 192; popular, 163, 211; procedural, 144; of SCAF, 136
Lenin, Vladimir, 30, 91–92, 114
lèse-majesté, 226, 232

Linz, Juan, 53–55, 82–83, 247
litigation, 68–73, 78, *81*, 83, 146–47, 234, 237; as dissent, 245, 249; as unmasking, 238; as veto power, 254. *See also* Majlis al-Dawla
lustration, 127, 164, 245. *See also* Ostracism Law
Lynch, Marc, 63

Madi, Abul Ela, 84, 184
Mahalla al-Kubra, 4, 7, 59, 66, 79
Maher, Ahmed, 219
majesty, of state, 209, 232
Majlis al-Dawla, 68–69, 72, 78, 80–81, 234–36, 273
Mann, Michael, 247
Maravall, José María, 258
martyrs, 19, 23, 25–26, 123, 128–29, 137, 216; families of, 102–3, 119, 132, 198, 206–7; Friday of, 9, 24; of Rab'a disbandment, 213; Tunisian, 1
Marzouki, Moncef, 232
Marzouq, Laila, 4
Masoud, Tarek, 34, 169
Maspero massacre, 119–20, 142, *215*
Maspero Youth Union, 95, 121, 130, 135, 260
al-Masry, Mahienour, 120, 219
massacres, 120, 142, 229, 231
Massey, Doreen, 97
Matariyya, 207
Mbembe, Achille, 214
McCain, John, 139, 152
media, 58, 75, 149, 155, 181, 228, 263; competitive, 67, 105, 107, 111, 237; in elections, 160, 155, 222; and framing,

63, 103, 113, 254–55, 262; international, 83, 178–79; and litigation, 69–70, 78, 234, 237; under Morsi, 173, 181, 185, 187, 191, 194, 200; opposition, 47, 52, 59, 67; progovernment, 18, 60, 82–83, 95, 206, 212, 220, 234; SCAF use of, 100–101, 113, 146, 160, 199, 200, 202; U.S., 22, 183; social, 4, 31, 127, 149
Mekky, Ahmed, 176
Mekky, Mahmoud, 178
Menoufiyya, *x*, 97, 157, 162, 189
memory, 1, 2, 16, 265: collective, 121; political, 45
military: in Constituent Assembly, 181; in constitution, 240, 236, 249; in economy, 99, 226–27; immunities, 118, 226–27; U.S. aid to, 99; use of force, 119–21, 204, 213, *215*. *See also* July 3, 2013; SCAF; al-Sisi, Abdel Fattah
military trials, 39, 57, *82*, 118, 217, 230, 246; campaigns against, 128–29; in constitution, 181; ruling against, 69
*milyuniyya* (mass assembly): April 2012, 153–54; April 2013, 194; and Constituent Assembly, 144, 150; and constituent power, 44; defined, 95–96, 273; first, 15, 135; November 2011, 97, 121–22, 140, 251, 262; October 2012, 182–83; as popular pressure, 100–101; as popular sovereignty, 44, 261; Red Card, 188
minimum wage, 24, 78, 79, 129, 132
Mink, Louis, 42
Minya, *x*, 11, 59, 90, 229–30
Mitchell, Timothy, 72

mobilization, 78, 257: cycles of, 28, 55; farmers', 58–60; judges', 74, 80, 186; mass, 17, 28, 64, 115; Muslim Brothers', 107, 11; opposition, 178. *See also* demobilization
al-Molla, Mokhtar, 123
monarchical presidency, 92, 140, 249
monarchy, 36, 110; Iranian, 203; Saudi, 173
Moore, Clement Henry, 52–53
morality tales, 33
Morland, Morten, *172*, 173
Morqos, Samir, 177
Morsi, Mohamed,110; approval ratings, 179, 193; cabinet appointments, 176–77, 190–91; and Constituent Assembly, 183–84, 262; coup against, 32, 35, 197, 199–202, 211, 253; death of, 232; Fairmont Meeting, 160–61, 176, 251; foreign policy, 173–74, 178, 193–97, 204; and judiciary, 174–75, 178, 193–95, 204; July 8 decree, 174–75; imprisonment of, 20, 202, 207–8; MB and, 154, 171–72, 190, 194–95; November 22 decree, 169, 171, 184–85, 244, *245*; opposition to, 169, 175–76, 185–90, 197, 205; perceptions of, *172*, 173, 244; police violence and, 168, 191–92; presidential election of, 40, 154–56, *157*, 158, *161*, 162–63, 246–47; protest law, 217; and SCAF, *172*, 177–78, 189, 192–93, 195, *196*, 197, 204
mosques, 14: al-Azhar, 28; Omar Makram, 103; as protest locations, 9, 11, *81*; al-Qa'id Ibrahim, 10, 86, 96; Rab'a al-'Adawiyya, 199, 213, 216; Salafi, 107
Mossadegh, Mohammad, 170, 203

Motyl, Alexander, 36
Moussa, Amr, 183, 204, 220; opposition to Morsi, 185, 187; presidential candidacy, 148–49, 155, *157*, 158
Moustafa, Tamir, 65, 290n76
Mubarak, Gamal, 51, 58, 64, 73, 209, *240*
Mubarak, Hosni, 2–3, 12–13, 14–15, 17, 24–25, 26; economic policies, 58, 68, 70–71; elections under, 2, 47–51, 55–58, 73–75, 80–81; funeral, *240*, 241; judiciary under, 68–73, 77–78; management of opposition, 52–55, 82; and military, 294n35; opposition to, 73–78, 84; protests under, 62–68, *81*, 84–85; regime philosophy, 52, 84; repression under, 78–80; succession plan, 55, 73, 242; trial of, 103; as trial witness, 231
Mubarak, Suzanne, 64–65
Muslim Brothers (MB): anticoup resistance, 212–14, *215*, 216–17, 219; arrests of, 9, 57, 78–79; attacks on, 167, 201, *215*; on Bishri panel, 104; in Constituent Assembly, 179, *180*, 181–83; and elections, 55, 74–75, 107, 193; as enemy, 206, 220, 229–30; failures of, 32–33, 121–22; fear of, 144, 150, 157, 162, 172, 204, 230; isolation of, 250–52; in Ittihadiyya clashes, 187–88, 191; and Kifaya, *76*; leaders of, 144, 166–67, 171, 190, 297n60; in opinion polls, 111, 155; as opposition, 80, 84; paternalism of, 252; and presidency, 40, 149–54, 157; and SCAF, 45, 120–21, 152
mystique, 99, 205, 224, 325n50
myth, 30, 35, 120, 295n48

Naguib, Sameh, 32, 302n111
al-Nahda, 210–11, 213–14, *215*, 216
Nakhla, Mamdouh, 69–70, 292n9
Nasserists, 109–11, 138, 182, 185, 200, 251, 299n82
National Defense Council, 99, 167, 181
National Democratic Party (NDP), *6*, 13, 48, 65, 74–75, 95, 106; dissolution of, 108, 147; domination of parliament, 2, 55, 57–58, 128; in municipal elections, 79; offshoots, 133, *134*; as succession vehicle, 55, 64. See also *fulul*
National Police Day (January 25), 3
National Salvation Front (NSF), 168, 200, 204, 213, 220, 222; formation of, 188; protests by, 166, 191, 201; and Tamarrud, 197
National Security Sector, 88, 103
Nazif, Ahmed, 66, 68, 224
"negative coalition," 84
Negri, Antonio, 31
Netanyahu, Benjamin, 15
networks: activist, 62–63, 75, *82*, 84, 94; corruption, 58, 264; familial, 117; grassroots, 110, 157; international, 83, 333n25; neighborhood, 107; of power, 25; protest, 52; shadowy, 200; spy, 87; transport, 23, 213
*New York Times*, 71
NGOs (nongovernmental organizations), 84, 137–9, 152, 155, 183, 228, 251, 286n19
Non-Aligned Summit, 179
Noujaim, Jehane, 32
Nour, Ayman, 4–5, 74, 80, 84, 109, 309n67

November 22 decree, 169, 171, 184–87, 193, 195, 244, *245*. *See also* Morsi, Mohamed
Nubians, 253
al-Nur, 110, *134*, 159, 177, 220, 223, 253, 313n27; in Constituent Assembly, *180*

Obama, Barack, 13, 15, 17, 21, 99, 108, 138, 149; administration, 122, 137
"object shift," 333n25
obligation, political, 265
O'Donnell, Guillermo, 112, 115, 130–31, 151, 256–57, 262, 303n117
"one person, one vote, one time," 57, 251, 286n17
ontology, 43, 83, 284n39
opinion polls, 111–12, 124, 149, 155–56, 171
Oslo Accords, the, 58
Ostracism Law (2012), 153, 158. *See also* laws; lustration
Owen, Roger, 2, 47, 55

Palestine: Gaza, *x*, 8, 64, 71, 183, 231; Hamas, 21, 207, 229, 231; Oslo Accords, 58; Second Intifada (2000), 63; solidarity with, 63–65, 67, 290n75; statehood, 179; West Bank, *x*, 63; women, 64
Panetta, Leon, 24
parliament, *6*; composition of 2012, 133, *134*, 135; and Constituent Assembly, 104, 109, 140, 142–47; dissolution of, 158–59, 160, 174, 185, *245*; elections to, 40, 127–28, 247; and judges, 164, 261; in Mubarak regime, 51, 56–57, 58, 74; "parallel," 80; as protest site, 23, 67, *81*, 128–29, 132; and popular sovereignty, 123, *131*, 135; and SCAF, 44, 123, 132, 135–39, 244; in Sisi regime, 223, 230, 235–36; Tahrir as, 96, 135; upper house of, 184–85, 193–94
patriotism, 11, 17, 212
Pentagon, the, 100
performance(s): of collective identity, 97; Kifaya, 74, *76*; as metaphor, 31–32; political, 54; prescribed, 219, 285n9; protest, 96, 218
petitions: anticorruption, 301n100; to courts, 78, 186; drives, 193; to parliament, 128–29; to president, 173; of protest, 63, 115. *See also* litigation; Tamarrud
Pierson, Paul, 258
Pioppi, Daniela, 170
plebiscitary election. *See* elections
pluralism, 53, 263
police, 18, *76*, 116–17: and April 6 strike, 79–80; brutality, 2, 171, 191; in counterrevolution, 208, 216–18; in Eighteen Days, 13, 15, 16, 18, 21–22, 26; inaction, 136–37, 168, 191, *215*; impunity, 103, 124; military, 87–88, 102, 137, 153; and Morsi, 168, 188, 191–92, 232; preemption, 79, 216–17; protests, 59–65, 74–75, *82*, 137, 216; protests by, 101–2, 192, 199, 201, 246; rulings against, 78; state, 90, 142, 172; trials of, 100, 102, 185, 192; violence, 47–48, 65, *82*, 102–3, 121–22, 137, 167–68, 207, *215*. *See also* massacres; political violence; SSI; state
political economy, 58, 117, 291n6

political fear(s), 29, 91, 117, 265: of ancien régime, 125, 164; in constitution-writing, 140, 183; of future, 262; of hidden power, 108, 144; of Islamists, 112, 148, 158, 250; of mass demonstrations, 135; of MB, 150, 157, 172, 204, 230; of military intervention, 145, 147, 154–55; 164; of Salafis, 135; of Supreme Constitutional Court, 185

political violence, 168, 200, 256, 286n16; in Eighteen Days, 7–9, 11, 14, 18–19, 21–22; in elections, 2, 48, 50, 56–57, 74; as factional fighting, 168, 183, 188, 201; military involvement in, 119–20, 123–34, 192, 213, *215*; police involvement in, 60, 62–63, 74, 77, 79, 121–22, 167, 191–92, *215*

*Politics, The* (Aristotle), 36

Pope Shenouda, 62, 78, 95. *See also* Copts

Pope Tawadros II, 199. *See also* Copts

popular sovereignty. *See* sovereignty

Port Said, *x*, 23, 64, 189, 192, *215*; stadium disaster, 136–38, 166–68, 251

Portugal, 117

Post, Erika, 55

power: absolute, 190; abuse of, 69, 114, 146, 170; agenda-setting, 261–62; balance of, 12, 94, 105, 108, 164, 170, 202, 249; blocs, 38–40; contests, 91, 175, 211, 245; crowd, 95, 131; devolution of, 94, 123, 248; dual, 92, 127, 133; foreign, 22, 231; governmental, 14, 20; hidden, 108, 144, 238; holders, 55, 78, 122, 163, 214, 227–28; people, 17, 261; public, 73, 249, 258; relative, 94, 100, 204,

rotation in, 252, 256; seizure of, 37, 91, 93, 101, 108, 139, 221; separation of, 163, 169; sharing, 104, 109, 125, 252–53; ultimate, 93, 260; and unaccountability, 72, 264. *See also* constituent power; emergency; sovereignty; state; transfer of power; veto

preemption, 3, 78, 240; by Morsi, 187; by police, 79, 216–17

Presidential Election Commission (PEC), 149, *157*, *161*, 198

prestige: of judiciary, 73; 194; state, 37, 46, 57, 206, 209–10, 241, 273. *See also* Haybat al-Dawla

privatization, 56, 58, 61, 66, 68, 69–71, 238, 263

property tax collectors, 67, 116, 128

prosecutor-general (PG), 184–185, 193, 232, 323n24

"prosecutorial narratives," 32–3

prosecutors, 60, 102, 118, 136, 138, 228–30, 236; military, 301n100; protests by, 182, 186, 193–94

protests: associational, 63–66, 77, 79; in canal cities, 167–68, Copts', 61–62, 98, 119–120; laws on, 60–61, 217–19, 227, 234; neighborhood, 60–62; "sectional," 113–14; three strands of, 24, 62; workplace, 66, 79, 113–15, 119. *See also* Eighteen Days; *milyuniyya*; sit-in(s); strikes; Tahrir Square

Przeworski, Adam, 164, 221, 243, 247, 258

public politics, 52–54, 68, 80–82, 110

public space: assembly in, 67; "inviolable spaces," 218; laws regulating, 60–61,

217–19; occupying, 92, 214; policing of, 26, 81–82, 218; and political identities, 97; and sovereignty, 214, 216. *See also* sit-in(s)

Qandil, Hisham, 176
Qasr al-'Aini Hospital, 14
Qena, *x*, 88–90, 96, 214

Rab'a massacre, 212–14, *215*, 216
railways, 16, 60, 79, *81*, 89–90, 192, 213, 218
referenda, *220*; April 2019, 236; December 2012, 188–89, 245, 255; January 2014, 220–21; March 2011, 105–10, 113, 151, 189, 251; May 2005, 73–74; on presidential selection, 56, 285n12, 314n39; as protest demand, 115, 201
"refolution," 34
regime(s), 54, 83, 101, 203; authoritarian, 28, 35, 53, 79, 242, 253, 259; change, 28, 30, 36–37, 43, 209, 243, 256–57; Franco, 53; military, 111, 239–40, 295n48; mixed, 28, 94; Nasser, 53; presidential, 29, 94. *See also* counterrevolution; Mubarak, Hosni; al-Sisi, Abdel Fattah
religion: in constitutional debates, 180–81; minority, 61–62, 70, 140, 253; on national IDs, 70; political parties and, 110–11; in referendum controversy, 107; and state, 112–13, 183, 239. *See also* al-Azhar; Copts; Islamistsecularist divide; Salafis
repertoire of contention, *81*, 96

repression, 3, 51, 55, 57, 164, 238, 253, 263; in Algeria, 209; chain of, 228; and concessions, 15, 20, 61, 117; of farmers, 59; legal, 227–28, 254; of protest, 65–66, 79–80, 221, 235
*Republic, The* (Plato), 36
republicanism, 263
reserve domains, 99, 196
restitution, 123, 129, 132, 140
reverence. *See Haybat al-Dawla*
revolution(s): constitutional, 34; and democracy, 34, 124, 247, 265; dual power in, 92, 127, 133; as experience, 41–42; French, 36, 29, 92; Iranian, 41, 179; as factional conflict, 37; myth of, 35–36; Russian, 36; subconcepts of, 35, 29; as treason, 232
revolutionary outcome, 35, 37, 41, 91
revolutionary situation, 30, 34–35, 42–43, 85, 171, 208, 211; as contested sovereignty, 44–46, 214, 249; defined, 37; genealogy of, 91–93; as interregnum 238, 256–57, 261; as maximum conflict, 46, 130, 255; as multiple sovereignty, 40, 93–94, 123, 131–32, 164, 203–4; as power fragmentation, 37, *245*, 249; as uncertainty, 99, 106, 133, 146, 204, 243
Revolutionary Socialists, 4, 84, 120, 302n111
Revolution Youth Coalition (RYC), 94–5, 110, 128, 137, 152, 260; in Constituent Assembly, *180*
Reynolds, Andrew, 34, 169
riot(s), 36, 60, 63, 84, 218, 239, 261

Rip Van Winkle, 90
Roads and Bridges Authority, 61
Robinson, James, 31
Rouquié, Alain, 125, 239
Rule, James, 34
Russian Revolution, 36, 92, 256

El Saadawi, Nawal, 296n59
Sabahy, Hamdeen, 7, *49*, 110, 158, 204; arrest of, 65; opposition to Morsi, 167, 183, 188, 198; parliamentary election battle, 47–51, 57, 80; presidential candidacy, 148, 156, *157*, 222–23
sabotage, 60, 145, 206
Sadat, Anwar, 13, 53, 56, 222, 236, 328n80
Said, Atef, 99
Said, Khaled, 2, 7, 275n4; Facebook page, 3–4, 23
Said, Mohamed Sayed, 77–8
Salafis, 90, 107, 121, 133, 163, 181, 220; in Constituent Assembly, 142, 145, 180–81; and Copts, 89, 97–98; and July 3 coup, 202; and MB, 252–53; and Morsi, 177, 192, 194, 250; political parties, 110–11, 122, 128, *134*, 135, 146, 155, 159, 174; and Sufis, 97. *See also* Abu Ismail, Hazem Salah; al-Nur
Saleh, Sobhi, 104, 144
Sanafir, *x*, 197, 224, 233, 235, 237, 239
al-Saqqa, Mahmoud, 128
Saudi Arabia, *x*, 147, 150, 173–74, 179, 209, 224, 233–34, 245
Sawiris, Naguib, 109, 111
Sayigh, Yezid, 98–99, 294n39, 332n8
SCAF (Supreme Council of the Armed Forces): and constituent power, 44, 142, 160, 164, 261; and constitution, 107–8, 123, 181; decrees, 116, 132, 159–60, 295n51, 301n100; formation of, 24, 28–29, 98; and Mohamed Morsi, 172, 177–78, 189, 192–93, 195, *196*, 197, 204; and Muslim Brothers, 149–153, 159; opposition to, 118, 121–24, 135–39; and parliament, 44, 123, 132, 135–39, 244; and presidential elections, 154; public outreach by, 101, 107, 113, 120, 146, 154; seizures of power, *245*; use of force, 119–20, 123, 213, *215*
Schedler, Andreas, 55
Schmitter, Philippe, 112, 130–31, 151, 256–57, 262, 303n117
Seif, Ahmed, 20
semipresidentialism, 182
Shadid, Anthony, 14, 17
Shafiq, Ahmed, 171, 179, 200, 225, 251; cabinet 96, 100, 296n52; presidential candidacy, 148–49, 156, *157*, 158, *161*, 222
Shahin, Mamdouh, 101, 160, *196*, 298n72
Sharaf, Essam, 61, 96, 115. *See also* cabinet
Sharon, Ariel, 63
al-Sharqawy, Pakinam, 177
Sharqiyya, *x*, 60, 157, 162, 188, 192, 232
al-Shater, Khairat, 149, 153–54, 172, 309n61
show trials, 230–32
Shubra, 5, 11
*al-Shurouq* (Cairo), 95, *180*
Sidi Bouzid, 9, 27
al-Silmi, Ali, 120
Silmi document, the, 120–23, 140, 159
Sinai, *x*, 8, 177, 196–97, 209, 215, 226, 233; Sharm al-Shaykh, 3

al-Sisi, Abdel Fattah, 18, 20, 27, *240*;
counterrevolutionary regime of, 209,
239–41, 248–49; as Defense Minister,
177, 189, 193, *196*, 197, 206, 210, 211; and
executive dominance, 223, 236; July
3, 2013 coup, 199–202, *245*; and legal
repression, 227–230, 217–219; on the
MB, 212, 214; personalized regime of,
226; plebiscitary elections, 219–26;
supporters, 207, 220, 226; Tiran and
Sanafir controversy, 224, 232–37; 2019
constitutional amendments, 236, 245
sit-in(s): 63, 67, *81*, 154, *215*: associational,
65, 77; cabinet, 123–24, 219; Ittihadiyya, 187; by police, 119; Qena, 89–90;
Rabʿa, 201, 212–13; Tahrir, 7–8, 22, 26,
103, 118, 121, 136, 296n57; workplace,
60, 66, 114; laws criminalizing, 102,
117, 129, 132, 219, 230; students', 88
Skocpol, Theda, 41
slogans, 44–45, 71, *81*, 178, 220; in Eighteen Days, 3, 6, 10, 14, 16, 22, 25; in
elections, 50, 148, 162; against MB,
144, 150, 167, 182; against Morsi,
171, 186–87, 191, 198, 205; against
Mubarak, 74, 76–77; against SCC, 187;
against Sisi, 233, 235; in Sudan, 244;
of 2011, 88–89, 114, 129, 211, 263
Snow, David, 259
soccer. *See* Port Said stadium disaster;
Ultras
social contract, 263
Social Democratic Party (SDP), 110, 128,
*134*, 158, 175
Socialist Popular Alliance, 110, 121
social movement, 66, 80

social sciences, 33, 35, 41, 243
solidarity, 77, 88, 121, 125, 128, 161, 212; in
Eighteen Days, 5, 11, 17, 19; Ministry
of Social, 96; pro-Palestine, 63–64,
65, 67
Soliman, Samer, 56, 287n35, 291n6
sovereign ministries, 176, 248
sovereignty: acts of, 71; contested, 44–46,
214, 249; as indeterminate concept,
211; as master concept, 261; military
appropriation of, 160, 261; multiple,
40, 93–94, 123, 131–32, 164, 203–4;
national, 138; popular, 39, 40, 44,
93, 123, 135, 211; twofold, 92. *See also*
constituent power; legitimacy; power
Soviet, Petrograd, 39, 92
Springborg, Robert, 53, 280n2, 294n35,
295n44
SSI (State Security Investigations): in
Eighteen Days, 8–9, 22; fixing elections, 57, 88; managing protests, 62,
67; relabeling of, 103; headquarters'
storming, 86, *87*, 96–97
state: agents of, 81, 91; Arab, 93, 150;
authoritarian, 92, 247; authority, 101,
115, 160, 248; civil (*dawla madaniyya*),
112–13, 236, 240; coercion, 14, 35, 38,
64, 125, 236, 238; elite, 99, 190, 209,
232, 246, 248; institutions, 81, 90, 103,
106, 112, 123, 164–65, 199, 204; mass
killing by, 102, 193, 214, *215*; media, 95,
220, 222; military (*dawla ʿaskariyya*),
113; police, 87, 90; powers, 91, 107,
131–32, 185, 236, 243–44, 246, 249;
religious (*dawla diniyya*), 112–113, 183;
unelected enclaves in, 164, 248

state protective legislation, 227–28, 239. *See also* law(s)
State Security Courts, 60, 230
Stepan, Alfred, 250, 254
Stilt, Kristen, 139, 298n73
Stinchcombe, Arthur, 94, 100, 127, 133, 164, 240, 261, 299n80
strikes: April 6 aborted, 79; civil servants', 28, 67, 93, 102, 114–15; hunger, 60; labor, 27, 52, 66, 113, 279n53; policemen's, 192, 246; prosecutors', 182, 186; rulings on, 232; SCAF decree criminalizing, 102, 116–17, 132; teachers', 119. *See also* sit-in(s)
students. *See* universities
Sudan, 174, 179, 196, 243–44
Suez, x, 28, 129: during Eighteen Days, 7–9, 16, 22, 25; protests, 167–68, 186
Suez Canal, 196–97; canal cities, 168, 217
Sufis, 15, 97, 110, 158, 172
Suleiman, Omar, 13–15, 20, 24, 26, 231; presidential candidacy, 153–54
Sultan, Essam, 112, 128
supermajority, 55, 133, 135, 140
supralegislative device, 253
supralegislative status, 164
Supreme Administrative Court (SAC), 69, 71, 234, 330n100. *See also* Majlis al-Dawla
Supreme Constitutional Court (SCC), 112, 198, 248: chief justice, 210, 236; competence, 235; and Constituent Assembly, 143, 182, 185, 245, 310n75, 314n38; dissolution of parliament, 151, 158–59, 179, 244; executive dominance of, 236; landmark ruling, 74

Supreme Judicial Council, 195, 319n89
surveillance, 82, 86, 167, 216
"synoptic judgment," 42
Syria, 54, 179, 233; refugee women, 213

*Tagamhur* (Assembly), 60, 218
Tagammu', *134*, 148
Tahrir Square, 5, *6*, *19*, 29, 63, 65; Battle of the Camel, 18–19, 27, 136, 184, 278n50; crowd capacity of, 16, 96; as foreign conspiracy, 22; Morsi oath in, 162–63; as open-air parliament, 96, 103, 135; as popular sovereignty, 39, 44; as revolutionary campground, 97; as state-led carnival, 207. *See also* Eighteen Days; *milyuniyya*
Tamarrud (Mutiny), 197–200, 202, 212
Tantawi, Mohamed Hussein, 15, 98, 100, 124, 136; and Morsi, 163, 165, 176, 177; and November *milyuniyya*, 122; and parliament, 132–33, 138
Tarrow, Sidney, 44, 132, 260
*terra nullius*, 33
terrorism, 16, 225, 230; "circuits," 229, 232, 236; list, 326n62; "war on," 56, 57, 207, 220, 226
"Third Square," the, 212
Thompson, E. P., 63
Tilly, Charles, 37, 46, 54, 86, 91, 218, 284n3, 335n50
*Time*, 31, 179
time, 42, 55, 81, 103–5; historical, 35, 117; as object of contention, 44; as political resource, 261–63; "time bomb," 109; *See also* chronopolitics

INDEX 375

Tiran, *x*, 197, 224, 233, 235, 237, 239, 326n59
toleration, 54, 81, 84
torture, 21, *82*, 141; charge against Mohamed Morsi, 231; and forced confessions, 229; by military, 192, 279n58; by police, 3; solitary confinement as, 227
trade unions, 129, 132, 144, 172, 180, 228, 263, 298n76
transfer of power, 21, 95, *131*, 164, *245*; and enduring conflicts 46, 255; November 2011 *milyuniyya* demand, 122
Transport Ministry, 196
treason, 232
Trotsky, Leon, 1, 92, 203
Tunis, 1
Tunisia, 2–3, 9, 17, 27, 30, 34, 92; constitution-making in, 297n62; elected president of, 232; military of, 307n44; slogans from, 6, 263, 274; 2008 protests in, 275n11; transition in, 250; women, 323n17
tutelage, 95, 112–13, 205, 283n32
Twitter, 24, 225

UAE (United Arab Emirates), 147, 150, 197, 200, 209, 225, 233
al-Ulaimy, Ziad, 137, 178
Ultras, 4, 6, 136–37, 166–67, 218
UN High Commissioner for Human Rights, 187
United States: American Chamber of Commerce in Egypt (Amcham), 58; Assistant Secretary of State, 175; election-monitoring, 75; House Intelligence Committee, 24; invasion of Iraq (2003), 63, 64–65; media, 22; Middle East policy, 56–57; military aid to Egypt, 99, 138; NGOs case, 137–39, 152; Secretary of Defense, 197; Secretary of State, 123; US-Egypt Presidents' Council, 58. *See also* Clinton, Hillary; Graham, Lindsey; McCain, John; Obama, Barack; Panetta, Leon; Wisner, Frank
universities, *81*: anticoup resistance in, 216–17, 219; elections in, 88, 193; faculty, 64, 116, 173; laws regulating, 56, 228, 230; rulings on, 78, 232, student protests in, 4, 62, 88, 114, 129. *See also under individual universities*

venality, 117
Venezuela, 19, 170, 203
verstehen, 42
veto, 29, 94, 120, 132, 144, 159, 253–54; "players," 258
violence. *See* political violence; state
"virginity tests," 119, 296n57. *See also* women
*vlast*, 292n15
voting behavior, 48, 54, *81*: as acclamation, 221, 223; in Constituent Assembly, 187, 314n41; versus electing, 221; sincere vs. strategic, 158, 162

al-Wafd, 4, 109, 111, 120–21, 223; in Constituent Assembly, 143 *180;* in 2012 parliament, 128, *134*, 135
Waldron, Jeremy, 141, 242, 264
Wallis, George, 262
war-making, 65, 181, 209, 226

al-Wasat, 110, 128, *134*, 155, 192, 252; in Constituent Assembly, *180*, 184; FJP and, 135, 194, 299n82; women in, 110
Weber, Max, 41, 221
West Bank. *See* Palestine
Wisner, Frank, 15, 17
Wolf, Eric, 259
women: assaults against, 74, 129, 137, 167; in Constituent Assembly, 143, 179, *180*, 183; Coptic, 62, 98, 130; demonstrations by, 97–98, 123, 144; exclusion of, 296n59; in Fairmont Meeting, 161; National Council for, 182; Palestinian, 64; on party lists, 110; in parliament, 128; in Rab'a sit-in, 213; rights in constitution, 315n51, 317n68; "7 a.m. girls," 219; Syrian refugee, 213; "virginity tests," 119, 296n57; voters, 48, 220; in Wasat party, 110

Yack, Bernard, 261

*zabbaleen*, 71
Zaghlul, Saad, 11, 198
al-Zainy, Noha, 75
Zaki, Mohamed, 199, 202
al-Zarqa, Bassam, 159
Zeinhom morgue, 136, 213, 323n19
Zirzara, 23
Žižek, Slavoj, 30, 32

Stanford Studies in Middle Eastern
and Islamic Societies and Cultures

*Joel Beinin and Laleh Khalili, editors*

EDITORIAL BOARD
Asef Bayat, Marilyn Booth, Laurie Brand, Timothy Mitchell,
Jillian Schwedler, Rebecca L. Stein, Max Weiss

*Paradoxes of Care: Children and Global Medical Aid in Egypt* 2021
RANIA KASSAB SWEIS

*The Politics of Art: Dissent and Cultural Diplomacy in
Lebanon, Palestine, and Jordan* 2021
HANAN TOUKAN

*The Paranoid Style in American Diplomacy: Oil and Arab Nationalism in Iraq* 2021
BRANDON WOLFE-HUNNICUTT

*Dear Palestine: A Social History of the 1948 War* 2021
SHAY HAZKANI

*A Critical Political Economy of the Middle East and North Africa* 2021
JOEL BEININ, BASSAM HADDAD, AND SHERENE SEIKALY, EDITORS,

*Archive Wars: The Politics of History in Saudi Arabia* 2020
ROSIE BSHEER

*Showpiece City: How Architecture Made Dubai* 2020
TODD REISZ

*Between Muslims: Religious Difference in Iraqi Kurdistan* 2020
J. ANDREW BUSH

*The Optimist: A Social Biography of Tawfiq Zayyad*   2020
  TAMIR SOREK

*Graveyard of Clerics: Everyday Activism in Saudi Arabia*   2020
  PASCAL MENORET

*Cleft Capitalism: The Social Origins of Failed Market Making in Egypt*   2020
  AMR ADLY

*The Universal Enemy: Jihad, Empire, and the Challenge of Solidarity*   2019
  DARRYL LI

*Waste Siege: The Life of Infrastructure in Palestine*   2019
  SOPHIA STAMATOPOULOU-ROBBINS

*Heritage and the Cultural Struggle for Palestine*   2019
  CHIARA DE CESARI

*Iran Reframed: Anxieties of Power in the Islamic Republic*   2019
  NARGES BAJOGHLI

*Banking on the State: The Financial Foundations of Lebanon*   2019
  HICHAM SAFIEDDINE

*Familiar Futures: Time, Selfhood, and Sovereignty in Iraq*   2019
  SARA PURSLEY

*Hamas Contained: The Rise and Pacification of Palestinian Resistance*   2018
  TAREQ BACONI

*Hotels and Highways: The Construction of Modernization Theory in Cold War Turkey*   2018
  BEGÜM ADALET

*Bureaucratic Intimacies: Translating Human Rights in Turkey*   2017
  ELIF M. BABÜL

*Impossible Exodus: Iraqi Jews in Israel*   2017
  ORIT BASHKIN

*Brothers Apart: Palestinian Citizens of Israel and the Arab World*   2017
  MAHA NASSAR

*Revolution without Revolutionaries: Making Sense of the Arab Spring*   2017
  ASEF BAYAT

*Soundtrack of the Revolution: The Politics of Music in Iran*   2017
  NAHID SIAMDOUST

The authorized representative in the EU for product safety and compliance is:
Mare Nostrum Group
B.V Doelen 72
4831 GR Breda
The Netherlands

www.ingramcontent.com/pod-product-compliance
Lightning Source LLC
Chambersburg PA
CBHW031845220426
43663CB00006B/501